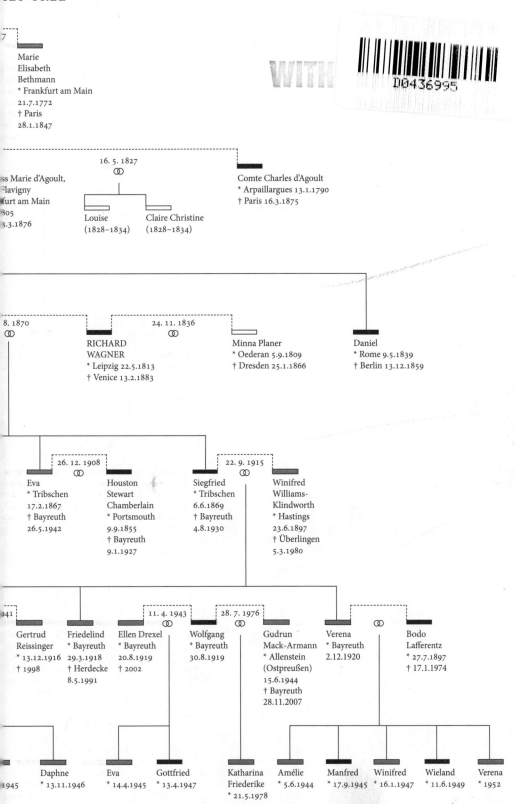

7

Marie
Elisabeth
Bethmann
* Frankfurt am Main
21.7.1772
† Paris
28.1.1847

16. 5. 1827
⚭

ss Marie d'Agoult,
Flavigny
furt am Main
805
.3.1876

Louise
(1828–1834)

Claire Christine
(1828–1834)

Comte Charles d'Agoult
* Arpaillargues 13.1.1790
† Paris 16.3.1875

8. 1870
⚭

24. 11. 1836
⚭

RICHARD
WAGNER
* Leipzig 22.5.1813
† Venice 13.2.1883

Minna Planer
* Oederan 5.9.1809
† Dresden 25.1.1866

Daniel
* Rome 9.5.1839
† Berlin 13.12.1859

26. 12. 1908
⚭

22. 9. 1915
⚭

Eva
* Tribschen
17.2.1867
† Bayreuth
26.5.1942

Houston
Stewart
Chamberlain
* Portsmouth
9.9.1855
† Bayreuth
9.1.1927

Siegfried
* Tribschen
6.6.1869
† Bayreuth
4.8.1930

Winifred
Williams-
Klindworth
* Hastings
23.6.1897
† Überlingen
5.3.1980

941

11. 4. 1943
⚭

28. 7. 1976
⚭

⚭

Gertrud
Reissinger
* 13.12.1916
† 1998

Friedelind
* Bayreuth
29.3.1918
† Herdecke
8.5.1991

Ellen Drexel
* Bayreuth
20.8.1919
† 2002

Wolfgang
* Bayreuth
30.8.1919

Gudrun
Mack-Armann
* Allenstein
(Ostpreußen)
15.6.1944
† Bayreuth
28.11.2007

Verena
* Bayreuth
2.12.1920

Bodo
Lafferentz
* 27.7.1897
† 17.1.1974

1945

Daphne
* 13.11.1946

Eva
* 14.4.1945

Gottfried
* 13.4.1947

Katharina
Friederike
* 21.5.1978

Amélie
* 5.6.1944

Manfred
* 17.9.1945

Winifred
* 16.1.1947

Wieland
* 11.6.1949

Verena
* 1952

COSIMA WAGNER

COSIMA WAGNER
THE LADY OF BAYREUTH

OLIVER HILMES
TRANSLATED BY STEWART SPENCER

YALE UNIVERSITY PRESS
NEW HAVEN AND LONDON

T 124554

First published in English by Yale University Press in 2010

English language translation copyright © 2010 Stewart Spencer

Originally published under the title *Herrin des Hügels, Das Leben der Cosima Wagner* by Oliver Hilmes © 2007 by Siedler Verlag, a division of Verlagsgruppe Random House GmbH, Munich.

For information about this and other Yale University Press publications, please contact:
U.S. Office: sales.press@yale.edu   www.yalebooks.com
Europe Office: sales@yaleup.co.uk   www.yaleup.co.uk

Set in Minion Pro by IDSUK (DataConnection) Ltd
Printed in Great Britain by TJ International Ltd, Padstow, Cornwall

Library of Congress Cataloging-in-Publication Data

Hilmes, Oliver.
    [Herrin des Hügels. English]
    Cosima Wagner: The Lady of Bayreuth / Oliver Hilmes; translated by
Stewart Spencer.
        p. cm.
    Includes bibliographical references and index.
    ISBN 978-0-300-15215-9 (cl: alk. paper)
    1. Wagner, Cosima, 1837–1930. 2. Opera producers and directors–Germany–
Bayreuth–Biography. 3. Wagner, Richard, 1813–1883. 4. Wagner family. 5. Bayreuther
Festspiele. I. Title.
    ML429.W133H5513 2010
    782.1092–dc22
    [B]
                                                                                        2009038775
A catalogue record is available for this book from the British Library

The translation of this work was funded by Geisteswissenschaften International –
Translation Funding for Humanities and Social Sciences from Germany, a joint initiative
of the Fritz Thyssen Foundation, the German Federal Foreign Office, the collecting
society VG WORT and the Börsenverein des Deutschen Buchhandels (German
Publishers & Booksellers Association).

10 9 8 7 6 5 4 3 2 1

Whatever she was resolved should never see the cold light of day was doomed to remain forever locked away in Stygian archival gloom.

Contents

Illustrations

Unless otherwise acknowledged all illustrations belong to the Nationalarchiv
der Richard-Wagner-Stiftung, Bayreuth.

Prologue

Bayreuth in midsummer: a white-haired Wolfgang Wagner can be seen standing next to his wife, Gudrun, and their daughter, Katharina, in front of the Festspielhaus, while themes from his grandfather's operas waft down from the open-air balcony and women in long dresses and men in dinner jackets mill all around the theatre. The international press has also assembled here. Music critics from all over the world are filing reports on the performances for their readers at home, and television crews are on hand to film the offstage spectacle. 'Did you see last year's *Parsifal*?' visitors can be heard whispering. 'What did you think of Schlingensief's production?' The prominent guests are now beginning to arrive. Black and silver-grey limousines drive up and stop at a long red carpet that leads straight into the theatre. The countless onlookers, all standing at a respectful distance, watch as the federal chancellor, Angela Merkel, arrives with her husband, followed by the Bavarian prime minister, Edmund Stoiber, and his wife Karin. Also in evidence are Claudia Roth; Guido Westerwelle; the minister for health, Ulla Schmidt, and her cabinet colleague Ursula von der Leyen; two former German presidents, Walter Scheel and Roman Herzog; the ambassadors of Italy, Japan and France; and sundry local dignitaries.

This was the scene in 2006, but the description could apply to any year: the cast may change, but the production remains the same. While the brass players on the balcony intone a motif from *Der fliegende Holländer*, the countless photographers call out the names of their subjects: 'Foreign Minister, could you turn this way?' Hans-Dietrich Genscher bestows a friendly smile on the cameras. 'Frau von der Leyen, what's your husband called?' 'Heiko.' Not to be outdone by so many prominent politicians, the world of show business is no less well represented: Margot Werner, Grit Boettcher, Roberto Blanco and Thomas Gottschalk make the pilgrimage to Bayreuth almost every summer.

Their number used to include the eccentric Munich fashion designer Rudolph Moshammer and his Yorkshire terrier, Daisy.

What are all these people doing here? Why have they come to this normally sleepy town in the Upper Franconian provinces? If Bayreuth has become the playground of high society, it is ultimately because of one woman alone: Cosima Wagner.

More or less everything about Cosima Wagner seems extraordinary. She was the illegitimate daughter of the leading pianist of the nineteenth century, Franz Liszt, and the French writer Marie d'Agoult. She spent a parentless childhood in 1840s Paris under the iron rule of unloving governesses. Her life then took her to the Berlin of the 1850s, where she was introduced to her first husband, Hans von Bülow, who was her father's eccentric favourite pupil and, much later, the principal conductor of the Berlin Philharmonic. Even while they were still on their honeymoon, the Bülows stopped off in Zurich and called on Richard Wagner, Bülow's friend of many years' standing. Cosima's marriage to Bülow was clearly a terrible mistake that ended in heart-rending tragedy following a scandal-fuelled episode in Munich. For years Cosima carried on an affair with Wagner behind her husband's back and had already borne him three children before she and Bülow were divorced and she married Wagner, her elder by twenty-four years. 'It is an occupation I have not sought after or brought about myself,' she wrote in her diary on 1 January 1869. 'Fate laid it upon me.'[1]

Cosima's first language was French. Her use of the German word *Betätigung* ('occupation' or 'activity') speaks volumes here, for her marriage with Wagner was no ordinary relationship. Rather, she saw the marriage as a mission. When Wagner died in 1883, Bülow commented scornfully that his former wife should now marry Brahms, a joke that Cosima felt was in singularly poor taste. The only thing that Wagner's forty-five-year-old widow wanted was to carry out what she regarded as her late husband's final wishes. Not baulking at even the most drastic measures, she cut off all her hair on the day of Wagner's death and sewed it into a velvet cushion, which she then placed in his coffin. Her gesture was intended to show the world that she had no life beyond Wagner's and that nothing should remind her contemporaries of her own individual identity. She spent the next forty-seven years successfully identifying with her late husband's person and works, so much so that the dead 'Meister' seemed to live on in Cosima, who was duly dubbed the 'Meisterin'. As a result, it is difficult even for the most hardened Wagnerians to form a clear picture of Cosima's personality. We may know what Wagner looked like as a person, but the outlines of his wife's physiognomy remain strangely blurred, and for the most part her personality disappears behind her self-appointed mission in life. But was her ego really so inextricably linked with Wagner's?

Who was Cosima Liszt-Bülow-Wagner? What remains of her more than 170 years after her birth? And what was her particular attraction, an attraction so seductive that not even a critical contemporary like Count Harry Kessler could escape from its spell? 'Cosima rules the social roost here,' he wrote in his diary after meeting her in Berlin. 'A position like hers is unique: princesses, ambassadors' wives and countesses all tremble before her and blush with joy whenever she deigns to address them.'[2] Even Maximilian Harden, who could not abide her, was obliged to concede that 'this Bayreuth is the creation of her own brain, and she alone is its deity'.[3] Coming from Harden, this was a compliment, no matter how venomously it may have been worded. And it aptly sums up the way in which, following Wagner's death, Cosima helped the Bayreuth Festival to achieve its international breakthrough. What had been no more than a provincial experiment in Wagner's hands became a flourishing family concern and a social institution. But how did Cosima bring this about? How was it that in an age when women were for the most part tied to the kitchen sink she was able to become a successful business manager, the Bayreuth Festival personified? How can we best do justice to a woman like Cosima Liszt-Bülow-Wagner? Only by examining the most private sources available to us in the form of uncensored letters and diary entries.

My search began in Bayreuth, in the National Archives of the Richard Wagner Foundation, in January 2005. This institute is housed in the Siegfried Wagner House, an annexe of the Villa Wahnfried, where the papers of the far-flung members of the Wagner family are now to be found. After a long and tiring train journey – in this respect nothing has changed since Cosima's day, for Bayreuth is still not served by high-speed trains – I alighted at the station and made my way through the well-kept town to the Siegfried Wagner House, where I was welcomed by one of the archivists, Kristina Unger. Soon afterwards I was introduced to the director, Sven Friedrich: 'You've certainly landed yourself in it,' he greeted me with a mixture of irony and sarcasm.

By the end of my first day in the archives, the import of Sven Friedrich's remark had become abundantly clear to me. The main problem for anyone writing a life of Cosima Wagner is not the lack of material, as might perhaps have been expected three-quarters of a century after her death, but the exact opposite. The Wagner archives are filled from basement to attic with documents of every description. Cosima was born in 1837 and so she belonged to a generation that grew up without the telephone as a means of mass communication. It was not until the mid-1880s that telephone lines were laid between the larger German cities such as Berlin and Hamburg, and not until many years later that telephone exchanges were opened in provincial backwaters like Bayreuth. In short, anyone wanting to communicate with anyone else would have recourse only to pen and paper or in an emergency would send a telegram. As a result, the Bayreuth archives contain thousands of letters to Cosima and her family.

In the course of time countless letters written by Wagner and his wife found their way back to Wahnfried, which either bought them up at auction or acquired them through donations. A few examples, drawn from the immediate family circle, may give an idea of the numbers of documents involved:

Cosima to Hans von Bülow	37
Cosima to her daughter Eva Chamberlain	167
Cosima to her maidservant, Dora Glaser	156
Cosima to her administrator, Adolf von Groß	491
Cosima to her daughter Daniela Thode	268
Cosima to her son Siegfried Wagner	220
Siegfried Wagner to his half-sister Daniela Thode	418
'Wahnfried' (one of Cosima's pseudonyms) to Daniela	2,078
Letters and telegrams on Cosima's ninetieth birthday	238
Letters and telegrams on Cosima's death	1,380

This list could easily be extended. Of particular importance are the unpublished papers of Cosima's son-in-law, Houston Stewart Chamberlain, which are also lodged in Bayreuth. Here I found letters and diaries, all of which are uncatalogued but which throw an entirely new light on Chamberlain's dubious activities. But I also discovered other, often sensational documents in the course of my research in other archives. The detailed correspondence surrounding the so-called Beidler case was previously thought to be lost, but I discovered it among the unpublished papers of Isolde Beidler's lawyer, Siegfried Dispeker. The estate of her personal physician, Ernst Schweninger, in the Federal Archives in Berlin, was also found to contain some remarkable documents.

All in all, these archives contain countless documents of inestimable value, papers which, remarkably enough, have until now been largely ignored by Cosima's biographers. There are various reasons for this. Those writers who attempted the earliest biographies during the 1920s and 1930s were generally able to publish only what the Wagner family permitted. At this date there were still no critical editions, and Cosima's papers were not available to independent scholars. True, the family's privileged writers were granted access to the archives, but this access was entirely arbitrary. It is also true, of course, that these authors were not interested in a balanced account of Cosima's life but were concerned, rather, to glorify the family. The result was a series of biographies notable for their sycophantic, hagiographic tone.

The classic example of an uncritical and, linguistically speaking, risibly bombastic account of Cosima's life continues to be Richard Du Moulin Eckart's biography, which appeared in two volumes between 1929 and 1931; its 2,000 or so pages referring repeatedly to its subject as 'the mistress of Bayreuth', the 'greatest woman of the century' and 'the guardian of the Grail', it effectively treated her as a latter-day saint. The foreword to the second volume of the German edition (only the first volume was translated into English) ends, significantly, with the words: 'May God protect Wahnfried and Bayreuth!' Such a sentence says all we need to know about the scholarly seriousness of these hernia-inducing volumes. As it happens, the author's readiness to toe the party line failed to impress Cosima's daughter Eva, who complained that Du Moulin Eckart had burnt insufficient incense to the greater glory of the Wagners.

The situation did not improve with the publication of Ilse Lotz's biography of 1935 or Max Millenkovich-Morold's of two years later. Both authors were beholden to the National Socialist spirit of the times. And both exuded the most sickly sentimentality. Ilse Lotz described her study as 'a novel about the life of a German woman', Cosima's French provenance being conveniently swept under the carpet. Cosima was held up as a German National mother figure, her life story commended to readers in Hitler's Germany as a model worth emulating.

All these trashy titles have long since gone out of print and sunk into well-deserved oblivion. In an altogether different league are Franz Wilhelm Beidler's writings on his grandmother, for even though he was denied access to the Bayreuth archives, he was able to relate the many published sources to one another and in that way produce a convincing picture of Cosima's character and of the age in which she lived.

During the decades following the end of the Second World War, the situation regarding the Bayreuth sources remained frustrating for journalists and scholars like. Anyone wanting to conduct research in the Bayreuth archives had to establish a good working relationship with the Wagner family and in particular with the much-feared Wahnfried archivist Gertrud Strobel. Even as late as the early 1970s a French musicologist was sent packing with the message that he need not return until Alsace-Lorraine was once again a part of Germany. This German National attitude slowly began to change only when, in April 1973, Winifred Wagner ceded the Festspielhaus, Wahnfried and the Wagner Archives to the city of Bayreuth. In turn, the city entrusted these assets to a newly established foundation in a deal that brought the Wagner heirs the handsome sum of 12.4 million marks. The archives were now a public institution, and when Gertrud Strobel retired three years later, it was no longer necessary for visitors to prove their political allegiances. Since then, access to the archives has been regulated by public law, a development warmly welcomed by Wagner scholars throughout the world.

One of the first fruits of this new openness was the publication in 1978 of the correspondence between Cosima Wagner and Richard Strauss. Two years later, Dietrich Mack, who has published widely on the history of the theatre in general and on Bayreuth in particular, brought out an edition of some 350 letters from Cosima under the title *Das zweite Leben* (The Second Life). In 1996 the correspondence between Cosima and King Ludwig II of Bavaria was published for the first time. And yet even now Cosima's biographers rarely see the inside of the Bayreuth archives. This is certainly true of the French journalist Françoise Giroud, whose 1996 biography, *Cosima la sublime*, was translated into German two years later. A slender volume, it attempts to deal with its subject's ninety-two-year life in under 50,000 words and deliberately eschews a comprehensive account. 'To go into detail would be pointless,' the author admits at an early point in her narrative, fobbing off the inquisitive reader once and for all.[4] She adopts a similarly dismissive tone in dealing with Cosima's anti-Semitism and the disastrous influence of her subject's son-in-law, Houston Stewart Chamberlain, contenting herself with the comment that the ultra-right-wing ideologue was a 'historian' who was 'a natty dresser and a fine speaker' and writing off his *Foundations of the Nineteenth Century* as 'just a little fanciful.'[5] This is the level on which Madame Giroud engaged with one of the most influential racial thinkers of the twentieth century. Of any sign that she ever set foot in the Bayreuth archives there is not the slightest trace.

In 2006, finally, Joachim Köhler published a novel under the title *I, Cosima*, an account described by its author as a 'fictional confession'. Yet even the title is misguided, for if ever Cosima had written such a confession, she would surely have called it 'He, the Master'.

No matter how varied they may be, all the biographies of Cosima that have appeared to date have one major disadvantage: they are based on incomplete sources. In general, it remains a mystery where their authors obtained their information. As for myself, it was my intention from the outset not to perpetuate yet more myths about Cosima. Rather, I was determined to write a historically sound biography based as far as possible on original sources. In all, I spent several months in the Bayreuth archives, investigating Cosima's life in depth. Ironically, though, the wealth of material available in Bayreuth also has its drawbacks. So as not to become bogged down in detail and so that the biography does not assume the most monumental proportions, the biographer must be prepared to be selective. My concern, therefore, was not to quote from as many sources as possible, but to paint a picture that would be true to life and make sense to Wagnerians and non-Wagnerians alike. It should also, of course, be gripping.

The documents that I have analysed tell the life of a pugnacious woman who, no matter how much she may be respected, is by no means uncontroversial within the Wagnerian community. They supplement and add extra detail to the lives of Cosima's contemporaries, while revealing her skill as a manipulator standing in the wings. Even as the young Frau von Bülow, Cosima was already a cunning tactician with a certain social influence. She went on to cultivate the company of crowned heads of state, including King Ludwig II of Bavaria and Kaiser Wilhelm II, frequenting the leading European houses and, in the course of her long life, corresponding with such eminent figures as Emma and Georg Herwegh; Hedwig and Ernst Dohm; Friedrich Nietzsche and his sister; Heinrich von Stein; Gustav Mahler; Richard Strauss; Hermann Levi; Felix Mottl; Adolf von Hildebrand; Theodor Mommsen; and Gerhart Hauptmann. But the documents also tell of Cosima as a housewife and as a mother, not infrequently reduced to apparent despair by her second husband's spendthrift lifestyle. She is revealed as a loving mother who none the less committed serious mistakes in bringing up her charges. When, in later life, she laid aside her widow's weeds, she could reveal a sense of humour and a laugh that was said to 'cause the very earth to shake'. She was fond of the odd glass of beer and also smoked the occasional cigarette.

But Cosima's life is also the story of the rise of a powerful dynasty. It is a tale of money – a lot of money – and of Cosima's claim to enjoy the sole rights to a corpus of works of art. And it is a tale, finally, of political influence. If Bayreuth became a magnet for the ultra-right in the early years of the twentieth century, this was because of a shift in political emphasis in the reception of Wagner's works. And it was Cosima who determined the direction that this development took, so that the cult of Wagner became the cult of an aggressive German nationalism. To that extent neither anti-Semitism nor Hitler nor all that he stood for came out of the blue in the Bayreuth of the 1920s. Brigitte Hamann's study of Winifred Wagner – 'A Life at the Heart of Hitler's Bayreuth', to quote the subtitle of its English translation – had a prehistory, and it is this prehistory that is recounted here. The Wagners would not be the Wagners if their lives were not beset by constant gossiping, quarrels and intrigues. Even in Cosima's day the Master's family could be counted on for a good scandal. We learn about a dog that underwent surgery at Bayreuth's Municipal Hospital, we read about sexual escapades, insidious attempts at extortion, hush money, suicides, illegitimate children and dubious machinations, and finally we are forced to stand by helplessly while discovering that the dynasty was almost ruined by a bizarre court case on the eve of the First World War. In short, the life of Cosima Liszt-Bülow-Wagner is grand opera at its grandest. Beginners onstage for Act One, please.

Oliver Hilmes
Berlin, February 2007

A Childhood Without Parents

(1837–55)

Années de Pèlerinage

From every side, Lake Como offers one of those delightful vistas that are unique to Italy's northern lakes. Surrounded by elegantly arching mountains and luscious vegetation, the town extends picturesquely along a gently sloping valley at the southern edge of the western arm of Italy's most beautiful lake, to which the town also gave its name. Along its shore and both to the north-east and north-west, the hills are clothed in vineyards and dotted with olive groves and clumps of chestnut trees, all of them shimmering with Italianate splendour in the bright golden sunlight.[1] Thus Franz Girard begins his description of Lake Como in the 1910 edition of Bruckmann's *Illustrated Travel Guide*. Girard also writes enthusiastically about the good-natured, peace-loving inhabitants of the town: 'Almost all of the girls are graceful, while the men are of handsome stock,' although 'hard work often destroys the women's beauty'.[2]

Among the countless musicians, artists and writers who over the years have fallen in love with Lake Como were the composer and pianist Franz Liszt and his mistress Marie d'Agoult. The couple arrived at the lake in the middle of August 1837. 'A long avenue lined with plane trees, acacias, lime trees and chestnuts leads to Como,' Marie d'Agoult wrote in her memoirs. 'The lake is wonderfully attractive.'[3] During the weeks that followed, the couple explored almost the whole of the lake's southern and eastern shores. They visited the sixteenth-century Villa Pliniana at Blevio and the Villa Melzi, with its impressive grounds, at Bellagio. But their programme of activities also included visits to Milan, some thirty miles to the south. In early September, they finally settled down to a life of 'utter solitude' in Bellagio: 'What is there more beautiful in the world than work, contemplation and love?'[4] While Liszt spent most of his afternoons at the piano, composing, Marie kept her diary or read plays by Corneille and Molière. 'I am living in the most beautiful country in the world,' Liszt rhapsodized in a letter to his mother. 'I am the happiest man on earth.'[5]

On 22 October they celebrated Liszt's twenty-sixth birthday: 'At nine in the morning we set off into the mountains,' Marie d'Agoult noted in her diary. 'Mounted on a "sommarello", the term of affection used hereabouts for a donkey, I made my way across gently rolling expanses covered in chestnut and scattered olive trees.'[6] Such an excursion must have been something of a strain for the thirty-one-year-old countess, who was seven months pregnant, although, oddly enough, her diaries nowhere mention that she was in the family way at this time.

In early November, as the time of her lying-in drew nearer, Marie and Liszt withdrew from Bellagio to the Hotel dell'Angelo at Como, where their daughter, Francesca Gaetana Cosima, was born on the afternoon of 24 December 1837. Even at that date, the name Cosima was unusual. It derives not from Lake Como, as has often been claimed, but from Saint Cosmas, an Arab physician active at the end of the second century AD who practised his profession without taking payment, encouraging many of his patients to convert to Christianity. He and his twin brother are the patron saints of doctors and apothecaries, and their feast day was 26 September, which is also the date on which Cosima celebrated her name-day. The child was baptized on 26 December 1837 in the cathedral at Como. Marie d'Agoult did not attend the ceremony as she was still recovering from what had been a difficult birth. The register of the child's birth poses a number of puzzles, for although Liszt is named as the father, the mother is said to be Caterina de Flavigny.[7] Why? At this point we need to examine the couple's former lives.

The Joys of Love

The tale of Franz Liszt and Marie d'Agoult is one of the great love stories of the nineteenth century. The countess had for years been unhappily married when she abandoned her husband and their young daughter and ran off with a man six years her junior.

There is no doubt that what began in a Paris salon in January 1833 was an intense, passionate and, for the time, exceptional relationship. 'When I entered Madame Le Vayer's salon at ten o'clock,' Marie d'Agoult recalled in her memoirs, 'everyone was already assembled.' She had been assured that Liszt would turn up. 'Madame Le Vayer was still speaking when the door opened and a strange apparition presented itself to my eyes. I say "apparition", because I can think of no other word to describe the extraordinary sensation caused by the most extraordinary person I had ever seen.' Liszt was then twenty-one and universally regarded as a sorcerer of the piano. The whole of Paris was talking about an exceptional artist who had begun his career as a child prodigy in his native Hungary and, starting with Vienna, conquered half of Europe. Extended tours had taken him as far as England, bravura pieces such as his *Grand galop chromatique* eliciting veritable storms of applause and turning women's heads. Marie's first impression was of a man who was 'tall and excessively thin, with a pallid complexion and large sea-green eyes in which the swift flash of light glistened like waves catching the sunlight, a face that expressed both suffering and power, a hesitant step that seemed less to press down on the floor than to glide over it and an air of absent-mindedness and unease, like that of a ghost about to be summoned back into the darkness.' When Marie d'Agoult returned home that night, it was a long time before she could get to sleep: 'I was visited by strange dreams.'[8] Had she fallen in love with Liszt?

Marie d'Agoult's family background is complex and requires some explanation. On her mother's side, she was descended from the influential Frankfurt banking family of the Bethmanns. Widowed when she was only eighteen, her mother Maria Élisabeth almost immediately remarried, her choice on this occasion falling on the young Viscount Alexandre de Flavigny, to whom she bore three children, Eduard, Maurice and Cosima's mother, Marie-Catherine-Sophie, who was born on 31 December 1805. But by October 1819, the Viscount, too, was dead, and the barely fourteen-year-old Marie was sent to live with her strict grandmother in Frankfurt. Marie hated the old woman. Two years later she was despatched to the famous Sacré-Cœur school in Paris, where she gained entry to high society and was courted by countless admirers, one of whom was the forty-five-year-old Count Auguste de Lagarde. Marie found herself on the horns of a dilemma, and the end of her affair plunged the now twenty-one-year-old woman into a serious crisis of indecision from which she emerged by marrying the first suitor to take her fancy. Charles d'Agoult was a cavalry colonel fifteen years her senior. Wounded while serving under Napoleon in the Battle of Nangis in 1814, he now walked with a permanent limp. Marie married Count Charles d'Agoult in Paris in May 1827. Their first daughter, Louise, was born in 1828, followed in August 1830 by a second daughter, Claire Christine. Whatever Marie may have felt for her husband, it was not love. 'I did not enjoy a single hour of happiness from the day I married,' she wrote in her autobiography.[9] Her husband must have suspected this: even before he married her, he had promised to release her from her vow if she ever came to regret her decision to wed him.

Six years into her unhappy marriage, the twenty-seven-year-old Marie was feeling particularly frustrated when in January 1833 she met the young, good-looking and altogether fascinating Franz Liszt. Within months they were lovers, and by March 1835 they had decided to leave Paris, so great was their fear that their liaison might provoke a social scandal. Before leaving for Basel, Marie wrote a letter of farewell to her husband: 'Your name will never pass my lips, unless it be spoken with respect and the esteem that your person deserves. As for myself, I ask only for your silence in the face of a world that will shower me with insults.'[10] There is no doubt that her decision demanded a great deal of courage. For a grande dame from high society, such a step was singularly foolhardy. Heedless of social conventions, she turned her back on the world of the French aristocracy. But Charles d'Agoult proved that he was a gentleman and kept his word, releasing his wife from her marriage vows and taking charge of their four-year-old daughter Claire Christine, Louise having died in December 1834. Father and daughter retired to the family estates at the Château de Croissy.

In the summer of 1835 Liszt and his mistress moved to Geneva, and it was here, on 18 December, that their first daughter, Blandine-Rachel, was born. The register of births names Catherine-Adélaïde Méran as the child's mother.[11] As was to be the case two years later, when Caterina de Flavigny was named as Cosima's mother, the entries were the assumed names of Marie d'Agoult, such obfuscation being necessary to draw a veil over her adultery. Although Liszt acknowledged both girls as his children, even this admission was to prove problematic in the future.

The Sorrows of Love

Blandine was entrusted to a wet nurse immediately after she was born and within months had been placed in the care of a pastor in Geneva, where she spent the next three years. A similar fate befell Cosima: she too was looked after by a foster mother. Today's readers must think it heartless of a mother to give away her children before they have even been weaned, but during the period under consideration this was standard practice in all well-to-do circles. The parents resumed their former lifestyles. Liszt gave over 1,000 concerts between 1839 and 1847, sometimes appearing three or four times a week.

From Saint Petersburg to Lisbon and from Glasgow to Constantinople he travelled the length and breadth of Europe, a revolutionary who not only wrote pioneering works that opened up a new world of expression but who also effectively invented the profession of the international concert pianist. He was the first to perform the whole of the existing repertory from Bach to Chopin and to do so, moreover, from memory. He was also a distinguished composer in his own right: in 1838 alone he completed three important collections of piano pieces – his first versions of the *Grandes études de Paganini* and the *Études d'exécution transcendante* and the bulk of the 'Italian' volume of the *Années de pèlerinage*.[12] Disconcerting though it must seem to us now, Liszt essentially had no time at all for his children.

At the end of March 1838 the lovers settled in Venice. Liszt fell in love with the city, but his mistress felt only loathing and disgust. There was nothing about La Serenissima that she liked: on one occasion she complained that the city's shops stocked only items that had remained unsold in Paris, while on another it was the bookshops that aroused her ire for selling titles fit only for maidservants. Her complaints knew no bounds: 'During the night a bunch of flowers left on the table makes me ill. I am sometimes afraid that I am going mad. My brain is tired. I have shed too many tears . . . My heart and mind have grown dry. It is an illness with which I came into the world. Passion raised me aloft for a moment, but I feel that there is no life principle in me.'[13]

Marie d'Agoult was not merely melancholic, she was plagued by regular bouts of depression and throughout her life suffered from psychosomatic illnesses. In this regard she was by no means alone in her family. Her half-sister, Auguste, was also mentally unstable and later took her own life, hence the reference to her own innate sufferings. But behind her emotional outbursts there was also a deep-seated dissatisfaction with her life at Liszt's side. She regarded herself as his muse but was forced to admit that this is precisely what she was not. 'You are not the woman I need,' he once told her. 'You are the woman I desire.'[14] The realization that she was not playing the role that she wanted to have in Liszt's life resulted in a painful sense of disillusionment. Her jealousy caused more and more scenes between them, and it seemed that their relationship had reached the point of no return.

To make matters worse, Marie found that she was pregnant again. The couple moved to Rome, where their son, Daniel, was born on 9 May 1839. He, too, was abandoned to a wet nurse, and it was not until the winter of 1841 that the parents saw their third child again. During these post-natal months, Liszt and Marie d'Agoult wandered aimlessly around Italy, visiting Lucca, San

Rossore and Pisa, among other places. They finally parted company in
Florence, Liszt travelling to Vienna via Trieste in order to give a series of
concerts in the Austrian capital, while Marie d'Agoult returned to Paris via
Genoa, taking her two daughters with her. It was the first time in months that
she had spent any time with them. Blandine ('Mouche') looked like her
mother, whereas Cosima had inherited her father's profile, including his
striking nose. In a letter that she wrote to Liszt on 23 October 1839, Marie
d'Agoult assured her former lover that 'feature by feature' Cosima 'resembles
the adorable Mouche, but she is much less beautiful and, above all, less distinguished. Their *education* is identical: her nurse says that she should be given
everything she wants *without delay*, otherwise she will die. I am going to try to
teach her to live a different life.'[15]

In December 1839, Marie d'Agoult took a large apartment in the Rue
Neuve-des-Mathurins in Paris. It had two reception rooms, a large salon, a
library and space for several servants in keeping with her social standing. 'I
had no fixed plans when I returned to Paris,' Marie later recalled. More than
four years had passed since she had fled the city – how should she behave
towards her family? 'The desire to make up for the harm I had inflicted on
others and to the best of my abilities to assuage the suffering that I had caused
was very powerful.'[16] She decided not to return to the family hearth, still less
to ask her husband to forgive her. Instead, she was determined to take charge
of her life. This sounds very much like a decision to break free from Liszt,
even if the ultimate breach did not take place until May 1844.

Marie attempted a cautious rapprochement with the Flavignys, a move
prompted not only by her regard for their aristocratic mores but also by the
matter of public opinion. Her mother, Madame de Flavigny, wanted nothing
to do with three illegitimate children, who simply did not exist in her eyes:
'Do not mention Blandine in my mother's presence,' Marie once asked the
poet Georg Herwegh. 'Her obdurate silence is a protest at the very existence
of these children, and she gets terribly worked up whenever their names are
mentioned.'[17] In the circumstances, it is clear that if Marie was to make a fresh
start in Paris, it would have to be without her offspring. But who would be
willing to take charge of them? For a time Liszt toyed with the idea of sharing
a house with his mother, Anna, and his three children as 'Mme d'A. herself
intends to look for an unfurnished apartment that suits her and that she can
occupy on her own'.[18] In the event things worked out rather differently. Liszt's
European tours meant that he would in any case spend little time in Paris, and
so Daniel remained in Rome, while Blandine and Cosima moved in with their

grandmother in Paris. Marie d'Agoult protested vehemently against this turn of events. 'Tomorrow they [i.e. the children] will sleep with your mother,' she wrote to Liszt in mid-November. 'Mouche is delighted, whereas I am immensely sad.'[19] But Liszt was insistent: 'I have already told you that I am entirely of the opinion that the Mouches should be brought up by my mother. There is absolutely nothing to weigh up here.'[20] Marie d'Agoult gritted her teeth and accepted this solution, while commenting maliciously on Liszt's mother in the letters that she wrote to her former lover. Anna Liszt, she claimed, was stupid and common, and it was beneath her to have any contact with such a woman. In January 1841, for example, she threatened to remove the children from Anna Liszt's custody: it was an 'idée fixe' and altogether absurd 'for two women like her and me to live together under a single roof'.[21]

Who was this woman who in the years to come was to be the children's most important point of contact? Following the early death of her husband, Adam, in August 1827, the thirty-nine-year-old Anna Liszt had settled in Paris in order to devote herself to her only son. A baker's daughter from Krems, she had worked in her Austrian homeland as a nursemaid and as a maidservant. She was a simple soul who already had problems with the German language and now had to learn French as well. All the more remarkable, therefore, is the ease with which she adapted to life in Paris and fulfilled the social duties of a woman about town, demonstrating great devotion and no less skill. Whenever Liszt was away on tour, she would sort out his business affairs for him, receiving important visitors, corresponding with his publishers, paying his bills and dealing with all the tasks and errands that it fell to her to take care of.

With hindsight we must regard it as a stroke of good fortune that Cosima and Blandine were placed in the care of Anna Liszt at the end of 1839. Their natural parents had no idea what to do with them and could not in any case be regarded as suitable guardians. Anna Liszt loved her grandchildren and offered them something approaching maternal affection for the first time in their lives. The period between the end of 1839 and the end of 1850, when they were separated from their grandmother, was arguably the happiest in their lives until then. Amid the many arguments that flared up between Liszt and Marie d'Agoult over the welfare of their children, Anna Liszt seems to have been the only person whom the sisters could regard as an ally. Their apartment in the Rue Pigalle and later in the Rue Louis-le-Grand was their first real home. Liszt assumed sole responsibility for his children's education and livelihood, while Marie d'Agoult failed signally to make a single contribution. He regularly sent his mother relatively large sums of money so that financially, at least, they would not go short.

Liszt and his former mistress saw each other only infrequently. Between 1841 and 1843 the couple spent their summer holidays together on the island of Nonnenwerth near Bonn, but their relationship was almost certainly unwinding by then. It was a gradual process that dragged on until 1844, both parties adding to their difficulties with their minor irritations and petty jealousies. It comes as no surprise, therefore, to discover a note of stridency entering their still voluminous correspondence. Marie d'Agoult was turning her Paris salon into a meeting place for left-wing men and women of letters and republican politicians: frequent visitors included writers such as Victor Hugo, Eugène Sue, Alphonse de Lamartine, Charles-Augustin Sainte-Beuve and Georg Herwegh. Among regular callers at the apartment in the Rue Neuve-des-Mathurins was the English diplomat, Henry Bulwer-Lytton (not to be confused with his more famous brother, Edward George, first Baron Lytton). Marie was evidently flattered that the sensitive Englishman was interested in courting her. She wrote to Liszt in Vienna: 'Hier soir M. Bulwer. Encore M. Bulwer! toujours M. Bulwer. Il a l'air de s'amuser beaucoup avec moi.'[22] Some weeks later she even asked Liszt for 'une petite permission d'infidélité'. Liszt seems to have seen through her game: 'You're asking for my permission to commit some infidelity! Dear Marie, you don't give a name. I assume it's Bulwer, though it matters little. . . . I want you to have your freedom, and I like it that you do, as I am convinced that you will always use it nobly and tactfully. Until the day when you say to me: this or that man has felt more strongly than you and understood more intimately than you who I *am* and what I can *be* – until that day there can be no talk of infidelity, and nothing, *absolutely nothing* will change between us.'[23]

Marie d'Agoult was not in fact interested in an affair with Bulwer: she was simply bluffing and wanting to make Liszt jealous. His diplomatic answer initially took the wind out of her sails, and so she returned to the attack, writing to him at the end of February 1840: 'B[ulwer] asked me yesterday if he could adopt the little one [Blandine].'[24] It was an absurd idea, and Liszt lost no time in dismissing it, but his former lover would not relent and wrote back to say that she was convinced that Bulwer 'loves me with complete disinterested-ness'.[25] Elsewhere she described the visitors to her salon: 'All these men are more or less in love with me. . . . Will that cause you a lot of suffering?'[26] There is no doubt that Marie d'Agoult was playing with her partner in a desperate attempt to draw attention to her own unhappy situation.

Among the men who were 'more or less in love' with Marie d'Agoult was presumably the influential publisher Émile de Girardin, who was responsible for a decisive turn of events in her life when he suggested that she should become a regular contributor to his newspaper, *La Presse*. As a sample of her abilities she submitted a piece on an exhibition at the École des Beaux-Arts. Girardin was ecstatic. Whatever his protégée wrote, he would publish it. Marie d'Agoult felt flattered but initially declined the invitation as she did not want to cause her family further unpleasantness: 'If I am to be criticized in the papers, I do not want anyone to feel honour-bound to defend me.'[27] Girardin had a solution to this problem, too: she should publish her articles pseudonymously. A suitable nom de plume was soon found: Daniel Stern. Marie d'Agoult's remarketing as Daniel Stern marked the start of an impressive career in journalism. Her brilliant and often caustic style struck a chord with the age, and for decades her three-volume *Histoire de la Révolution de 1848* was a standard work that is still worth reading today.

No less important is her novel *Nélida* – an anagram of the name Daniel – which she completed in 1844. But its significance was of an entirely different order from that of her history of the 1848 revolution, for it signalled the definitive end of the affair between its author and her former lover. Its genesis was bound up with a woman who would otherwise be barely worth mentioning, Lola Montez, a twenty-six-year-old dancer whom Liszt met in Dresden in late February 1844. Lola Montez was not in fact her real name, but was the product of a perfervid imagination. She was born Marie Dolores Eliza Rosanna Gilbert. Nothing about her seems to have been genuine. Although it pleased her to pass herself off as the very embodiment of a hot-blooded Spanish dancer, she was in fact born in Ireland. It may likewise be doubted whether as an artist she could be taken seriously. It would probably not be doing her much of a disservice to describe her as an adventuress. Be that as it may, she performed in Dresden in the early months of 1844 and met Liszt. It seems that she already had her eye on the world-famous pianist and hoped to be able to use him to advance her own career.

Whatever may have taken place between the two of them, it was in all likelihood no more than a casual encounter, but the alleged liaison between the notorious dancer and the demigod of the keyboard had all the makings of a sensational scandal. Rumours were rife in the salons of the period: Lola Montez was said to be Liszt's mistress, she was accompanying him on one of his tours and he had even obtained an engagement for her at the Académie Royale de Musique. By the time that Marie d'Agoult got wind of all this, she had had enough and was all too ready to lend credence to the rumours. Liszt arrived in Paris in early April 1844. The couple met and argued. What had been a difficult situation now seemed utterly hopeless. But what Liszt did not know is that by this date Marie d'Agoult had been working on *Nélida* for a good six months. By the summer of 1844, the manuscript was finished. In short, the 'Lola Montez affair' was not the outward reason for the novel but merely a kind of catalyst. The relationship between Liszt and Marie d'Agoult had long since been under strain.

Nélida has regularly been described as an autobiographical novel, but the plot is based less on real facts than on its author's imagination and on wishful thinking. Be that as it may, it is doubtful whether the tale of Nélida de la Theiellaye and Guermann Regnier is one of Marie's better literary efforts. Such doubts were raised from an early date, notably by the poet Pierre-Jean de Béranger, who was one of the first to read the finished manuscript and who advised against publication. 'Some people will think that they recognize themselves in the characters,' Béranger argued. 'You'll be accused of having painted real-life portraits.' But Marie d'Agoult refused to be deterred by these objections. 'I felt a need – blind, perhaps, but none the less almost irresistible – to emerge from an isolation of heart and mind that had more than once driven me to thoughts of suicide. I needed to break free from myself and find some new interest in life.'[28] Marie d'Agoult's 'irresistible need' was at bottom the desire to wreak vengeance on her lover of many years' standing. She was simply unable to forgive him for the fact that he had never regarded her as his muse and as a source of inspiration and that he was not dependent on her as an artist. In one of the key scenes in the novel, the author accuses Guermann Regnier – who bears markedly Lisztian features – of artistic impotence as a painter. It is an episode that lays bare Marie d'Agoult's own complexes and frustrations: in her eyes Liszt was artistically impotent because he spurned her inspiration. In public, Liszt reacted with astonishing calm to this tasteless attack on him, commenting laconically that he had never intended to become a painter. But it seems clear that such frontal attacks wounded him very deeply. The two of them would now go their separate ways.

Years of Happiness

'Your news of the children, which I received in Lyons, was a source of great pleasure to me,' Liszt wrote to his mother from Nîmes in early August 1844.[29] He had set out a good three months earlier on an extended tour that took him through southern France to Spain and Portugal. At this point he could scarcely imagine that it would be nine years before he next saw his children. Once again, then, the children effectively had no father. What was to become of them, especially now that their parents had separated for good? Blandine was eight and old enough to start regular schooling. From 1844 she attended the girls' select boarding school run by Louise Bernard and her daughter Laure in the Rue Montparnasse. Madame Bernard was regarded as an excellent and loving teacher who made sure that her young charges knew everything they needed to know as future members of Parisian high society. The timetable at her school included reading, German and English, an introduction to history and even excursions into the world of Greek tragedy. 'Yesterday I went to see blandin [*sic*] with Cosima,' Anna Liszt informed her son; 'she's always infinitely happy to see us.'[30]

In the weeks and months after their separation, Liszt was keen to ensure that for the sake of their children the break-up should be amicable. He was at pains 'as far as possible to avoid all friction on this side,' he assured his mother. 'Sooner or later matters will take whatever course they must, but for the present we must simply possess our souls in patience.'[31] A few weeks later he got wind of the rumour that 'Mme d'A. is wanting to return to her husband'. Although this rumour proved unfounded, Liszt's immediate reaction was one of relief, because Marie d'Agoult would have had to renounce all rights to the children if she had returned to Charles d'Agoult. 'This arrangement suits me down to the ground, it could not be better and strikes me as the only sensible solution. It was bound to happen sooner or later – and the question of my children would be much simplified.'[32]

His children? Blandine, Cosima and Daniel were illegitimate, but Liszt had acknowledged them as his own, and so, according to French law, he alone had the right to care for them. If a child's mother was involved in its upbringing at this time, she owed this to an agreement with the father, since, strictly speaking, she had no legal claim to it. It was an arrangement that worked after a fashion. 'It seems to me that the children's education is a source of inextricable annoyance for you,' Liszt wrote accusingly to Marie. 'And on the day that you set yourself up as my enemy, it will be impossible for me to agree to hand them back to you.'[33] Marie d'Agoult struck an equally implacable note in her reply, showering Liszt with reproaches and ultimately accusing him of trying to steal from her 'the fruits of a mother's womb'. 'From now on, Monsieur, your daughters no longer have a mother. That is what you want.' And she went on: 'One day your children may ask you where their mother is. And you'll reply: "It didn't suit me that you should have one." '[34] On another occasion she resorted to threats, telling her former lover that she would fight for her children like a lioness. But it was an empty threat. Marie withdrew from the fray and did not see Blandine and Cosima again until the beginning of 1850.

These constant wranglings affected Anna Liszt, too. She was worried about what would become of her grandchildren. 'Blandine and Cosima should both remain where they are,' Liszt reassured her: 'Blandine should stay with Madame Bernard, Cosima with you.' If Marie d'Agoult were none the less to attempt to take the children, he would 'answer force with force and come to Paris in order to take all three to Cologne or somewhere else. But I hope that she will not oblige me to take this painful step and that a glimmer of sound common sense will come to her aid.' Above all, his 'dear mother' should not be afraid of thunderbolts raining down on her from the direction of the Rue Neuve-des-Mathurins: 'They will certainly not prove fatal.'[35]

For the present, then, the situation remained as it was. But in mid-1846 Liszt decided that Cosima, too, should become a pupil at Madame Bernard's boarding school, a suggestion that initially left Anna Liszt distinctly unenthusiastic. 'She is getting on perfectly well at home and has certainly not missed out on her education,' Anna Liszt sought to reassure her son, who was once again away on tour, this time in Hungary. 'She is still quite sickly, although she has grown a lot' – no doubt Anna Liszt's culinary skills played a part in this. In her stilted German, Anna reports spoiling her eight-year-old granddaughter with cutlets, steaks and whole legs of lamb. In short: 'All she needs is good food. But if you really want her to go to boarding school in October, I'll hand her over, but I believe I shall soon have to take her back when she falls ill and that the money will be thrown away.'[36] Liszt was able to dispel his mother's misgivings, and in early October 1846 Cosima was placed in Louise Bernard's care.

And so Liszt's younger daughter was now introduced to the realities of the world. In fact, Cosima seems to have enjoyed life in the Rue Montparnasse, not least because the two sisters remained in close contact with their grandmother, whom they both loved. They spent their weekends and school holidays with Anna Liszt, so that little had really changed. It goes without saying that music played an important role in the syllabus at the boarding school. Cosima had shown a certain talent on the family piano at home, and so it was decided that she would be properly trained, but when the music teacher at the boarding school, a Mademoiselle Chazarin, learnt that she was to teach the daughter of the world-renowned Franz Liszt, she grew understandably nervous. Liszt responded with characteristic charm, assuring her that he had complete trust in her and informing his mother that 'it is really not necessary to prescribe a method to such an intelligent teacher as clearly talented as Mademoiselle Chazarin'.[37] As for Daniel, Liszt's youngest child had moved to Paris in the autumn of 1841 and had lived with his sisters at his grandmother's house. From October 1846 onwards he was taught privately by a Monsieur Harlez, whose boarding school he entered two years later in order to prepare for the prestigious Lycée Bonaparte.

To judge by all that we know about Liszt, it would be difficult to describe him as a good father. But unlike Marie d'Agoult, who contributed nothing to their upbringing, Liszt made it possible for Blandine, Cosima and Daniel to enjoy an excellent and expensive education. He regularly sent his mother money from his countless concert tours. In February 1847, for example, we find him writing to her: 'In approximately two weeks you'll receive fifteen thousand francs, which I don't need, and you'll have another ten thousand on my name-day. There will then be a break till the end of the autumn as I shall probably need the little money I have to survive the summer in reasonable comfort'.[38] But a happy childhood involves far more than this. Decades later Cosima was still complaining that she had 'come into the world curiously disinherited'.[39] Her comment suggests how difficult and even painful her early years must have been without any parents. All three children regarded their father as a kind of force of nature. On another occasion, Cosima recalled that 'from my childhood, when I would see him flit past, until the very end, the impression that he left on me was that of a fantastically legendary phenomenon'.[40] Her choice of words is significant: Liszt was a fleeting phenomenon like a comet passing briefly across the heavens and disappearing again as quickly as it had come. It was undoubtedly difficult to be the daughter of Liszt and Marie d'Agoult.

During the nine-year period from 1844 to 1853 when Liszt did not see his daughters at all, he gave Paris the widest possible berth, so keen was he to avoid all contact with his former lover. Time and again he announced that he would be visiting the city, prompting a veritable frenzy of anticipation in his children, but on each occasion he stayed away. Even plans to meet elsewhere failed to materialize. Only through his letters did Liszt continue to take an interest in his children's lives. He enquired about their daily routine at school, asked about their achievements in class and even discussed the books that they were reading.

All in all, the relationship between Liszt's children and their 'cher père' was extremely formal and reserved. They addressed him as 'Sie', reserving the informal and affectionate 'du' for their grandmother. As long as they could remember, they were conscious of the fact that their father was world-famous. Visibly proud, they collected cuttings from newspapers and magazines, hoarding everything about him that they could lay their hands on. Although they scarcely needed encouragement, Anna Liszt additionally urged her charges to love and honour their father. It comes as no surprise, therefore, to discover that their letters to him seem solemn and awkward. In June 1846, for example, we find Cosima writing to her father: 'Thank you a thousand times for taking the time to write such a lovely letter to me.'[41] A little over a year later, she reported on her progress on the piano – she was currently practising Weber's *Invitation to the Dance*: 'It is a very difficult piece for me, as I do not have much strength, but I shall try to play it without making any mistakes.' Success at school was another favourite topic of conversation: she was now in a new class, Cosima reported, and must make much more effort. At the same time, she hoped to win several of the popular school prizes 'for it would be shameful of me not to get one.'[42]

There is no doubt that these are the letters of a young woman anxious to please her father. Both girls showed considerable skill in their attempts to lure Liszt to Paris. On one occasion they promised to practise the piano more assiduously than ever if he were to visit them, while on another they even announced that they were praying for his return. But Liszt did not even attend their first Communion, an absence that understandably saddened the sisters. Cosima put a brave face on it: 'You have long postponed this visit, which would have made us so very happy, but I am sure that it is not your fault and that you, too, cherish the desire to see us.'[43]

The Princess

The Ukrainian city of Kiev lies some 1,250 miles to the east of Paris. It was here, in early February 1847, when the city was still a part of Russia, that Liszt gave a handful of concerts and was introduced to the woman who was to exert a decisive influence on his own and his children's lives. She was Jeanne Élisabeth Carolyne von Sayn-Wittgenstein. On the day after their first meeting this princess invited the virtuoso pianist to her feudal estates at Woronince, 150 miles to the south-west of Kiev. Liszt remained there for several weeks, a stay that continues to be shrouded in mystery. All that we can say for certain is that Anna Liszt had cause to complain that the letters she regularly received from her son had dried up to a mere trickle. Had he fallen in love and forgotten the world around him? And who was Carolyne von Sayn-Wittgenstein?

Carolyne was born in 1819 and was the only daughter of an immensely wealthy Polish landowner, Peter Iwanowsky, and his wife, Pauline Podowska. Their wealth must have bordered on the fabulous, for it is said that they needed 30,000 serfs to work the lands that they owned.[44] Carolyne's parents separated when she was eleven. She remained with her father and was brought up by a French governess. Peter Iwanowsky's relations with his daughter seem to have been eccentric, to put it mildly. At all events, he had no problems offering the young lady his cigars, an offer she was happy to accept. From this period dates her love of smoking and character traits best described as droll. In April 1836 she married Prince Nicholas von Sayn-Wittgenstein, the youngest son of Field Marshal Ludwig Adolf Peter von Sayn-Wittgenstein, a veteran Russian soldier, and thus acquired the title of princess. Their only daughter, Marie, was born the following February. But their marriage proved an unhappy one, and within four years they had gone their separate ways.

Let us return to 1847. Following his visit to Woronince, Liszt initially resumed his tour of the Ukraine, renewing contact with Carolyne in Odessa, from where the couple returned to her estates. Here they remained until the autumn. News of the affair between the famous pianist and the eccentric princess spread like wildfire, eventually reaching Paris, where Anna Liszt was already concerned about her son's well-being. While conceding that his new mistress was 'an admirable woman', she attempted to dissuade him from any further involvement with 'high-born ladies' – 'you've already paid dearly for this!'[45] But her maternal advice, including her monitory reminder of Marie d'Agoult, came too late, for Liszt and the princess had already decided that their lives were inextricably linked.

Events now moved swiftly. Liszt left Woronince in January 1848 and travelled to Weimar, while the princess, after a period of nerve-wracking indecision, sold her estates and together with her money and daughter fled to Germany under conditions that verged on the traumatic. Since 1842 Liszt had held the honorary title of 'Kapellmeister-in-Extraordinary' at the Weimar court, although it was not until January 1844 that he had conducted his first concert in the town. By 1848 he was tired of constant travel and decided to settle with Carolyne in the city of Goethe and Schiller. A home appropriate to his standing was quickly found in the Altenburg, a vast villa on a small hill slightly away from the inner town. The three-storey building had space for Liszt's study, his extensive collection of scores, his various musical instruments ranging from a spinet once owned by Mozart to several grand pianos and a 'piano-organ', the latter a combination of the two instruments specially designed for Liszt. Carolyne's needs were similarly catered for. There were also several guest rooms, allowing friends and – in increasing numbers – Liszt's private pupils to be accommodated on the premises, often for relatively lengthy periods of time.

Initially, however, Carolyne lived at the Altenburg alone, while Liszt stayed at the Erbprinz Hotel, an official arrangement prompted by the fact that the princess was attempting to persuade Tsar Nicholas I to annul her existing marriage. Social and aristocratic conventions had to be upheld if the case was not to be jeopardized. But when the tsar turned down the request in the autumn of 1848, Liszt abandoned all pretence and moved into the Altenburg with his mistress.

Carolyne von Sayn-Wittgenstein was a woman to whom it was impossible to remain indifferent, her autocratic manner and effusive way of speaking positively inviting contradiction. But it was not easy to stand up to her, as a clearly impressed Hans von Bülow – currently studying with Liszt – wrote to tell his mother: 'The next day I lunched with Liszt and had an opportunity to get to know the princess a little better, especially to hear her speaking, for she talks for hours on end and scarcely allows her interlocutor half a minute to reply. . . . Liszt was not present at this conversation, which the princess conducted with admirable perspicacity, constantly making new assertions that were never superficial and all the while smoking the strongest imaginable cigars that produced a terrible, noxious cloud of smoke.'[46]

Liszt's biographers, especially those of an earlier generation, rarely had a good word to say about the princess. She appeared to them to be the complete opposite of Marie d'Agoult and, worse, the antitype of feminine beauty: short, swarthy and ugly. She was dismissed as 'Baba Yaga', a wicked Russian witch whose influence on Liszt was said to be entirely malign. Such a view is both offensive and unjust. Liszt and the princess loved each other: of that there is no doubt. And Liszt found in her a partner who took a real interest in his ideas, his plans and his compositions. It seems beyond question that Liszt's years in Weimar would have been far less productive if Carolyne had not been there. But it is no less true that as a fanatical Catholic Carolyne turned Liszt into the centre of a bizarre and almost pseudo-religious cult and that her influence radically affected his relations with his three children. His letters to Cosima, Blandine and Daniel reflect this develop-ment all too plainly: from now on he is no longer an artistic father figure, good-natured in his own way, but a strict patriarch all too ready to chide his offspring.

The first of his children to feel this change was Daniel when Liszt wrote to inform his mother that he would 'make short work' of his son as 'it can only upset me to see a person persist in leading a life of stupidity and idleness'.[47] Once again it was Anna Liszt who took up the cudgels on behalf of her grand-children and placated their unjust father. But the most decisive change of all took place in early January 1850, when Blandine happened to discover Marie d'Agoult's address. The very next day, while they were out walking, she and Cosima decided to call on their mother. The girls rang the doorbell and were admitted. When mother and daughters found themselves reunited so unex-pectedly after more than five years' separation, they fell into each other's arms, and there is no doubt that both parties were happy to see each other again. Back at home, they said nothing to their grandmother about what had just happened. A few days later, on 8 January, Anna Liszt travelled to Weimar to visit her son and his mistress, leaving the children alone for the first time in Paris. During this period further meetings took place between Marie d'Agoult and her daughters. In February, a good four weeks after her first visit to the Rue Neuve-des-Mathurins, Blandine wrote to her father in all innocence: 'We've seen Mama again, and so great was our pleasure that it made us forget the pain of such a protracted separation.'

At the Altenburg the alarm bells rang. Liszt was shell-shocked, and his anger knew no bounds, although his reproach amounted to little more than a reminder that after prior arrangement Marie d'Agoult could have visited her children whenever she liked at Madame Bernard's boarding school. The fact that for five years she had made no use of this right meant that she herself was not entirely guiltless in the matter of her estrangement from her children. But why now? And why in this way? In Liszt's eyes the meeting represented a flagrant breach of trust for he felt that his daughters and their mother had gone behind his back. He was also afraid that his former lover might interfere in his children's lives, a fear that was not without foundation: 'Mama longs to see more of us,' Blandine informed her father.[48] He replied with some asperity: 'You were wrong, and you have done me wrong by assuming that it was not for good reason that I have until now refused to allow the sort of relationship between you and your mother that should of course have existed.' Only now can the girls have realized what had happened, not least because Liszt was not sparing in his emotional blackmail. Their grandmother, he went on, had wept 'bitter tears' at their misbehaviour. As a punishment they would have to leave

Madame Bernard's school and live with their grandmother again. 'You've behaved badly,' he scolded the two girls. 'What's done can't be undone, and so you must make every effort to put things right, and this is possible only if from now on you cease all correspondence and all contact with your mother at least until such time as I instruct you otherwise.'[49]

Blandine and Cosima were left with no choice but to offer a meek apology and mend their ways. They begged their father to relent, but in vain. Liszt remained implacable, and the two children were obliged to say goodbye to Laure Bernard, a teacher whom they had both come to love. Meanwhile, at the Altenburg, Liszt and the princess had to decide how best to deal with the situation in Paris. The girls' return to live with their grandmother was no more than a makeshift solution, as Liszt was convinced that his mother was far too good-natured and forbearing. At this point Carolyne suggested despatching her own former governess to Paris, a suggestion that was to lead to a further dramatic change in the lives of Cosima, Blandine and Daniel.

Brainwashing

Madame Louise Adélaïde Patersi de Fossombroni was already seventy-two years old when she received Carolyne's cry for help. She was then living in retirement in Saint Petersburg. A French national, she had fared badly at the hands of fate. She had been widowed early in life and had been abandoned by her only son when he was twenty-five. Madame Patersi then found a sense of purpose in her life by educating the children of leading aristocrats, among them the Countesses Isaure de Foudras and Ludemille de Thermes, Princess Zénaïde de Wagram and Carolyne Iwanowska, better known as Princess Carolyne von Sayn-Wittgenstein. There is no doubt that Carolyne was the driving force behind Madame Patersi's appointment. After all, the old woman was not only regarded as an outstanding teacher, she was particularly loyal to her former pupil. Carolyne could rely unconditionally on Madame Patersi and would effectively be installing her own vice-regent in her new position in Paris.

The fact that the new governess held strict moral views and was not a woman to be tangled with became clear from her journey to Paris. Dressed, as always, in black, she boarded the train in Saint Petersburg and spent the entire journey sitting bolt upright in her compartment. The reason? She would have felt it indecorous to relax against the cushion provided for her comfort. By the time she arrived in Weimar, where she was to receive her final instructions, the torturous travails of her journey had left her so ill that Carolyne had to spend the next two months keeping a vigil by her sickbed in the Altenburg. But Liszt was reluctant to waste any time and insisted that his mother should hand over Cosima and Blandine to Madame Patersi's elder sister, the unmarried Madame Thomas de Saint-Mars, who lived in the Rue Casimir Périer. The matter was one of immense importance to him, as he made unmistakably clear in a letter to his mother pre-empting Madame Patersi's eventual arrival in Paris: 'I have asked Madame Patersi never to let my daughters go out without her and to visit you often. I am convinced that you will soon get to know her so well that you will come to value and love her for the good that her guidance will bring to my children. She will decide what they should fittingly be permitted to do and what should be forbidden them; she is thoroughly familiar with my ideas on the subject of their upbringing and of their future, ideas that coincide in every way with her own.'[50] It broke Anna Liszt's heart to have to give up the grandchildren she loved so much and to move into a smaller apartment in the Rue Penthièvre. Her household was broken up, and part of its contents, including Liszt's library, was handed over to the children's new governess.

Louise Adélaïde Patersi de Fossombroni's teaching programme was as terrifying as her name. What began at the end of 1850 and lasted until August 1855, by which date Cosima was nearly eighteen, amounted to an authoritarian regime similar to that used for breaking in horses. Even in their sleep, her charges had to know what a young lady from high society should think about art, literature, music and history and what opinions she should express on such matters. Madame Patersi had played practically no part in the social and political upheavals that had shaken France since 1830 and so she viewed the term 'high society' as synonymous with the *Ancien Régime*, an absolutist form of rule swept aside by the French Revolution. The politician Charles-Maurice de Talleyrand-Périgord argued with dewy-eyed nostalgia that only those who had lived before 1789 could know how sweet life was. This was a view shared by Madame Patersi, who had been born in the Brittany village of Saint-Hilaire-de-Chaléons in 1778. She and her sister brought up the children to despise the values of the post-revolutionary world and taught them a profound contempt for all things 'bourgeois'.

Madame Patersi's dismissive attitude to the present often had curious consequences. She hated all forms of entertainment, so that even free tickets for a concert were an abomination in her eyes, and she felt that it was unseemly to accept such gifts. As Cosima commented in a letter to her father, 'In general, Madame Patersi is so dissatisfied with everything that she even abhors tickets

that have been given to her.'[51] Their governess demanded total subordination
on their part and was not fastidious about the means that she used to achieve
that end. Childish defiance or rebellion and resistance were broken on the
wheel. During their initial period in Madame Patersi's care, Blandine and
Cosima were often reduced to tears – not that this made any impression on the
two old ladies in the Rue Casimir Périer. 'Tears are just water' was one of their
watchwords. Nor did the elderly sisters shy away from spiritually terrorizing
their charges. Only a few months after she arrived in Paris, Madame Patersi
dragged the two girls off to see Father Ventura at the Madeleine, telling the
reverend father that they had been exceptionally naughty. The desired reprimand was not slow in coming: 'My children, you must obey your father blindly,
even when you do not understand his reasons for acting as he does. You
will discover them much later and see that he acted solely for your own well-
being.'[52] Father Ventura ended by bestowing his blessing upon his visitors and
giving them a crucifix and some medals blessed by the pope. The Catholic
Church was also called upon to prepare the young women for their future roles
as wives. And so we find Cosima writing to inform her father that Abbé Gabriel
had told her that a woman's entire life was 'a sacrifice and that she has to be a
living host'.[53] Only a few weeks later, Blandine reported that Madame Patersi
was implacable in her attempts to train them both to be good wives: 'She
assures us that our husbands will no longer let us get away with all the things
for which she now reproaches us.' And she went on: 'We have little experience
in these matters but understand very well that she is perfectly right.'[54]

There are many incidents in the sad lives of Cosima and Blandine at which
we might be inclined to smile, were it not for the fact that those incidents had
such unpleasant consequences for them both. Once, when Cosima had left
her room in a mess, she had to write an essay and send it to her father. In it
Cosima describes an imaginary conversation between a certain Madame de
Mahn and her daughter Herwig: 'My dear mother, when you reprimanded me
this morning about the mess in my room, you promised to tell me a story that
would make it clear what terrible consequences such a mess can have. Will
you tell me this story now, dear mother?'[55] But Cosima had to break off her
little tale before it was finished, as Madame Patersi was too impatient to wait
for the end. But she seems to have achieved her aim: Cosima had understood
that disorder – in this context synonymous with disobedience – could have
the most 'terrible consequences'.

The two sisters no doubt felt instinctively that there was something mendacious about this education, but they had no one in whom to confide their

feelings – least of all Liszt and the princess – and so they vented those feelings of unhappiness in the form of the written word. Blandine's unpublished papers, now in the Bibliothèque nationale in Paris, include a number of amusing and yet depressing plays that throw light on the intellectually cramped confines of the Rue Casimir Périer. The following thoroughly banal 'Scène de la vie intime' took place on 20 March 1855. It is nine o'clock in the morning and the characters are still in their nightclothes. Suddenly there is a ring at the door:

THE PORTIÈRE: I'm coming, Madame! A policeman has sent me. You're to receive a fine!

MADAME DE SAINT-MARS *(gruffly)*: What? We'll see about that! But why, if I may ask?

THE PORTIÈRE: He saw a wet facecloth fall from a fourth-floor window. I didn't want to come up, but he made me.

MADAME DE SAINT-MARS: Oh, how droll! We're respectable women, and yet we're accused of throwing wet facecloths on to the heads of passers-by! It's appalling! Send the oaf up at once, assuming he'll condescend to come!

The Portière withdraws, while Cosima and Blandine get dressed in their room.

COSIMA: It's a joke. What are we being accused of? I'm a little surprised. In fact, I bet it was Patersi who threw out the facecloth. Hurry up. I want to see the end of this farce.

BLANDINE: Just wait a moment! It takes a while to climb to the fourth floor. But it's funny to see how seriously these women are taking it – it's as if a murder had been committed.

COSIMA: Yes, but a moral murder, as Patersi would say.

The conversation is interrupted by the arrival of the Policeman.

MADAME DE SAINT-MARS *(to the Policeman, respectfully)*: What's got into you, calling on us this morning like this?

THE POLICEMAN *(calmly)*: I've come because a wet facecloth fell from the fourth floor.

MADAME DE SAINT-MARS: You're wrong. Who do you think dropped it? The maidservant is away, and the young ladies are dressing in their room.

THE POLICEMAN: It may have been these young ladies.

MADAME DE SAINT-MARS: These young ladies never open their window unless we ourselves are present.

THE POLICEMAN *(with an ironic laugh)*: That's possible, but I know only that I saw a facecloth fall from this window.

MADAME PATERSI (*deeply troubled*): From my window, Monsieur? That's impossible! I was busy ironing ribbons, Monsieur.

THE POLICEMAN: When someone is ironing ribbons, it's quite possible to throw a troublesome facecloth out of the window.

MADAME DE SAINT-MARS: It must have come from the fifth floor.

THE POLICEMAN: It came from the fourth.

MADAME DE SAINT-MARS: Let's get this straight. We live on the mezzanine on the third floor.

THE POLICEMAN: No, no, it came from this window. I just happened to be looking up when the cloth fell from the window. It couldn't possibly have flown up to your window as it was a wet facecloth.

MADAME PATERSI: Monsieur, I don't own a facecloth as I use a sponge when washing.

THE POLICEMAN (*very calmly*): I don't know what the cloth was used for. I just know that it fell from the window.

MADAME PATERSI: I swear to you by God, Monsieur, by the Gospel, by all that's sacred, Monsieur, I didn't drop the cloth.

THE POLICEMAN: You can swear as much as you like.

MADAME DE SAINT-MARS: We're respectable women. Remember whom you're talking to.

MADAME PATERSI: Yes, respectable women! We're God-fearing and not sanctimonious. We follow the teachings of the Abbé Lonvot. We weren't picked up in the street, Monsieur!

THE POLICEMAN: I know very well that you weren't picked up in the street. But that's where the cloth was found.

MADAME DE SAINT-MARS (*put out, leaning for support on a sofa*): And you think we're lying and that we'd be capable of lying to our consciences because of some pitiful fine? When I swear to you, I do so by my honour. (*She strikes her own breast.*) Be off with you, and make your enquiries on the fifth floor.

THE POLICEMAN: They'll just tell me exactly the same.

MADAME DE SAINT-MARS: What do you mean? 'Exactly the same'? Do you think they'll demean themselves . . .

MADAME PATERSI: Yes, that they'll demean themselves for a few sous?

MADAME DE SAINT-MARS: Do you really think that you're dealing with rag-and-bone men from the Faubourg Saint-Marceau? You think I don't know what I'm capable of?

THE POLICEMAN: Very well! This time I'll let it pass, but don't try it again.

MADAME DE SAINT-MARS: Oh, you can rest assured that we shan't try it again, especially since it wasn't us today.

THE POLICEMAN: I'm not entirely convinced of that.

MADAME DE SAINT-MARS: Is there something you're not telling us? Oh, that would be terrible, appalling! How much is this fine? I ask not because I intend to pay it – after all, I haven't deserved it. You see, if I go to the police, I don't know what I'd say, yes, I'd say that the police should take good care that the people they employ have good eyesight.

THE POLICEMAN: Oh, my eyesight is fine – sometimes too good.

MADAME PATERSI: That is Monsieur's prerogative.

MADAME DE SAINT-MARS: What do you mean, it's his prerogative? Was it you who dropped it? If only the maidservant were here, but she's gone out, and our reputation is such that people shouldn't even think of accusing us of anything.

THE POLICEMAN: It's like this. Madame's window was open. Why else would she have closed it when she saw me?

MADAME DE SAINT-MARS: Oh, Monsieur, that's quite impossible. In her condition, my sister never stands by the window. She is far too fastidious to stick her nose out of the window in a nightcap and dressing gown.

MADAME PATERSI: Also, I was holding a large hand towel.

THE POLICEMAN: Madame, I couldn't see everything you were holding. But I could certainly see the facecloth.

MADAME PATERSI: Monsieur, you're the first person who has dared to doubt our morals. Ask everyone in this quarter who we are and if I would be so tasteless as to own a facecloth and throw it out of my window. Never, Monsieur! My reputation is spotless. I have brought up the most distinguished women in France and Poland, and neither I nor any of my pupils has ever been accused of such a thing before . . .

THE POLICEMAN: That's of no concern to me. But I know that a facecloth fell out of the window. On this occasion I'll let it pass.

MADAME DE SAINT-MARS: Watch what you're saying! We've never lied, and we certainly shan't start lying over a facecloth. What kind of an example would that set these young ladies? . . .

The Policeman leaves, laughing to himself as he does so. Laughing out loud, Blandine enters the room in which Cosima is standing, half dressed.

BLANDINE: What do you make of this dramatic scene?

COSIMA: I heard only half of it. It's the most farcical thing I've ever seen. It's just like the story about the coachman.

MADAME DE SAINT-MARS *(entering with a smile)*: Well, we seem to have got off lightly. At least no one was killed.
MADAME PATERSI: Except the policeman. His bad conscience will undoubtedly be the death of him and of his sense of morality.
COSIMA *(quietly to Blandine)*: You know that it was Patersi who dropped the facecloth and that the policeman was right?[56]

Incredible though it seems, the scene clearly took place just as described. The atmosphere in which Blandine and Cosima grew up was one of hypocrisy, repression and false etiquette. From the very beginning of their rule of iron, Madame Patersi and her sister censored their charges' letters. In June 1853, for example, we find Blandine writing to her father: 'Madame Patersi doesn't post any of the letters that we write to you in French without reading them first. She permits me to inform you that she alone is responsible for the delay to this letter.'[57]

So severe was the censorship to which they were subjected that the only letters that Cosima and Blandine could write to their father in faraway Weimar were those designed to please him and to praise him. In December 1851, for example, Cosima wrote to him: 'We'd give anything to be able to make you content, you who feel such great love for us and who are so kind to us. We're surrounded by the maternal care and genuine interest on the part of these ladies and shall proceed along the lines you desire.'[58] Blandine, too, joined in this enforced chorus of praise: 'Madame Patersi is excellent for us, she gives us really motherly advice, and every day I grow increasingly fond of her. Sometimes we argue, but that certainly doesn't alter our feelings of affection.'[59]

All that really concerned the girls fell victim to the censor's red pencil. In this way they were infected with the curse of self-censorship and self-mortification even as teenagers. Hand in hand with this controlling influence went a certain superficiality in their correspondence. Unable to say what they felt, the two girls had to content themselves with expressing suitably sensitive views on works of music, books and paintings. And since their governess had given them to feel that their father was far too grand to concern himself with them, they struggled to please him with every sentence they wrote. The skill that Madame Patersi was trying to implant in her pupils was the ability to make stimulating small talk and to hold a cultivated salon conversation over tea and biscuits. Liszt was fully aware of the sham nature of this upbringing. When Blandine went into raptures over a piano sonata by Weber, he reacted indignantly: 'Why, in fact, is this sonata more congenial in your view? And why in particular does it impress you? I should be grateful if in your next letters you could provide some details on this matter, because expressing such generalizations is tantamount to saying nothing at all.'[60]

Why did Liszt do nothing to resist the crass regime to which his daughters were subjected? He must have been aware that their governess was merely carrying out the instructions of the new woman in his life and that nothing happened in Paris without Carolyne's knowledge and consent. After all, it could be argued that Madame Patersi's most important function was to drive a wedge between Marie d'Agoult and her children and to hold up the princess as a new and above all a better mother. And so we find Cosima writing to her father: 'I hope that God will answer my prayers and make it possible for us to call Madame la Princesse our mother before too long, for she already occupies that place in our hearts.'[61] In this regard, too, the censor was functioning efficiently, so that it is difficult to know how sincere were the children's protestations of their love for Carolyne.

That the dividing line between hypocrisy and fawning subservience is fluid emerges from a letter written jointly by Cosima and Blandine to Carolyne: 'Madame (or, rather, dear mother), for how else could we address you since you yourself call us your daughters and the tenderness that you express in your letters is that of a mother. Yes, Madame, please be our mother, for you have long been so in our eyes.' Madame Patersi had clearly done her work. Perhaps the old governess was standing behind her pupils when they elevated their stepmother to well-nigh saintly status: 'All the teachings that your letter contains, dear mother, were taught us long ago by Madame Patersi. We are keenly aware of Madame Patersi's merits. She certainly does not spoil us, and yet we are grateful to you for having entrusted us to her care. She often tells us about your afflictions, and, believe us, dear mother, that our hearts go out to you and that the day that brings an end to those sufferings will be blessed a thousand times in our sight, as it will be by all who love you.'[62] At around the same time Cosima assured her father that she and her brother and sister were taking very seriously the advice that he had given them and that Madame Patersi repeated on a daily basis. They were all very happy, she went on, at the tender relations that had developed between themselves and the princess.[63]

It is doubtful if Liszt suspected the emotional conflicts caused in his daughters by this subtle form of brainwashing. Although he noted a 'predisposition to burst into tears and create scenes', he never stopped to consider its causes.

For him, it was merely one of those characteristics 'that are among the most annoying in women and especially in yourselves, for I find such a quality extremely unsympathetic'. Comfort and consolation could clearly not be expected from such a father. 'Tears are attractive only on festive occasions, which, thank God, are infrequent enough. This blubbering is a parody of those beautiful tears, and as such I abhor it.'[64]

Unsurprisingly, the young Cosima Liszt reacted to this reign of mental terror with not so much as a single word of protest or provocation, but with a characteristic mixture of pride and humility. In this she received guidance from a book that every good Catholic family owned at this time alongside the family Bible. The book in question was *De Imitatione Christi* by Thomas à Kempis, a fifteenth-century Augustinian monk from Agnetenberg near Zwolle, who was one of the principal exponents of what has been called *devotio moderna*. This 'new piety' is characterized by a meditative approach to the life and sufferings of Christ as well as to God and the individual soul. Its author preaches a life of atonement and selflessness, for only in this way, he argues, is it possible to follow in Christ's footsteps. Our saviour appears here as a close friend offering comfort in the midst of life's calamities. It is entirely possible that Madame Patersi placed a copy of Thomas's tome on Cosima's bedside table – decades later she described *De Imitatione Christi* as 'the book of my youth'. When Cosima's own daughter, Daniela, grew depressed and melancholic in January 1881, she advised her 'to start at the beginning and read a chapter a day first thing in the morning'. She went on to quote her favourite passages from the work: 'Moreover, our entire peace in this miserable life consists more in humble suffering than in our exemption from that suffering'; and ' "He who best understands how to suffer will have the greatest peace" – thanks to this sentence I regained the peace of mind that had been taken from me by my grief at my own perceptions. And when you read: "A passionate man changes good into evil and easily believes in evil, whereas the peaceful and good man makes everything good again", you will understand me and appreciate many of my admonitions.'[65]

The belief that suffering could help her to grow and that she was a kind of martyr was Cosima's strategy for dealing with the world psychologically. In short, she accepted the many emotional wounds that she suffered early in life as so many challenges. If Cosima withstood these trials with humility, then her inner logic dictated that she was destined to walk in the footsteps of Christ. As a result, she developed an almost pleasurable propensity for suffering that was caught up with a submissive willingness for self-sacrifice on the one hand and a mixture of pride and absolute self-control on the other.

But there was also something specious about these characteristics: they were, after all, only a small step away from affected suffering, counterfeit emotion and showy gestures. Had not the Abbé Gabriel described the married woman as a 'living host' and likened her life to a constant 'sacrifice'? Cosima seems to have taken this to heart, for her marriage to Wagner many years later was notable for its altogether masochistic emotionalism. Everything from Wagner's passing remarks ('the Master's words') to his marital infidelity was invested with a theatricality of positively histrionic proportions. In February 1878, when Cosima discovered that her husband had been having an affair with Judith Gautier, her reaction was to adopt the attitude of a Christian martyr: 'May God help me!' she wrote in her diary. 'Oh, sorrow, my old companion, come back and dwell within me; we know each other well – how long will you stay with me this time, most loyal and dependable of friends?'[66] There is no doubt that Cosima had read De Imitatione Christi extremely closely and attentively.

Changes

How often had Cosima, Blandine and Daniel prayed for their father's return, but in vain! Not until the autumn of 1853 were those prayers finally answered, and the prospect of a reunion finally seemed to be close. In the Rue Casimir Périer there was naturally feverish activity and a tremendous sense of excitement. Nine years had passed since their last meeting, nine years during which much had happened. Blandine and Cosima had still been children when their father had last seen them in 1844. How would he now look? Had he changed? And how should they greet him? Questions upon questions. But Liszt did not come alone, suggesting that after such a lengthy separation he was nervous at the thought of renewing contact. After concert engagements in Karlsruhe, he had travelled to Basel, where he met Carolyne and her daughter, Marie. They were joined on their journey to Paris by one of Liszt's colleagues and friends, Richard Wagner.

Liszt had little time and, it seems, even less inclination to take any interest in his three children. Many years later, Cosima recalled that throughout the week-long visit, 'we were never taken along but found it entirely natural that he went out with Caroline [sic] and Marie'.[67] Carolyne tried to break the ice by giving small gifts to her stepchildren, but the general impression left by the visit was one of distance and stiff formality. Writing retrospectively, Wagner proved himself a perceptive observer:

One day Liszt invited me to spend an evening with his children, who lived a
secluded life in Paris under the care of a governess. It was a new experience
for me to observe my friend in the company of these girls, who were already
growing tall, and his son, who was just entering adolescence. He himself
seemed a bit bemused by his role as a father, from which over the years he
had derived only the cares and none of the satisfactions.[68]

All the parties felt inhibited, and even between the fifteen-year-old Cosima
and Marie von Sayn-Wittgenstein, who was more or less the same age, there
was a sense of shyness and reserve. Decades later, Marie recalled that 'poor
Cosima was in the throes of adolescence – tall, angular and fair-skinned, with
a large mouth and long nose, the very image of her father. Only her long
golden hair was of rare lustre and great beauty.'[69] The family gathering in
the Rue Casimir Périer took place on the evening of 10 October 1853.
Madame Patersi served a simple supper, after which the company retired
to the salon, where Wagner declaimed the final act of *Götterdämmerung*: 'It
was suddenly a lot for three children who thought themselves cut off not
just from the world but also from their family,' Cosima later wrote. 'All I could
do was stare at the ground, my poor eyesight and timidity of mind allowing
me to take everything in only furtively, as it were, for I knew that it was
not really there for me.'[70] Cosima seems to have left no real impression on the
man who was to be her second husband. 'I can still see Cosima's ecstatic
expression as the tears ran down her pointed nose,' Marie wrote dismissively.
'At that time Wagner had no eyes for the ugly child who was one day to
become his Isolde.'[71] In his autobiography – dictated to Cosima – Wagner
adopted a rather more charitable tone, attributing to both daughters an
'invariable shyness'.[72]

Within just over a week the visit was over, and the comet-like Liszt and his
satellites had disappeared as quickly as they had come. Life in Paris went on
as before. Cosima and Blandine continued to write to their father, proudly
informing him of their successes at school. They had a crash course in English
and German, learnt more about geography and studied the history of the
Middle Ages. Liszt's works often lay open on the piano. In the spring of 1854
we know that Cosima worked on her father's *Réminiscences de Don Juan*,
while Blandine learnt to play his *Réminiscences de Robert le diable*, both of
them difficult pieces. In June the girls fell ill with a fever and for a time
were confined to their beds, Cosima reporting that 'throughout our indispo-
sition Madame de Saint-Mars has looked after us admirably and spared

neither effort nor exhaustion in her attempts to bring us relief, so that I can assure you, dear father, that no mother could have looked after us any better; Madame Patersi, too, was very kind to us, and we are both now fully recovered'.[73]

As if to make up for his lack of interest in them the previous year, Liszt now invited his daughters to join him in Brussels. The two young women could scarcely believe their own luck. In the company of Madame Patersi they travelled to Belgium in mid-July 1854 and put up at the Hotel Bellevue in Brussels. Liszt evidently made an effort to spend more time with his visitors, inviting them out to eat and taking them on a tour of the Antwerp Zoo. 'They're good, they look good and are good-hearted,' Liszt wrote to Carolyne. 'I have been chatting with them or, to be more accurate, I speak to them and for them. Madame Patersi continues to be the perfect and excellent person that we know and love – she always keeps perfect order, even amid the pros and cons of a certain number of confused ideas.'[74] This hardly makes it sound as if father and daughters spent a genuinely enjoyable time together. At all events, the 'perfect order' praised by Liszt – a synonym for total control – could be maintained only at great cost. More than ever, Cosima, Blandine and Daniel were keen to renew contact with their mother. Unappealing though this idea must have seemed to Liszt, he also understood that he could not keep his children away from Marie d'Agoult for ever, especially now that they were almost grown up. At the end of a series of tenacious and wearisome negotiations, the parties finally worked out a modus vivendi: the countess must accept Madame Patersi as the children's governess and could meet her offspring only after due consultation and with the necessary prior agreement.

Since the end of 1851 Marie d'Agoult had been living at the Maison Rose, a magnificent villa in the Champs-Élysées not far from the Arc de Triomphe. On their weekly visits to Marie's salon, the children met well-known writers, philosophers and politicians. It was the first time that they had encountered anything approaching an intellectual challenge outside school. Marie read the French classics with them as well as works by Goethe and Plato. Years later, Cosima recalled that 'when she had read enough, she would take us to the Louvre and even – when our two old guardians permitted it – to the theatre. . . . I cannot describe the impression made on me by these Sunday visits; I can still see myself gazing hungrily at my mother's wonderful library, and when we returned to the cramped confines of our pedantically strict lives with two seventy-year-old governesses, these impressions continued to live on in us, as if we had just emerged from a world of bliss.'[75]

It required a certain diplomatic skill on the children's part to see their mother without incurring the wrath of the Altenburg. Blandine in particular was a mistress of deception. After each meeting with her mother, she would despatch an unctuous letter to Weimar in an attempt to keep the princess sweet. It was clear to them that their stepmother hated Marie d'Agoult and that if she had had her way, she would have ended all contact for good. 'I've written a short letter to our father,' Blandine warbled on in December 1854, 'in which I told her about our visit to see our mother, and I now feel the need to tell you, my dear, that no matter what the situation we may find ourselves in, we shall continue to be the same people in your eyes, we shall always love you with all our hearts and that you can count on us, just as we count on you. Have you not always been a mother to us?'[76]

A few days later Blandine reported on their next meeting: 'We spent Saturday with our mother, as arranged with Madame Patersi, there was just her, her daughter and little Daniel de Charnacé. It all passed off very simply and as was fitting. We arrived at five o'clock. Supper was at six.' And she went on:

We cannot thank our father enough for his sincere and tenderly paternal ideas on this matter, we never had any other thoughts, while our mother announced no wishes in this regard and simply told us that in future, if an opportunity were to arise, we might occasionally go to a museum together. You must understand, my dear, that we could never regard our mother's return to us as a way of distancing ourselves from our father. It is he who protects us and who will continue to protect us and we want only his protection, and this is so clear to us that it seems impossible that our mother could ever have any other ideas, she certainly shows no sign of doing so but is very calm and reserved and full of respect and concern for Madame Patersi, a point on which we are very glad. We belong body and soul to our father, and I do not know who could ever think of changing anything about our feelings in this matter.[77]

Perhaps Cosima and Blandine over-egged the pudding, for the naturally suspicious princess seems not to have believed the children's effusive asseverations of their love. Her mistrust was fuelled in no small part by Madame Patersi, who sounded out her charges, spying on them and informing Weimar of her findings. 'We are not afraid to tell her [Marie d'Agoult] about you,' Blandine defended herself, 'for what could we say to her that would not be filled with gratitude, love and respect for you?'[78]

The situation worsened in the early part of 1855, when Madame Patersi fell ill. Now seventy-seven, she suffered from a painful abscess that was repeatedly lanced by her doctors but which showed no signs of healing. The old woman was visibly declining: 'I feel so sorry for her and am so upset', Blandine assured the princess, 'that I no longer know where I am; I forget the days and hours and think only of this poor sick woman, who has been so inhumanly tested throughout her life and shown only a soul full of selflessness, strength and endurance, of which we have seen repeated signs and which we shall always remember.' For Madame de Saint-Mars, the task of looking after her sister, running the household and as far as possible keeping an eye on the two girls proved too much of a strain. Chaos descended on the Rue Casimir Périer, and we find Blandine writing to Carolyne: 'My dear, the outgoings on the house amount to around 2,150 francs, and we still have a number of smaller expenses such as two hats and the cost of having our brown clothes made. Madame de Saint-Mars is spending a lot of money on her sister's illness and can't advance us anything, and so we would ask you, my dear, if you would be kind enough to send us some money towards our upkeep.'[79] Cosima, too, was unwell. Dr Godart put his money on an upset stomach 'as she felt an intense and lasting pain and looked very poorly, but otherwise he would give us no further details and said only that this was to be expected from a chronic complaint'.[80]

With Madame Patersi in poor health, Cosima ill and Madame de Saint-Mars hopelessly overburdened, there was cause for considerable concern at the Altenburg. The situation could not be allowed to continue. But what should become of the children? Who could take them in? Marie d'Agoult? This was out of the question – Liszt would never have tolerated such a solution. Anna Liszt? She too was ailing and by now too old. What about Liszt himself? But he and the princess were still living in sin, a state of affairs that had already led to a certain disquiet at the Weimar court. A solution had to be found that took account of aristocratic sensibilities and that meant, therefore, that Liszt was unable to house his illegitimate children under his own roof. But it would also be true to say that he had little interest in doing so.

Liszt initially thought of sending his daughters to stay with an acquaintance in Dresden, a suggestion that in the end came to nothing. It was against the background of this muddled situation that it occurred to Liszt to ask Franziska von Bülow, the mother of his favourite pupil, to help him. Carolyne and her daughter travelled to Berlin at once to discuss the situation with Frau von Bülow. It seems that the two women quickly came to an agreement, for on 13 August Liszt wrote to his mother to inform her that she would be receiving visitors from Berlin. He had failed, however, to put his cards on the table when he claimed that he was merely wanting to spend a few days with his children: 'Frau von Bülow is being kind enough to collect them from Paris and bring them to Weimar, where I plan to house them in a style that they will always be pleased to recall.'[81] Cosima and Blandine were beside themselves with joy, and for the present everything looked just like a normal holiday. Only Anna Liszt was suspicious. 'I was extremely surprised', she told her son, 'because when I was in Weimar I heard you say more than once that I couldn't bring Cosima and Blandine to the town.'[82]

The girls travelled to Weimar with Franziska von Bülow, while Carolyne set off for Paris in order to deal with Madame Patersi. Soon after arriving in Paris, she called on Anna Liszt and initiated the old woman into the callous plan: Blandine and Cosima would not be returning to Paris but were being taken to Berlin under a pretext. There they would be living with the Bülows. 'The princess told me this with complete indifference', Anna Liszt complained to her son. 'There's practically nothing I could say, except that the children are now too big for yet another upheaval.'[83] Anna Liszt was upset at not being able to say goodbye to her grandchildren. The whole unhappiness of the last five years suddenly boiled to the surface: Carolyne would have done better to have left Madame de Patersi in Russia, for by the time she arrived in France she was already too old to look after the children, whom she had never really loved. And so she went on. But it was all to no avail. Liszt struck a conciliatory note in his letter of reply, but his resolve was utterly implacable.

Throughout this period Cosima and Blandine had no idea what was to happen to them. They spent two carefree weeks with their father, laughing and turning the Altenburg upside down with their boisterous behaviour. But when they found out about Liszt's plans for them, they predictably started to howl. They browbeat him and begged him to change his mind, but in vain. On 4 September 1855, Liszt, Cosima and Blandine travelled to Merseburg, where Franziska von Bülow was to collect her new charges, but after they had visited the local cathedral, Blandine persuaded her father to allow them to spend a few more days together in Weimar. Liszt proved amenable and took his children back with him. But after four days the girls moved to Berlin, while Daniel remained in Paris, completing his education.

'Blandine and Cosima are submitting willingly to their fate', Anna Liszt informed her son at the end of September. 'They've written to tell me that you've promised to visit them in Berlin this winter, they are looking forward to seeing you and live in hope that you'll come.'[84] Initially, everything was terribly strange and unfamiliar. Above all, the two young women missed their grandmother. Only for Madame Patersi and her sister did they shed no tears. For all that they were old and frail, the two governesses still felt sufficiently sprightly to rummage through the effects that Blandine and Cosima had left behind them in Paris. Here they discovered three letters that Marie d'Agoult had written to Blandine in August, letters containing derogatory remarks about Carolyne von Sayn-Wittgenstein. Madame Patersi suspected treachery and arranged for copies of all three letters to be forwarded to Weimar. When Liszt read these missives from his former mistress, his anger knew no bounds and he sent a detailed reply to his 'chers enfants', involuntarily admitting that he had received these documents from Madame Patersi in distinctly under-hand circumstances. Blandine was outraged, describing this act of indiscretion in a letter to her brother Daniel in Weimar as 'base and contemptible'. This in turn provoked Liszt into writing a further sharply worded rejoinder in which he praised Madame Patersi for her 'act of responsibility and morality', while accusing his daughters of seeking to 'rebel' against his wishes. 'And since when', he concluded, 'have three tiny tots like you been justified in setting yourselves up as supreme judges in matters of conscience and morality?'[85]

2

A Marriage of Convenience

(1855–64)

From Bad to Worse?

The Bülows are members of an aristocratic German family that can trace back its origins to the thirteenth century. The dynasty is said to have been founded by Gottfried von Bülow, who is described as a Mecklenburg knight in a document dating from around 1230. During the centuries that followed, the Bülows have brought forth an impressive roster of high-ranking soldiers, diplomats, politicians, writers and musicians, and a draughtsman and actor, Bernhard Victor Christoph Carl von Bülow, better known to German audiences as Loriot. Many members of the family have been well-to-do, while others have got by as best they could.

Among the second group were Carl Eduard and Franziska von Bülow. Franziska von Bülow née Stoll was fifty-five when she assumed responsibility for Cosima and Blandine in September 1855. Fate had treated her badly. Her first marriage to the Leipzig businessman and banker Jacob Kaskel had ended after only a few years, and in August 1828 she had married the writer Carl Eduard von Bülow, her junior by three years and a popular novelist in his day. He also translated and published works from English, French and Spanish and edited the writings of Novalis. Their first son, Hans Guido, was born in Dresden in January 1830. A sister, Marie Isidore, followed three years later. A second daughter, Oda Elisabeth, who was born in 1834, appears not to have reached adulthood. But this marriage, too, was joyless and ended in a divorce. Carl Eduard von Bülow remarried in 1847 and died in Switzerland in 1853.

The children had an unhappy childhood marked by mental torments and physical beatings applied with pedantic rigour.[1] By the age of four they were already required to memorize fairytales and poems, to study French and take riding and dancing lessons. There was no thought of leisure, still less of entertainment. Music lessons inevitably played a major role, Hans's teachers even including Clara Schumann's father, Friedrich Wieck. As a boy, he showed exceptional talent, but the last thing that Franziska von Bülow wanted for her son was an artistic career, so obsessed was she by the almost morbid ambition to make 'something respectable' out of him. The best profession, she felt, would be that of a civil servant, and so he initially had to study jurisprudence. But in 1850 he attended the world premiere of Wagner's *Lohengrin* in Weimar and, in spite of his parents' violent opposition, resolved to pursue a career in music.

Bülow had attended the world premiere of *Rienzi* in Dresden as early as 1842 and four years later had got to know Wagner in person. In September 1850 he fled to Zurich to be with his idol and under the latter's supervision gained practical experience of conducting. Although his mother continued to fulminate from a distance and for a time even refused to have any further dealings with her son, Bülow's mind was made up: Wagner, he told his sister, was 'the greatest artistic phenomenon of our century, perhaps even in the whole history of the world. It has become clear to me that I could be this man's famulus, I'd like to become his pupil and apostle, and with such an ambition and such a goal, life would seem to be worth living'.[2] Bülow was utterly charmed by the charisma of a man seventeen years older than himself. Even more crucially, his hero worship had allowed him to discover his own true self. From now on his one aim in life was to serve Wagner as a pianist, conductor and writer.

Bülow began studying the piano with Liszt in Weimar in the autumn of 1851. He stayed with his teacher and Carolyne von Sayn-Wittgenstein at the Altenburg and soon became the darling of the household. Liszt even saw in him his 'legitimate successor, my heir by the grace of God and by virtue of his talent',[3] which was certainly quite a claim. Even Carolyne found a small place in her heart for the sophisticated and cultivated young man with his aristocratic manners. She spoke only imperfect German and so she enjoyed conversing with Bülow in flawless French. After undertaking an initial series of recital tours and briefly working as a private tutor, Bülow was appointed to a teaching post at the Stern Conservatory in Berlin in April 1855. For a time he lived with his mother in the Behrenstraße, but with the arrival of Cosima and Blandine in early October 1855, the family moved to a larger apartment at 86 Wilhelmstraße.

Hans von Bülow was one of the leading musicians of the nineteenth century. As a pianist he toured the length and breadth of Europe and even visited the United States, where he gave no fewer than 139 concerts during the

1875–6 season alone. Although there were critics who described his playing as academic and understated, his immaculate technique, his tremendous musical intelligence and his encyclopaedic memory all ensured that he was universally admired. In spite of the slights that he suffered, he spent the whole of his professional life championing Wagner's works. Unlike many of the composer's other followers, he also showed his independence by conducting the music of Brahms, a bipartisanship viewed askance by the Wagner camp. As both pianist and conductor, he also promoted the music of as yet unknown contemporaries such as Richard Strauss and Camille Saint-Saëns. Among the many works inextricably bound up with Bülow's name is Tchaikovsky's Piano Concerto no. 1 in B flat minor, which he introduced to the world in Boston in October 1875.

In addition to the kind and solicitous mentor whose charm and warmth could be beguiling, there was, however, a second Hans von Bülow, a man widely seen as an unpredictable and eccentric cynic who frequently shocked his contemporaries. Wherever he went, he caused a furore. His predilection for cutting puns and sarcastic comments was legendary, and the list of anecdotes ascribed to him is correspondingly lengthy. When a composer showed him a failed transcription of a piece by Chopin, he is said to have remarked: 'What ideas people have when they have none!'[4] On another occasion a man of some distinction stopped him in the street, adding with some embarrassment: 'Oh, Herr von Bülow, I bet you don't recognize me?' 'You've won the bet,' quipped Bülow and continued on his way.[5] Especially famous was a speech he gave at a Beethoven concert in Berlin in March 1892, when he described the values of the French Revolution – 'liberté, égalité, fraternité' – as 'illusory words': 'In the face of freedom, equality and fraternity, the positive watchword is "infantry, cavalry and artillery"!'[6] Conversely, it is no longer possible to say with any certainty if it was Bülow or some other contemporary who described Anton Bruckner as 'half genius, half simpleton', for the quotation has also been attributed to Mahler. Edith Wolff, the daughter of Bülow's agent in Berlin, Hermann Wolff, summed up the situation when she noted that 'the atmosphere around Bülow was always somehow electric, so that an explosion could follow at any given moment and was often triggered by altogether unforeseen events or encounters'.[7]

There were evidently various reasons for Bülow's complex personality: a strict and loveless upbringing, his parents' unhappy marriage, the many enervating arguments within the family circle to which the youth was witness and that culminated in his parents' divorce, and the early loss of his father. It seems from all we know about her that Franziska von Bülow was a cold, domineering and probably neurotic woman unable to show her children the love she undoubtedly felt for them. Following the failure of her second marriage, she clung increasingly desperately to her elder son, tying him to her apron strings and watching jealously over his life. He resisted her attempts to control him by seeking refuge in cynicism. But a further reason for Bülow's behaviour must surely be sought in his poor state of health. Even as a child he is said to have had no fewer than five bouts of meningitis, which he survived only because of his tenacious hold on life. But he was never really well, suffering all his life from severe headaches, anxiety states and various other complaints that provide his letters with a constant counterpoint. His sixty-four years of life resemble nothing so much as an odyssey through the world of medicine, a world inhabited by doctors who mistreated him with their highly questionable methods. When his headaches later became unbearable, he fell back on morphine and cocaine, resulting in substance dependency.[8] One is left with the impression that with his caustic and offensive behaviour Bülow was unconsciously trying to demonstrate the strength and virility denied to his ailing body.

This, then, was the family background that awaited the seventeen-year-old Cosima and the nineteen-year-old Blandine when they joined the Bülow household in the autumn of 1855: a strict, suspicious, cold and deeply frustrated matriarch with two failed marriages behind her, and her highly gifted, eccentric and perpetually sickly son.

Self-deception

'As for my girls,' Liszt wrote to the twenty-five-year-old Bülow in September 1855, 'you must allow me to tell you the great importance that I attach to your making them work very hard, for I believe that they are sufficiently advanced in their musical studies to be able to profit from your lessons.' But he should not allow the 'little girls' to act up: 'They already respect you, and so it won't be hard for you to drum things into them.'[9] It is evident from this letter, which Liszt addressed to Bülow even before the girls had arrived in Berlin, that he already had a clear idea of his daughters' immediate future: in essence, the regime that they had endured for so long in Paris was to be continued unchanged in Berlin. Franziska von Bülow was to step into Madame Patersi's sensible shoes, while her son oversaw their musical education. Friends of Bülow gave them lessons in harmony and theory and they attended lectures in the history of music. Italian lessons were also a part of the syllabus. Bülow himself assumed responsibility for their piano lessons. 'As for their musical abilities, they are not merely talented but performers of genius. They are indeed the daughters of my benefactor, quite exceptional creatures.' And, no doubt to his benefactor's particular delight, Bülow noted in passing that 'they are not amusing themselves unduly in Berlin'.

From the outset, Bülow felt drawn to Cosima, who filled him with 'admiration' and 'exaltation': 'I was moved and deeply touched to recognize Liszt himself in Mademoiselle Cosima's playing!'[10] There is no doubt that Cosima was exceptionally gifted as a pianist. But did she really have her father's genius? Or was Bülow's letter not rather intended to flatter the teacher whom he loved and whom he thought he could detect in his daughter? There is much to be said for the second suggestion. Cosima certainly resembled the young Liszt: in contemporary paintings and drawings we can see a tall and strikingly thin young woman with a long, slender neck and an unusually large and well-defined nose, hence her siblings' nickname for her, 'la cigogne', or 'the stork'. Bülow was clearly impressed and 'exalted' by this physical resemblance between Cosima and her father. Moreover, both Blandine and Cosima displayed a certain snobbishness, leaving observers in no doubt that they felt that they had come down in the world in their new home and that they emphatically disliked Prussia. It would have been easy for observers to have seen in this the empty affectation of two teenagers, but Hans von Bülow was no ordinary observer. His respect for Liszt and the haughtiness of the latter's two daughters instilled a regular sense of inferiority in him. To one of his female friends, he admitted that 'I am embarrassed by their obvious superiority, and the impossibility of appearing sufficiently interesting in their sight prevents me from appreciating the agreeable nature of their company as much as I should like to do.'[11]

The question must inevitably be asked: why, if she was so talented, did Cosima not become a pianist? Did she not have Clara Schumann – her senior by eighteen years – as a model? The answer is clear. Unlike Marie d'Agoult, Liszt had no interest in such a career for his daughter. Years later he told Carolyne von Sayn-Wittgenstein that Marie had asked him 'why I prevented Cosima from pursuing her true vocation and embarking on an artist's career!!' Liszt's next sentence makes it clear how absurd he found this idea: 'After *Nélida* this would have been most fitting!'[12] In Liszt's eyes, *Nélida* – an act of novelistic revenge on the part of Marie d'Agoult – disqualified his former lover from engaging in any kind of artistic activity and rendered such displays of female artistry fundamentally risible in his sight. In any case, he had other plans for Cosima. Within the not too distant future, both Cosima and Blandine would marry, he calculated, and, as Liszt's daughters, they would be expected to show a certain musical accomplishment. But that was all.

Within six weeks of Cosima's arrival in Berlin things had started to happen. On the evening of 19 October 1855 Bülow conducted an orchestral concert that included the overture to *Tannhäuser*. Tensions in the Bülow household were inevitably greater than ever, and the audience at the concert itself naturally included Franziska, Cosima and Blandine, all of them there to lend their support. Even Liszt came specially from Weimar to boost his protégé's morale. As his pupils proudly noted, Bülow conducted 'with fire and nobility',[13] but the audience responded dismissively, hissing and whistling the performance. Bülow was beside himself and suffered a nervous breakdown in the green room, briefly losing consciousness. Liszt and a number of the conductor's colleagues attended to his needs, while Franziska and the girls returned home. Liszt reported on the aftermath in a letter to Carolyne: 'It was around two in the morning when I shoved Hans through the front door of his house in the Wilhelmstraße. There was still a light burning in the building, but I didn't go up, and I shan't return to see the girls until around ten.'[14] What Liszt did not know is that Cosima had sat up on her own, waiting for Hans to return. The two of them then spent the rest of the night in the living room, where Cosima did what she could to comfort Bülow. It was then that they became engaged. Many years later she recalled in her diary: 'I remember my betrothal fifteen years ago, under the auspices of the *Tannhäuser* Overture in Berlin.'[15]

The night's events did not go unnoticed. When Franziska von Bülow heard what had happened, she complained to Liszt, accusing Cosima of making sheep's eyes at her son. Liszt sought to placate his outraged correspondent by insisting that Hans was not interested in marriage: 'And even if he later decides to get married, it will not be hard for him to find a far more advantageous match than my daughters.'[16] Liszt had already written to the princess on this score in the July of that year, pointing out that 'my daughters are possessed of enough sound common sense to avoid unnecessary excitement'.[17] Evidently he saw in the autumn's events no more than an adolescent crush, an assessment that all too soon proved to be spectacularly wide of the mark, for he had simply not reckoned on the couple's resolve. In late November 1855 Liszt and Bülow met in Berlin to discuss the situation, and in the course of their meeting Hans declared his intentions. By April 1856 he was officially asking for the hand of Liszt's daughter in marriage: 'It is more than love that I feel for her,' he explained. 'Rather, the idea of drawing even closer to you, whom I regard as the principal instigator and animator of my present and future existence, sums up all the happiness that I can expect to feel here on earth. In my eyes Cosima Liszt towers over all other women not only because she bears your name but also because she resembles you so much and because so many of her qualities make her a faithful reflection of your own person.'[18]

This was a remarkable declaration of the writer's love, aimed, as it was, less at his future wife than at her father. Liszt was in a difficult situation. On the one hand, he was familiar with Bülow's complex personality and no doubt suspected that married life would not be easy for him, while on the other hand it was difficult, if not impossible, for him to reject his favourite pupil's request out of hand, for all in all Bülow was a good match. As a prospective father-in-law, Liszt showed great skill and diplomacy in initially postponing the decision, arguing that Cosima was still too young to commit herself to a lifetime of marriage and that it would be better to wait a year. By testing the couple's resolve he wanted to be certain in his own mind. If their feelings for one another were to survive the period of waiting, he reckoned that there would no longer be any objections to the wedding. Meanwhile tensions were mounting in Berlin: 'Hans has been in Weimar for a week,' Franziska von Bülow wrote to inform her daughter. 'He hasn't written, which is extremely tiresome, not least because his future will presumably be decided there.'[19]

On his return to Berlin, Bülow was able to reassure his mother: in principle Liszt had agreed to the wedding. But when Marie d'Agoult discovered what was going on, she did all in her power to put a spanner in the works, despatching Cosima's half-sister, Claire, to Berlin and seeking by all the means at her disposal to prevent the wedding from taking place, convinced, as she was, that Cosima was the victim of an arranged marriage and suspecting a conspiracy on the part of her arch-enemy, Carolyne, and of the latter's 'accomplice', Franziska von Bülow.[20] But Claire's mission achieved nothing, and so Marie d'Agoult invited her daughters to spend the summer with her in Paris. The sisters stayed with Anna Liszt and met their mother on several occasions. Painting a picture of the blackest hues, the latter did what she could to discourage Cosima from marrying Bülow, but her efforts were all in vain. Two months later Cosima returned to Berlin on her own, while Blandine, against Liszt's wishes, remained with her grandmother in Paris. In October 1857 she married the thirty-two-year-old lawyer, Émile Ollivier.

What did Hans von Bülow and Cosima see in each other? Let us begin with Cosima's much later version of events:

I spent two years in the strangest state, telling no one of our engagement. And even now I do not know how we ended up getting married. One thing I do know, however, is that I never once asked for an explanation. I enjoyed being loved, and as for the rest, I gave it no thought. . . . The wedding came about without any feeling of capriciousness on my part, without my making any move of my own and above all without any brooding on the matter.[21]

Cosima's self-analysis is revealing: she became Frau von Bülow because she never once reflected on the decision that had been taken and because she maintained a state of almost total passivity from the moment that she and Hans von Bülow had sat up all night together in October 1855. Bülow himself was in despair, his letter to Liszt soliciting Cosima's hand in marriage attesting to the fact that he was making the most terrible mistake.

As for Cosima, she was, of course, impressed by Bülow and will have felt flattered that he had preferred her to her prettier sister. Of course, she wanted to be seen as a grown-up woman and to escape from the control of both Liszt and the princess. Even so, she could have withdrawn from the match at any time and, like Blandine, have decamped to Paris, not least because there were still plenty of voices eager to talk her out of marriage. But none of these factors can have been decisive against the background of a prescribed wait of two whole years. The main reason for Cosima's insistence on going ahead with the wedding must be sought elsewhere. During her period of waiting, she had ample opportunity to get to know Bülow more closely, and it will have become clear to her what it would mean to be the wife of an eccentrically brilliant and hypersensitive musician. He lived under constant pressure and was permanently overwrought. In short, one did not need to be a clairvoyant to see the problems that lay ahead. But these very prospects, which would have tended, rather, to deter other women, seem to have been a positive incentive for Bülow's bride-to-be. She felt sorry for her fiancé, for 'poor Hans', as Blandine significantly called him, and clearly confused self-sacrificial friendship with true love. Perhaps it was during these months of waiting that Cosima reread Thomas à Kempis's *De Imitatione Christi*, the book that she had known since her adolescence. Be that as it may, there are certainly signs here of Madame Patersi's teachings: of the need for humility, the denial of personal needs and an empty display of emotion. Cosima wanted to sacrifice herself to her ailing and unstable fiancé and to look after him. To her, such pity was synonymous with love. Many years later she wrote in her diary: 'It was a great misunderstanding that bound us together in marriage; my feelings toward him are today still the same as twelve years ago: great sympathy with his destiny, pleasure in his qualities of mind and heart, genuine respect for his character, however completely different our temperaments.'[22]

As for Bülow, the composer Peter Cornelius thought that 'his marriage to Cosima was a sacrifice offered up by a friend to his master, Liszt; his aim was to give the natural child a brilliant, honourable name and thereby give the father a profound sense of satisfaction and a lifetime's solace. It was an act of gratitude.'[23] Cornelius knew what he was talking about. After all, he had studied with Liszt and knew all the actors in the drama personally. His account of the situation has much to be said for it, but in its present, exaggerated form it confuses Liszt's and Bülow's roles. There is no doubt that Liszt was keen to see his daughters married off, but the idea that it should have been Bülow who walked down the aisle with Cosima is one that he initially dismissed as more or less insane. In other words, he did not expect this 'sacrifice on the part of a friend' and certainly did not ask for it. The prime mover was Bülow, and there seems little doubt that various emotions conspired to persuade him to act as he did. In the first place, there were the romantic and tragic circumstances of that night in October 1855, to say nothing of Cosima's genuine feelings of sympathy and fellow suffering, all of which had a profound effect on an artist as sensitive and unstable as Bülow. There was also the fact that Bülow saw in Liszt the man who was his 'instigator and animator'. Last but not least, Bülow was still so uncertain of himself that he allowed himself to be impressed by Cosima's 'evident superiority'. Even as late as June 1856, by which date the wedding had long since been agreed, he complained that he did not 'seem sufficiently interesting' to her. His need for an emotional prop and for understanding, his respect for Liszt and his persistent feelings of inferiority all came together to produce an unwholesome brew. On the eve of the wedding ceremony, he wrote to his friend Richard Pohl: 'My wife is such a perfect friend to me, it is almost impossible to imagine a more ideal situation.'[24] This says it all. Decades later the elderly Cosima told her daughter-in-law Winifred, 'Herr von Bülow should never have married.'[25] This was self-regarding to a fault. It would have been more accurate to say, 'Herr von Bülow should never have married me.'

In the weeks leading up to the wedding, a few bureaucratic obstacles still had to be overcome. The ceremony was due to take place in Berlin, and so the groom first had to become a Prussian citizen. At this date there was no possibility of a civil ceremony – there were no registry offices in Prussia until 1874. Only a church wedding could be considered, and since the bride was Catholic, it had to be a Catholic service. Only when these formalities had been sorted out could the ceremony go ahead at Saint Hedwig's Church on the morning of Tuesday 18 August 1857 in the presence of mainly family members. Bülow wanted to avoid a social free-for-all, and so only the immediate family was invited. The witnesses were Liszt and Paul von Bülow, a cousin of Hans's late father.[26] Marie d'Agoult, Anna Liszt, Blandine and Daniel were all absent. The newlywed husband informed the world of the event in the briefest of public announcements:

> I have the honour of announcing my marital union with Fräulein Cosima Liszt, the daughter of Herr Dr Franz Liszt, kapellmeister to the Court of the Grand Duke of Saxony. The ceremony took place today in Saint Hedwig's Cathedral in Berlin.
> Berlin, 18 August 1857
> Hans von Bülow[27]

A Journey into the Future

The newlyweds' honeymoon took them first to Weimar, where they were accompanied by Liszt, and thence to Baden-Baden and Lausanne. There the couple met Karl Ritter, an old school friend of Bülow's, and his wife, who had themselves only recently tied the knot. Their next port of call was Zurich, where Wagner and his wife were now living in a spacious summer house – the 'Asyl', or 'Refuge' – placed at the composer's disposal by the immensely wealthy, retired silk merchant Otto Wesendonck at a peppercorn rent. The house was attractively situated on the slopes overlooking Lake Zurich. In visiting the Wagners, Bülow was making good a promise that he had been obliged to make to his idol that spring, when Wagner, in a display of singularly poor taste, had written: 'Assuming that you have no one to dishonour that night and are thus free to spend it with me, I would ask you to consider how you might set about visiting me this summer. If you were to come with Cosima, that would be quite splendid.'[28]

The Bülows duly came and initially put up at a hotel. Almost immediately problems arose, when Bülow succumbed to a rheumatic fever and had to remain in bed. When he recovered two days later, the newlyweds joined the Wagners in the 'Asyl'. Other visitors included Emma Herwegh, the wife of the revolutionary poet, Georg Herwegh, the composer Robert Franz and the Swiss writer Gottfried Keller. Wagner was in the best of spirits, and the company drank and made music. Bülow played from *Das Rheingold* and *Die Walküre*, while Wagner sang all the parts. Bülow must have imagined such happiness stretching away into the infinite future as he compared himself to 'a pope in Avignon'[29] and had eyes only for Wagner, whom he idolized to distraction. He wrote to his mother: 'I hardly think of myself as a husband at all but feel as free as I need to be for my own peace of mind.'[30] The next day we find him writing to another correspondent: 'What I'm now celebrating could hardly be more different from a normal honeymoon, but my wife isn't jealous.'[31]

Jealousy is in fact the wrong term, for Cosima, rather, was seriously put out. The situation, moreover, could hardly have been more delicate, for apart from Wagner's wife Minna, to whom he had been married for over twenty years, the guests also included his current mistress, Mathilde Wesendonck. The fact that Minna was as yet unaware of the affair that was going on between her husband and the wife of his financier merely added to the sense of awkwardness. The atmosphere in the 'Asyl' was charged to an unusually high degree. When Wagner had seen Cosima for the first time in Paris in October 1853, she had still been a teenager. Four years later she found herself in the presence of a man who both enchanted and appalled her. He was a charismatic figure who addressed others with a directness bordering on the forceful and who was capable of a captivating thoughtlessness and lack of consideration. But what Cosima saw was a vain peacock strutting and mincing around like a Venetian patrician, joking, blaspheming, doling out compliments aplenty and generally ensuring that he remained the centre of attention. For a young woman who set such store by etiquette, all this was bound to be profoundly unsettling. For years Madame Patersi had impressed upon her an understanding of what was fitting and, above all, what was not. And Cosima now found herself in the presence of someone whose directness and coarse humour were a kind of declaration of war on all that she understood by *savoir vivre*. One evening, Wagner read his recently completed libretto to *Tristan und Isolde* to the assembled company, causing Cosima to burst into tears. The impact left on her by his reading and by his uninhibited personality was simply too much, and she retired to her room, too upset to remain. All in all, we may surmise that the impression that Cosima formed of Wagner during this period was far from favourable.

The Bülows left the 'Asyl' at the end of September 1857, breaking their journey in Weimar, where they spent some weeks at the Altenburg. Bülow then remained behind with Liszt, while Cosima travelled alone to Berlin in order to set up their first home together. They had found a property at 11 Anhaltische Straße not far from the station of the same name. Franziska von Bülow, who until then had lived with her son, moved into a new apartment of her own in the nearby Wilhelmsplatz.

During the early months following her encounter with Wagner in Switzerland, Cosima's attitude to the composer was one of distinct reserve. In her letters to Carolyne's daughter Marie as well as to the Herweghs she repeatedly made fun of this curious ménage à trois involving Wagner, Minna and Mathilde. In one letter we find her making light of Wagner's financial problems and in another she writes disparagingly of Minna's sour expression ('la face de citron'), which Minna assumed in the presence of 'la belle Mathilde'.[32] One has the impression that Cosima found the scenes on the Wesendoncks' estate mendacious and embarrassing: Wagner had written a Serenade for the fair Mathilde; all that he needed to compose now was a Nocturne for Otto.[33] And she could only smile at the personal communications that she received from 'Richard de Zurich'. He had, she reports contemptuously in July 1858, written her a stupid letter that could only have been intended for a child: 'I refrained from replying by telling myself that this droll exuberance was the result of a paroxysm of passion for the fair Mathilde'.[34]

Cosima's attitude to Wagner began to change only after she and her husband had travelled to Zurich for a second time in mid-July 1858. If their stay at the 'Asyl' in 1857 had been a time of unadulterated pleasure, this was certainly not the case in 1858. Minna Wagner had found out about her husband's affair with Mathilde Wesendonck only a few months earlier, and since then dark storm clouds had hung over the two households, generating an atmosphere that could explode at any moment. One such scene took place on 19 July, when a violent argument between Wagner and his wife was witnessed by Bülow. 'I'm sorry about the poor reception you were given on this occasion,' Wagner apologized the next day. 'My wife asks you to move in with us at once; she also hopes that your visit will help us to renew contact with the Wesendoncks, something we very much need to do, and she says that you are both most welcome here.'[35] Although the Bülows moved out of their hotel in Zurich and stayed at the 'Asyl', their presence was hardly calculated to solve the Wagners' marital problems. To make matters worse, they were joined by Marie d'Agoult, who wanted to see Cosima again and to get to know her new son-in-law.

The atmosphere remained tense. Towards the end of her visit, Cosima travelled to Geneva in the company of Karl Ritter to see her sister Blandine. A close

friend of Bülow, Ritter was another of Wagner's youthful admirers, his brother
Alexander additionally being married to Wagner's niece, Franziska. The visit
almost ended in disaster. Ritter was unhappily married, and Cosima was no
less frustrated after twelve months of married life. In the course of a boat trip
on Lake Geneva, they both admitted that their lives were unbearable, at which
point Cosima apparently asked her companion to drown her. But when Ritter
declared that he wanted to die with her, they rowed back to the shore and went
their separate ways. This, at least, is the version of events given by Wagner,
whom Ritter drew into his confidence only a few weeks later. On Cosima's
return to Zurich the Bülows prepared to leave. She was abnormally agitated,
Wagner later recalled, 'and this found expression more especially in convul-
sively violent intimacies towards me. While she was saying goodbye the next
day she fell at my feet, covered my hands with tears and kisses, so that, aston-
ished and shocked, I pondered the mystery, without being able to solve it.'[36]

What had happened? It seems from the incident in Geneva that Cosima was
in the throes of a particularly severe emotional crisis. 'It was a great misunderstanding that bound us together in marriage,' she recalled in 1869. 'In the very
first year of our marriage I was already in such despair over this confusion that
I wanted to die.'[37] The emotional turmoil of the events in the 'Asyl', her encounter
with the equally unhappy Karl Ritter and her dramatic outing to Geneva all
made it clear that, for her, married life consisted of an indifferent sameness.
What she missed so painfully in her relationship with Bülow was the very thing
she had discovered in abundance in Zurich and Geneva: boundless passion. But
this does not mean that she had fallen in love with Wagner. In Cosima a 'dark
desire for love' seethed 'as in a volcano', Marie von Sayn-Wittgenstein later
recalled: 'The sickly, overwrought and essentially desiccated Bülow was not the
Siegfried who in the longer term could tame this wild young Valkyrie.'[38]

Wagner, too, clearly recognized that the Bülows were having marital problems. 'For today, give my very best wishes to your Mazeppa stallion,'[39] he
wrote to Bülow in February 1858. But his jokes hid a gentle warning: 'As for
her health, Cosima's worst enemy is her temperament: she is of quite extraordinary provenance and is therefore difficult to look after!'[40] It is doubtful if
Bülow had any idea what was going on in his wife's head. Certainly, it was not
until many years later that he found out about the incident in Geneva. The
couple set off back to Berlin on 16 August 1858. Wagner meanwhile had made
up his mind: he would leave his 'Asyl' the very next day, disband his household and find refuge on his own elsewhere. Three years were to pass before he
saw Cosima again.

Coffee Mornings in Berlin

Back in Berlin, Bülow threw himself into his work, leaving him without a moment's peace and quiet. In addition to his post at the Conservatory, he also had to prepare for a series of concerts in Berlin, Brandenburg and Hamburg, not to mention an extended tour of Königsberg and Danzig in early December 1858. There were also all manner of major and minor errands to be run for Liszt and Wagner. Whether he was required to obtain money for the notoriously destitute Wagner or prepare a vocal score of *Tristan und Isolde*, Bülow naturally dropped everything else as soon as he received a call from one or other of his musical gods.

There seems to have been no place for Cosima in this hectic round, so it is hardly surprising to find that she soon grew disillusioned. To make matters worse, she was initially far from happy in Berlin. Although she had become a Prussian citizen as a result of her marriage to Bülow, she remained authentically Parisian from a social point of view and was bound to find Berlin a provincial and boring city. In 1855 Berlin numbered some 440,000 inhabitants and was still far from being the brilliant metropolis of the 1870s. By way of comparison it is worth remembering that in 1846 Paris already had a population of over 1 million. In the mid-1850s Paris's prefect, Baron Georges-Eugène Haussmann, was already starting on his 'grands travaux', a major reconstruction of the inner city that would thrust the French capital into the very centre of the modern world. Haussmann oversaw the construction of endlessly long, straight boulevards and of the city's many squares and parks, but he also established a modern infrastructure, including a sewerage system. For a long time Berlin was unable to keep pace with such developments. The public monuments were in dubious taste, while the modest pretensions of Prussian cooking and the earthy humour of the Berliners were bound to strike a false note with a young French woman concerned with the rules of etiquette.

Cosima was not alone in harbouring these misgivings. 'The railway journey into the Prussian capital is glacial, unchanging and lifeless,' Jules Laforgue, the French reader to Empress Victoria, complained: 'The station in the most remote sub-prefecture in France would have no truck with the buffets of Berlin's stations.'[41] Cosima thought exactly the same. In a letter to Georg and Emma Herwegh we find her lamenting that 'Berlin is so dead that you could rain down a mass of blows on it and it would still move no more than a corpse.'[42] In particular, she missed the sophisticated lifestyle that she knew from her youth in France. Most of all, she abhorred the private invitations to coffee and tea. 'I have just returned from a Berlin café,' she told the Herweghs in February 1858

> where people meet at five o'clock and leave at nine minutes past, having failed to sate their hunger and having conducted a frightful belletristic conversation that normally leaves me with such indigestion that not even sleeping round the clock is enough to put me back on my feet, or, rather, to reactivate my brain.[43]

Laforgue, too, found life in Berlin garish and insincere. 'Addressing others by their titles comes so naturally to them that even people who have been in close contact with each other for years continue to use such titles when speaking with one another. I shall never get over my astonishment at my memory of a woman who, on meeting a friend of hers, said: "Wie geht es Ihnen, Geheimrätchen?" '[44] (The expected form would be 'Wie geht es Ihnen, Geheimrätin?' – 'How are you, Frau Privy Councillor?' But the speaker has used a diminutive form, like Evchen or Liebchen, as a term of endearment.)

But we should not imagine Baroness von Bülow as a home bird who never went out. From 1858 she worked as a translator and as the Berlin correspondent of the French *Revue germanique*, a monthly magazine established in January 1858 by two French journalists, Auguste Nefftzer and Charles Dollfus, with the aim of informing its French readers about the intellectual lives of their neighbours to the east. Both editors hailed from Alsace and were acquainted with Marie d'Agoult. Other contributors included Claire de Charnacé – Marie's daughter and Cosima's half-sister – and her husband, Guy. But the laudable venture was also supported by such eminent individuals as the elderly Alexander von Humboldt and the famous historian Leopold von Ranke. It was a remarkably heterogeneous journal, containing, as it did, articles on politics, history, theology, philosophy and literature as well as translations and pieces on art and music. The *Revue germanique* was not commercially successful – by the end of six months it still had only 300 subscribers, including five in Germany, whereas it needed between 450 and 500 to be able to remain afloat. Its deficit continued to grow, and from 1861 the editors were obliged to publish pieces on English, Italian and Spanish topics in order to survive. But even this strategy proved ineffectual, and in February 1868, Dollfus, financially ruined, had to sell the paper.[45]

Remarkably enough, Cosima's work for the *Revue germanique* has for the most part passed unnoticed. Her early biographer, Count Richard Du Moulin

Eckart, typically muddied the waters in an attempt to prevent his readers from seeing that his heroine had sullied her hands with journalism, even misspelling the names of the two editors as Neffzer and Dollfuß. The assiduous count should have known better as he spoke fluent French (a glance at the title page would have sufficed) and he was in close contact with Wahnfried throughout his work on his book. But by the late 1920s his paymasters in Bayreuth clearly had no desire to be reminded of their mistress's journalistic past.

Cosima's first contribution was a French translation of Friedrich Hebbel's tragedy *Maria Magdalena* which appeared between late May and late June 1858. Thirty years later, she recalled that she had been 'literally wild' about Hebbel but that she 'would not look at it now at any price'.[46] The translation was evidently awkwardly worded because we know that Nefftzer was required to make substantial changes to it.[47] We shall not go far wrong in assuming that during this early period Cosima still had difficulty with the German language: after all, she had spent the first seventeen years of her life speaking almost exclusively French. It is clear from all that we know that her German was later flawless, and yet the letters that she wrote in German often have an element of artificiality about them, their sentences seeming strangely otherworldly and antiquated for the time. 'What she says is almost always intelligent,' recalled one contemporary, 'in other words, it is well thought through; but one has the feeling that it has been thought through for a long time in advance, so that the ideas are inflexible and fail to adapt to the actual conversation.'[48] Decades later, Winifred Wagner described her mother-in-law's German as that of a 'very well trained linguist'.[49] In short, it was always possible to tell that German was not Cosima's mother tongue.

The *Revue germanique*'s regular Berlin correspondent, Felix Werner, retired in December 1860, leaving Cosima free to file reports on the Prussian capital. Unfortunately, the situation is made more complicated by the fact that she never used her own name but preferred pseudonyms and initials as a byline. Dollfus's biographer, René Martin, worked through the editor's unpublished papers and managed to identify some of these pen names.[50] Cosima frequently used the initials 'C. F.', although in November 1861 she signed an article 'F. Hoffmann', and another one in the spring of 1862 was signed 'E. Franz'. We can only speculate on the reasons for this obfuscation, but perhaps she was concerned about the reputation of her husband, who was after all in the full glare of the city's cultural headlights.

Whatever the answer, Cosima contributed articles on a wide range of different subjects. In January and April 1862, she commented on the recent publication of the diaries of Karl August Varnhagen von Ense; she also reported on performances of works by Bach, Gluck and Robert Schumann; and she wrote warmly on her visit to a Christmas market. Occasionally she would strike a particularly pessimistic note in describing life in Berlin, berating its inhabitants for their austere charm and their inhospitable local climate: 'This place, Protestant to a fault, raises aridity to the level of a natural wonder, and all the ovations, all the torchlit processions and formal banquets will not find a home beneath our inclement sky in so unwelcoming a city and in these minds of ours, so sandy is the ground.'[51] For Cosima, Berlin was simply Poussièropolis, the City of Dust and Grime. She wielded a deadly pen, and her French arts features are linguistically accomplished, witty, ironical and sometimes even mocking in their tone. When Wilhelm I was crowned king of Prussia in October 1861, she wrote witheringly about the expense, which was excessive by the city's standards: 'Judge for yourselves on the strength of the rumours that circulated here in a city in which the demureness of local customs can be compared only with the complacency of local manners. Prussian pedantry and meanness have sweated blood and water in recent days. It was a question of at least keeping one's composure, for want of anything better.'[52] Cosima's contributions to the *Revue germanique* came to an abrupt end in May 1862, when she submitted an unsolicited translation of a short story by Alfred Meißner and the editors turned it down, citing lack of space as their reason and prompting the offended translator to resign by way of protest.

'During the early years of her marriage,' recalled Marie von Sayn-Wittgenstein,

Cosima made an honest attempt to be her husband's loyal and brave companion. She was also an excellent housewife, active in every area, and cheerfully tolerated her husband's morbid whims and constant moroseness. True, she was not mild-mannered and gentle by nature. Quite the opposite, in fact. Her exaggerated self-esteem and innate causticity meant that she offended most of the women and many of the German men in her circle, who accused her of lacking femininity.[53]

Among those who failed to submit to Cosima's sometimes cool and austere charms was her mother-in-law. Time and again minor skirmishes and major arguments broke out between the two women. These were not always the usual family bickerings. Rather, Marie von Sayn-Wittgenstein claims that Franziska von Bülow took against Cosima and Blandine from the start:

'Hailing from utterly foreign climes, they offended against all her bourgeois ideas.'[54] In fact, Cosima seems to have convinced herself that her mother-in-law, far from harbouring bourgeois ideas, was utterly lacking in firm convictions and fixed views. Years later she was still complaining to Bülow that his mother 'did not have what it takes to turn childhood into a paradise on earth and provide the basis for a noble and pure existence.'[55] Cosima could hardly have expressed herself more clearly. Not without reason she contemptuously referred to her mother-in-law as 'Lady Perhaps', a woman of straw whose life was one of perpetual vacillation.

These differences were naturally passed over in silence by Bayreuth's official chroniclers. After all, no shadows could be allowed to fall across the path of the later First Lady of Bayreuth. Like so much else put about by Wahnfried, the suggestion that it was Franziska von Bülow of all people who introduced her daughter-in-law to sophisticated society in Berlin belongs in the realm of legend. Bülow's mother did not move to the city until the spring of 1855 and had no obvious entrée to its salons. Moreover, the Bülows were not members of the higher aristocracy and lacked financial means. If Cosima had become a part of the social establishment by the early 1860s, then this cachet seems to have been the result of her own endeavours. She began by persuading her husband to introduce weekly visitors' hours in keeping with contemporary practice, even advertising them in Berlin's post-office guide. In 1862, for example, she was at home every Wednesday and Saturday between four and five o'clock, when visitors could present their *cartes de visite* and pay their respects. Cosima also organized sizeable soirées. The guest list for one that she held in early March 1859 emerges from a letter from Liszt to Carolyne von Sayn-Wittgenstein: in attendance were not only Liszt and Franziska von Bülow but also Emma Herwegh, the sculptress Elisabeth Ney, Ernst and Hedwig Dohm, the actresses Ellen Franz and Lila von Bulyowsky, the journalist Eduard Fischel, the history painter Carl Becker, the politician Ferdinand Lassalle and a number of other personalities. A singer performed a selection of Liszt songs and the maestro himself obliged with two of his virtuoso piano pieces, rounding off the evening by performing piano duets with Bülow. The cultural fare was exquisitely chosen, while the lady of the house took care of her guests' bodily needs: 'The supper was most respectable,' even the fastidious Liszt was forced to concede. 'There was ice cream aplenty and all manner of different dishes to satisfy all and sundry.'[56]

Cosima's later development and in particular her flirtation with the ultra-right seem hard to square with the views of her left-wing friends. But the contradiction is merely apparent as Cosima's political thinking was largely unaffected by Lassalle, Dohm, Bruno Bauer and the Herweghs. At no point in her life did she have any time for the women's movement that found such a powerful champion in Hedwig Dohm. Her ideas on marriage and, indeed, on everything under the sun were all marked by the hierarchical, authoritarian thinking propounded by Madame Patersi. In Cosima's eyes a wife must submit to her husband's wishes, an outlook apparently confirmed by memories of her own childhood, when Marie d'Agoult's relationship with Liszt had foundered on the former's wish to break free from the shackles of an unemancipated life. It is clear that Cosima's contacts with left-wing intellectuals and artists were essentially social in character. Many years later she wrote about the theologian Bruno Bauer: 'As a young woman, I liked him a lot, his proud poverty and forceful character pleased me, and he did not demand that I should read his books.'[57] That says it all.

In Berlin Cosima was also introduced to Marie von Buch, who was to become her best friend. Marie married Alexander von Schleinitz in 1865. He had initially been Prussia's Minister of Foreign Affairs, and from the end of 1861 to his death in 1885 he was Minister of the Royal Household. As the later Imperial Chancellor Bernhard von Bülow recalled, Schleinitz was not especially popular in Prussian high society. With his 'hair dyed black, the slimness of his figure apparently due to a corset, his saccharine smile and his affected way of speaking', he got up the noses of many of his contemporaries, including Otto von Bismarck. 'That Bismarck did not like Schleinitz was entirely understandable,' Bernhard von Bülow commented sardonically.[58] Thirty-five years younger, his wife kept a salon frequented by *tout* Berlin. According to the twenty-year-old Prince Wilhelm, who fell in love with her, Mimi, as she was invariably called, was 'practically the only woman in the whole of Berlin society with whom one could talk about things other than clothes and the art of flirting'.[59] She also made quite an impression on Wagner, tirelessly collecting money for his Bayreuth Festival project.

The friendship between Marie von Schleinitz and Cosima Wagner continued after Alexander von Schleinitz's death and Marie's remarriage to the Austrian diplomat Count Anton von Wolkenstein-Trostburg, whom she accompanied to Paris and Vienna. But she was a far from uncontroversial figure. Harry Kessler, for example, called her 'narrow-minded and fanatically "German": Luther above all. Ibsen, she said, was sick: she hated all that was sick.'[60] And Bernhard von Bülow recalled her as being 'mannered in outlook, demeanour and language and in the whole way she presented herself, often even in her thought processes. She would have greeted Molière's *précieuses ridicules* as her sisters. She was also exceedingly vain, in a way that sometimes encouraged ridicule.'[61] Cosima's upbringing meant that she too was inclined to engage in emotionally charged affectation and to lend an air of undue solemnity to even the most everyday occurrences. In both women, a grand manner went hand in hand with piqued petty-mindedness. And yet – or perhaps precisely because of this fact – Mimi von Buch was one of the few people who enjoyed Cosima's unconditional trust, a trust reflected in more than 400 surviving letters.

Storm Clouds

'How is Daniel?' queried Anna Liszt in a letter that she wrote to her son in mid-September 1859. 'Cosima hasn't mentioned him for the past twelve days, I only hope he's on the road to a full recovery.'[62] Four weeks later, she returned to the subject: 'Cosima said nothing about him in her last letters and has never said anything at all even though I long since asked her what illness he's suffering from. She told me it doesn't have a name.'[63]

There were good reasons for Cosima's reticence as the feelings of Daniel's seventy-one-year-old grandmother needed to be spared. Daniel Liszt had gone to stay with his sister and brother-in-law in Berlin at the end of August. He had just completed an exhausting year of study at the University of Vienna and wanted to relax with the Bülows. He felt tired and unwell even on his arrival in the Prussian capital. It seemed initially as if he was suffering from some common-or-garden fever, but one morning he woke up and started to cough blood. The doctor who was summoned had no idea what the problem was, and to that extent Cosima was right when she claimed that the illness had no name – they were groping around in the dark. Daniel grew weaker during the weeks that followed, wasting away before his hosts' eyes. 'It's sad in the house, too,' Bülow complained to a friend in early October; 'poor Daniel still refuses to get better – he's been in bed for almost two months!'[64] For a time Bülow moved out of the apartment in order not to disturb the invalid with his musical activities, while Cosima self-sacrificially saw to her brother's needs, keeping vigil with him at night and reading to him or simply holding his hand. Liszt arrived in Berlin late in the evening of 11 December. By the time that he had made his way to the Bülows' home the next morning, Daniel was already close to death. The family doctor explained that the situation was hopeless. Liszt remained at his son's side throughout the rest of the day. The mood was one of valediction.

Daniel Liszt died on the evening of the following day, 13 December 1859, at the age of only twenty. Cosima was kneeling by the bed. A few minutes passed, then Liszt said: ' "I can't hear him breathing." Cosima placed her hand on his heart, but it was no longer beating. A little later we heard a sigh: he had passed away.'[65] As if it were entirely natural, Cosima washed her brother's body and dressed him in a shroud. The funeral took place two days later on the fifteenth. The family was represented only by Liszt, Hans and Cosima von Bülow, and Franziska von Bülow and her daughter Isidore. The precise cause of death remains uncertain. 'It was a wasting disease, a gradual fading away,' Bülow claimed, 'his élan vital had been sufficient for only twenty years.'[66]

The whole family was badly affected by Daniel's death. Liszt and his mother seemed paralysed, while Cosima and Blandine were numb with grief. Both sisters had been very fond of their brother. For years, the three of them had formed a secret conspiracy against Madame Patersi and the princess. With Daniel, a part of their childhood had died. When Blandine heard of his death, she wrote a heart-breaking letter to Cosima in which she communed with her brother: 'Daniel, Daniel, you are no longer among us,' she sighed. 'But why did you have to leave us so soon? We still needed you. . . . How proud our grand-mother was of us and especially of you. "Do you know," you once said to her, "three children like us will never be found elsewhere." ' And, turning an accusing finger to Cosima: 'I shall always regret not being with him during his final moments. Why didn't you summon me? Why didn't you tell me the truth about his condition? . . . There is no comfort for me, because unlike you and my father I was unable to lighten his final hours. My dear Cosima, look after yourself, take care of yourself, keep yourself well for the sake of those who love you, for your Blandine who worships you, I too would like to be with you in order to speak to you, to embrace you and to overwhelm you with my love.'[67]

For years Cosima continued to relive those December days from 1859, while bitterly reproaching Carolyne von Sayn-Wittgenstein, for 'it was on her advice that Daniel was sent to Vienna' to study law, even though the climate in the Austrian capital was bound to harm his permanently delicate health.[68] Her accusation is undoubtedly unjust, for conditions in Vienna were not substantially worse than those in Paris. But her hatred was deep-seated, and in Cosima's eyes Carolyne was to blame for Daniel's death. 'Princess W[ittgen-stein] described us to my father as having been born under a curse,' she noted in her diary in January 1881, 'and the preservation of our lives was thus of no special account.'[69] But she also felt that she herself was to blame for what had happened, berating herself 'for not having saved him by going with him to

Cairo; also I fear that I did not consult the right doctor when he was lying ill in my house'.[70]

A little over a month after these terrible December days, Cosima became pregnant, but the joys of motherhood did nothing to lift the mood of depression in the Bülows' household. It was certainly not a happy pregnancy, for Bülow unintentionally made life hell for his wife. Throughout the early months of 1860 he himself was in a wretched emotional state, plagued as he was by self-doubt and by bouts of depression, causing him to react gruffly and sullenly and not infrequently to shout at his young wife. Excruciating headaches added to his problems, forcing him to spend whole days at a time lying apathetically in bed. Cosima was so desperate that she did not even dare inform her husband of the good news. Some years later she wrote to him that 'you will remember that when I was expecting Loulou [Daniela] I did not dare tell you about it, as if my pregnancy were illegitimate, and that I told you about it in a dream'.[71]

The Bülows' first daughter was born at four o'clock in the morning on 12 October 1860, the loud scream with which she greeted the world encouraging her proud father to claim on the day of her birth that his daughter would become a Wagner singer, 'a future Isolde'.[72] Her Catholic baptism took place in Berlin on 24 November in the very room in which Daniel had died eleven months earlier: Cosima prepared a small chapel, and the cathedral chaplain presided over the ceremony.[73] The child was called Daniela in memory of her mother's dead brother (the registry of births spells the name Daniella), while her second name, Senta, was intended as an act of homage to the heroine of Wagner's opera *Der fliegende Holländer*. But throughout her life she was known as Loulou, Lulu or Lusch. Although the birth was not difficult, it took Cosima a long time to recover her strength – she remained dependent on medical help until January 1861. When Liszt arrived in Berlin to act as godfather, he was shocked at his daughter's appearance and insisted on her returning with him to Weimar in order to recuperate.

At the Altenburg, however, Cosima's condition showed few perceptible signs of improvement. She suffered from a persistent cough that prevented her from getting a good night's sleep. Blandine evidently had no illusions about the real reasons for her sister's problems and wrote to Liszt: 'Bülow is himself ill, he'll probably worry about Cosima for a moment, but she'll tell him that nothing is wrong with her, and that will reassure him. As for his mother, Madame von Bülow, you know as well as I do that all she is capable of is empty words. Cosima may be dead in six months if she has only this company to look after her.'[74] Not only was Cosima in poor health, but her relations with Bülow had reached an emotional impasse. The couple were clearly incapable of coexisting in a relaxed and trusting manner. Out of consideration for her perpetually ailing husband, Cosima did not dare to speak openly about her condition or her needs, a situation that could not be maintained in the longer term.

During the summer of 1861 the Bülows decided to take the waters at Bad Reichenhall near Berchtesgaden. Cosima's health improved noticeably and she went on a number of excursions into the surrounding area, Bülow reporting to a friend that 'so hale and hearty is my wife that we've been walking for six to eight hours a day'. But the stay came to an abrupt end for Bülow: 'At the end of next week I have to go to Weimar and abandon my wife to her fate here. My father-in-law is very keen that I should take an active part in the Society of Musicians' meeting – as a conductor.'[75] In mid-August, by which date Bülow had returned to Berlin on his own, Blandine and her husband, Émile Ollivier, arrived in Bad Reichenhall in the company of Wagner, whom Cosima had not seen for three years. The two were clearly not especially interested in each other as Cosima spent most of the time with her sister. Wagner recalled the occasion in his autobiography:

> Ollivier and I, however, were mostly excluded from the hilarity that soon set in here as well, as the two sisters, who laughed so incessantly that their presence could be determined from far away, usually locked themselves in their rooms for privacy so that I could only resort to conversations in French with my political friend.[76]

Only when they were saying goodbye in the hallway of the hotel did Wagner catch 'a look of almost timid inquiry from Cosima'.

But Cosima's recovery was short-lived, and on her return to Berlin her life resumed its sad old course. Her husband was once again 'in a very disagreeable state'.[77] But her bags had scarcely been unpacked when Cosima was called away to be with her father in Löwenberg in Silesia: he insisted on seeing her. To make matters worse he returned with his daughter to Berlin and proceeded to spend time in the Anhaltische Straße. 'My wife is totally preoccupied by her father,' Bülow complained, 'she has to be Martha and Mary in one and the same person. Thanks to my rheumatism, there's nothing at all I can do to help her!'[78]

Cosima found herself increasingly disillusioned by life at Bülow's side. And Bülow himself? He seems at least to have been vaguely aware of the problematic nature of his marriage: 'Cosima has achieved the admirable trick of enduring life with me,' he told his sister in June 1862, 'but my own nature has a hint of the feminine about it, and my wife is very strong-willed. Unfortunately she is so little in need of my own protection that she is able to protect me instead.'[79] One of Cosima's concerns was to inspire her husband to write music of his own. Although he regarded composition as a self-evident aspect of his artistry and for a long time had thought that his true vocation was that of a composer, his life's work from the early 1860s onwards had become increasingly centred on performing music. His work-list is correspondingly small. By 1863 some fifteen works had appeared in print, mostly piano music and a few songs but also three major orchestral works. As with so much else in his life, his creative work was a constant struggle with his own whims and passions and his fluctuating state of health. 'You've no idea how much I yearn to do something in which I can immerse myself heart and soul,' he had admitted to Richard Pohl in the summer of 1858. He was referring to the legend of Merlin, which he wanted to turn into a grand opera. 'My life and health depend on Merlin!'[80] Pohl was supposed to provide the libretto, but when he started to hang fire and finally abandoned the project altogether, it was Cosima who took over, inviting her friend Ernst Dohm to provide a text. Dohm duly obliged, only for Bülow's creative urge to burst like a bubble when Wagner demanded that he should prepare a vocal score of *Tristan und Isolde*. In the wake of this work, Bülow lost all his self-confidence and came to regard his own compositions as clumsy occasional pieces. It was now, he felt, completely mad even to consider writing music of his own, and so he failed even to make a start on *Merlin*. Cosima, who was particularly looking forward to becoming her husband's muse and acolyte, could only look on as Bülow was paralysed by Wagner's overpowering genius. It is unclear how she reacted to this turn of events, but we may assume that she was disappointed.

A similar incident happened a few years later, in the summer of 1862. 'You've no idea how much I have to do here for Wagner or at least to try to do,' Bülow told Pohl at the end of July. 'I've just completed a copy of *Die Meistersinger* – 145 quarto pages; my fingers are stiff from working eight hours a day for five days in the most appalling heat.' His work on Wagner's latest opera plunged him into another existential crisis. 'I wish it were time to sleep and that everything were over. I've lost all my self-esteem and, with it, my love of life. Where does one start with an impotent piety?' And he goes on:

> If there were a convenient way to bidding farewell to life, I should not have hesitated for so long. . . . You simply don't know what is going on around me

and within me. By constantly sacrificing myself to this and that person I have lost myself and my own individuality – 'anyone finding the said object is requested to return it etc.' I'm no longer of any use to myself or to anyone else.

Bülow was burning the candle at both ends. But it was Wagner in particular, he felt, who was destroying him. The 'impotent piety' that he felt in the presence of *Die Meistersinger*, for example, left him feeling numb and undermined his self-worth. 'With Wagner as a neighbour, everything else seems wretchedly shrivelled up and becomes childish and null and void,' he went on in his letter to Pohl. He was not even capable of reading the proofs of his songs that his publisher had just sent him: 'It all strikes me as so pitiful and paltry that I simply can't bear to look at it.'[81]

Bülow's psychological dilemma conflicted with Cosima's understanding of marriage. All that she could have given her husband – a creative stimulus and creative courage: in a word, the love of a muse – turned out to be of no avail. Even while they were still engaged, Bülow had been afraid that Cosima would find him 'insufficiently interesting', but now what he regarded as his failures as man and artist were bound to leave him feeling desperate: 'Never would he have lost me if Fate had not brought me together with the man for whom I had to recognize it as my task in life to live or die,' Cosima wrote in her diary in 1869.[82] In other words, Bülow would never have lost Cosima if he had completed *Merlin* and not capitulated in the face of Wagner's genius. And yet it must be stressed that in the summer of 1862 neither Wagner nor Cosima thought that they would ever be more than friends. Against this background, it is important not to overestimate the significance of the events that were to follow.

In early July, the Bülows spent some weeks in Biebrich, a small town on the Rhine where Wagner was currently living in rented accommodation. They spent a turbulent time there, for as always with Wagner there was plenty going on. Other visitors included his current muse, Mathilde Maier, who was the daughter of a Mainz lawyer; the actress Friederike Meyer, with whom he had likewise become very friendly; and the tenor Ludwig Schnorr von Carolsfeld and his wife, Malvina. Much later, Cosima recalled that everything about Biebrich had been 'sad, beautiful and boundlessly innocent! Mathilde Maier was in financial control, while Mathilde Wesendonck sent poems, Friederike Meyer fascinated us with her wit and talent and I myself was as aloof as you can imagine.'[83] Remarkably, she does not mention her husband even once. There are no doubt good reasons for this, as it seems that these weeks in Biebrich were far from being as 'boundlessly innocent' as Cosima wanted her daughter Daniela to believe. Writing in his autobiography, Wagner recalled that

> Cosima appeared to have lost the shyness she evinced toward me during my visit to Bad Reichenhall the previous year . . . When I had played and sung 'Wotan's Farewell' for my friends one day in my own special way, I noticed on Cosima's countenance the same expression she had showed me, much to my surprise, at that leave-taking in Zurich; but this time the ecstasy had dissolved into a serene transfiguration. Here everything was silence and mystery, only now the belief in her belonging to me came over me with such certitude that in my eccentric exuberance I became boisterously high-spirited.

In short, there was little of the sadness described by Cosima in her letter to Daniela. Nor did the situation change in Frankfurt, where Wagner accompanied the couple at the end of their visit to Biebrich:

> When I was conducting Cosima across an open square back to her hotel it occurred to me to dare her to jump into a wheel-barrow which stood empty nearby so that I could wheel her back to the hotel: she was game for it at once, whereas I, again struck by astonishment, lost the courage to carry out my mad project.

It is striking that Cosima later deleted the following sentence:

> Following behind us, Bülow had witnessed the incident; Cosima explained to him unabashedly what it was all about, but unfortunately it did not appear that he could share our high spirits, for he cautioned his wife to be more careful in such things.[84]

Before Wagner saw the Bülows again in Leipzig in late October 1862, the family was visited by a further tragedy when Cosima's sister Blandine died on her husband's estates at La Moutte near Saint-Tropez on the Côte d'Azur. She was only twenty-six. What had happened? On 3 July she had brought into the world a son who was named Daniel in memory of her dead brother. The birth was straightforward, but complications arose when Blandine's left breast became inflamed. The swelling grew and finally became infected. In mid-August Blandine's doctor, Charles Isnard, decided to operate but evidently failed to take the steps necessary to prevent sepsis: it was the height of summer, and the painful procedure took place in a private house. As a result, the patient contracted blood poisoning. The doctor prescribed arsenic and laudanum (a mixture of alcohol and opium), but to no avail. Blandine had a high temperature, was unable to eat and grew increasingly weak. Her suffering finally came to an end in the early hours of 11 September 1862. Less than three years after Daniel Liszt's death, the family had been afflicted by this second blow of fate.

Blandine's widower, the thirty-seven-year-old Émile Ollivier, was inconsolable, blaming himself for placing his credulous trust in his late wife's doctor. So distraught was he that he was even afraid that Blandine might have fallen into a coma and been buried alive.[85] There were no grounds for his suspicion, and yet it was negligent of him to allow such an operation to go ahead in conditions that were far from hygienic. 'Presumably there was a lack of expert medical help,' Bülow ventured a cautious reproach. Liszt and Cosima – now his only child – were likewise distraught, but it was Anna Liszt who was most affected by the tragedy. As Bülow noted, 'she was forced at the end of her life to watch one after another of her grandchildren die, grandchildren to whose childhood she had devoted the true cares of a mother.'[86] Cosima and her daughter Daniela travelled to Paris in September and spent some weeks with the elderly Anna Liszt, who, increasingly alone, was herself in poor health following a femoral neck fracture. She wanted the Bülows to move to Paris, but this seemed a vain hope, not least because Bülow was currently trying to hold down his position as court pianist in Berlin, a city to which he was tied in a variety of ways. Anna Liszt spent the remaining years of her life in Paris, where she was looked after by Émile Ollivier and where she died in early February 1866.

On the Run

On their return to Germany in late October 1862, the Bülows travelled to Leipzig. Here, in a concert at the Gewandhaus on 1 November, Bülow played Liszt's Second Piano Concerto and Wagner conducted his own *Meistersinger* Overture. There had been problems in the run-up to the concert, and Wagner was in one of his difficult moods. At a rehearsal, he later recalled,

> I suddenly felt utterly transported by the sight of Cosima, sitting in a corner of the hall, very pale and in deep mourning yet smiling at me warmly. . . . She now appeared to me as if stepping toward me from another world. Our

emotions were so solemn and so deep that only our absolute surrender to the joy of meeting again could help us bridge that abyss. All the events of the rehearsals struck us as an oddly amusing magic lantern show, at which we looked on like laughing children.[87]

What Wagner fails to mention is that Cosima was now five months pregnant. But, just as had been the case three years earlier, there could be no question of the joys of incipient motherhood suffusing the Bülow household. If we may believe her later diary entry, the birth of her second daughter on 20 March 1863 was a heartless and emotionally sterile affair:

How wearily and gloomily I brought my baby into the world, without any assistance; how indifferently did the father greet it! Only Richard, far away, was concerned about me, and I did not know it. How dreary, how empty, how inwardly disturbed was my life at that time! How could I ever thank R. enough for what his love has done for me? At that time I was feeling so wretched that I told nobody that my labour pains had come, and that the baby was already there when they summoned the midwife. My mother-in-law was living in the house, Hans was at home, there were servants in plenty, and I was walking up and down in the salon all by myself, wriggling like a worm and whimpering; a cry I could not suppress woke the household and they carried me to my bed, where Boni then crept out. In every home a coming child is a time of joy, but I hardly dared tell Hans that I was pregnant, so unfriendly was his reaction, as if his comfort were being disturbed.[88]

Blandina Elisabeth Veronica Theresia – called Blandine and nicknamed Boni or Ponsch – was baptized into the Catholic Church on 29 April. The witnesses were Carolyne von Sayn-Wittgenstein and Cosima's brother-in-law, Émile Ollivier.[89] Although Cosima's recollections of the birth of her second child receive some support from all that we already know about life in the Bülow household, it none the less remains impossible to know to what extent her account reflects the true facts of the matter. In the first place, her diary entry is self-contradictory: Cosima claims that she brought the child into the world alone, without any help, and that the baby had already been born before the midwife was called, whereas only a few lines later we learn that she had been carried to her bed, 'where Boni then crept out'. And what are we to make of the fact that it is clear from Bülow's letters that he was by no means as indifferent to the birth of his second daughter as Cosima would have us believe?

Her reference to Wagner's ostensible concern is likewise coloured by hindsight: after all, he had worries of his own at this period and is unlikely to have had much time for Cosima's physical and emotional well-being.

Wagner's life was in a mess at this time. In a letter that he wrote to his publisher, Franz Schott, in October 1862 he compared himself to a 'drowning man'[90] – the image was provoked by the fact that work on *Die Meistersinger* was progressing only slowly, leading Schott to withhold any further advances. And there was also his inability to sort out his private life. Although he had visited Minna in Dresden following his concert in Leipzig, it was to prove their final meeting. Minna died in January 1866 at a time when Wagner was again on the run, this time from himself. Having vacated his apartment in Biebrich, he travelled to Vienna with Friederike Meyer, whom he hoped would be engaged by the Burgtheater while *Tristan und Isolde* was in rehearsal at the Court Opera. Neither hope was to be realized. When Wagner saw that his affair with Friederike Meyer was resented by her sister, the soprano Louise Meyer-Dustmann, who was rehearsing the role of Isolde, he packed her off to Italy as a cure for her failing health. Once she was out of the way, he rented palatially spacious rooms on the ground floor of a villa in the Viennese suburb of Penzing, overlooking the park at Schönbrunn, and from May 1863, with the help of borrowed money, began to furnish the apartment in squirearchical splendour. The result was a riot of silks and satins, Wagner's predilection for the accoutrements of luxury once again outclassing his distinctly modest financial means.

His search for the woman of his life continued apace. 'I lack a home,' he appealed to Mathilde Maier, 'not in terms of a place to live, but in terms of people. . . . I lack a womanly being who might resolve – in spite of everything & everyone – to be to me what only a wife can be in such pitiful circumstances, and *must* be, I say, if I am to survive.'[91] He could not divorce Minna, he explained, for her heart was so weak that she would not survive such a course of action, and so he suggested that he and Mathilde Maier should live together in sin. Mathilde found the invitation supremely resistible and, appealing to social convention, turned it down. But Wagner had other irons in the fire, notably Lisbeth Völkl, the daughter of a Viennese pork butcher. She was 'young, modest and poor', he explained – incongruously – to Mathilde Maier, and he was resolved to try his luck with her and 'see if she will be what I need'.[92] She was not, and so Wagner brought other young complaisant women to his rooms in Penzing, carrying on like the cock of the walk, flirting and philandering, while making it clear that his true feelings still belonged to

Mathilde Wesendonck: 'Whatever the intoxicating and flattering pleasures that life may have to offer, one loves only once,' he admitted to a female friend; 'I know only too well that I shall never stop loving her, and her alone.'[93]

Wagner remained on the run, his life increasingly unsettled. In early November 1863 he conducted two concerts in Prague and in the middle of the month met Mathilde Maier in Karlsruhe, before moving on to Zurich, where he spent four nights with the Wesendoncks – the last time that he was to stay with them. If he had hoped that Otto Wesendonck would rescue him from his present financial impasse, he was mistaken: Wesendonck was unforthcoming.

After leaving Zurich, Wagner spent the night of 26 November under Mathilde Maier's roof in Mainz, then continued his journey to Berlin, where he arrived on the twenty-eighth. His next port of call was Löwenberg in Silesia, where he was not initially planning to stay, but the local choir was performing Bülow's orchestral ballad *Des Sängers Fluch*, and so Wagner allowed himself to be talked into remaining by Bülow and attending the concert. Fate now took its course. While Bülow spent the Saturday afternoon rehearsing, Wagner and Cosima took a cab ride through Berlin: 'This time we fell silent and all joking ceased,' Wagner wrote in his autobiography several years later. 'We gazed mutely into each other's eyes and an intense longing for the fullest avowal of the truth forced us to a confession, requiring no words whatever, of the incommensurable misfortune that weighed upon us.' The following sentence was struck out by Cosima when preparing the first published edition of *My Life* in 1911: 'With tears and sobs we sealed a vow to belong to each other alone.' Then, as if nothing had happened, Wagner and Cosima turned up at the evening's concert in Löwenberg. Their avowals had 'lifted a great weight from our hearts. The profound tranquillity which ensued gave us the serenity to attend the concert without any sense of oppression.'[94]

Throughout the years that followed, it is clear from Cosima's diaries that 28 November was a day of special significance. On 28 November 1869, for instance, we read: 'Six years ago R. came through Berlin, and then it happened that we fell in love; at that time I thought I should never see him again, we wanted to die together. – R. remembers it, and we drink to this day.'[95] Two years later we read: 'Eight years ago today he declared his love for me, it was on a Saturday; he left immediately afterward, and I had no thoughts, but was sad unto death.'[96] And three years after that: 'On Saturday the 28th, we celebrate our first union eleven years ago!'[97]

It must be stressed, however, that with the passage of time events invariably become much clearer and we learn to discern continuities and the workings

of fate in ways that were scarcely apparent at the time. To that extent, it would
be wrong to attach too much importance to Wagner's version of events in his
autobiography. The avowal that the couple allegedly made in Berlin, agreeing
to 'belong together' in future, pre-empts what actually happened. When we
read Wagner's retrospective account of his feelings, then his behaviour after
this ostensible 'union' assumes a number of puzzling aspects. Writing to his
'dearest sweetheart', Mathilde Maier, five days later, he announces: 'I had to
spend a day in Berlin. The Bülows had arranged this extremely cleverly. What
a wild time we had; he gave a grand concert in the evening. Sheer devilry!'[98]
This does not sound like the grand passion of Wagner's life – leaving aside the
question of whether or not the wild 'devilry' is a reference to the romantic cab
ride. Three days later, on 6 December, we find Wagner writing to his current
mistress, Maria Völkl, the sister of the pork butcher's bashful daughter with
whom he had had no luck the previous June:

> Now, my darling, prepare the house for my return, so that I can relax there
> in comfort, as I very much long to do. . . . . *And plenty of perfume: buy the best
> bottles, so that it smells really sweet.* Heavens! how I'm looking forward to
> relaxing with you again at last. *(I hope the pink drawers are ready, too???)* –
> Yes, indeed! Just be nice and gentle, *I deserve to be well looked after for a
> change.*[99]

One hardly gains the impression that in the weeks after his 'union' with
Cosima, Wagner had thought of nothing else. Rather the opposite seems to
have been the case. But this much is certain: in November 1863 there were still
barriers in the way of a lasting union between Wagner and Cosima, both of
whom were in complex dependent relationships as a result of the bonds of
family and friendship between Bülow, Liszt and Wagner himself. It would
require the intervention of a third party before these barriers could be
removed, and until that happened in May 1864, Wagner's ship of state was to
continue its wayward course towards the reefs and shoals of disaster. One after
another, his plans and hopes all burst like bubbles, as he sank further and
further into debt and could no longer pay his creditors as the result of a series
of transactions involving dubious bills of exchange. It was in order to escape
from the threat of a debtor's prison that he fled from Vienna on 23 March 1864.

Wagner was fifty years old, fleeing from his creditors, with no home to call
his own. Where should he go? Where *could* he go? The Wesendoncks declined
the pleasure of his company. And so, after passing through Munich, Wagner

travelled to Mariafeld near Zurich, arriving there on 26 March and throwing himself at the mercy of a female friend, Eliza Wille, who put him up for a month. A family friend of the Willes, Friedrich von Bernhardi, recalled Wagner's arrival in Zurich:

> On the run from his creditors, he alighted from a first-class compartment, declined to take the steamer to Meilen but insisted on a carriage, which he could no more afford to pay for than for the journey from Vienna to Zurich, then bought the most expensive cigars he could find, which he asked to be placed on Wille's account, ordered a red silk dressing gown – again at Wille's expense – and told everyone that he was staying with the Willes only as a favour.[100]

No matter how badly things may have been going for him, Wagner remained true to himself and with a casualness bordering on the ridiculous demanded the luxuries that he believed were his by right. He continued to cut the capers of a deposed but still boundlessly self-confident monarch. Eliza Wille was not a little surprised to be told one day:

> Mine is a different kind of organism, I have sensitive nerves, I must have beauty, radiance and light. The world owes me a living! I can't live the miserable life of an organist like your Master Bach! Is it such an outrageous demand to say that I deserve the little bit of luxury that I can bear? I, who can give pleasure to thousands?[101]

Wagner got increasingly on his hostess's nerves, and his visit ended after a month. His next hideout was Stuttgart. Here, on 3 May 1864, the long-awaited miracle finally happened, when the cabinet secretary to the young King Ludwig II of Bavaria, Franz Seraph von Pfistermeister, tracked Wagner down to his hotel in the town and invited him to Munich, where Ludwig demanded to see him. Ludwig's top civil servant informed the bemused composer that the king was resolved to support a musician whom he revered and to ensure that his future was free from the cares and calamities of everyday life. Wagner was free at a stroke: he had finally achieved his breakthrough. Before leaving for Munich, he dashed off a letter to his saviour:

> I send you these tears of the most heavenly emotion in order to tell you that the marvels of poesy have entered my poor loveless life as a divine reality! – And

this life, with its ultimate outpouring of verse and music, now belongs to you, my gracious young King: dispose of it as you would of your very own property![102]

Redemption

By the afternoon of Wednesday 4 May 1864 Wagner was standing before his redeemer in the royal residence in Munich.

That same day he wrote to Eliza Wille:

> He is, alas, so fair and intelligent, so soulful and glorious that I fear his life will melt away like a fleeting, divinely inspired dream in this vulgar world of ours. He loves me with all the inwardness & ardour of one's first love: he knows everything I have written and understands me as I understand my own soul. He wants me to remain with him for ever, working, resting and performing my works; he means to give me everything I need; I am to complete the *Ring*, which he is determined to perform in the way I want. I am to be my own absolute master, not a kapellmeister, nothing but myself, and his friend. And he understands all this with exactly the same seriousness as if the two of us – you & I – were talking to one another. All want is to be lifted from my shoulders, I am to have whatever I need – only I am to remain with him. What do you say to this? – What do you say? – Is it not unprece-dented? – Can it be other than a dream?[103]

In informing Mathilde Maier of his first encounter with the king, Wagner described the meeting as 'one great love scene that seemed as if it would never end. He shows the deepest understanding of my nature & of my needs. He offers me everything that I need to live, to create, and to perform my works. I am to be his friend, nothing more: no appointment, no functions to fulfil. It is all I ever wished for.'[104] Ludwig reacted in no less ecstatic terms, assuring his idol:

> Unconsciously you were the only source of my joys from my tender youth onwards, a friend who spoke to my heart as no other did, my finest teacher and tutor. – I shall do all in my power to repay you for this! – Oh, how I have looked forward to the time when I should be able to do this! – I scarcely dared entertain the hope that I should so soon be in a position to prove my love to you.[105]

The story of the misanthropic king and his charismatic favourite composer began as a fairytale. But is that really what it was? Scarcely. Even the term 'friendship' seems ill suited to describing their complicated relationship. Rather, the relationship between Wagner and King Ludwig II of Bavaria was one of misunderstandings, exaggerated hopes and false assumptions. One of Wagner's German biographers, Martin Gregor-Dellin, even saw in this ostensibly fairy-tale episode 'an intermezzo of the most shameful and insidious kind'.[106] By the end of the relationship, Ludwig, who had confused dreams with harsh reality, was simply left behind, and the same was true of Hans von Bülow, who lost both his wife and his children to Wagner. But one thing at a time.

Ludwig was born in August 1845, the first son of Crown Prince Maximilian of Bavaria and Crown Princess Marie, herself the daughter of Prince Wilhelm of Prussia. In March 1848 Maximilian's father, King Ludwig I, abdicated, not least in consequence of his affair with the notorious Lola Montez. He was succeeded by Maximilian, whose two-year-old son now became crown prince in turn. The boy's upbringing was cold and loveless, and it seems that Ludwig drifted away from his parents at a very early age. Not even with his tutors could he develop any close relationships: 'I hated him,' Ludwig said of his tutor Professor Steininger, 'just as I hated all my teachers.'[107] To judge by what we know, the quality of Ludwig's schooling was not of the best, a surprising fact, given the involvement of the Bavarian royal family. The crown prince later began to study at the University of Munich and even attended Justus von Liebig's class in chemistry, but his education was abruptly interrupted by his sudden accession to the throne. It was, however, his interest in Wagner that was to prove of central significance in his life. Even while he was still only twelve, his imagination was fired by Wagner's essay *The Artwork of the Future*. In other words, he knew Wagner's theoretical writings before he knew his stage works. His first Wagner opera was *Lohengrin*, which he heard in Munich in February 1861 and which proved to be a seminal experience. On that day, he later enthused in a letter to Cosima, 'I began to live, you can imagine that the hour of my own death, too, will strike when He is no more.'[108]

Ludwig's interest in Wagner deepened in the course of 1863. He bought all the books about the composer that were then available, reading them enthusiastically and making a note of his impressions in his diary. Now and then he even dreamt about his idol, but it was not until the winter of 1863/4 that he was seized by the desire to make contact with the composer. Not until Ludwig had succeeded his father in March 1864 was such contact finally made. At this date Ludwig was eighteen years old, an exceptionally tall and handsome young man, but a loner, dreamy, misanthropic, melancholic and homosexual. 'For me, the last year was the most beautiful in my entire life,' Ludwig wrote to Wagner on New Year's Eve 1864, 'for me it was happy and blissful in every way: "No one went, but someone came!" '[109]

This, then, was how Ludwig summed up his first year on the throne: 'No one went, but someone came!' The death of his father evidently meant nothing to him, whereas Wagner's arrival in his life meant everything. From now on Ludwig saw it as his duty to relieve Wagner of the cares of the quotidian round in order that he could devote himself to his work. It is unclear, however, to what extent Ludwig really understood this music. His piano teacher thought that his eminent pupil was altogether unmusical, apparently incapable of telling the difference between a waltz by Strauß and a sonata by Beethoven. It seems likely, therefore, that it was the mythical characters in Wagner's world of Germanic legend that fascinated the king. From the outset, Ludwig's civil servants at the Munich court were sceptical about his enthusiasm for the composer. In a letter to Cosima, Cabinet Secretary Pfistermeister spoke diplomatically about 'the highly unusual gifts of our dear and most gracious lord', a delightful euphemism for Ludwig's increasingly rapt otherworldliness. Pfistermeister went on to report a conversation that he had had with Ludwig, in which the latter had explained how

recently, after a long hunt, I took a warm bath at night and was standing in the large bath tub when I chanced to strike the surface of the water with both hands, one after the other, with differing force. The sound that it produced immediately reminded me of the final motif from Tristan, so that this whole scene – Isolde beside Tristan's body – resounded in my ear, with all the details of the music, as if conjured out of thin air.

Pfistermeister's comment could hardly be more significant: 'Is that not strange indeed?'[110]

No less strange is the correspondence that passed between the king and the composer, a total of some 400 letters, not including all the poems and telegrams. The reader is struck first and foremost by the effusive, infatuated tone that sometimes acquires a note of ecstatic frenzy. A few examples may serve to illustrate this point: 'Light of my life, my one and only friend' (Ludwig II, 11 December 1864); 'O my King! Thou art divine!' (Wagner, 11 December 1864); 'Ultimate, highest, most beautiful being of my life! Wondrous King!' (Wagner, 31 December 1864); 'O Saint, I worship Thee' (Ludwig II, 5 January 1865);

'My noble, glorious friend! My beautiful will, my loving providence!' (Wagner, 21 March 1865); 'Ardently beloved, my only friend!' (Ludwig II, 23 March 1865); 'I laud and magnify Thee who art more than Man, Thou art imbued with the Spirit of a God' (Ludwig II, 12 July 1865).

It has often been suggested that there was a homoerotic element to Ludwig's relations with Wagner, and it is undoubtedly possible that this was true of Ludwig, at least on a subliminal level. But it was certainly not true of Wagner. Within only a few years the latter had started to find these terms of endearment distinctly embarrassing. When Cosima admitted in July 1878 that she had read some of his letters to Ludwig, 'he says, "Oh, those don't sound very good, but it wasn't I who set the tone." '[111] But the overwrought encomia of their early letters were plainly sincerely felt. Both men were completely blinded by their first encounter with one another. Ludwig met his 'finest teacher and tutor', while Wagner found himself standing in the presence of his 'redeemer'. Ludwig not only freed him from the hopeless entanglements in which he was embroiled in early 1864 but opened up new prospects for him. Without Ludwig, it is more than likely that *Die Meistersinger* and the *Ring* would not have been completed and *Parsifal* would probably never have been written at all. The Bayreuth Festival, too, would not have been established. And it was Ludwig who, albeit involuntarily, brought about the marriage between Richard and Cosima Wagner.

But it is no less true that this 'royal friendship', as it has been dubbed, soon proved to be a misalliance. Politically speaking, Ludwig ascended the throne at a difficult time. The world of politics was dominated by the 'Schleswig-Holstein Question', with Bavaria as the third-largest power after Prussia and Austria, both of which were currently contending for hegemony in the German-speaking world. The second German–Danish War that was fought over the duchies of Schleswig, Holstein and Lauenburg ended in 1864 with the defeat of Denmark, allowing Prussia to make territorial gains in northern Europe, an accretion of power inevitably contested by Austria. There were also arguments over the future of the Customs Union, a trade agreement between seventeen German states.

It is unlikely that the adolescent Ludwig had the stature to find his own way in life and, having found it, to pursue it with any real commitment. He was too young to assume such a heavy burden of office, his father's relatively early death having meant that on the dynastic career ladder a whole generation had been passed over. And so he required political advisers. But posterity is bound to ask if those advisers needed to include Wagner. It is clear from Ludwig's letters that he had a detailed knowledge of Wagner's theoretical writings. In July 1864 Wagner wrote a programmatical essay for him under the title 'On State and Religion', an essay in which he put his case to a monarch who was above party politics and argued that Ludwig would find 'redemption' in his own art. Ludwig got the message and allowed the political forces of the day to pursue their course unchecked.

Bavaria needed a powerful king who should have been partisan in the best sense of the term, but instead Ludwig withdrew into Wagner's cloud cuckoo land. 'My beloved has often wanted to know more about my political views', Wagner insinuated in September 1865. 'I have already divulged certain things. Would my beloved know more?'[112] This was the period of the Gastein Convention, convoked to discuss the fate of the three duchies of Schleswig, Holstein and Lauenburg. Instead of placing Bavaria's foreign policy on a new footing, Ludwig begged the 'light of his life' to inform him of his own opinion on the matter. Wagner prepared a series of orotund diary entries, which he then sent off to Ludwig. What happened next could hardly have been more grotesque: Ludwig prepared copies and distributed them among his ministers, who were instructed to 'carry out the ideas set down herein', as Wagner himself wrote to inform a friend with a mixture of pride and bemusement. 'I do not need to tell you the almost comical confusion to which this has led!' There is no doubt that Wagner had some influence over his royal friend and was more than capable of using it. He went on in the same letter: 'I have ruthlessly told him my opinion about his officials, ministers etc.'[113] It is clear that Wagner's ruthless opinion was scarcely flattering to the individuals concerned. The Catholic king's unfortunate dependence on his Protestant Rasputin was bound to bring Wagner's enemies out of the ornately carved woodwork, enemies who envied Wagner and opposed his ideas. But until such time as these people had asserted their authority and Wagner had been driven from Munich in December 1865, the honeymoon period continued.

Last-minute Panic

It was not until the middle of May 1864 that Hans and Cosima Bülow learnt about their friend's remarkable rescue. Wagner was then in Vienna, sorting out his creditors – Ludwig had given him 4,000 florins to this end (about 20,000 euros at today's prices). 'My happiness and my power are now so great', Wagner wrote to Bülow on 12 May, that I am concerned only not to incur the charge of abusing that power. Hence my concern not to demand any favours but only to accept them. The fuss & the envy are such that we were obliged to pretend that the annual stipend that the king has made over to me of his own free will is extremely small. Stick to this story when addressing the world and my own: but I can tell you that I am amply provided for and that I am using all my additional income simply to pay off my debts – all of them.[114]

As the future was to demonstrate, Wagner's fears were well founded, for Ludwig spared no expense in gratifying his passion. In addition to an annual stipend of 4,000 florins, the king also gave the composer a similar amount as a contribution towards the cost of moving from Vienna to Bavaria. And on 10 June, Wagner received a gift of 16,000 florins – some 80,000 euros at today's prices. For the *Ring* it was agreed that he would receive a fee of 30,000 florins. All in all, Wagner received a grand total of 131,173 florins and 46 kreutzers from the court secretariat between 1 May 1864 and 31 December 1867. By way of comparison, a professor earned between 600 and 1,200 florins a year at this date. Munich's court kapellmeister, Franz Lachner, was paid 4,000 florins, and a minister received 12,000. In the space of three and a half years, therefore, Wagner received the equivalent of ten ministerial salaries. None the less, it has to be conceded that these sums all came from the privy purse – the so-called 'civil list'– and that in comparison to the amounts of money that Ludwig lavished on his extravagant building programmes, Wagner's appanage was negligible. And yet there were influential contemporaries unwilling to draw this distinction. 'Wagner's aims were initially not political at all, but purely egotistical', complained Ludwig von der Pfordten in his unpublished reminiscences.[115] Both von der Pfordten, who was Bavarian prime minister from 1864 to 1866, and other prominent figures saw the composer only as a rapacious predator threatening to eviscerate the Bavarian state.

Wagner returned to Munich from Vienna on 13 May 1864 in the company of his two servants, Franz and Anna Mrazek, their three-month-old baby, Auguste, and Wagner's dog, Pohl. Having waited on Wagner in Penzing, the Mrazeks now ran his household in Kempfenhausen, an out-of-the-way village on the north-eastern shores of Lake Starnberg that was the setting for the Villa Pellet, a twenty-two-room manor house that Ludwig had leased for his idol within a short distance of Schloß Berg, where he himself resided from time to time. Anna Mrazek later recalled that 'initially it was relatively quiet in the large villa. Wagner went to see the king almost every day. He returned

between three and four in the afternoon, accompanied by this or that
gentleman from the royal household, who remained with him all evening.
This peaceful existence must have lasted about three weeks.'[116] During the
hours that they spent together, Wagner read to Ludwig, and they gave themselves up to their fantasies.

The idyll came to an end when Ludwig left for Bad Kissingen on 18 June.
Wagner was now on his own, and it suddenly became painfully clear to him
that, although his financial worries may have been resolved, he still lacked a
suitable woman to make his happiness complete. So boisterous was his mood
that he was incapable of being alone. He began by trying to tempt Hans von
Bülow to his new home on the banks of Lake Starnberg to help him while
away the hours: 'My dear, don't waste the summer sweating away at your
work! I beg you! – You'll live here & stay as long as you want, without
spending a single kreutzer. Given the arrangements here, you won't be
disturbing me in the slightest. Your travel expenses and so on will all be
completely indemnified (or, rather, reimbursed); I too owe you a certain
amount of money, which you can collect on this occasion.'[117] Bülow evidently
demurred, for a week later we find Wagner returning to the attack: 'I invite
you, together with your wife, child and maid, to take up residence here this
summer for as long as you like.' And he went on: 'Populate my house, at least
for a while! – This is my most heartfelt request! Just think! This is the most
important thing to have happened to me in my entire life: a great era, its most
significant section! Let us collect our thoughts and together see what all this
means and – the meaning that it may yet have for us! . . . For heaven's sake,
children! Children! I won't take no for an answer! I couldn't bear it!'[118]

Hans and Cosima hesitated. But when Wagner repeated his invitation even
more insistently in a letter to Cosima on 16 June, a decision was finally taken.
Wagner suggested that Bülow should abandon his position in Berlin and settle
in Munich as 'Vorspieler', or pianist, to the king. He claimed to have discussed
this new appointment at court, where Ludwig was said to have been enthusiastic about the idea. Pfistermeister guaranteed him a salary of at least 1,500
florins a year. The offer seemed attractive, not least because Bülow had for
some time been tired of his post at the Stern Conservatory in Berlin. Whether
Wagner had an ulterior motive and was planning to install Cosima in his
vicinity is something we can only surmise, but it is striking that in his decisive
letter to Cosima, he avoided addressing her by the intimate 'du' and used the
more formal 'Sie' instead, even though they had been on intimate terms since
their days together in Biebrich. But presumably Wagner knew that Bülow

would read the letter, too, and wanted to make his friend think that there was still a certain distance between himself and Cosima. That no complicitous plot was involved seems clear from the fact that it was at precisely this time that Wagner resumed his courtship of Mathilde Maier, to whom he wrote on 22 June, addressing her as 'du': 'Will you come and run my house for me? I beg you, come in September, have a look round, help me – and impose whatever conditions you want, but just make sure that I get you here!'[119] Wagner even wrote to Mathilde's mother, Josephine, in an attempt to allay her objections and worries: 'Do you have the courage to face the world and the necessary trust in me to relinquish your Mathilde to me?'[120] And in a monumental show of poor taste, Wagner even assured Frau Maier that he would 'give some thought' to asking for Mathilde's hand following the death of his wife, Minna. Wagner's last-minute panic is clear. By the time that he fired off his letter to Mainz, the Bülows had already announced their visit. All in all, a cabal could have been planned more skilfully than this. But Wagner's double-dealing may be a reflection of his own fear that his courage was about to fail him. Perhaps he suspected what would happen when Cosima arrived at the Villa Pellet. Perhaps his approach to Mathilde was an attempt to thwart this development. We simply do not know.

Cosima arrived in Starnberg on 29 June 1864, accompanied by her two daughters, Daniela and Blandine. Bülow was still tied up in Berlin but planned to follow as soon as he could. From now on things moved quickly, but, thanks to the sworn testimony of Anna Mrazek, the events of these weeks can be reconstructed in some detail. Fifty years later, in May 1914, she told a court: 'I am convinced that Frau Cosima then gave herself to Richard Wagner. In general, it was easy to tell in Starnberg at that time that there was something going on between Frau Cosima and Richard Wagner. The two of them were always together and were always walking in the grounds, arm in arm.'[121] While Blandine and Daniela were sleeping next door, the adulterers sealed their union. Nine months later Cosima gave birth to Wagner's first daughter, Isolde.

When Bülow arrived in Kempfenhausen on 7 July he was again very ill, suffering from a rheumatic fever that had almost paralysed his left arm, while his nerves were again in shreds. He had no idea what was going on, and this was hardly the time to discuss marital problems. The situation was awkward, not least because Wagner was inevitably concerned not to forfeit the friendship of so brilliant a pianist and conductor. And so Cosima and Wagner decided to keep him in the dark. As Anna Mrazek recalled much later, the plan worked, at least in the shorter term: 'To the extent that he noticed anything at all, Bülow seemed not to make much of it. At the time I thought that he regarded the relationship as one between friends, although I myself already regarded it as one between lovers.' But disaster soon followed. Franz Mrazek was working in the house and, as his wife explained, he saw 'Bülow wanting to enter Wagner's bedroom, but the door was locked as Frau Bülow was inside with Wagner. (My husband knew that Frau Bülow was in the room with Wagner.) My husband went on to say that Bülow returned to the living room and threw himself on the ground, shouting and screaming and beating the floor with his hands and feet like a madman.' It seems barely conceivable, but there was evidently no subsequent argument between Bülow and his wife, no emotional scene, no attempt at clarification, as we might have expected. Bülow did not even demand an explanation from his rival. The main characters in this farce just carried on as usual, as if nothing untoward had taken place. 'No one said anything,' Anna Mrazek recalled, 'I did not hear a word about it.' Only Bülow vented his frustration on Anna Mrazek, presumably in the belief that she and Cosima were in league with one another. In 1914 Anna Mrazek told the court: 'Frau Cosima stood behind her husband's back and placed her index finger to her lips by way of a warning.'[122] Bülow was not to know what was going on.

Realizing which way the wind was blowing, Wagner now regretted his letters to Mathilde Maier and her mother and wished he had never written them. On 19 July, he wrote to Mathilde to say that he was now in the sort of mood 'in which I would not accept any sacrifice that might be made to me'.[123] In other words, Mathilde Maier need not bother to come as Wagner had in the meantime made other plans.

Bülow's health continued to give cause for concern. Although he was barely able to stand, he and Wagner travelled to Munich every day for a whole week, performing excerpts from Wagner's new works for the edification of the king. But the situation could not go on: Bülow needed medical treatment. The Bülows left the Villa Pellet on Friday 19 August. Bülow himself moved into the Bayerischer Hof Hotel in Munich, where he could be seen by a doctor, while Cosima travelled to Karlsruhe to see her father, who was appearing at a music festival in the town. Evidently she felt the need to speak to Liszt and initiate him into her secret and ask for his advice. She remained in Karlsruhe for six days, during which time Liszt unsurprisingly took her to task. Perhaps he reminded her of the marriage vows that she had taken in Saint Hedwig's Church in Berlin. Perhaps, too, he drew her attention to Wagner's poor reputation. And perhaps he explained that adultery is a mortal sin. We may be certain that the impending breakdown of the Bülows' marriage was a heavy burden for him to bear. His principal concern was of course the fate of his daughter and his favourite pupil. But he also suffered from religious scruples. His partner of many years' standing, Carolyne von Sayn-Wittgenstein, had moved to Rome in 1860, the better to pursue her attempts to have her marriage to Prince Nicholas annulled. But her attempts failed, and during the years that followed, Liszt turned increasingly to religion in general and to the Catholic Church in particular as a source of consolation. In April 1865 the then fifty-three-year-old composer received the tonsure and in the course of the coming months entered the four minor orders, orders that dated from a time when the Church had a different order for each liturgical function – Liszt's four were Doorkeeper, Lector, Acolyte and Exorcist. Cosima's adultery must have pained him not just as a father but also as a future Abbé. Years later, Carolyne recalled that 'I was with him during the deaths of his son, his daughter Blandine and his mother, but nothing compared to his despair over this.'[124]

Cosima returned to Starnberg with Liszt on 25 August 1864. It was three years since Wagner and Liszt had seen one another, but their reunion took place in circumstances that could hardly have been more unfortunate. Initially they retained their composure and even made music together, but on the afternoon of 30 August a violent argument broke out, in the course of which Liszt showered his friend with reproaches. 'There were also many other reasons to be agitated,' Wagner hinted mysteriously in a letter to Mathilde Maier, 'Liszt's visit – against such a background etc.'[125] It was clear that Liszt would side with Bülow. Equally clearly Liszt must have believed that he could still drive a wedge between Wagner and his daughter, otherwise he would scarcely have advised Bülow to accept Ludwig's offer of a post in Munich. During the weeks that followed, Liszt did all in his power to keep Cosima away from Wagner.

The Bülows left Starnberg on 3 September. Bülow himself was still very weak, and it was only with great effort that Cosima was able to get him to the station, where she manoeuvred him into a compartment for the journey back to Berlin. Here Bülow's health improved. 'But things are getting better only very slowly,' he told a friend, 'which is all the more regrettable in that domestic upheavals demand a quicker pace.'[126] By 'domestic upheavals' he was presumably thinking first and foremost of his imminent move to Bavaria. It was paradoxical that he accepted Ludwig's offer of a post set up for him by Wagner and that he was moving to Munich as the king's private pianist. He now had to sell up in Berlin and plan for his resettlement in Munich. Although Cosima too had her hands full, she left for a two-week break with her father in early October. They travelled first via Eisenach to Paris, where they saw Anna Liszt and Marie d'Agoult, and from there they moved south to Toulon and Saint-Tropez, where they visited Blandine's grave. They resumed their separate journeys on 15 October, Liszt travelling on to Rome, while Cosima returned to Germany. The tour was evidently intended by Liszt as a way of distracting his daughter and of opening up a rift between her and Wagner. As the future was soon to make painfully clear, his attempts were all in vain.

3

Wagner
(1864–83)

Tristan and Isolde

Wagner left the Villa Pellet on Lake Starnberg in October 1864 in order to settle in Munich, moving into a palatial villa at 21 Bienner Straße that was placed at his disposal by King Ludwig II. He was now living close to the Königsplatz, Munich's most exclusive residential area, facing the Propyläen and Glyptothek, his new home being no less elegant than its surroundings: the two-storey mansion, with its characteristic bay at the front, offered its new occupant ample room to expand, while the park-like garden invited him to relax in the shade of its ancient trees. The focal point of the upper floor was a large salon that could be used for receptions and that housed Wagner's Érard grand piano. To the right a door led to the composer's holy of holies, his 'satin chamber'. The select few who were permitted to enter this study were generally overwhelmed by what they found here, for the room's furnishings – entirely Wagner's own creation – were a riot of light and colour and an orgy of velvet and satin. The walls were lined with yellow satin, while the pink silk curtains in front of the windows bathed the room in a roseate glow. Throughout the room were draperies, artificial roses and decorations made from precious fabrics such as damask and satin. In the middle of the study was a couch covered with a floral moiré fabric.

Such extravagant luxury was no more than a reflection of Wagner's own view of himself. Earlier that same year, as we have already noted, he had asked his hostess at Mariafeld, Eliza Wille, whether a man who could 'give pleasure to thousands' should reasonably be denied a modicum of luxury.[1] With Ludwig's money his dreams could come true, and he was able to create the atmosphere that he believed he needed to work. The task of running his household for him was entrusted to Franz and Anna Mrazek and to Verena ('Vreneli') Stocker-Weidmann, whom he knew from his time in Lucerne.

The Bülows arrived in Munich in late November 1864 and moved into a much smaller house at 15 Luitpoldstraße just round the corner from Wagner; with his annual salary of 2,000 florins, Bülow could not compete with his idol. 'You can well imagine that it will be some time before we are back in the swim of things,' he complained to his mother in Berlin. Dozens of crates and cases still had to be unpacked, and to make matters worse, renovation work on the building was progressing only slowly: 'Our annoyance at the unreliability and incompetence of the workmen has lost some of its force now that we have got used to what simply cannot be helped, things are becoming less temporary, and the definitive arrangements may well turn out to be attractive.'[2]

Bülow was still not fully restored to health when on 25 December he gave his first concert in his new post at the city's Odeon Theatre. The programme included solo works by Bach and Mozart and, accompanied by the Court Orchestra, Beethoven's Fifth Piano Concerto. Even King Ludwig turned up in honour of the occasion, causing a minor sensation as the king had little time for 'absolute music', and it was the first and last time that he set foot in the Odeon. Perhaps Bülow realized that his activities performing for the king would serve little useful purpose, for he described his principal task as that of serving Wagner. 'He is so lonely and so forlorn that even the mere presence of a few unquestioning supporters such as Peter Cornelius and myself is bound to be of value to him. My duties are clearly laid out: to concentrate exclusively on the Wagnerian challenge.'[3] The arrangements could hardly be more delicate, with Bülow as Wagner's satellite and Cosima as his mistress.

Thanks to Peter Cornelius we are reasonably well informed about life in Wagner's circle of influence in the early months of 1865. Cornelius was born in 1824 and studied with Liszt in Weimar before settling in Vienna in 1859. There he had got to know Wagner and quickly became his friend and disciple. But like all who came too close to Wagner's fire, he ran the risk of being burnt. 'Wagner's genius had an annihilating force to it,' he wrote in 1862. 'When I recognized it again today, I was forced to tell myself that whereas he draws on unlimited resources, what I'm producing is simply botched! The man is a genius right down to his nerve endings!'[4] But Cornelius differed from Bülow in that his feelings of self-worth were not undermined by Wagner's genius. When Wagner summoned him to Munich two years later, his initial reaction was to turn down the invitation: 'He wants me to be his Kurwenal. W. doesn't understand that although I may have some of the qualities needed for doglike devotion, I unfortunately also have a little too much independence of character and talent to be no more than a footnote to his own private history.'[5]

Wagner needed the presence of his friends, and with his love of casual camaraderie he wanted to be with people. And so he refused to take no for an answer and even persuaded Ludwig to pay Cornelius an honorarium. But Cornelius saw through his plan: 'For Wagner, the king's thousand florins are merely a new way of saying: "Come to me!" . . . The atmosphere around Wagner is tremendously sultry, he burns me up and robs me of the air I need to breathe.'[6] Elsewhere we find him complaining that 'Wagner is too much caught up in himself; in his proximity I'd hatch only Wagnerian eggs.'[7] But no matter how much he hesitated and delayed, he could not resist the summons and on 30 December 1864 he arrived in Munich and became Wagner's factotum, 'a stick of intellectual furniture.'[8]

Within two days Cornelius had paid a courtesy call on the Bülows. 'Hans was ill,' he noted in his diary, 'his condition is giving some cause for concern. They are both noble, sophisticated people, but heavens only knows what may happen, given the way they live together – in time this will become clear to me.'[9] Even if Cornelius did not yet know what had happened during the previous six months, he was perceptive enough to sense that something was not quite right. Cosima, he observed mysteriously a good two weeks later, was living a 'sad life between her husband, who is slowly fading away, and her eccentric fatherly friend'.[10] Her 'eccentric fatherly friend' was, of course, Wagner, who was increasingly taxing Cornelius's patience. 'Wagner neither knows nor understands what a strain he places on people,' he told Josef Standthartner with a sigh, before going on to describe a typical encounter:

We recently called on Frau von Bülow! Wagner picked up Schack's translation of Firdausi and read a number of cantos about Sohrab and Rustum. Meanwhile Bülow had finished his lesson – it lasted barely twelve minutes – and by now we were deep into *Tristan und Isolde* – the whole of the first act was sung. In the meantime tea had been served – we'd barely drunk half a cup before Wagner was well into a retelling of his *Parzival* – and so it went on all evening until we all went our separate ways.

And Cornelius concluded: 'Our great friend simply has to talk about himself and read and sing to others, otherwise he feels unwell.'[11]

It was at this period – early February 1865 – that the first storm clouds gathered over Wagner's head, dampening his exuberant enthusiasm. It started on 6 February, when Franz von Pfistermeister called on Wagner at his new home in the Brienner Straße. It is unclear what they talked about, but it seems that Wagner again transgressed the bounds of tact and good taste by referring to Ludwig as 'my lad'. Pfistermeister lost no time in retailing this incident to the king, presumably dramatizing the remark and turning a moment of tactlessness into a terrible gaffe. Ludwig was piqued, to say the least, because in spite of his closeness to Wagner, he was still keen to maintain a sense of courtly etiquette. No one described the king of Bavaria as 'my lad' and went unpunished, and when Wagner turned up that Monday afternoon for an audience arranged the previous day, he was sent packing. The king, he was told, was displeased. Wagner could leave. Such an incident could not be kept quiet for long, and within days it was being rumoured that Wagner had fallen out of favour, prompting Ludwig to write to the composer on 14 February to complain about 'the wretched and short-sighted people who can speak of disfavour, but who have no inkling of our love and who can have none!'[12]

But this formal apology was scarcely calculated to end the gossip. Five days later, on 19 February, the Augsburg *Allgemeine Zeitung* launched its scattergun attack, the author of the piece, Oskar von Redwitz, accusing Wagner of arrant profligacy: 'His demands in matters of ordinary life and comfort seem to be of so exquisitely sybaritic a nature that an oriental potentate need not recoil from the prospect of putting up permanently in his house near the Propyläen and sitting as a guest at his table.' Worse, the composer was said to be abusing Ludwig's generosity: 'Or is it perhaps worthy of a really great and noble artist that Wagner, installed in his luxurious surroundings, should spend thousands on carpets alone, for instance – out of the purse of his generous benefactor – in the ostentatious role of a modern Croesus?' Redwitz advanced an argument that was extremely clever, not to say cunning, in his attempts to open up a rift between Wagner and his patron. The poor king, he went on, had no idea of the machinations of his decadent favourite and must therefore be protected from the composer. 'Otherwise we shall have to praise the day when Richard Wagner and his friends, this time really and truly "overthrown", will have to turn their backs on our good Munich and on Bavaria itself. For however exalted Wagner and his music may be, our king and our love for him stand, for us, a hundred times higher.'[13]

Bülow felt that he too was implicated in this assault on the composer's 'friends' and lost no time in branding Redwitz a 'dishonourable backbiter'. The residents of Wagner's Munich colony had never imagined that life would be quite like this in Ludwig's brave new world. 'The whole thing is a cabinet intrigue,' Cornelius suspected,[14] and in this he was probably not wrong. Wagner was caught in the political crossfire. In fact, it was less his financial extravagance that outraged his enemies than his influence on the king. Indeed, there were even people who attempted to exploit that influence, when powerful circles around Prince Maximilian Karl von Thurn und Taxis sought Wagner's help in installing one of their own favourites as cabinet secretary. Wagner would have received shares in an agricultural bank in return for his services, but this sop was unacceptable to him and so he refused his support. When Pfistermeister found out what was going on, he offered Wagner generous financial assistance in turn. There was considerable fear and uncertainty in both camps. On 11 March, Wagner finally demanded a vote of confidence from Ludwig: 'Should I leave? Should I stay? I want only what you want.'[15] Ludwig replied by return of post: 'Stay, stay here, all will be just as wonderful as it was before.'[16]

For the present, oil had been poured on troubled waters. The next day, 12 March, Bülow set off on an extended tour that took him initially to Utrecht and from there to The Hague, Amsterdam, Hamburg, Dresden and Jena. By the time that he returned to Munich on 2 April, Cosima's latest pregnancy had almost run its course. The fact that he was prepared to leave her alone for more than three weeks during a period bound up with all manner of difficulties and troubles once again throws light on the couple's relationship. She was delivered of her third daughter – Wagner's first child – at 8.40 on the morning of 10 April 1865. Named Isolde Josepha Ludovika, she was described in the baptismal register of Saint Boniface's church in Munich as the 'legitimate daughter' of Hans and Cosima von Bülow. The Catholic baptism took place on 24 April in the 'parents' home' at 15 Luitpoldstraße. The witnesses were Josephine von Kaulbach, the wife of the local painter Wilhelm von Kaulbach, and none other than Wagner himself, the child's natural father.[17] The Bülows' marriage had long been a sham, although it is difficult to say for certain if Bülow really thought he was Isolde's father.

The events surrounding the child's conception in the summer of 1864 were hardly open to doubt. Or could Bülow have been mistaken? Only a few days after the birth, he wrote to a friend to announce that 'for the third time' he had 'become a "mother"', as they say in Berlin when daughters put in an appearance'.[18] If Bülow was convinced that he was the father, this can mean only that Cosima was intimate with both men at the time that the child was conceived. But perhaps Bülow was merely trying to put a brave face on an impossible situation. If he had admitted that Isolde was not his child, he would have ensured at a stroke that he and his wife, and Wagner too, were social pariahs in Munich. Perhaps he was too embarrassed to admit this fact and recoiled from the truth, preferring for better or worse to acknowledge the child as his own. At all events, Cosima's midwife was in no doubt as to the father's true identity. Much later, Anna Mrazek recalled that 'whenever she went to see Frau Cosima during her lying-in period, the midwife told me that she always found Richard Wagner sitting by her bedside'.[19] Bülow was in any case otherwise engaged, as he was preparing for the world premiere of Wagner's *Tristan und Isolde*, ruining his already failing health in the service of his rival while Wagner and Cosima were fussing over their first child together.

Bülow's behaviour raises a number of questions. Why did he put up with it all? Why did he not take Wagner to task? Why did he not simply announce that their friendship was over? After all, this would have been an entirely natural step for him to take. Unlike Peter Cornelius, however, Bülow never managed to escape from Wagner's gravitational pull but continued to feel strangely drawn to the charismatic composer, whom he served with slavish docility. Cornelius suspected that the Bülows' fatal dependence on Wagner was the result of their artistic 'impotence'. 'None of them has any creative talent, they bring to light nothing from the depths of their hearts. That is why they blindly and unconditionally say "yes" to Wagner.'[20] This would certainly explain Bülow's commitment to *Tristan und Isolde*. As so often, he spared neither himself nor his musicians. In addition to numerous sessions with individual players, he conducted a total of twenty-one orchestral rehearsals in the course of which the inevitable gaffes occurred. One eyewitness reports that 'neither Wagner himself nor the Bülows had any idea of the peculiar nature of the ground on which they were now standing and as a result committed a number of serious errors'.[21] The people of Munich were a good-natured and friendly bunch, Rosalie Braun-Artaria recalled, but they were never able to tolerate arrogant outsiders. Among the errors of judgement that she mentions were the insults that Bülow heaped on the audience. During one of the rehearsals he asked for a row of seats in the stalls to be removed in order for the stage to be enlarged. When the theatre's technical director objected that thirty seats would be lost, Bülow commented that it was a matter of supreme indifference to him 'whether we have thirty *Schweinehunde* more or less in the place'. It was the sort of indiscretion to which Bülow was notoriously prone and that was scarcely calculated to improve the standing of Munich's Wagnerian coterie.

The first night had to be postponed at the last minute when the Isolde, Malvina Schnorr von Carolsfeld, lost her voice. 'The shock was tremendous', wrote Josephine von Kaulbach:

No one would believe it. People assumed that the police had arranged it all because they were afraid of a riot. The students were planning to pelt Bülow with apples and rotten eggs and to greet him with children's rattles when he stepped up on to the conductor's podium.... We have nothing but sympathy for the good Frau von Bülow, who really has to be admired for the calmness and amiability with which she has put up with all this.[22]

Cosima seemed not even to notice all this unpleasantness. She saw herself as a distinguished Parisian and regarded gossip and scandal as altogether beneath her. And so she busied herself with the task of distributing tickets for the final dress rehearsal on 11 May. One such recipient was Josephine von Kaulbach, who immediately after the performance complained to her husband that the work was 'too much for our feeble nerves and ears. The singing consists in strident howling; they bawl and rant and rage, and throughout it all they are accompanied by the most ingenious dissonances in the orchestra: timpani, trumpets, cymbals and other newly invented instruments rise to a pitch of absolute frenzy'. She concluded her account by noting that 'the good Frau Bülow' spent the entire performance 'beaming with pleasure'.[23] It was no doubt a matter of some indifference to Cosima whether or not Josephine von Kaulbach understood the work and whether or not she liked it. After all, the artist's wife was merely a more or less useful contact. 'Were you at Frau von Kaulbach's?' she enquired of Malvina Schnorr von Carolsfeld. 'If you visit her, sound her out about me; if she is as friendly and as well-disposed as she used to be, tell her that I'll be writing to her; but if she has been worked on, then you should simply give her my regards.'[24]

There is no doubt that these were the words and actions of a consummate politician inasmuch as Cosima was concerned to ensure that the first night was a major event in the social calendar and to rally Wagner's local supporters to his cause. Opera-goers were to be given the feeling that they were members of an exclusive and sophisticated coterie. Her plan worked. 'It struck me as very strange', Rosalie Braun-Artaria complained,

that it was precisely those people who until then had been thoroughly unmusical who now declared that they finally knew what music was. The whole of the Wagner community at that time had all the hallmarks of a sect, and there was nothing in the least attractive about the thought of joining it. And so I remained loyal to my old gods, Mozart, Beethoven and Schubert, even after I had become personally acquainted with Frau von Bülow, who was always keen to acquire new friends. But I knew that other, less awkward customers would soon be drawn into the charmed circle of 'those who belonged', a circle into which she welcomed everyone as if as a matter of course with that calculating amiability of hers.[25]

Tristan und Isolde finally opened on 10 June in the presence of the king and proved a huge artistic triumph. The audience cheered demonstratively at the end, and when Wagner and his singers took their curtain calls, they were visibly moved and overwhelmed. The audience even overlooked the sheer bulk of the leading singers, whose excessive weight went 'far beyond our idea of what such ideal lovers should look like'.[26] Later that evening, many of the performers and their friends assembled in Wagner's house and garden for a glittering first-night party. Only one thing blighted the occasion: the non-attendance of old friends such as Otto and Mathilde Wesendonck, Carl Bechstein and Franz Liszt, all of whom were conspicuous by their absence.

Power and Influence

'I need a secretary, but of the kind that *I* need', Wagner wrote to Heinrich Porges in late May 1864:

> He must be able to deal with my business correspondence, keep my manuscripts in order, prepare literary and musical fair copies and make arrangements of my scores etc. – in a word, he must be completely versatile. Do you wish to take this on?[27]

Porges was a writer on music who had become friendly with Wagner in Vienna. He hesitated before accepting the composer's insinuating invitation, and by the time he arrived in Munich in the summer of 1865 it was already too late, because by then Wagner had already found a secretary: Cosima. It was not as if he had offered her the post. Rather, she had obtained it through her own skill and tenacity. The lovers thus extended their liaison to the workplace, Cosima having made herself indispensable. She led a strenuous double life, not only performing her own domestic duties but making her way each day to the Brienner Straße, where she organized Wagner's schedule, dealing with his correspondence and superintending the running of his household.

By now her relationship with her husband was more of a part-time occupation than a full-time marital commitment. When Bülow was not in the theatre or away on tour, the atmosphere in the Luitpoldstraße was strained and even hostile. More than once Bülow would commit the unforgivable transgression of striking his wife. Years later Cosima noted in her diary how Wagner 'recalls scenes, at which he was present, when Hans struck me, and says he was horrified at the calm indifference with which I had borne this'.[28] Perhaps her mind was distracted from Bülow's beatings by her thoughts of the book she had first read in her youth, Thomas à Kempis's *De Imitatione Christi*, in which she would have read at one point: 'If you wish to be raised to Heaven, you should debase yourself here on earth.' Cosima bore all this because she had found her true vocation in life: to serve Wagner and to sacrifice herself to him. But which of them was the controlling force?

'Since then Wagner has been completely and utterly under her spell,' Cornelius noted in his diary. 'It is no longer possible to speak to him on his own, no letters get through to him without her first breaking them open and reading them to him.'[29] This was the situation by the summer of 1865 at the latest. In mid-July Wagner began to dictate his autobiography, thereby satisfying one of Ludwig's requests: 'Every available hour I now fill by faithfully retelling what my friend then carefully writes down.'[30] They made rapid progress in their work on *My Life* and within five days had completed forty pages. But Cosima could not have played the dominant role ascribed to her by Cornelius if she had done no more than 'carefully' write down whatever Wagner told her. While freeing him from those enervating tasks that it gave him no pleasure to perform, she also revealed a high degree of independence and a willingness to act on her own initiative.

In essence she saw herself as a business manager, to use a modern term. The first person to find out what this meant was Mathilde Wesendonck. As early as January 1865 Cosima had already launched a plan of action designed to round up Wagner's stray manuscripts: many of the original drafts of his essays and compositions were now in the hands of friends and acquaintances, the composer having adopted an extremely liberal attitude to his autograph manuscripts in the past, giving them to contemporaries to whom he owed money or to whom he felt indebted in other ways. Cosima now demanded the return of these precious papers. Mathilde Wesendonck responded by writing to Wagner himself:

In a letter that I received from her today, Frau von Bülow has asked me for some of your literary manuscripts that are in my possession. I have gone through the portfolio, but it is impossible for me to send anything, unless it be your own personal wish. You will presumably barely remember which lost leaves, some of which are only very brief, have found their way into my hands, and so I am sending you a list of the entire contents of the portfolio and would ask you to let me know if and what I should send you.[31]

Mathilde Wesendonck's dig at 'Frau von Bülow' was clearly intentional, otherwise she would have replied to her in person, rather than appealing to Wagner, who clearly found Cosima's initiative embarrassing. He dismissed the whole thing as Ludwig's idea, but this was only a half-truth as the ruthlessly businesslike manner in which Cosima importuned Wagner's followers could hardly be in the king's best interests.

Carl Tausig and Peter Cornelius were among other friends of the composer who received such letters from his self-appointed secretary and who were invited to hand over an incomplete manuscript of *Tannhäuser* that Wagner had given them several years earlier. But it transpired that Tausig had passed on the score to Brahms, a man whom Wagner could never abide. Cosima refused to let go, but proceeded to bombard the hapless Brahms with urgent entreaties, which the latter studiously ignored. Instead, he told Cornelius that he had the 'disagreeable feeling that they merely want the manuscript out of my hands'. In Tausig's place, he went on, he would 'refuse to hand over' something that had been given to him in this way.[32] Brahms remained obdurate, and it was not until ten years later that Wagner saw his score again. For Tausig, however, this unfortunate episode was not yet over, for in the summer of 1865 Cosima also demanded the return of the original score of *Tristan und Isolde*, causing Tausig to complain with some warmth about the activities of the 'Delphic oracle', as he called her: 'Wagner recently had the extremely odd idea of getting the Delphic oracle to demand the return of the original score of *Tristan*, which she did in an extremely uncivil manner, claiming that she wants to give it to the only person who understands Wagner's music, the king, and that the latter will one day bequeath it to Germany.'[33] A brilliant pianist who had studied with Liszt, Tausig was understandably reluctant to have his own musicality compared with that of the dilettante king. As he angrily told Cornelius, he preferred not to reply 'to this unreasonable demand'.

It may have been in jest that Tausig compared Cosima to an oracle, but the future was to prove him right. Even during her time in Munich, she developed a psychological strategy that she was to refine in the coming decades and that involved invoking Wagner's ultimate authority. It was a strategy that was as simple as it was effective. In the final analysis, Tausig could not of course know if it was ultimately Wagner who wanted him to return the score as the ostensible request had been delivered by an 'oracle'. This lack of clarity was Cosima's greatest strength. Unlike Mathilde Wesendonck, Tausig shied away from contacting Wagner directly, a reluctance that is the best possible proof that Cosima's ability to present herself as Wagner's mouthpiece was functioning well-nigh perfectly. On Wagner's death, it was almost inevitable that she became the 'Meisterin', for the dead 'Meister' seemed to live on in her. Even then it remained unclear to what extent this or that remark or orally transmitted instruction really stemmed from Wagner. But no Wagnerian believer would have dared doubt the 'Master's words' as interpreted by his widow. Her late husband's authority had passed to her in its entirety.

In 1865, Cosima was twenty-seven. Her outward appearance, her charisma and, more generally, the whole aura surrounding her abetted this process of subversion. Eyewitnesses such as Rosalie Braun-Artaria praised her 'great art of holding an engrossing conversation. She was a highly attractive combination of grande dame and a personality entirely animated by artistic and literary interests.' She was not a beautiful woman, 'but her slim, elegant figure, with its characteristic facial features and abundance of blonde hair, created an emphatically attractive impression in spite of her rather large nose'.[34]

Although Cosima could draw others into her sway, she none the less radiated a certain coolness and distance. A pointed remark or imperious gesture could cause the temperature in a room to fall by several degrees, a situation that Cornelius witnessed for himself on more than one occasion. At the end of October 1865, for example, Heinrich Porges and his wife, Minna, held a flat-warming party at their new home in Munich. Bülow was away on tour, and so Wagner and Cosima were able to attend as a couple. Carrying on like minor royalty, the 'divine couple', as Cornelius contemptuously called them, began by keeping the company waiting for an hour. When they finally arrived, Wagner was wearing a morning suit, Cosima a 'grey silk dress with pink trimmings'. The evening then pursued its unedifying course. Wagner, Cornelius recalled, was 'caught in a kind of half-light between paterfamilias and local demigod'. After a few arguments over art and religion, Cosima wrested the conversation round to herself and proceeded to dismiss Carl Tausig with all the charm of an executioner, a dismissal apparently due to the fact that following the row over the score of *Tannhäuser*, he had fallen into disfavour with her. 'He has no touch,' Cosima opined. 'He can't be numbered among the great pianists, he is a caricature of Liszt, he has no individuality whatsoever.' According to Cornelius, 'these were the four main tenets in her papal bull

excommunicating Tausig. Now would have been a good moment for Wagner
to have refuted this nonsense and to have defended his friend, but instead he
chose to say nothing. Meanwhile, the lady of the house was serving various
delicacies, including Indian and Italian lettuce with capers, caviar and eggs
washed down by a late Burgundy. While the other guests tucked in, Wagner
and Cosima ate nothing but held their hands over their glasses and plates,
demonstratively insulting their hosts. 'When the demigods finally drove away
in their carriage,' reports Cornelius, 'poor Minna broke down in tears, and we
then held a long discussion about it all, a discussion both consoling and
enlightening.' The presence of the 'demigods' had turned the get-together into
a 'cold and blasé evening when one is glad when it is all over'.[35]

Cosima's behaviour was undoubtedly impolite, not to say shameless. But
the tale also throws significant light on her aims, for she was attempting to
drive a wedge between Wagner and his old friends while at the same time
seeking to deify her lover. As Cornelius was forced to concede, the plan
worked: 'I am suspicious enough to believe that in the deepest recesses of his
heart Wagner already regards Porges and his wife as a burden. Just like me.
Because he now sees everything through another's eyes.'[36] As Cornelius hints,
these were Cosima's eyes, their authoritarian and hierarchical way of seeing
things conditioned by the education that she had received. She claimed to
have the sole right to represent Wagner and as a result had to deny his past
and, with it, his old friends, while his political ambitions of the 1840s were
necessarily a closed book to her. She despised his revolutionary activities and
it is doubtful if she ever really understood them. In December 1865 she celebrated her twenty-eighth birthday, so that she was still a young woman at this
time, but, curiously, her social and political response to life was that of a
member of a bygone age, a representative of the *Ancien Régime*. For years she
had watched Carolyne von Sayn-Wittgenstein turning Liszt into the centre of
mythic cult, and although she had as a child suffered from this, she now
proved to be Carolyne's best pupil, organizing an elitist cult of Wagner's genius
that moved increasingly in the direction of wholesale deification on a truly
transcendental scale.

Wagner himself was no doubt aware of the fact that his friends were
drifting away from him, and it seems from all we know that for a time he
secretly tried to resist this move. It is hard to say why he ultimately allowed
himself to be elevated to the status of a demigod. Of course, he loved Cosima,
which on the most trivial level may go some way to explaining his complicity
in this development, while his vanity was undoubtedly flattered by the solemn

dignity and sublimity fostered by Cosima's cult of him. But the decisive factor should probably be sought elsewhere: Wagner needed Cosima. For him, as for many composers, writing music was a process verging on the intimate and could happen only in a 'pleasurable' atmosphere. Unlike Mahler, who shut himself away in austere log cabins in order to write his music and had no need of Alma, Wagner liked to talk about what he was working on and to sing aloud from his new scores. Cosima created this comfort zone by always being there for him, lightening the cares of everyday life, dealing with his hated correspondence and, to put it crudely, watching Wagner's back. In this way she succeeded in making herself indispensable both as a lover and as a manager. Even Pfistermeister and his officials accepted her as Wagner's proxy. Indeed, the servants of the state valued Frau von Bülow as a woman with whom they could do business in plain and simple terms. 'Your inspired, clear and calm mind', wrote Pfistermeister, 'is the best possible mirror in which to reflect Wagner's unquestionably brilliant views.'[37]

In August 1865 Cosima joined in Wagner's correspondence with King Ludwig, enmeshing her own life yet further with that of her lover. Wagner no doubt welcomed her intervention as he did not always have a sufficiently clear head to reply to Ludwig's letters with the appropriate degree of detail and hymnic fervour. There was an element of calculation, therefore, in his words when in a letter to the king he praised Cosima as a 'noble, profoundly sublime creature': 'If you wish to have accurate and detailed information about any aspect of me that you do not understand, you should address your enquiries to this rare creature, who will reflect everything back at you like the primeval wellspring of the Norns.'[38] But Ludwig was not allowed to know that Wagner and Cosima were lovers, and to that extent this three-way correspondence was mendacious on one decisive point.

When we examine the 127 letters and telegrams that Cosima addressed to Ludwig – for the most part between August 1865 and the beginning of 1869 – then Wagner's image of a wellspring with a reflective surface acquires a certain ambiguity. Many of these letters have no real substance apart from their Wagnerian basso continuo; they served as a forum for exchanging various ill-defined feelings rather than as an expression of concrete ideas. Cosima held up to her correspondent a mirror in which Ludwig could read whatever he wanted to read – not that this excluded confidences and a certain closeness and intimacy in the sentiments that were expressed. But Cosima also reflected the ideas which in Wagner's opinion the king was entitled to know and read about him. In this respect, too, Cosima was Wagner's mouthpiece or, rather, his echo. And just as any echo involves a change in the quality of the original sound, so Cosima occasionally modified Wagner's original, increasing or decreasing the volume, changing the pitch or altering the speed. In November 1867, when Ludwig was toying with the idea of engaging Paul Heyse as the artistic director of his theatre company, Wagner, who hated Heyse, stood aside and left Cosima to go on the offensive. In a letter that reads more like an official memorandum, she launched a savage attack on the writer, who in 1910 went on to win the Nobel Prize for literature:

> My objections to him are as follows: 1) his Jewish extraction – in this respect I beg our august and dear friend most humbly not to see a harsh prejudice but a profoundly well-justified fear of a race that has caused the Germans much harm; 2) his inexperience of conditions in the theatre; 3) his own productivity ...; 4) his inability and profound reluctance to share our friend's [Wagner's] views on art, since one naturally regards oneself as a completely different type of poet; and 5) the trouble that one would have (if the experiment were to turn out not to your satisfaction) in removing P. Heyse from his post. It would result in a regular scandal, the whole of the literary coterie, the newspapers, the whole of Israel, whether under cover or out in the open, would rise up as a man in his defence![39]

Above and beyond all her spiteful calumnies, Cosima was trying to say that there should be no other gods but Wagner. That was why Heyse's own creativity was a shortcoming and why she proposed as an alternative appointment the writer Hermann Schmidt, a 'simple director' and a 'subaltern', who had no ambitions of his own and who therefore posed no threat. It was a clever move as it touched on a sensitive spot with Ludwig. After all, she knew that he had no desire for a new scandal that was even remotely related to Wagner. If Heyse were not to be appointed, she implied, then Bavaria, too, would benefit, otherwise the city ran the risk of being plunged into an artistic civil war. Needless to say, it was from Wagner that Cosima had picked up her 'arguments' against Heyse. But she was able to express them more convincingly and more effectively than Wagner would have dared to do. The plan worked. 'What you say about P. Heyse,' Ludwig wrote back, 'I fully agree with, and I am more than willing to try Hermann Schmitt [sic], which I am confident will work out.'[40] The first round had gone to Cosima.

Intrigues in Munich

'I've not previously told you that Wagner is also in a political relationship with the king and has become a kind of Marquis of Posa,' Peter Cornelius informed his fiancée, Bertha Jung, in mid-November 1865. 'The king is said to have asked him for his opinion on matters relating to Germany, and Wagner has expounded his views in regular letters since then.' When Cornelius thought about it afterwards, he felt only a sense of horror: 'I saw the beginning of the end in this. For an artist to have a decisive influence on the life of the state is bound to end badly.'[41] Cornelius was to be proved right. But what lay behind his mysterious references? During the second half of September, Wagner prepared some notes on the essential quality of 'German-ness' for Ludwig's edification. Years later he expanded these notes and published them under the title 'What is German?' After arguing over the concepts of beauty and nobility in the German spirit, Wagner came to the point and demanded the foundation of a new political newspaper under the editorship of two of his friends, Heinrich Porges and Franz Grandauer. He also advocated building up a people's militia. When Ludwig passed these musings on to his ministers with instructions that they should 'execute the ideas set down therein', alarm bells started to ring in the corridors of power. This time Wagner had gone too far, it was claimed in the halls of the court secretariat, and the break with Pfistermeister now seemed to have become inevitable.

Wagner himself dated this decisive disagreement to 11 October 1865. And money was again the main issue. On the 16th Wagner wrote to Ludwig: 'Be generous with your princely largesse and leave it to my conscience, just as I shall one day return this princely trust!'[42] Behind this priceless expression lay some outrageously exorbitant demands. Wagner demanded 200,000 florins, some 1 million euros at today's prices. Of this, 40,000 were to be paid at once, the remainder invested at an annual interest of 5 per cent for the rest of Wagner's life. Instead, Wagner received 40,000 florins in cash and an annual stipend of 8,000 florins that could be terminated at any time and that amounted to more or less the same as interest at 5 per cent. When Cosima went to collect the money on 20 October, the treasury officials decided to play a trick on her and claimed to have no banknotes in stock, with the result that they gave her 40,000 florins in coins. Cosima pretended not to notice and ordered two cabs, with which she returned to Wagner's house in the Brienner Straße, taking with her the innumerable bags of money. This incident may have been trivial, but it shows how charged the atmosphere in Munich was at this time. An explosion could occur at any given moment.

It is doubtful if Wagner even noticed what was brewing. Instead of attempting to calm the situation and place a certain distance between himself and the king, he did the exact opposite and in mid-November went to see Ludwig at Hohenschwangau. The seven days that the two men spent together were the high point of the Munich period but at the same time they proved to be its swansong. While in Hohenschwangau, Wagner organized concerts every morning and read to Ludwig from his memoirs, after which king and composer would ride off into the surrounding countryside in a coach and four. Their activities did not pass unnoticed. His mind clouded by his feelings of euphoria, Wagner committed the error of demanding a change of personnel at the very top of the political hierarchy. 'Pfi' and 'Pfo', as he called Franz Seraph von Pfistermeister and Ludwig von der Pfordten in an extraordinary show of frivolity, had become intolerable in his eyes, and so he demanded the dismissal of both the king's cabinet secretary and the prime minister of the state of Bavaria. No good could come of this, and on his return to Munich, Wagner found himself staring into the abyss. A newspaper article appeared, describing Wagner as a parasite and likening him to one of the plagues of Egypt, while in another, evidently backed by 'Pfi' and 'Pfo', it was said that the demand for Pfistermeister's removal from office was prompted by a wish 'more easily to satisfy certain lustful desires to exploit the king's exchequer'.[43]

Wagner walked straight into the trap when he dashed off a note to the king:

> Your secretary feels that he is more powerful than you are: he orders the far-flung host of the favourites in his pay to denigrate his supreme master – and this is precisely what happens. The most worrying rumours fill the city: that you are neglecting the business of running the country and merely pursuing your idle fantasies, from which I myself am said in turn to derive the food for shameless demands – this is the one aspect under which people deign to view Our Relationship.

Wagner demanded 'Pfistermeister's immediate dismissal . . . But, my King, be quick and resolute!'[44] But Ludwig had now had enough and refused to listen. In a final desperate act, Cosima fired off an open letter to one of the local newspapers, the *Neueste Nachrichten*. Although published anonymously, it had in fact been written by Wagner. 'I venture to assure you,' the article concluded, 'that with the removal of two or three persons who do not enjoy the least respect among the Bavarian people, both the king and the Bavarian people will once and for all be rid of these annoyances.'[45] But it was all to no avail. On 1 December von der Pfordten issued an ultimatum to the king: 'Your Majesty stands at a fateful parting of the ways – you have to choose between the love and respect of your loyal people and the "friendship" of Richard Wagner.'[46] As if the pressure were not already enough, the masses too were now mobilized: a committee collected nearly 4,000 signatures among the citizens of Munich, demanding Wagner's removal. Ludwig had to decide – and he did so in favour of his people. On 6 December, he sent his cabinet secretary to the Brienner Straße to instruct Wagner to leave Bavaria. Four days later, at daybreak, Wagner set off for Switzerland in the company of his servant, Franz, and his dog, Pohl.

At the station to wave Wagner off were Cornelius, Porges and Cosima. (Bülow himself was again away on tour.) Wagner looked unwell, and the mood was understandably muted in the extreme. When the train left, taking Wagner into a life of exile that would be lavishly paid for by Ludwig, Cornelius seemed to 'see a vision fade away'.[47] As for Cosima, she wrote to Malvina Schnorr: 'How can I describe my final days with Richard and my parting from him? That one can survive such emotions – is it a sign of strength or of weakness?'[48] Whatever the answer, Cosima herself was completely broken and close to tears. As Cornelius observed, 'there is a real relationship between Wagner and Cosima. It may even be supposed that she will follow him with the children. Once we had taken our leave of him, she returned not to her own house but to Wagner's. . . . But how will this affect Bülow?' he wondered. 'Has he abandoned his wife entirely to Wagner as part of some ultra-romantic deal?'[49]

Involuntary Exile

Following his expulsion from Bavaria, Wagner resumed his life of aimless wandering, calling for longer or shorter periods in Berne, Vevey, Lyons, Toulon, Hyères, Marseilles and Geneva. Meanwhile, one annoyance followed another with remorseless implacability. In early January a newspaper reported that he was allowing his wife Minna to vegetate in utter poverty in Dresden. When Cosima heard about these reproaches, she seized the initiative and asked her Dresden friend Malvina Schnorr for help:

Try to persuade the woman to sign the following declaration: 'I have just learnt of the calumny directed against me and my husband in a Munich newspaper and I consider it my most sacred duty to declare that in good times as in bad my husband has always looked after me adequately. I am pleased that through this declaration of mine I may at least silence one of the shameless calumnies that has been directed at my husband.' I beg you, my dear, to persuade the woman to do this (only don't mention my name); tell her that it would be magnanimous of her to speak the truth in this way, that in doing so she would move her husband to a quite incredible extent, that it will render her immortal, that it would be a truly beautiful, nay sublime thing to do as she is now so embittered with regard to her husband. And do this soon, my dearest, so that I can publish it in the local papers.

Cosima knew that Wagner's enemies were rubbing their hands with glee at calumnies which, for all that they were thoroughly baseless, were calculated to deal him yet another blow. And so Cosima begged her correspondent to 'go to the wretched woman'. 'My version of the text', she concluded, 'seems to me to be the right one, it has to be very clear, very absolute.'[50]

Cosima's crisis management worked, and three days later – 9 January 1866 – Minna signed a formal statement in defence of her husband couched in terms very similar to those just outlined. It was to be her last token of her love for Wagner for she died in Dresden on 25 January 1866. Wagner was then on the Côte d'Azur and did not attend the funeral. Wicked tongues claimed that on the day of the funeral Cosima deliberately turned up at the theatre in Munich wearing a white dress, but this is almost certainly untrue. At all events, Bülow leapt to his wife's defence.

Meanwhile, Cosima was doing everything in her power to engineer Wagner's return to Munich and by 5 March she had even managed to arrange an audience with Ludwig von der Pfordten. It was a step that required a good deal of courage as Bavaria's prime minister was widely regarded as Wagner's most powerful adversary. His manner was cool and formal, and when Cosima bravely took him to task, he went on the offensive and, as he later recalled in his memoirs, lost his composure in the face of a woman: ' "And so you're now his [Wagner's] guardian angel?" I retorted. She blushed and left.'[51] However much Cosima may have longed for her lover's return, the road back to Munich was blocked, and so Wagner remained in exile, while the Bülows maintained their sham marriage. When Cosima and her elder daughter travelled to Geneva to see Wagner in early March, Bülow explained away the visit as a courtesy call 'in order to provide a little company for the poor great solitary man'.[52] It was now a question of finding a comfortable place for Wagner to settle in his involuntary exile. In their search for such a home, Cosima, Daniela and Wagner arrived in

Lucerne on 30 March, and it was during a boat trip on Lake Lucerne that they suddenly caught sight of their dream home, the whitewashed Villa Tribschen on a spit of land jutting right out into the lake and facing the 7,000-foot Pilatus. It was a breathtaking sight. The following day Cosima and Daniela returned to Munich, while Wagner leased the whole house and surrounding estate for 5,000 francs a year, a rent that was paid for by the king. The composer moved into his new home in the middle of April 1866.

The Bülows had in the meantime left for Amsterdam, where they met Liszt. 'Cosima is making the trip in order to be reconciled with her father,' Cornelius reported, adding that Liszt had taken it amiss 'that she had gone to see Wagner in Geneva'.[53] Liszt's attempts to mediate were evidently unsuccessful, because on 11 May, nine days after her return to Munich, Cosima again set off for Lucerne, taking her daughters with her. 'I feel almost as if I shall never see them again,' Cornelius wrote to his fiancée; 'that would suit me down to the ground! I no longer have any contact with her, my whole nature is completely alien to her.' Bülow, too, breathed a sigh of relief when his wife left, for, as Cornelius astutely observed: 'He's so agreeable when she's not there, he's then a completely different person.'[54]

If Wagner had expected to find some peace and quiet in Switzerland after the turbulent months in Munich, he was to be bitterly disappointed. The first of a whole series of novel forms of annoyance came on 22 May, when Ludwig II travelled in secret to Tribschen in order to help Wagner celebrate his fifty-third birthday. What had been intended as a friendly surprise ended as a diplomatic disaster, for Ludwig's romantic outing took place only weeks before the outbreak of the Austro-Prussian War, prompting tremendous outrage among the Bavarian population, many of whom thought that their ruler had run off and left them in the lurch. They vented their collective frustration on Hans and Cosima von Bülow. On 29 May a sharply worded attack on Wagner's 'accomplices' appeared in the *Neuer Bayerischer Kurier*. In particular, the anonymous writer complained about the 'wretched role' played in the affair by 'Herr and Madame Dr Hanns [*sic*] de Bülow: how cunning is the assault that has been mounted on the king's privy purse, how sophisticated the attempts by this fine company to keep the king sweet by all manner of deceptions and lies and to isolate him from the people appropriate to his position'.[55] To make matters worse, the relationship between Wagner and Cosima now came into the journalist's line of fire, 'Madame Dr Hanns de Bülow' being mocked as Wagner's 'carrier pigeon', an allusion that the readers of the *Neuer Bayerischer Kurier* did not need to have spelt out for them. Two days later, the

Volksbote added more fuel to the fire: 'It is not even a year since the well-known "Madame Hans de Bülow" collected 40,000 florins from the royal exchequer in the famous two cabs for her "friend" (or whatever), but what are 40,000 florins?' As if that were not bad enough, the writer went on, 'the self-same "Madame Hans", whom the general public has known by the eloquent name of "Carrier Pigeon" since last December, is currently in Lucerne with her "friend" (or whatever) and was also there at the time of the visit by a certain exalted person.'[56]

The whole of Munich knew how much money Wagner was receiving from the king's private coffers, and so from that point of view the article contained nothing that was new – apart, that is, from the parenthetical references to Frau von Bülow's 'friend'. Behind the laconic remark 'or whatever' lay the shocking truth, a point understood by Bavaria's burghers and farmers. The nerve ends in the Bülow household were now fully exposed, and it was in some desperation that Cosima wrote to Malvina Schnorr from Tribschen: 'Hans forbids me to come to Munich, and Richard, striking a note of mystery, says that he's right.'[57] But Bülow now committed the error of publishing a clumsy rebuttal that merely made the situation worse. And, as if enough damage had not already been done, he even challenged the editor of the *Volksbote* to a duel, a challenge that the editor fortunately declined. In a final attempt to extricate himself from the situation, Bülow asked the king to relieve him of his post, and this he was duly granted. With that, he set off for Zurich. Cosima, meanwhile, had returned to Munich and now went on the offensive, penning a letter to Ludwig in which she invited the king to attest to her marital fidelity. In terms of its sheer hypocrisy and mendacity, this letter takes some beating. The full extent of her deception becomes painfully clear when we recall that Cosima was already carrying Wagner's second child, Eva:

> How could my husband work in a city in which the honour of his wife has been impugned? My royal liege, my friend, I have three children to whom it is my duty to transmit their father's honourable name unsullied. For the sake of these children, that they may not some day revile my love for our Friend [Wagner], I beg you, my most exalted friend, to write this letter.[58]

Cosima met Bülow in Zurich, and the couple then continued their journey to Tribschen. 'No one must know that we're going to Lucerne,' she impressed on Malvina Schnorr. 'If you see Frau Kaulbach, give her my best wishes and tell everyone that we were in Zurich and are in good spirits and that we'll remain in Munich even if Hans is dismissed (so that they don't think we're leaving).'[59] The Bülows arrived at Tribschen on 10 June. 'Today is the anxiously awaited day of decision in Lucerne,' Cornelius informed his fiancée. Was Bülow planning to call his wife and his rival to account? 'I know what will happen. Cosima will remain with Wagner, for this must happen if Cosima's destiny is to be fulfilled. And Wagner's.'[60]

We shall probably never be able to say for certain exactly what Bülow knew by this stage and what he merely suspected. It is equally unsure what the three of them ultimately discussed at Tribschen. Some time later Bülow wrote to one of his friends: 'Since February 1865 I was in absolutely no doubt about the extremely peculiar nature of the situation. But never in my wildest dreams did I imagine that the situation would become public, still less did I have nightmares about it.'[61] If we take this at face value, we shall be forced to conclude that Bülow knew about his wife's affair with Wagner. But perhaps the fact that Isolde was Wagner's daughter was something he would never have dared imagine even in his wildest dreams. Or was this merely a lie designed to cover himself? We simply do not know. Bülow was a very proud person, and his honour was a matter of the gravest concern to him, and so he let Wagner and his wife pull the wool over Ludwig's eyes. Once Wagner, too, had asked the king to declare the Bülows' honour inviolate, Ludwig duly signed a press release drafted by Wagner and dated 11 June:

> Since, moreover, I have been able to form the most accurate impression of the noble and high-minded character of your honoured wife, who has stood by the side of him who is her father's friend and her husband's exemplar, offering him her comfort through her most sympathetic concern, it remains only for me to investigate the inexplicable nature of those criminal public calumnies in order that, having obtained the clearest insight into these shameful goings-on, I may ensure that the evildoers receive their just deserts according to the full rigours of the law at its most implacable.[62]

It cannot be stressed too much that Cosima and Wagner browbeat the king into committing an act of perjury, and revenge was not slow in coming. Intimates such as Porges and Cornelius were in no doubt as to who was behind these machinations. The good people of Munich likewise appeared reluctant to believe their king's asseveration that Cosima's reputation was spotless, but at least the press exercised self-restraint: after all, no one contradicted His Majesty and went unpunished.

The Bülows remained at Tribschen until early September 1866, even if it is difficult to imagine how this remarkable ménage à trois actually functioned. Although violent arguments between Wagner and Bülow often bubbled to the surface, Bülow lacked the strength to draw a line under the affair. Time and time again a decision was deferred *sine die*. Instead, Cosima went on long walks or took boat rides on the lake in the company of her husband and lover, a modus vivendi that the other members of Bülow's family found altogether incomprehensible. And so we find Carolyne von Sayn-Wittgenstein writing to one of Liszt's cousins: 'Between the two of us, I have to say that I am afraid Cosima has lost her reason. A great misfortune for a woman! They could have retained their place in Munich . . . if Wagner, who summoned them there, had disassociated himself from them quietly, without giving way.' And she went on:

> The Bülows, who place themselves on a par with Wagner, have behaved better following his departure than this patron of theirs deserves. And I am convinced that in doing so they have contributed to the fact that it is now impossible for them to remain in Munich any longer. I am deeply saddened by this. It is very painful for me to have to stand by and watch Liszt's own children abandoning all that they could have been both for him and for the world of art for the sake of a scoundrel of a genius like Wagner.[63]

It was at this point – at the height of an already turbulent period – that the Austro-Prussian War broke out on 14 June. Even during the 1850s Prussia's dashing prime minister, Otto von Bismarck, had already come to the conclusion that there would be a battle for supremacy between Germany's two leading powers, Prussia and Austria. Central to the current tensions were their differing views on the Schleswig-Holstein Question, differences that the previous year's Gastein Convention had only temporarily resolved. When Prussia proceeded to occupy Holstein, Austria demanded that the federal army be mobilized, prompting Prussia to announce that the federal treaty had been broken and to declare war on Austria. The German states then aligned themselves with one or other of the major powers in what was effectively a civil war. Among the twelve German states that sided with Austria was the kingdom of Bavaria, while Prussia's allies essentially included the smaller and medium-sized north German states and Italy. The Prussian armies won a decisive victory at Königgrätz on 3 July 1866, a victory due above all to the use of modern military technology: the percussion-needle rifle allowed five shots a minute to be fired, while rapid large-scale troop movements were now possible thanks to the use of the telegraph and railways. Austria could simply not compete. The Treaty of Prague brought Bismarck one step closer to his goal: the formation of a German national state excluding Austria and dominated by Prussia. But he knew that France would not stand idly by while north and south Germany were united under Prussian hegemony, and so the North German Union was initially limited to the German states that were north of the Main. In his regard Bismarck moved with considerable astuteness, ensuring that the North German League's constitution of 17 April 1867 incorporated rules that might later make it possible for the originally independent southern German states to enter the League under German federal law.

Bavaria's defeat plunged Ludwig into a state of deep depression. He was politically out of his depth and wanted nothing so much as to abdicate, even going so far as to ask Cosima for her permission to do so: 'I feel the urge to tell you that it has become completely impossible for me to live any longer apart from Him who is my All. I cannot bear it.'[64] His declaration of love was directed, of course, at Wagner, who, needless to add, had no desire at all for a privatized monarch. Ludwig was of interest and importance to him only as a ruler. Both Cosima and Wagner urged the king to stay calm, while Wagner used the opportunity to inveigh against his old enemies, this time successfully. Pfistermeister resigned in October and Ludwig von der Pfordten was dismissed at the end of December.

The Bülows returned to Munich from Tribschen on 1 September in order to sort out their affairs in the city. Two weeks later Bülow travelled to Basel, where for a time he lived on his own, while Cosima and the children returned to Switzerland in late September. Bülow accepted all this with a typical dash of cynicism, writing to tell a friend that he was fortunate 'to own a wife who has not only the keenest understanding but also the right emotional instinct. Unfortunately I've nowhere to live, and so I have to get by without my wife and children. The former is coming for a week-long visit to my bachelor's apartment, which is charming, if small, in order to attend the more interesting of my concerts. My pen is slipping from my fingers – almost.'[65]

The time for the couple's definitive separation seemed to be at hand, only for a new source of annoyance to arise in the middle of November, when Wagner's first Isolde, the now distinctly cranky Malvina Schnorr von Carolsfeld, suddenly turned up at Tribschen with her pupil, Isidore von Reutter, and launched into a series of absurd prophecies, claiming that her late husband had assured her that she was now destined to marry Wagner, while Isidore von Reutter – also active on the side as a clairvoyant – was Ludwig's promised bride. His two strange visitors increasingly tried Wagner's patience, and when Malvina made the mistake of threatening to expose Cosima and Wagner, he threw her out of the house. Swearing that she would be avenged, Malvina went straight to the king and told him what she had seen in Tribschen: a woman in an advanced state of pregnancy, playing the housewife, and no doubt much else besides. This embarrassing affair dragged on for almost two years. Initially the king seemed not to believe the gossip, but this all changed at the end of 1867, when he wrote to his new court secretary, Lorenz von Düfflipp: 'I have grown completely and utterly tired of the constant arguments and complaints on the part of Wagner, Bülow, Porges, Froebel and their hangers-on. I have shown so much consideration and patience to these people and granted them so many favours that they have every reason to be satisfied and grateful; but my patience is now starting to wear thin.'[66] When Düfflipp drew the king's attention to the fact that there was something not quite right about the whole business, Ludwig finally began to have doubts about Wagner's and Cosima's honesty: 'Might there be some truth to the sad rumour, a rumour I could never entirely bring myself to believe? Might adultery really be involved here? Woe betide them if it is!'[67]

The lovers' adultery – to pick up Ludwig's expression – entered a new phase when Cosima was delivered of Wagner's second daughter, Eva Maria, at Tribschen on Sunday 17 February 1867. Bülow arrived at Tribschen from Basel that same afternoon. It had been a relatively easy birth, and Cosima was already holding the child in her arms. Bülow sat down beside his wife's bed and said 'Je pardonne', to which Cosima apparently replied: 'Il ne faut pas pardonner, il faut comprendre' (It's not a question of forgiving, but of understanding). As if the situation were not already difficult enough, Wagner travelled to Munich in early March 1867 in order to discuss Bülow's reappointment in the city with the king. Wagner remained true to himself, acting not out of sincere friendship, a guilty conscience or even compassion but for reasons of self-interest and tactical advantage. He was hoping to complete *Die Meistersinger von Nürnberg* in the not too distant future and wanted the first performance to be conducted by Bülow. His negotiations were crowned with success, and after a certain hesitation Bülow was appointed court kapellmeister, an appointment he regarded as his rehabilitation. He moved back to Munich in the middle of April 1867.

But Wagner had to pay a high price for this coup as Cosima, for better or worse, was obliged to return to her husband. Bülow now held a prominent position at court, and this, together with the king's declaration that Cosima's honour was inviolate, meant that the latter could no longer remain at Tribschen, otherwise the gossip and suspicions would start up all over again. And so the parties put on a show and during the coming months pretended that the Bülows' marriage was still intact. 'My wife is extremely well, thank God,' Bülow wrote to Joachim Raff at the beginning of May, 'and has spent the last twelve days furnishing our home here, a task that is now complete.' Wagner seems to have found it impossible to be separated from Cosima – after all, they had long been a couple – and so he travelled to Munich on 21 May. As Bülow explained in his letter to Raff: 'To this end we have taken a larger apartment in which two self-contained rooms are permanently at his disposal.'[68] But Wagner remained for only a few days with the Bülows in the Arcostraße, then moved to a villa near Starnberg that Ludwig had leased in his name. Here he worked on *Die Meistersinger*, then returned to Lucerne in mid-June.

Meanwhile, Bülow and his wife continued to lead separate lives. While he underwent an unsuccessful course of treatment in Sankt Moritz, Cosima headed back to Tribschen to discuss the hopelessly intractable situation with her lover. Presumably she was thinking of a separation, but it was unclear how this could be effected. When she and her daughters returned to Munich in mid-September, she was at an even greater loss than ever. Her life resumed its former course, and if she was unable to see Wagner, at least she could make do with performances of his works. Every so often Bülow would put a spoke in her wheel as if seeking to be avenged on his faithless wife in an exquisitely subtle way. On 22 September 1867, for example, a performance of *Tannhäuser* had been announced under Bülow's direction, but the all-powerful court kapellmeister declined to admit Cosima to the rehearsals, claiming that some administrative regulation or other prevented her from attending. But Cosima was a cunning adversary capable of giving like for like, and so she wrote to Düfflipp, the court secretary responsible for such regulations: 'My husband is such a stickler for the rules that he refuses to admit me to today's rehearsal because no special permission has been granted him. Perhaps you would be good enough to let me know that I may indeed attend.'[69] Permission was duly given.

Decisions

The first half of 1868 was entirely dominated by preparations for the world premiere of Wagner's new opera, *Die Meistersinger von Nürnberg*. The composer himself travelled to Munich in May to superintend the final rehearsals and naturally stayed with the Bülows in the Arcostraße. Once again, husband, adulteress and lover lived under the same roof with their four children, two of whom had been fathered by the husband, two by his rival. As if their domestic arrangements were not already sufficiently fraught, Bülow and Wagner also had to work together as artists. On this occasion, however, the rivals were no longer able to keep control of their feelings, and the tensions between them frequently threatened to disrupt the rehearsals: 'Heavy, dull sense of Hans's profound hostility & alienation,' Wagner noted in his Annals at this time.[70] In spite of this, the first performance of *Die Meistersinger von Nürnberg* took place under Bülow's direction on 21 June 1868 and proved a sensational success. The audience cheered the performers to the rafters and gave Wagner a standing ovation. Three days later he left Munich for Lucerne, alone.

On his arrival in Tribschen, Wagner fell ill, although it needed no doctor to diagnose his illness as psychosomatic. 'Increasing clarity at my condition & at the state of things,' he complained. 'The most profound lack of courage and inability to act: realized that the reason for my complete incapacity of will lies in the fate of my relations with Cos. & Hans. It is all futile: the Munich experiments have been a total failure. Now regard it as indispensable that I never return there.' On 22 July Cosima arrived in Switzerland and the two of them evidently decided to grasp the nettle: 'Difficult communications over decision: Plutonian & Neptunian solutions! – Agreed on the main point!'[71]

For Wagner, the 'main point' was the realization that things could not go on as they were and that the Bülows would have to separate. This realization developed a momentum of its own when on 14 September Wagner and his mistress set off for a two-week tour of Italy that took them over the Sankt Gotthard Pass and Stresa to the Borromean Islands in Lake Maggiore and finally to Genoa and Milan. On 28 September, two days after Cosima's name-day, they visited her birthplace at Como and the following day returned to Switzerland. In Ticino they were overwhelmed by a terrible storm: torrential rain buried whole communities under mudslides, bridges were washed away and streams were transformed into raging torrents. Wagner and Cosima were reduced to covering long stretches of their journey on foot amidst all manner of filth and debris. At Faido they found a simple room at the Hôtel de Poste and spent 'three evil but profound days' in the course of which their third child, Siegfried, was conceived. It was this overwhelming mixture of a mood bordering on the apocalyptic and the intimacy of her relationship with Wagner that persuaded Cosima to clear the air and abandon her double life.

On 3 October 1868 she wrote to her husband from Faido, a decisive letter in which she presumably – the letter has not survived – declared her intention of leaving Bülow and of moving in with Wagner. When the lovers arrived back in Tribschen on 6 October after further rigours en route, Wagner wondered in his diary: 'What did fate want?'[72]

We cannot be certain how Bülow reacted to the letter from Faido, but he is said to have been beside himself with anger: Cosima's first biographer, Richard Du Moulin Eckart, even claims that he practised using a pistol in order to challenge Wagner to a duel, although no evidence has ever been found to authenticate this assertion. On 14 October Cosima travelled to Munich with her four daughters and asked her husband for a divorce. Bülow prevaricated, giving the children's well-being as his reason. The confusion on all sides was understandably great, and so desperate was Cosima that she even had the idea of converting to Protestantism in the hope of facilitating a divorce. When she told her lover of her resolve to go to Rome, presumably to confer with her father, Wagner lost his nerve. He knew that Liszt was on Bülow's side and was afraid – for good reason – that the Abbé would try to talk his daughter out of a divorce. At the eleventh hour, therefore, Wagner asked Claire de Charnacé to go to Munich to persuade her half-sister to abandon her resolve. Claire came – and Cosima was furious. 'Wilful meddling makes existence unbearable,' she cabled Wagner. 'Most anguished bitterness at this game with the weary woman's peace of mind.'[73] Cosima was so angry that within the hour she had fired off a further telegram to Tribschen: 'Claire's arrival has had the most repugnant outcome for me, your refusal to let me go to Rome is the saddest thing that could ever have happened.'[74]

Only now did Wagner realize what he had done and that he could not treat Cosima in this way. His guilty conscience evidently plagued him sufficiently to draw him to Munich on 1 November, but his visit was ill-timed for the Bülows' eleven-year marriage was currently receiving its last rites, and so he left the very next day for Leipzig, where he stayed with his sister Ottilie Brockhaus and her family. Back in Tribschen, he received a telegram from Cosima on the fifteenth: 'Am not writing as a precaution. Leaving tomorrow. Will cable again. In good health, calm.'[75] It was the calm before the storm, for on the afternoon of the sixteenth she 'said farewell to Hans for ever'. Out of respect for his feelings, she left Daniela and Blandine in Munich, at least for the present. The year 1868 went down in the Wagnerian annals not just as the year of *Die Meistersinger* but also as a year of decision: 'R. says my religion dates from this Hegira, I pray with all my heart.'[76] Once again Wagner proved to be a keen-eyed observer. Just as the Hegira – Muhammad's departure from Mecca to Medina in AD 622 – marked the start of the Islamic calendar, so Cosima's decision of November 1868 marked the creation of her own religion, a religion that henceforth bore the name of Richard Wagner. 'My single prayer: one day to die with Richard in the selfsame hour. My greatest pride: to have rejected everything in order to live with him. My supreme happiness: his joy.'[77] If Madame Patersi's teachings had already fuelled her love of bombastic, theatrical emotion, she now raised her separation from her husband to positively pseudo-religious heights: 'That I had to leave Hans appears cruel to me, but then I have to ask myself on whose account this cruelty arose. Also I feel plainly how within me some divinity rules, which determined my course – *I did not wish or choose*.'[78]

As for Bülow, he felt his male pride had been wounded, and the failure of his marriage was obviously a matter of such deep embarrassment to him that he was reduced to lying, and he tried to convince even close friends that Cosima was not with Wagner: 'She is hiding away with her sister, Countess Charnacé, in Versailles and writes occasionally, but only to the children.'[79]

Guilt and Atonement

You shall know every hour of my life, so that one day you will come to see me as I am; for, if I die young, others will be able to tell you very little about me, and if I live long, I shall probably only wish to remain silent. In this way you will help me do my duty – yes, children, my duty. What I mean by that you will find out later. Your mother intends to tell you everything about her present life, and she believes she can do so.[80]

With these words Cosima von Bülow began her diary on New Year's Day 1869. The final entry in her *journal intime* is dated 12 February 1883, the eve of Wagner's death. The fourteen years between these two dates are described in intricate detail, the record of her daily life running to twenty-one note-books and more than 5,000 pages. Normally a diarist commits to paper things that he or she would otherwise be unable or unwilling to discuss with others. Some chroniclers commune with themselves in secret, while others write private or confidential letters to themselves. But this was not the case with Cosima. From the outset her diary was intended to be read by her children, foremost among them being Siegfried, who was born in 1869. She wanted to account for herself in their eyes. In the event, her only son never saw these diary entries for himself, an omission for which he had to thank his sister Eva but which was never his mother's intention. When the diaries finally appeared in print in two volumes in 1976 and 1977, they ran to 2,500 printed pages and were hailed as an editorial feat and a milestone in Wagnerian biography. (Geoffrey Skelton's English translation appeared in 1978 and 1980.)

In fact, Cosima's memoirs are a unique record of the bond between her and Wagner. Once readers have become used to the sometimes old-fashioned and laboured style, they will discover an infinite number of details about life at the side of a genius, Cosima offering a meticulous account of Wagner's daily routine, his moods and whims, his views and his work, his many minor and major illnesses and, more generally, the age in which he lived. Cosima kept an assiduous note of all that her husband said, thereby documenting the development of his religious, political and philosophical thinking. In quoting the Master literally, she was at pains to be as accurate as possible, giving her style a certain lofty solemnity.

But Cosima's diaries also attest to her tremendous sense of guilt towards her first husband. Time and again she refers to her 'guilt' and 'failure' and even dreamt about him. Countless pages are filled with comments that are positively masochistic in tone: 'How constantly I suffer about Hans! I should like to die before him, so that he might realize how every hour I suffered with him, through all happiness and all blessings.'[81] Cosima dealt with these emotional conflicts by deifying her new lover. Whenever Wagner spoke to her, it was 'always divine, unique'.[82] She worshipped him to the point of idolatry, and more than once we find her writing that 'every utterance from him is doctrine to me'.[83] The more she revered Wagner and the more godlike he appeared to her, the sooner she could come to terms with her 'guilt'. She compensated for her complexes with regard to her first husband by suggesting that she had abandoned him for a demigod and, indeed, that she had had no choice in the matter. She was determined to serve this divine being at all costs and in that way to atone for the failure of her marriage to Bülow.

Cosima's self-reproaches were fuelled by a powerful sense of inferiority. 'My feelings of unworthiness mount daily,' runs a diary entry in late November 1877.[84] Elsewhere she complains about an 'ever-deeper recognition of my own unworthiness' and observes an 'ever more cheerful and voluntary atonement for this unworthiness, a more radical negation of self-will, repudiation of all life's vanities, concentration on the one single aim'.[85] The reasons for this aspect of Cosima's character lie in a crisis of self-esteem and disturbed identity.

Madame Patersi's reign of mental terror had produced in her a complex of suffering that found expression in feelings of inferiority. Her loveless childhood, her unhappy marriage with Hans von Bülow, the failure of that relationship and even the fact that her husband beat her – she made no attempt to rebel against all this but bore it in silent suffering in the spirit of *De Imitatione Christi*. Her diary contains countless entries that seem profoundly disconcerting: 'The more deeply I suffer,' we read in February 1876, for example, 'the stronger grows this strange ecstasy of suffering within me.'[86]

For Cosima, this 'ecstasy of suffering' was no doubt a kind of moral masochism. The term 'masochism' was not in fact coined until 1886, when it was used by the German neurologist and forensic psychiatrist Richard von Krafft-Ebing with reference to the writer Leopold von Sacher-Masoch, whose short stories repeatedly discuss the desire for pain and submission. Modern psychologists would prefer to refer to a 'self-harming personality disorder'. People who harm themselves are unable to come to terms with their own lives but see themselves in a disproportionately critical and negative light, writing off those lives and constantly blaming themselves. The last thing I want to do is to criticize Cosima or turn her into a psychotic study. She was not sick, and the passage of time makes it impossible to treat her life as a case history. But if we take the theory of self-harm as our starting point, then Cosima certainly showed fundamental features of this personality disorder by reacting to positive experiences with tormenting self-reproaches and feelings of guilt. If ever something gave her pleasure, she was unable to acknowledge this and enjoy it, but preferred to avoid opportunities for activities that might afford her any enjoyment. A further sign of this predisposition was her immoderate desire to sacrifice herself to Wagner, an attitude that found expression in theatrical, emotional and self-destructive posturing.

In common parlance, masochism and its counterpart, sadism, are generally seen as sexual practices. But Cosima's masochism was not sexually motivated. Indeed, one has the impression that she found active sexuality distinctly unappealing, noting on one occasion that 'the one single difference between R. and myself is that he takes pleasure in comfort and in pretty things, while I tend almost to prefer abstinence to enjoyment'.[87] 'Abstinence' was emphatically not for Wagner, and so we find Cosima complaining a few months later: 'In the afternoon some concern that R. cannot be persuaded to curb his inclinations.'[88] For Cosima, prudishness seems to have been something of a moveable feast: 'If only we could curb passion – if only it could be banished from our lives!'[89] And six months later she notes tersely: 'I think I am ripe for a convent.'[90] By the date in question – the middle of November 1870 – Wagner and Cosima had been married for barely three months. There was probably no question in their marital relations of smouldering eroticism or sexual fulfilment. Cosima felt no need for a physical relationship, while Wagner looked elsewhere. When she launched into yet another lecture on the virtues of chastity, he told her bluntly: ' "Yes, yes, I know, you would dearly like to introduce some of that renunciation stuff here, but –" He broke off his banter. My main aim is certainly to dispel all passionate feelings and in this way to atone until I can make things good again.'[91] Wagner was an astute observer and clearly saw through his wife's compulsions: 'Your feminine dignity was offended,' he told her in September 1871, 'and so you took refuge in religion!'[92]

Cosima's masochistic personality disorder was a complementary phenomenon that helped her to compensate for her deficient sense of self-worth as a woman. Anyone reading her diaries is bound to gain the impression that she literally longed to be humiliated and to lead a life of submissive subservience. When Wagner completed the *Ring* on 21 November 1874, she wallowed in exquisite anguish: 'How could I express my gratitude other than through the destruction of all urges toward personal existence? Greetings, eventful day, greetings, day of fulfilment! If a genius completes his flight at so lofty a level, what is left for a poor woman to do? To suffer in love and rapture.'[93] Occasionally she even longed for 'self-destruction': 'When R. complains of his upset stomach, I blame myself for having lost the moral courage I once possessed and not warning him off. "So," says R., "I have destroyed you utterly, moulded you utterly anew?" I: "I hope so." '[94] That Cosima's desire for self-harm extended to her offspring is bound to be disconcerting, but it is not in fact surprising. In December 1871, for example, we read: 'Spoke very seriously with the children, wept and prayed with them, brought them to the point of asking me for punishment.'[95] What is so alarming is not that she punished her children but that she worked on them in such a way that they literally begged to be punished. This incident throws a poor light on Cosima as a mother, so keen was she to burden those around her with the onerous task of making good the wrong that she herself had caused her former husband. As we shall see, her eldest daughter, Daniela, was to be reduced to despair at this and to develop a serious inferiority complex of her own.

Our scrutiny of Cosima's diaries would be incomplete without a closer investigation of her latent anti-Semitism, for the reader's pleasure invariably palls whenever she expatiates on 'Israel' – her term for all things Jewish. Her diaries reveal a primitive view of the world in which 'Israel' stands for all that is bad and 'Germany' for all that is good. If a play or opera failed to please her, then it was the Jewishness of the actors and singers that was to blame: 'The declamation absurd throughout,' she wrote, dismissing a performance of Weber's *Preciosa*, 'much Israel, and in consequence everything a masquerade.'[96] But if a Jewish artist turned in a decent performance, then in Cosima's opinion he was merely mimicking non-Jews. This, she argued, was true of the pianist Josef Rubinstein, 'who in the way of Jews has copied all sorts of things from my father, much to his own advantage.'[97] Not infrequently she pried into her contemporaries' racial backgrounds with positively sleuth-like zeal: 'Strauß probably an Israelite,' she wrote off the theologian David Friedrich Strauß.[98] And if she was able to convict an individual of being a part of 'Israel', she felt that there was nothing of which that person was not capable: 'It reminds me that Count Bismarck's assassin was a Jew.'[99] She seems to have believed every malicious rumour and anti-Jewish horror story that came her way: 'Bad rations are said to have made the soldiers ill,' she noted in May 1876; 'the suppliers are all Jews and they deliver bad bread, bad meat, etc.'[100] Cosima's hatred of the Jews was evidently not free from paranoia, her visions of horror even encroaching on her world of dreams: 'Thoughts of R.'s being murdered by a Berlin Jew.'[101]

Remarks such as these are bound to strike the modern reader as offensive in the extreme, but they also allow us to gain a clearer picture of the overheated anti-Semitic atmosphere in Wagner's immediate circle. One might, of course, conclude from this that Cosima was merely writing down and repeating the anti-Jewish comments that issued daily from Wagner's lips. But although her diaries document the shift in Wagner's anti-Semitism during the final years of his life, they are far from being a mere reflection of that development. According to the German writer Dieter David Scholz, 'the essential difference between Wagner's and Cosima's remarks is that Wagner was always capable of revising his views and adopting a sense of self-critical distance, even demonstrating a certain ability to learn from his own experiences. This ability was coupled with a political awareness and a clear talent for observing social changes, whereas Cosima's judgements were unchanging.'[102] This assessment certainly does not imply that Wagner's anti-Semitism was more sophisticated or more intelligent, still less that it was 'better' than Cosima's. Such attributions are in themselves absurd and would in any case be in the worst possible taste as Wagner was equally capable of vulgar and completely unforgivable remarks about Jews. But Scholz is right to argue that in terms of their narrow-mindedness, their simplicity and their credulity, Cosima's views were in a class apart from Wagner's.

As for the reasons for Cosima's hatred of Jews, it seems likely that she was first infected with the virus of anti-Semitism during her years as a young woman in the Paris of the 1850s and that she may have caught it from the rabidly Catholic Carolyne von Sayn-Wittgenstein or the no less fanatical Madame Patersi de Fossombroni. Liszt, too, was not entirely free from anti-Jewish sentiments, and her first husband, Hans von Bülow, can certainly be described as an anti-Semite of the first order. No doubt all these factors played a part in the development of Cosima's own anti-Semitism, but they still cannot provide a convincing explanation. If, however, we take as our starting point Cosima's low self-esteem and disturbed personality, we may find that we have a more complex and subtle measure of the situation, for with Cosima masochism and anti-Semitism were two sides of the same coin. She reviled the Jews and everything Jewish because she herself lacked the ability to see herself as a fully integrated person. She was never at peace with herself but felt weak and inferior and found in the Jews a group that in her own estimation was beneath even her. In spite of all her complexes, she could point the finger of blame at these people. In that way the fact that someone was Jewish gave her the chance to play the card of her own Aryan 'superiority'. That is why her anti-Semitism was so simplistic, so conceited and so intractable, because it did not depend on insights, findings and experiences of any kind but was an integral part of her masochistic personality.

All this means that she was necessarily opposed to the assimilation of the Jews and to their ever being granted equal rights. The process of Jewish eman-cipation did not really begin in Germany until after the revolutions of 1848 and made appreciable progress only during the 1860s. It was during this decade that laws were passed in Bavaria, Baden and Württemberg granting the Jews equal rights and making the Jewish religion merely one denomina-tion among others. For assimilated Jews this development often meant that they turned their backs on their old religious laws. This was not invariably a voluntary process, for non-Jews often demanded that Jews should be baptized if they were to be socially accepted. As Heine wryly noted, 'A certificate of baptism is the entrance ticket to European civilization.' To many Jews, baptism alone seemed to offer them the chance to prove themselves 'worthy' of eman-cipation and to underscore their membership of the host nation. It is striking that at the height of Jewish integration in Germany Wagner decided to repub-lish an older tirade against the Jews.

In order to understand this development, we need to cast our eyes back to 1850, when Wagner had a price on his head following his participation in the failed Dresden Uprising of May 1849 and was living in exile in Switzerland, out of the reach of the German police. Under the significant pseudonym of 'K. Freigedank' (Free-Thought) he published his notorious essay 'Jews in Music' in two instalments of the *Neue Zeitschrift für Musik* in September 1850. In under ten pages he argued that the Jews had never had any art of their own, and so Jewish musicians were condemned to a life of non-creativity and could merely reproduce and imitate what others had created. This claim was followed by a number of wayward criticisms, all of which boiled down to what was at best a half-baked ideology. When he declared the various causes of widespread anti-Jewish resentment to be the very essence of Jewishness, Wagner was guilty of 'projecting'. The original publication of the essay attracted little attention and evidently disappeared from sight soon afterwards, but by the time it was republished nineteen years later, this time under its author's real name, the world had changed: Wagner was now a famous European composer. Even within his own circle of friends the appearance of the pamphlet in March 1869 was greeted with disbelief. Heinrich Esser, one of the conductors at the Vienna Court Opera, wrote to Wagner's publisher, Franz Schott: 'I do not understand how Wagner could commit such an act of lunacy and repeat a folly that he committed many years ago and that had in the meantime been forgotten, for in this way he is bound to make a fool of himself now and for evermore.'[103]

Jens Malte Fischer hits the nail on the head when he notes that there was no outward need to republish the essay, which he sees as a fall from grace.[104] On this occasion its impact extended far beyond the confines of Germany and Austria, the contents of the pamphlet being hotly debated as far afield as England and North America. What was particularly unfortunate about its republication was the fact that Wagner chose to reissue it at the height of Jewish emancipation and attempted to poison the still strained relationship between Jews and non-Jews. To that extent the pamphlet is a key text in nineteenth-century anti-Semitism and was a major catalyst in the vast wave of anti-Semitism that swept across Germany in the 1880s. In German National circles, *Jews in Music* was hailed as a manifesto expressing 'the awakening conscience of the nation', as Wagner's later son-in-law, Houston Stewart Chamberlain, was gleefully to claim.[105]

And Cosima? 'He has sent off the essay on the Jews,' she noted on 11 January 1869, 'which makes me apprehensive, yet I did not try to prevent it.'[106] Her misgivings stemmed from her worries about possible protests on the

2 Cosima's mother, Marie d'Agoult, shown here in a portrait painted in 1839 by Henri Lehmann. Under the pseudonym 'Daniel Stern', she wrote historical works that were well regarded in their day.

1 Cosima's father, the leading pianist of the nineteenth century, Franz Liszt.

3 A childhood without parents: together with her brother Daniel and her elder sister Blandine, Cosima (seen standing at the back) lived with her grandmother, Anna Liszt, in Paris. Their father left their education to strict governesses such as Madame de Saint-Mars (right). 'Since when', Liszt demanded, 'have three tiny tots like you been justified in setting yourselves up as supreme judges in matters of conscience and morality?'

4 Cosima Liszt *c*.1852. Marie von Wittgenstein recalled her step-sister the following year: 'Poor Cosima was in the throes of adolescence – tall, angular and fair-skinned, with a large mouth and long nose, the very image of her father. Only her long golden hair was of rare lustre and great beauty'.

5 A picture of unhappiness: Cosima and Franz Liszt in Munich. Only when she became pregnant with Wagner's first child did Liszt discover the full extent of the Bülows' unhappy marriage.

6 There are few surviving photographs that show Cosima and Hans von Bülow together. Still less are there any wedding photographs. By the time the present photograph was taken in Pest in 1865, their marriage was long since over. The violinist Heinrich Wilhelm Ernst is seen here standing beside Cosima, with Liszt seated at the piano.

7 Baroness Cosima von Bülow around 1865. She was Wagner's secretary, housekeeper and secret lover. 'Since then Wagner has been completely and utterly under her spell', Cornelius noted in his diary. 'It is no longer possible to speak to him on his own, no letters get through to him without her first breaking them open and reading them to him.'

8 Richard and Cosima Wagner in 1872: 'Every word of his is an article of faith to me.'

9 Cosima's children photographed by Adolf von Groß, *c.*1873: (left to right) Isolde, Eva, Siegfried, Blandine and Daniela. In educating her charges, Cosima was certainly not at all squeamish: 'Spoke very seriously with the children, wept and prayed with them, brought them to the point of asking me for punishment.'

10 and 11 The Bayreuth Festival Theatre, built between 1872 and 1876 by Otto Brückwald after designs by Wagner and with considerable financial assistance from Ludwig II's privy purse. The auditorium (below) originally had wooden seating for 1,460. The present photograph shows the sets for the temple of the Grail at the time of the first performances of *Parsifal* in 1882.

12 Group portrait with children and dogs on the steps at Wahnfried, August 1881. Top row: Blandine, Siegfried's tutor, Heinrich von Stein, Cosima and Richard Wagner and the painter Paul von Joukowsky. Bottom row: Isolde, Daniela, Eva and a sad-looking Siegfried.

13 Important friends and assistants at the time of the Bayreuth venture: the conductor Hermann Levi, the painter Paul von Joukowsky and the theatre technician Fritz Brandt.

14 The front of Wahnfried *c.*1874, with Caspar Zumbusch's bust of Ludwig II.

15 The salon in Wahnfried. Cosima refused to allow anything to be changed here after Wagner's death, and the furniture and musical instruments that Wagner had used could not be touched under any circumstances. Cosima's daughter-in-law, Winifred, had difficulty adapting to Wahnfried's antiquated regime: 'No one had told me anything about it being a sacred chair.'

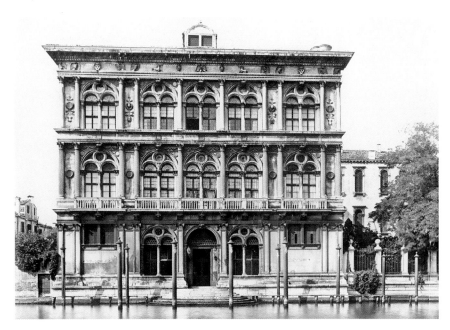

16 The Palazzo Vendramin-Calergi in Venice, where Wagner died in 1883. The building now houses the city's casino.

17 An intimate get-together: the conductor Hans Richter photographed by Adolf von Groß *c.*1890 with Cosima's children, Eva, Isolde, Siegfried, Daniela and Blandine.

18 Even in later life, Cosima's daily constitutionals were special events, when passers-by would pause and stare in reverence at the 'first lady of Bayreuth'. According to Winifred Wagner, 'She had a habit of going into individual shops in order to rest there. And so every shop owner was always delighted when she came and sat down in his shop.'

19 The composer Siegfried Wagner in the shadow of his all-powerful father: 'Mama! Mama! I've just had an idea – Papa's Redemption motif!' The upper part of William A. Wellner's 1904 caricature shows Cosima wrestling with Heinrich Conried.

20 The Beidlers in Bayreuth in 1905. Isolde Beidler, the first daughter of Richard and Cosima Wagner, fell out of favour in 1914 and from then on her name could no longer be mentioned. 'Just think,' Cosima is reported as saying about Isolde, 'it is as if my feelings in this regard have died.'

21 Regime change: when his mother fell ill in 1906, Siegfried took over the running of the Festival.

22 Houston Stewart Chamberlain reading to Cosima in Bordighera in 1913.

23 Cosima's father, Franz Liszt, died in Bayreuth on 31 July 1886. Thirty years later members of his family and family friends gathered to commemorate the event: (left to right) Hans von Wolzogen, Franz Stassen, Marie and Josef Pembaur, Siegfried Wagner and his young wife, Winifred, Hans Richter and Eva Chamberlain.

24 'What a model of the most sublime will-power our Mama is, even to the point of unapproachability!' (Eva Chamberlain).

25 The family line is assured. In this photograph, taken *c.*1924, the next generation of the Wagner family can be seen lined up on the steps leading down to the garden at Wahnfried: (left to right) Wolfgang, Verena, Siegfried, Wieland, Winifred and Friedelind.

26 Nazism comes to Bayreuth: German Day in 1923. 'Why doesn't Ludendorff become our dictator?' Cosima wanted to know.

27 A living monument: Cosima Wagner in 1928. She lived in a world of her own imagination, still carrying on as if she were running the Festival. According to Eva Chamberlain, 'She generally rehearsed the role of Kundry and put a conductor in his place!'

28 When Cosima died in 1930, the whole of Bayreuth turned out to mourn her passing.

29 Old friends: Winifred Wagner, Siegfried's successor as head of the Festival, welcomes Hitler to the theatre in 1937.

part of the general public, a reaction that was not slow in coming. But she did not doubt in the rightness of Wagner's actions. We shall never be able to say for certain whether Cosima actively encouraged Wagner to republish the 'Jewish pamphlet', as it was to be known from now on, as her diary entries on the subject are too vague to admit of ultimate certainty, but it is striking – at the very least – that the Jews came back into Wagner's firing line within months of the couple's cohabitation. Be that as it may, there is no doubt that she supported her partner's campaign. When the pamphlet was translated into French, it was Cosima who corresponded with the translator: 'Afterward he corrects my letter to the translator. "How we really do work together!" he says.'[107] And when an acquaintance complained 'that people blame the Jewish pamphlet on me', she noted with evident pride: 'Nice people!'[108]

One final example: it was at Cosima's suggestion that Wagner wrote his essay 'Know Yourself' in early 1881, a piece in which he criticized the age and, more especially, capitalism, linking his critique with further anti-Semitic tirades. This was also the first time that he formulated the idea that 'antagonism between the races' was responsible for cultural decline:

> When our friends have gone, he reads to me the revised ending of his article, which seems to me more fitting than the first, and R. himself says that he always meant to write about us, not about the Jews. And yet I have to tell him what strange feelings it arouses in me when he alters anything at my instigation; I say that for me every idea he has is sacred.

There is no doubt that Cosima not only encouraged Wagner to write this article, she also persuaded him to revise its final section. Jewish assimilation was a thorn in her flesh. To the extent that the Jews acquired equal rights in the eyes of the law, she herself lost the possibility of defining her own self-worth, for she needed the ostensible 'antagonism between the races' to enhance the value of her own deficient self. A few lines later she adds her own thoughts on the 'Jewish question':

> I say it seems to me that in their contacts with the Israelites the Germans come to grief on account of not only their bad qualities, but also their good ones: for example, their lack of desire, which makes them so capable of idealism; now, under the pressure of these rapacious people, this is turning into indolent insensitivity.[109]

Human, All Too human

Tribschen, 6 June 1869:

> R. at my bedside in great concern. The midwife arrives after 3, to wait in the
> adjoining room, since I do not wish to speak to anybody. Things appear to
> quiet down somewhat. R. decides to use this period to get a few hours' sleep
> in order to strengthen himself for the coming day. He goes downstairs and
> gets into bed, but is so tortured by restlessness that he gets dressed again and
> comes upstairs; he rushes in and finds me in the most raging pain, being
> tended by the midwife. I was startled to see him suddenly standing before
> me and imagined I was seeing a ghost; I turned away in horror, thus driving
> him from the room into the open salon next door; when he again hears my
> cries, he rushes in once more, since the midwife has left me alone for a
> moment; I gripped his arm as I writhed, but signified to him that he should
> not speak. The midwife returned, R. withdrew again to the neighbouring
> room; there he remained earwitness to the delivery and heard the cries of the
> labouring mother.[110]

It was on this day that Cosima brought her fifth and final child into the world:
Siegfried Helferich Richard. The birth of her only son marked a critical
turning point in her life, for in the wake of the 'significant change' that
Siegfried had brought about in their lives,[111] Cosima decided to ask her
husband for a divorce. Nine days later, on 15 June 1869, she wrote what must
have been the most difficult and at the same time the most painful letter that
she had penned at any point in a marriage that had now lasted almost twelve
years: 'I have never had any luck with my conversations with you. Whenever
I have tried to establish an honourable peace between us, you responded with
irony and when I've asked you for a definitive separation, you refused to
listen.' Even as recently as the November of the previous year, she had still
thought that it would be possible for the three of them to coexist after a
fashion. 'I was wrong, and we are now surrounded by the wreckage, and I have
to bear the weight of a grave accusation, that of being the cause of this
collapse.' Cosima was unsparing in her self-reproaches: 'I have never hidden
from myself the extent of the wrong that I have caused you, for you have done
no wrong except to have married me. . . . And yet I confess that I should never
have left you if I had not encountered the life with which my own life has
merged so absolutely that I no longer know how to break free from it.' She

ended her letter by asking for her husband's permission 'to bring up the children and to remain in contact' with him.[112]

Bülow's reply was not slow in coming: within two days he had written a detailed response, the intimate tone of which is moving even today. It was basically a love letter that he addressed to Cosima:

> But, alas, since you left me I have been deprived of my whole support in dealing with life and its struggles. Your spirit, your heart, your friendship, your patience, your indulgence, your sympathy, your encouragement, your advice – and finally, and above all, your presence, your gaze, your speech – all these shaped and constituted this support. The loss of this supreme being, whose full worth I appreciated only after its loss, has made me both morally and artistically insolvent – I am now a bankrupt.

This may have been the first time that Bülow told Cosima that he loved her and that he needed her. Perhaps it was also the first time that he told her what she meant to him. But his declaration of his love came too late. 'It is necessary for me to break with all that pertains to you and to R. W., since my previous life had only these two leading threads (to which I might perhaps add your father) – also in my thoughts, as far as this is humanly possible.'[113] He agreed with Cosima's proposals and entrusted to her the task of bringing up their two children.

Bülow was unwilling and unable to remain in Munich as the place reminded him of his failed marriage. Before handing in his notice and leaving the city for good, he conducted the Court Orchestra one last time at the request of King Ludwig II. On the programme was the very work with which he had begun his tenure in Munich four years earlier, *Tristan und Isolde*. The new production opened on 20 June and was followed two days later by a private performance for the king. Both performances were a huge personal success for Bülow, but this barely made amends for all that he had had to endure. In early August, he sold up in Munich and auctioned off his furniture. Cosima was badly affected by it all. 'As for myself,' she wrote to her half-sister, Claire de Charnacé, 'I have discovered in the cruellest way that all failings in this world are punished. After all, I have been an instrument of this inscrutable justice in punishing myself.'[114]

Bülow left Munich on 19 August 1869 and, after spending a few weeks in Wiesbaden and Berlin, finally settled in Florence. For the present he left Cosima in the dark about his plans, and she had to rely on their former cook for news:

Hans is sad and gloomy and doesn't know himself where to go. If people ask after him, they are to be told that he has disappeared. I was never as close to the thought of taking my own life than I was when I read these lines. It seemed to me that this was my supreme duty, and all thoughts of my children, love, etc. were no more than a cloak beneath which to hide my cowardice. I have got over this phase, just as I have got over all the others, but with less courage, as I spent the whole day sobbing, without being able to calm down.[115]

Throughout this period Cosima suffered from nightmares. In one of them, she and Bülow were pelted with stones while they were begging in the street. There is no doubt that Cosima's feelings of guilt were threatening to destroy her completely. Wagner was of little help in dealing with her emotional problems as he was the main character in the tragedy. He also had troubles of his own during the summer of 1869 as Ludwig was insisting, against the composer's wishes, that *Das Rheingold* be staged at the end of August. As Bülow's successor, Hans Richter – Wagner's assistant – was to conduct the world premiere. When Richter wrote to the Master in Tribschen, pointing out that local conditions in Munich were such that the performance risked becoming a fiasco, Wagner asked his young friend to boycott the performance. Richter did as he was told, and the events that followed did so with wearisome predictability: Ludwig, who had been looking forward to the performance, felt insulted and suspected that his orders were being undermined. In a letter to his secretary, Lorenz von Düfflipp, he inveighed against the 'theatre rabble' and described Wagner and his cronies as a 'pack of animals'. Such brazen behaviour, he went on, was unique in his experience.

The 'royal friendship' that had once existed between Ludwig and Wagner was now approaching a new low. The king finally dismissed Hans Richter, engaged a new conductor and gave instructions for the performance to go ahead on 22 September. Wagner travelled to Munich in a last-ditch attempt to persuade him to change his mind, but Ludwig refused even to see his favourite composer. As had been feared, the world premiere of *Das Rheingold* turned out to be an artistic disaster.

By way of a diversion during these turbulent weeks in Tribschen, Wagner and Cosima received a visit from some young Wagnerians from Paris: Judith Mendès-Gautier, the enigmatic daughter of the poet Théophile Gautier; her husband Catulle Mendès; and the aesthete Philippe-Auguste Villiers de l'Isle-Adam. Although the three visitors stayed at one of Lucerne's hotels, they spent much of their time in the company of their idol. Another visitor at this date was the twenty-four-year-old Friedrich Nietzsche, who had been Professor of Classical Philology at the University of Basel since February 1869 and who after his death was to become the most influential philosopher of his generation. Wagner had been introduced to him in the November of the previous year at the Leipzig home of his brother-in-law, Hermann Brockhaus, and had invited him to Tribschen. His first visit took place on 15 May 1869 and was to be followed by twenty-two more. Too busy preparing for his inaugural lecture to be able to attend Wagner's birthday celebrations on 22 May, he none the less wrote a long letter to the composer, thanking him for the hours that they had spent together 'because the best and loftiest hours of my life are associated with your name, and I know of only one other man, your great spiritual brother Arthur Schopenhauer, whom I regard with equal reverence, even *religione quadam*'.[116] Nietzsche even numbered himself among Wagner's 'pauci', a claim that no doubt flattered the composer's elitist view of himself.

If we ignore the note of homage, we shall discover here an exceptional friendship that was filled with a profound sense of sympathy that naturally included Cosima. 'I told Cosima that you come right after her, then there's no one else by a long distance,' Wagner told Nietzsche early in 1872.[117] There is little doubt that he meant this and that it reflected his feelings at that time. Cosima, too, regarded Nietzsche as 'the most important of our friends'.[118] Their discussions were not just about philosophy, for Wagner and Cosima also treated Nietzsche as a member of their own family. He was in Tribschen when Siegfried was born and he spent two successive Christmases with the family, helping Cosima to decorate the tree and painting the Christmas nuts gold. At Easter 1872 he hid the children's Easter eggs and on other occasions ran errands for the mistress of the house, including buying confectionary and Brussels lace for her. Not until much later were there signs of a gradual estrangement that ended in open hostility. But that is another story. For the present the sun shone down on Lake Lucerne.

'As for our visitors, we've only one who is at all agreeable,' Cosima wrote to Richter at the end of November, 'Professor Nietzsche from Basel, who loves and understands the Master and who therefore shows wit and a heart. Apart from the fact that we've all been unwell in our various ways, we can't complain about the state of our health in Tribschen; the whole of Lucerne has been afflicted by the measles, but until now we ourselves have been spared.'[119] It is interesting to note Cosima's whimsical explanation for Nietzsche's 'wit and heart': he owed such qualities to his reverence of Wagner. But however amusing such comments, it must be remembered that behind them lay a conscious strategy on Cosima's part.

With Cosima's definitive decision to throw in her lot with Wagner, her idolization of her partner entered a wholly new phase, a change that had already found expression in the very language that she used to describe him. Not yet officially divorced, she was unable to refer to him as her husband or spouse and so she spoke simply of the 'Master'. Even though it was not Cosima who invented this term, its immoderate use in her letters of this period is striking. Hand in hand with this usage went a certain hierarchical order, for the presence of a 'Master' presupposed the existence of 'apprentices' and 'journeymen'. In Cosima's eyes, the Master's servants and assistants had to keep out of the limelight, for only in this way could the Master's star shine brightest. It comes as no surprise, therefore, to find her asking Hans Richter 'to burn my letters as soon as you have read them', so anxious was she to obliterate all trace of her own existence and ensure that there was nothing to remind the world of her own individuality. 'I always write to you with complete frankness, that goes without saying, and it would be embarrassing if any words of mine were to cause ill feeling. You must keep all the Master's letters, for even if there were to be a burglary here and if what was stolen were to be published, it would be a matter of the utmost indifference, it can never do him any harm, for what he writes may and, indeed, *must* endure.'[120]

Cosima had good reason for this secrecy, for her outbursts against France and 'these terrible French people'[121] would hardly have pleased that country's Wagnerites. Elsewhere we find her complaining, 'The French know nothing about Christmas, but what do they know about anything at all?'[122] For a native Frenchwoman to express such opinions seems at first sight to be mere affectation, but in Cosima's case it was more than that, for her hatred of the French represents an attempt to come to terms with her past. 'For me, the French language has ceased to be the language of the heart,' she told her friend Marie von Schleinitz:

Everything that hurt me sounded French, everything that healed me German; my good old grandmother who loved me in my childhood spoke German, whereas my governesses and the adoptive mothers who took charge of me spoke French, the German language was a place of refuge that I and my brother and sister sought out in order to escape from their care; Herr von Bülow and I seasoned the wretchedness of our marriage with the pepper of Gallic wit. With the first letter that I wrote in German to

Wagner – and more generally too – the eternal hour of my liberation struck. My faith, my love and my hope are German, whereas nothing that affects my heart occurs to me in French.[123]

Cosima's loveless childhood in Paris under the iron rod of Madame Patersi, her difficult relations with her father, her poisoned contacts with the princess and, last but not least, her unhappy marriage to Bülow all had French associations for Cosima, so it was only logical that French should be the language in which she continued to correspond with the representatives of her wretched past, especially with Bülow. If we ignore the elementary errors, the missing subjects and objects and the basically non-existent punctuation, her French creates an oddly convoluted and stilted impression, even though, paradoxically, these letters are the outpourings of an uprooted Frenchwoman no longer able or willing to express herself in her native tongue and who, having found a new home for herself in a diffuse definition of 'German-ness', now thought only in German.

'The prelude to our divorce has begun,' Cosima reported in late November 1869 to her half-sister, Claire de Charnacé.[124] But the process dragged on and on, bringing with it all kinds of stress for Bülow and his wife. Throughout these months they relived the vexatious vicissitudes of their marriage. Cosima was keen to avoid an open war and to ensure that her husband could save face, but in March 1870 she heard a rumour that Ludwig's secretary, Lorenz von Düfflipp, had written to Bülow with the aim of speeding up the process. Cosima was beside herself with anger and wrote a strongly worded letter to Düfflipp, her defective German reflecting the full extent of her fury:

No one has the right to say a word in this matter; Herr von Bülow and I have agreed on a divorce, and when this takes place concerns only him and me. And just as Herr von Bülow and I left Munich in the wake of the shameful ordeals that we suffered in the city, so neither I nor any of my dependants will ever again set foot in Munich, whether or not my divorce is finalized.[125]

In the event, the rumours were untrue, and Düfflipp was able to clear up the misunderstanding. Several more months were to pass, however, before the divorce was finalized, months that tested the patience of all concerned. 'Letter from the lawyer in Berlin,' we read in a diary entry dated 21 June 1870, 'telling me of an order according to which I have once again to declare that I do not intend to return home; following this statement comes the final hearing, in which "presumably the divorce will be promulgated".[126] It was not until 18 July 1870 that the Bülows were finally divorced, an event that Bülow himself commented on with all his usual sarcasm when he wrote to a friend: 'Frau von Bülow no. 1 was far too big for me, in terms of her height, I mean.'[127] Cosima did not attend the hearing in Berlin, and it was not until a week later that she was told of the court's decision: 'There is no happiness on this earth, my children,' she noted in her diary, 'for at this news I had only tears.'[128]

Meanwhile, the world of politics too was in turmoil. On the day after the Bülows were divorced, France declared war on Prussia, an outbreak of hostilities preceded by arguments over the Spanish succession that dated back to 1868, when Bourbon rule had been swept aside and Queen Isabella II driven into exile. In their search for a suitable successor, the politicians set their sights on Prince Leopold von Hohenzollern-Sigmaringen, the husband of a Portuguese princess. After initially hesitating, Bismarck supported the prince's candidature as it offered him a chance to inflict a diplomatic defeat on France. After all, he knew that Napoléon III would have difficulty accepting the accession of a German to the Spanish throne. But he failed to reckon on the fact that after strenuous protests from the French, the prince would withdraw his candidacy on 12 July 1870. The very next day the French ambassador, Count Vincent Benedetti, spoke to King Wilhelm I of Prussia while the latter was taking his daily constitutional at the spa resort of Bad Ems and demanded that the Hohenzollerns should once and for all renounce all claims to the Spanish throne. Wilhelm declined politely but firmly and refused to see the ambassador again as he felt that the tiresome matter had already been resolved. That same evening an internal report on this essentially unspectacular affair landed on Bismarck's desk in Berlin. Bismarck saw his chance and rewrote the memorandum, sexing it up and giving the impression that Wilhelm had snubbed the French ambassador. He then circulated the report. France predictably felt both humiliated and insulted by what was to become known as the 'Ems telegram'.

It is one of the ironies of history that it was Cosima's brother-in-law, Émile Ollivier, who in the Chamber of Deputies advocated war with Prussia. The southern German states – minus Austria, which Bismarck had thrown out of the German Union – joined forces with Prussia, overwhelming the French army, which suffered a military debacle at Sedan in the Ardennes on 1 September 1870. Napoléon III was taken prisoner and the French Republic was proclaimed. Metz capitulated in October, and Paris, which had been under siege since September, followed suit at the end of January 1871. Even before a general ceasefire had come into force, Bismarck was already talking to the southern German states about their entry into his North German Union. Thus was born the German Reich. The king of Prussia was proclaimed the new German kaiser in the Hall of Mirrors at Versailles on 18 January 1871. The Germans now had their united empire and their Kaiser Wilhelm I. There was a widespread sense of national euphoria that extended as far as Lucerne, where Wagner and Cosima joined in the anti-French celebrations.

Wagner and Cosima were married at the height of the war, on 25 August 1870 – King Ludwig's birthday. The ceremony took place in the Protestant church in Lucerne, with Hans Richter and the writer Malwida von Meysenbug as witnesses. 'At 8 o'clock we were married,' the newlywed Cosima noted in her diary; 'may I be worthy of bearing R.'s name! My prayers were concentrated on two points: R.'s well-being – that I might always promote it; and Hans's happiness – that it might be granted him, separated from me, to lead a cheerful life.'[129] The day was undoubtedly emotionally confusing for the nine-year-old Daniela and the seven-year-old Blandine. Perhaps they wondered where their father was. And why was their mother marrying another man? Cosima explained to her daughters that 'because of his work their father would always be away on tour and was obliged to be permanently absent, whereas their Uncle Richard was always alone, so that Papa and Mama thought it more sensible if Mama remained in Tribschen and married Uncle Richard.'[130]

Liszt learnt of his daughter's marriage a week later from the newspapers. Cosima had not informed her father of this latest turn of events as she was afraid of his reproaches: after all, he had continued to side with Bülow in the affair. Indeed, her decision to marry Wagner marked a new low in her dealings with her father: their relationship seemed to be poisoned.

The year as a whole had been a turbulent one for Cosima, but it ended with a wonderful surprise. When she woke up on the morning of Christmas Day, it was to the strains of music of enchanting and intimate tenderness. A group of musicians under Wagner's direction was standing in the stairwell at Tribschen and performing a serenade for Cosima, who always celebrated her birthday on Christmas Day, even though she had been born on Christmas Eve. The music that first rang out on the stairs at Tribschen was later to become known as the *Siegfried Idyll*: 'After it had died away,' Cosima recorded her impressions in her diary, 'R. came in to me with the five children and put into my hands the score of his "Symphonic Birthday Greeting". I was in tears, but so, too, was the whole household.'[131]

The Early Reich

'But what is to become of me?' Wagner wrote to King Ludwig II on 1 March 1871. 'What is to become of my work, about which you have always been so enthusiastic and which you rate so highly, even regarding it as the greatest ever to be produced by the mind of man?' He was referring to the completion and performance of the *Ring*. It was during this period that his dissatisfaction with conditions in Tribschen began to grow and he realized that he would be unable to implement his idea of a festival – a synthesis of music, drama and theatre in a Wagnerian 'total artwork' – without a theatre and a power base of his own. With typical self-assurance, he offered the king a detailed account of his plan to set up a festival of his own, the running of which 'would naturally be placed entirely in my own hands'. Wagner even had a specific place in mind: 'It lies in Bavaria and thus has my august friend as its master. But its principal virtue consists in the fact that we would not even have to build a theatre there.'[132] Here, far from the cities that Wagner hated and free from all social dependencies, Wagner could stage his works at an annual festival.

Wagner had been reminded of the small town in Upper Franconia in the spring of 1871. Bayreuth is first mentioned in 1194, but it was not until the middle of the eighteenth century, during the reign of the Margrave Friedrich and his wife Wilhelmine – the favourite sister of Frederick the Great – that Bayreuth began to expand and flourish with the construction of numerous large buildings and parks, including the Margraves' Opera House, the rebuilding of the Eremitage, the erection of the Neues Schloß and Hofgarten and the large-scale expansion of the town along what is now the Friedrichstraße. When the Wagners arrived in Bayreuth in the middle of April 1871, they found an architectural jewel. The town then numbered 17,000 inhabitants and seemed well suited to Wagner's needs: 'The place ought not to be a capital city with a permanent theatre, nor any of the more popular or larger health resorts, which, especially in the summer, would attract quite the wrong sort of audience,' Wagner explained his choice. 'It ought to be situated close to the heart of Germany and be a Bavarian town, since I am also thinking of taking up permanent residence there and think it only right to do so in Bavaria, if I am to continue to enjoy the acts of kindness shown to me by the King of Bavaria.'[133]

The Wagners lost no time in visiting the Margraves' Opera House, an ornate Baroque theatre with an interior designed by Giuseppe Galli-Bibiena, but its pit proved too small for Wagner's *Ring* orchestra. None the less, the couple decided to settle in the town and to build their own festival theatre there. For the present, however, they avoided any official negotiations with the city fathers but instead continued their journey to Leipzig, Dresden and Berlin. Here they discussed the practical implementation of so costly an undertaking. Wagner was in his element, not only conceiving the whole idea but calculating the cost, drawing up plans and rejecting various suggestions put to him, before starting all over again. All in all, the total cost of building the theatre, including its fixtures and fittings, and of paying the artists and other staff amounted to some 300,000 thalers, or 7.5 million euros at today's prices. In the spirit of the 'Gründerjahre' – the early years of the German Reich, when countless new companies were floated – Wagner established a patrons' scheme that was a kind of public limited company intended to sell 1,000 patron's certificates to individuals at 300 thalers each in return for which they would be guaranteed free seats for the performances. The scheme was initially run by the pianist Carl Tausig, another of Wagner's young admirers, whose early death from typhoid fever in July 1871, when he was not yet thirty years old, prevented him from enjoying the fruits of his labours. He was replaced by Cosima's friend, Marie von Schleinitz, whose tenacity and guile went a long way towards raising the money that was needed. Cosima, too, proved a cunning cashier. When Hans Richter reported that a Viennese music lover was a fan of Wagner's works, she was disappointed to find that 'this consists simply in the acquisition of a patron's certificate worth 300 thalers'.[134] And to Peter Cornelius she wrote without further ado: 'What's happening with your brother and his inheritance?'[135] But by the beginning of 1875 only 490 certificates had been sold. To make matters worse, it had become clear that the number that needed to be sold now stood at 1,300.

The patrons' scheme had proved a failure, generating insufficient money for the project to proceed and leaving Wagner once again dependent on King Ludwig. On 3 May 1871 Wagner called on Bismarck in Berlin in the hope of enlisting the Reich's support. Two days later, in the presence of the kaiser and the Empress Augusta, he conducted a concert comprising a selection of his own works and Beethoven's Fifth Symphony. The concert was sensationally successful. Buoyed up by these impressions, the Wagners travelled to Leipzig, where on 12 May the composer let it be known that the first Bayreuth Festival would take place in 1873, even though the Bayreuth town council as yet knew nothing of its impending good fortune. Not until 1 November 1871 did Wagner make contact with the chairman of the council, Friedrich Feustel, a banker with a keen interest in the arts and an eye to the future. Within a week,

Wagner had received a letter from Feustel, offering him a plot of land, free of charge, on which to build his new theatre. From now on the project acquired a tremendous momentum of its own, and by mid-December Wagner was back in Bayreuth to conduct negotiations with the council. 'The plot of land that we have been given is quite wonderful,' Cosima reported to Marie von Schleinitz, 'and the mayor, town councillors and council chairman have outdone one another in their friendliness and good will.'[136] But an additional plot of land had to be found for the Wagners' new family home. On 1 February 1872 Wagner was able to buy such a plot next to the Bayreuth Hofgarten, a purchase facilitated by yet another generous donation from King Ludwig. It was here that the family home, the Villa Wahnfried, was shortly to be built.

For the most part, Cosima covered her husband's back, organizing the family's move to Bayreuth, packing chests and suitcases, disbanding the household at Tribschen and planning the festivities that were to accompany the ceremony marking the laying of the theatre's foundation stone. Following this official act, Wagner was to conduct a performance of Beethoven's Ninth Symphony, the famous final chorus of which is a setting of Schiller's 'Ode to Joy'. Wagner left Switzerland on 22 April 1872 and travelled to Bayreuth via Darmstadt. As the family still had no permanent home in the town, he initially took rooms at the Hotel Fantaisie a few miles to the west of Bayreuth. Cosima and the five children followed him a week later.

The foundation stone of Bayreuth's new Festival theatre was laid in pouring rain at eleven o'clock on the morning of 22 May 1872, Wagner's fifty-ninth birthday. King Ludwig sent a good-will message that was enclosed within the foundation stone, after which brass band music and various blessings rounded off the morning's events. At five o'clock that afternoon Wagner conducted Beethoven's Ninth Symphony, together with his own *Kaisermarsch*, in the Margraves' Opera House. 'In the opera house R. fetches me from my box to sit with the five children on the stage beside him,' Cosima noted in her diary. 'Very fine impression, even the gravest among the men have tears in their eyes.'[137] Following the gala concert, some 300 guests of honour were invited to a celebratory banquet, from which only Liszt was conspicuous by his absence. Instead, he sent merely a message of support. His demonstrative refusal to attend the ceremony and his continuing avoidance of the Wagners weighed heavily on the couple's minds, and in early September they travelled at short notice to Weimar, where Liszt maintained the third of his three homes after Rome and Budapest. Grand Duke Carl Alexander had placed a small apartment at his disposal in the Hofgärtnerei, and it was here that he received his visitors and taught his numerous pupils. 'I am terribly upset by my father's weariness of soul,' Cosima commented after their meeting.[138] During the days that followed, she spent a good deal of time with him. In turn he gave her a great deal of pleasure by playing works by Bach, Beethoven and Chopin, together with excerpts from Wagner's operas, but in general there was no denying the rift that had opened up between them. At table Wagner attempted to break the ice by cracking little jokes that brought a smile even to the Abbé's lips, but Cosima realized to her dismay that, although her father spoke to her, he almost never looked at her directly. 'I depart in sorrow,' she noted on the day that she and her husband set off back to Bayreuth. 'It is not the separation which pains me, but the fear of entirely losing touch.'[139]

His sad leave-taking with Cosima evidently preyed on Liszt's mind, and within six weeks he had set out for Bayreuth. The family was just having lunch on Tuesday 15 October when Dr Liszt's arrival was announced by one of the Wagners' servants. All were pleased to see each other again, and during the next seven days Liszt became one of the family. After attending church in the morning, he would take breakfast with the other family members. They would then visit the site of the Festival theatre or drive out to the Fantaisie. (A few weeks earlier, the Wagners had left their hotel and moved into an apartment at 7 Dammallee within the town itself.) Father and daughter used the occasion to discuss their situation at length:

> Long talk with my father; Princess Wittgenstein is tormenting him on our account – he should flee from Wagner's influence, artistic as well as moral, should not see me again, his self-respect demands this, we murdered Hans from a moral point of view, etc. I am very upset that my father should be tormented like this – he is so tired and is always being so torn about! Particularly this wretched woman in Rome has never done anything but goad him – but he goes not intend to give me and us up.[140]

This confession left Cosima feeling relieved. If she had initially feared that her father would reject her, she now knew that it was the princess who was hounding her and her family in Bayreuth. Perhaps Cosima was returning her father's confidence when she admitted that she was thinking of leaving the bosom of the Catholic Church. A year earlier she had written to Bülow, using the formal 'Sie': 'If I were to tell you that I am toying with the idea of converting to Protestantism with the children in order to be able conscientiously to fulfil this part of my task, how would this thought strike you? I need hardly add that I shall not take this step without your consent.' Cosima justified her decision by claiming that she was 'afraid' of her father confessor. During the divorce proceedings, she explained, she had repeatedly had to put up with indiscreet questions and reproaches, a fate from which she wanted her daughters to be spared:

> On the strength of the conflict currently facing the Catholic Church, I am afraid that – if I were to entrust our daughters' religious education to another Catholic priest just now – their Christian faith would be shaken to its foundations rather than being confirmed. Moreover, I would be unable to continue to accompany them to church or to supervise such an important aspect of their education, as I cannot bring myself either to deny or to confirm the pope's infallibility.[141]

Cosima officially converted to Protestantism in the vestry of Bayreuth's parish church on 31 October 1872: 'We set out at ten o'clock for the dean's house, where my conversion is recorded in front of the witnesses, Herr Feustel and the mayor; then to the vestry, where I receive the sacrament with R.; a deeply moving occasion, my whole soul trembles, our dean speaks from the depths of his heart. R. is profoundly touched.'[142] Siegfried had already been baptized into the Protestant Church, but it is no longer possible to say when Cosima's other children converted as the parish church's archives contain no record of the matter. But we may assume that the four girls, all of whom had been baptized as Catholics, converted to Protestantism as they all went to confirmation class.

Cosima's conversion was motivated less by religious conviction than by her desire to demonstrate her solidarity with her Protestant husband, and it was not long before her enthusiasm for her new faith began to wane. And so we find her noting in her diary on 6 April 1873: 'To church, and once more a long and dreary sermon.'[143] The truth of the matter is that Cosima remained a pietistic Catholic until her dying day, her thoughts not infrequently turning to non-Protestant confession and the absolution demonized by Luther. Cosima herself was aware of this and occasionally flirted with the idea, telling her friend Marie von Wolkenstein that 'basically I am a Catholic (Lulu calls me a Jesuit!)'.[144] Wagner, too, saw through his wife's ostentatious Protestantism, commenting mockingly on her 'Catholic expression – this is how he jokingly describes a look of exaltation he claims sometimes to see in me'.[145]

Although only the foundations of the Festival theatre had been laid, Wagner was already planning its inaugural production. Bound up with these plans was an extended tour of Germany on which he and Cosima set out on 10 November 1872. As the Bayreuth Festival's future director, he wanted to find out more about conditions in other German theatres and assemble a suitable cast for the *Ring*. Between 10 November and 15 December, the Wagners visited Würzburg, Frankfurt, Darmstadt, Mannheim, Stuttgart, Strasbourg, Karlsruhe, Wiesbaden, Mainz, Cologne, Düsseldorf, Hanover, Bremen, Magdeburg, Dessau and Leipzig. Train journeys at this time were long and uncomfortable. In each town or city Wagner had to talk to theatre managers and singers and submit to a round of receptions and dinners arranged by local dignitaries for the famous composer and his wife, so that it was often after midnight by the time the couple got to bed. After only a few hours' sleep they had to set off for the station again on the next stage of their journey. All in all, it was less an agreeable break than what we would now describe as a marketing strategy, leaving them weary beyond words. On their return to Bayreuth, they were reunited with their children who in the meantime had been entrusted to the care of governesses. Blandine and Eva looked thin and sickly, and the three-year-old Siegfried, too, was unwell. To make matters worse, the Wagners' five-week tour had produced only the most sobering results: what they had seen in the various theatres they had visited was of such an appallingly low musical standard that it could hardly serve as a model.

Their annoyances continued to grow, as the news from the Festival's board of management became increasingly unwelcome. The sale of the patrons' certificates had ground to a halt, and there was a general lack of money to fund the venture. In spite of poor health, Wagner set out on a concert tour in January 1873, the proceeds of which were intended to swell the Festival's coffers. This second journey took the composer to Dresden, Berlin, Hamburg, Schwerin and Chemnitz. On 4 February he conducted a concert in Berlin in the presence of the kaiser and his wife that raised a total of 5,400 thalers. Cosima acted as Wagner's agent, arranging schedules and skilfully negotiating fees. When an invitation arrived from Pest, she wrote to Hans Richter, demanding to know if 'the concert will result in a net income of at least 10,000 florins as he is refusing to appear in other places that are unable to guarantee this sum. Berlin has contributed 5,400 thalers, Hamburg 4,000.'[146] The Wagners were nothing if not choosy. By the summer of 1873 they had shifted no more than 340 patrons' certificates. Even with the additional income from Wagner's concert tour, this could not even begin to cover the cost of building a theatre and mounting the first Bayreuth Festival. And so Wagner drafted a kind of publicity leaflet, 'The Stage Festival Theatre in Bayreuth', a copy of which he even sent to Bismarck. But the chancellor had no interest in Wagner's plans and did not so much as deign to acknowledge the offprint.

Although the future continued to look bleak, the theatre's topping-out ceremony went ahead on 2 August. The whole of Bayreuth was festively decorated, the fine weather bringing out the townspeople. The shell of the building was consecrated to the strains of the march from *Tannhäuser*. The local dean spoke a few pious platitudes, and Wagner himself declaimed a poem that he had cobbled together at the last minute. Liszt, too, attended the ceremony, his presence a source of particular pleasure to the Wagners. The day ended with a funfair and fireworks. But appearances were deceptive, and only a few weeks later, on 30 August 1873, Wagner signed a circular to the patrons of the Bayreuth Festival, admitting that 'the planned performances cannot take place before the summer of 1875'.[147] The venture was on the verge of bankruptcy. Who could help? King Ludwig? Lorenz von Düfflipp held out little hope of any further assistance, limiting himself to drawing Wagner's attention to the 25,000 thalers that he had already received for his family villa. No more was available, not least because, as Düfflipp went on to emphasize, 'His Majesty would like to see his own projects being promoted above all else and to avoid everything that might in any way prevent or delay the realization of these plans.'[148] Ludwig's plans consisted – notoriously – in building increasingly fantastical fairytale castles that used up almost all his private fortune, the civil list. In spite of this snub, Wagner travelled to Munich on 20 November but was not even admitted to the king's presence. On his return to Bayreuth, Wagner reported that Ludwig was becoming more and more strange in his behaviour, and more and more reclusive: 'Every day he has some inspiration, and has hardly been persuaded out of it when he returns to it again. He no longer goes out of doors, takes his midday meal at 7 o'clock, has sixty candles lit in one small room, in which he remains, eating again at 11 o'clock and going to bed at 2 a.m., then, since he cannot sleep, taking pills.'[149]

In early January 1874 Wagner made a further attempt to engage the king's attention. Düfflipp, who was well disposed to the project, revealed a good deal of understanding for his predicament, but as before the approach ultimately ended in failure. Then, on 27 January, a letter from the king arrived in Bayreuth. Wagner was initially reluctant to open it at all as he expected the usual royal bickerings, and so Cosima read the letter to him: 'I see at once that it is very friendly. The king promises never to give up his mission in life, and says the delay was forced on him only by the state of his purse.'[150] What Ludwig actually wrote was: 'No, no and again no! It shall not end like this! Help must be made available! Our plan cannot be allowed to fail!'[151] Although this all sounded very vague, Wagner could still feel satisfied. In February the Festival's board of directors signed a contract with the court secretariat awarding the Festival credit facilities of 100,000 thalers, allowing Wagner to announce that the Festival would now take place in 1876. Ludwig was no longer willing to hand over large sums of money, as he had done in previous years, but made the funds available in the form of a loan. The Wagners were now in debt for many years to come and were obliged to pay back the loan from the Festival budget. This also meant rejecting one of the main ideas originally associated with the Festival: whereas Wagner had initially thought that his theatre would be open to all and that admission would be free, he now saw himself forced to sell tickets and to cut his idealist's coat to suit the reality of his cloth.

Daily Life in Wahnfried

By the spring of 1874 the Wagners' family villa next to the Hofgarten was finally nearing completion. More than once Wagner had had cause to berate the workmen for what seemed to him their slow progress, and there were times when he was even tempted to call it 'Ärgersheim' – a source of nothing but worry and trouble. But the Wagners were finally able to move in on 28 April 1874: 'It is not yet finished, far from it, but we shall conquer.'[152] Built by a local architect, Carl Wölfel, the house had been designed by Wagner himself and was typical of the artists' villas of the nineteenth century. Central to the three-storey building were its entrance hall and salon, which covered an area of 100 square metres, its large bay window overlooking the garden at the rear of the building. The entrance hall extended over all three floors to the skylight in the roof. It included a gallery at first-floor level and was intended to double as a recital room. It was here that Festival rehearsals were held over a period of several decades. The salon, conversely, was the family's living room and library, additionally hosting receptions. To the left of the hall lay Cosima's 'lilac salon', while to the right was the dining room. On the mezzanine floor were dressing rooms and bathrooms, and on the top floor were the bedrooms and Wagner's study. The building had no central staircase, and so narrow spiral staircases, each with its own stairwell, were incorporated into the walls. In this way the builders wanted to draw a conscious dividing line between the public area and the private rooms. Above the main entrance Wagner added a carved inscription: 'Hier wo mein Wähnen Frieden fand – Wahnfried – sei dieses Haus von mir benannt' (Here, where my illusions found peace, let this house be named 'Peace from Illusion'). Behind the house, henceforth known as the Villa Wahnfried, lay the couple's empty grave. One might regard this as a macabre detail, but, as Wagner told the king, it was important for him 'to have a clear idea of the place that will one day receive us in eternal rest on the land that we owe to the magnanimity of your love, land, moreover, that will one day be bequeathed to my son as his inalienable home'.[153]

Conceived on the grandest scale and furnished with Wagnerian luxury, the building was architecturally interesting but, as Cosima's daughter-in-law, Winifred Wagner, recalled, it was also 'insanely impractical' in terms of the family's day-to-day activities. Many of the rooms could be reached only by circuitous routes: if Wagner, working in his study on the top floor, rang, the servant had to run up three flights of stairs from the kitchen in the basement. Over the years the family employed a veritable army of servants to look after the house and maintain its extensive grounds. They included Wagner's personal valet, Georg, Cosima's maidservant, Sophie, a chambermaid, Afra, and a cook, Victoria, as well as a concierge, gardeners and governesses. Wagner was fond of luxury. But it was Cosima who was left to run the household, for as a general rule the master of the house was not interested in knowing if there was enough income from his royalties to pay for all these employees. And so we find Cosima confiding in her diary on 17 March 1875: 'I now have to take my badly disordered household in hand, and start right away, busying myself all day long with the linen. In the evening R. laughs and says, "I'm glad to see that I also married a housekeeper." '[154] Wagner did not take such mundane worries particularly seriously and evidently found it amusing to see his wife poring over the housekeeping books: 'I am still busy putting my whole household in order, and R. laughs when he sees me doing accounts with my cook.'[155] The results were sometimes alarming, as in April 1877, when Cosima noted that 'we spent 14,999 marks in the last quarter, which worries me very much'.[156] But somehow there was always enough money in the coffers, at least for the Wagners' private requirements.

While Cosima was organizing the servants, Wagner was busy running his 'Nibelung Chancellery', a motley assortment of young and enthusiastic musicians who helped in all manner of different ways. Early members of the group were the Russian pianist Josef Rubinstein, the Macedonian musician Demetrius Lalas, the Hungarian conductor Anton Seidl and the Saxon composer Herman Zumpe. They were later joined by the two conductors Felix Mottl and Franz Fischer and by Liszt's pupil Berthold Kellermann. Wagner's journeymen worked and lived at the White Lamb Inn, copying out the score of the *Ring*, preparing piano reductions and working as *répétiteurs* and production assistants during the actual Festival. The existence of this community was soon a matter of public knowledge, so that even letters addressed simply to the 'Nibelung Chancellery in Bayreuth' reached their destination. Wagner would look in on the group at least once a day to check up on what they were doing, after which he would invite his young friends to join him in a glass of beer. In the evening they often performed music at Wahnfried, 'claiming that it was only here that they learnt anything, certainly more than in the expensively run academies and conservatories'.[157] Wagner was nothing if not immodest.

Contemporary eyewitness accounts provide a rich fund of information about daily life at Wahnfried. Take the reminiscences of Wagner's publisher, Ludwig Strecker. Strecker had studied law and was only twenty-two when, soon after taking over the running of the venerable publishing house of Schott, he paid his first call on the Wagners in January 1876. 'The door was opened by a frock-coated servant who asked me politely what I wanted,' explained Strecker, recalling his surprise at such fuss and to-do. The Master and his wife were busy, he was told. He was invited to come back later that afternoon. When Strecker returned a few hours later, he happened to find Wagner in the garden. After engaging in a bout of friendly banter, they entered the salon, where Wagner lost no time in broaching his favourite subject: money. In the light of all the manifestly expensive objects scattered around the room, Strecker was not a little surprised to find Wagner complaining so bitterly at the high level of his debts.

After an hour or so, Wagner dismissed his visitor but invited him back that evening to spend some time with his family. 'When I returned,' Strecker later wrote,

> I found not only Rubinstein but also Frau Cosima, who was wearing a large green eyeshade to protect her eyes, but she then removed it – partly from vanity, I think, as her eyes are very beautiful. An interesting, narrow face, large nose, equally large mouth with splendid teeth, blond hair simply knotted, very beautiful, aristocratic hands and a very slim figure. When she becomes animated, her voice is agreeably deep, but normally the tone is somewhat blasé. At all events, she is a clever, interesting woman who can be

utterly charming, as she proved in the course of the evening and following day. . . . She worships the Master to distraction, following his every movement and hanging on his every word – he rewards her with exceptional and, as it appears, sincere gallantry and attentiveness.

Strecker returned for lunch the next day: 'It was a very fine meal, served by a servant who wore white gloves.' While Cosima proved a stickler for etiquette, her husband, who was 'in a very good mood, made various jokes with the children.'[158] Cosima seems to have been satisfied with her visitor, for she noted in her diary afterwards that 'he pleases us with his good manners.'[159]

In itself, this anecdote is trivial, and yet it confirms a point made by many of Cosima's contemporaries, who observed in her a certain aristocratic affectation. However much she may have suffered as a result of her rigid and pedantic upbringing, she remained Madame Patersi's best pupil. Even in the informal atmosphere of her family circle, appearances and perfect manners were a matter of supreme importance to her. She knew what was fitting and punished all who violated such customs, her pedagogic zeal not sparing even her husband. The famous soprano Lilli Lehmann watched Cosima trying to 'educate' the sixty-two-year-old Wagner 'if he, for instance, did not use his knife at table sufficiently in the English fashion, whereby many a dinner came to a speedy and unexpected end.'[160]

As was usual at this period, it was the lady of the house who had the task of bringing up the children. Daniela and Blandine initially attended a local school in Bayreuth before transferring to the select Luisenstift, a convent near Zwickau in Saxony. As boarders, they returned home only at weekends or in the school holidays. The three other children, Isolde, Eva and Siegfried, were taught by a governess in the Wahnfried nursery. From July 1875, their governess was Susanne Weinert, who described Cosima as 'the mistress'. Although Cosima repeatedly demanded to see the children's timetable, she rarely interfered in their teaching. Susanne Weinert reports that the children had to stand up when their mother came into the room. They also had 'to kiss her hand and are so accustomed to this demonstration of a child's respect for its parents that they will never forget it'.[161]

Siegfried was ten when he had his first tutor in the person of Heinrich von Stein. The whole of the Wagners' lives revolved around little 'Fidi', as Cosima called her son, turning him into the centre of a veritable cult. Susanne Weinert noted that the servants were expected to address the six-year-old stripling as 'Herr Siegfried'. Even by 1875 there were already signs of the dynastic principle that saw the son as the one and only heir who would take up his famous father's inheritance and continue the family line. As we shall see, Fidi's interest in following this calling is another story. His four sisters, meanwhile, existed to serve an ancillary function, their one purpose in life being to receive a solid education and marry into good families, but otherwise they would stand by their brother. Daniela, Blandine, Isolde and Eva had to lead lives of self-deprecating renunciation in order that Siegfried's light could burn the more brightly. Cosima could not imagine her daughters receiving a professional training or pursuing an artistic career, however obvious such a calling may have been. 'I do not consider it possible for a woman to live a public life and at the same time fulfil her feminine duties.'[162] There is no doubt that this picture of a woman's role in society was widespread at this time, and yet we should not forget that we are not dealing here with 'simple people' but with the family of an artist. Daniela, for example, was an outstanding pianist like her mother, but there was no question of a concert career for her. Cosima made the same mistakes with her own daughter as those that Liszt had committed many years earlier.

'Do not repeat things such as the claim that the king is mad,' Cosima admonished Daniela on one occasion. 'As a rule, you should draw a veil over whatever may embarrass another person.'[163] Cosima brought up her daughters to avoid drawing attention to themselves: they should not stand out from the crowd and should not rub people up the wrong way but should always be straightforward and unassuming. For Cosima, tact was one of a woman's finest qualities: 'Pay proper heed, my dear – note when it is time for you to disappear and do so, moreover, without others noticing that you want to be discreet. The gift of tact is the rarest in the world and almost the best of all because it renders everything much easier and makes it all possible.'[164] It was not always easy for the impulsive Daniela to conform to her mother's ideas, with the result that in most of her surviving letters to her daughter, Cosima had something to complain about: 'Do try, my child, to acquire a more attractive and elegant handwriting, yours is far too untidy and inexpressive.'[165] On another occasion she noted a certain 'vulgarity' in her eldest daughter and advised her to lower the pitch of her voice: 'When you raise your voice, your lively nature gives you a certain curtness, while your intensity adds an element of vulgarity (whereas your voice is most agreeable when you speak in moderate tones). I am citing this as an example of much that is not part of your true self but which is like an excrescence, which, like any good gardener, you must tear out by the roots.'[166] And there was no shortage of well-meaning advice on how to find a suitable husband. And so we find Cosima striking a typical note of prudishness when describing 'courtship' as foolish, 'only this is the way in which a man lets a woman know that he has singled her out from all the others. This is how it all starts; the man is like a woodpecker who then comes along and inspects the nearest tree, if he finds it hollow, he does not remain there like the bird extracting its worm but goes on his way or, rather, he lets it go on its way (if one can say that about a tree!)'[167] This, then, was sex education in 1881.

Daniela and Blandine called Bülow 'father', while Wagner was 'papa'. Wagner himself clearly drew no distinction between Bülow's two daughters and his own three children but played and joked with all of them whenever he had the time. 'Siegfried scampers around on the carpet in sheer delight and turns somersaults, most of which are unsuccessful. Often his papa joins him, takes the boy by the legs and to the sound of teasing from his sisters and their governess gets him to turn a cartwheel just as it should be done.'[168] Not infrequently Wagner himself got down on the ground, while his son clambered all over him. If one or the other of his daughters came into the room, Lilli Lehmann recalled, 'he would ask her, rather sarcastically, what was the word for lamp, cup, book, etc., in French, and tease her because the use of French in his own house was very distasteful to him.'[169] Wagner had a great propensity for mockery and colourful remarks, a trait that regularly excited his wife's displeasure. It is easy to imagine her piqued expression when he regaled his family at mealtimes with a dream that he had had when he had fallen asleep 'with a finger in his nose; he says it shows him a cave with stalactites, then a milk pond, and finally the pulpy brain substance!'[170]

First Night

By early 1875 Bayreuth was again on the brink of bankruptcy. The Festival planned for the following year risked having to be cancelled, and so Wagner was obliged to earn some extra money by conducting concerts in Vienna and Budapest in March. During the months that followed, he also travelled to Leipzig, Hanover and Berlin and back again to Vienna. Rehearsals for the 1876 performances began in Bayreuth in July 1875 under the supervision of Hans Richter. 'In '75 Bayreuth still belonged solely to the artists, and they simply turned it upside down,' recalled Lilli Lehmann. The singers would sit on the windowsills of their rooms, learning their roles, while dangling their legs inside. Music calls were held in every available space. In the evening they all met in one or other of the town's many hostelries. 'There was great merriment and afterwards dancing. Wagner was also "invited," of course, and was so delighted, so exuberant, that, in spite of Cosima's presence he stood right on his head, and, over and over again, clinked glasses with his dear old friend, Marie, my mother, and drained his glass.'[171] But the boisterous mood could not conceal the fact that the financial situation continued to be precarious. So serious was his predicament that Wagner resolved to write to Wilhelm I and ask him for a loan of 30,000 thalers. But the kaiser passed on the request to Bismarck's chancellery. When Wagner discovered that his appeal was to be debated in the Reichstag, he withdrew it in a fit of mortified pride. As Cosima remarked at the time, Wagner was 'deeply annoyed at being referred to the Reichstag, when he had appealed to the Emperor's grace'.[172]

A new source of income presented itself in February 1876, when Wagner received an invitation from Philadelphia to write a 'Grand Festival March for the Inauguration of the Centennial Commemoration of the American Declaration of Independence'. The commission bored him to tears, leading him to complain that in writing the work he would 'think of nothing but the five thousand dollars he has demanded and may never receive'.[173] Cosima's fears were unfounded, for the Americans paid the fee that Wagner had asked for, and Schott contributed another 9,000 marks for the publishing rights to the work. In early March the Wagners travelled to Berlin for the local premiere of *Tristan und Isolde*, and it was here that Cosima learnt of the death of her mother, Marie d'Agoult, in Paris on 5 March 1876: 'At first I am unable to believe it – I cable to Paris, but receive no answer. R. tells me that all the newspapers are reporting the same!'[174] The funeral took place two days later, so that Cosima was unable to accompany her mother to her final resting place. 'If she had been less talented,' Cosima complained to Marie von Schleinitz, 'she would undoubtedly have led a far more harmonious existence, but she would certainly never have admitted as much to me, and since she proudly continued to deny all personal sufferings, I shall prefer to assume that she found it easier to act as she did.'[175] To Daniela she wrote that 'there is nothing left for me to do except to grieve for the woman who brought me into the world. I hope that you will do the same, outwardly as well as inwardly; ask for your black dress and for black ruffles. But otherwise you should be silent and discreet.'[176]

This, then, was a difficult time for Cosima. It was against this background that the first Berlin performance of *Tristan und Isolde* took place on 20 March in the presence of the imperial couple and of the whole court. During the first interval Wagner was received by Wilhelm, who even promised to come to Bayreuth for the opening of the Festival. He also arranged for the net proceeds of the performance – 5,000 thalers – to be transferred to the Festival account, so that the Wagners' visit to Berlin was a complete success at least from a financial point of view.

The rehearsals for the first Bayreuth Festival began in early June with bad news: Friedrich Feustel reckoned that by the end of the month they would have run out of money. But then, on 29 June, at the very last minute, Munich declared its willingness to defer repayment of the credit that it had advanced, giving the Festival at least a breathing space. Wagner's nerves were in shreds, a state of affairs that was entirely understandable in the light of the countless worries with which he had to contend. As one eyewitness remarked: 'One cannot but admire the way in which he puts up with it all and fights! For ever young and on the ball, while maintaining a continuous correspondence and keeping his eye on the smallest detail, he somehow manages to keep on composing and does not simply collapse beneath the strain.' The author of these lines was the Dessau choreographer Richard Fricke, whom Wagner had met during his tour of Germany in December 1872 and whom he had signed up for the inaugural Festival. 'You must be everything for me,' Wagner had told Fricke on his arrival in Bayreuth. 'You must help me and will be a jack of all trades who can also do everything himself.'[177]

Wagner's words of praise reflected his current frame of mind, for there is little doubt that without Fricke the 1876 Festival would not have taken place at all. The two men were clearly kindred spirits. Richard Fricke was only five years younger than his famous namesake and was also born in Leipzig, so they shared a common bond. In the course of the rehearsals Fricke became altogether indispensable, acting as director, dramaturge, choreographer and translator all rolled up into one: 'Wagner talks quietly and indistinctly, while gesticulating wildly with his hands and arms; the final words of a sentence give a vague idea of what he wants, and you really have to pay the damnedest attention.'[178] Fricke was almost unique in his ability to deal with Wagner's whims, enabling him to mediate in arguments and defuse many an explosive situation. Cosima, too, held Fricke in high regard, with the result that he occasionally gave dancing lessons to her children. In general, he spent a good deal of time at Wahnfried, where he was able to observe family life at close quarters. One evening the composer handed out cigars to his guests: 'We were embarrassed to enter the salon with lit cigars, but lo and behold! Frau Cosima came towards us with a lit cigar in her mouth!'[179]

By the beginning of June, work on the theatre was sufficiently advanced for stage rehearsals to begin there in earnest. The architect, Otto Brückwald, had created something that at the time was altogether unique: with its original total of 1,460 seats, the auditorium is in the shape of a Greek or Roman amphitheatre, thus offering a democratic alternative to the traditional horse-shoe-shaped auditorium of a court theatre, with its boxes and balconies. The orchestral players are seated in a sunken pit between the stage and the first row of the stalls, where they cannot be seen by the audience. Wagner wrote in this context of a 'mystic abyss' dividing the reality of the auditorium from the ideality of the stage. Here the action of the music drama provides the only focus of attention. Equally remarkable is the double proscenium arch, framing the stage twice over and adding to the sense of depth. There were also a number of technological innovations that were regarded as sensational by the audiences of the time. For the three Rhinedaughters, the Darmstadt theatre technician Carl Brandt had designed three swimming machines of such terrifying instability that the singers, Lilli and Marie Lehmann and Minna Lammert, refused point-blank to be strapped into the cradles at the end of six-metre poles and trundled around the stage on four-wheeled carts. ' "No," said Lilli, "you can't expect me to agree to that, I'll not do it at any price, I've only just got over a serious illness, quite apart from my constant dizziness." ' But Fricke finally persuaded the women to agree to the ordeal. 'Among many "Oohs" and "Ahs" and squeaks and squeals we buckle them in and the ride begins, very slowly.'[180] The swimming machines were operated by members of the Nibelung Chancellery, including the young Austrian musician Felix Mottl. 'I'll spit on your head if you don't hold me still!' Lilli Lehmann threatened.[181] Brandt's contraption worked perfectly, Wagner was enthusiastic about it and at the end of the rehearsal he thanked the singers 'with tears in his eyes, petting them and smothering them with his kisses'.

These weeks were beset by constant vicissitudes. The poor weather – the months of May and June were exceptionally cold and wet – left everyone depressed, while Wagner additionally suffered from a painful abscess on his tooth, leaving him frequently ill-tempered and unable to attend a number of the rehearsals. There were also countless greater or lesser problems. The neck of the giant dragon, for example, got lost on its journey from London and did not arrive until the very last minute, while Carl Emil Doepler's costumes likewise caused much concern. 'The costumes are reminiscent throughout of Red Indian chiefs,' complained Cosima, 'and still bear, along with their ethnographic absurdity, all the hallmarks of provincial tastelessness.'[182]

Ludwig II turned up for the dress rehearsals between 6 and 9 August. But he was becoming increasingly eccentric in his behaviour, alighting from a special train at dead of night on an open stretch of track and, having been welcomed by Wagner and a mere handful of initiates, travelling on to the Eremitage. He now avoided his people and whenever he drove through the town it was behind closed curtains. He returned to Hohenschwangau during the night of 9/10 August but returned, incognito, for the third cycle of the *Ring*, which was staged between 27 and 30 August. The first cycle had been given on 13 August (*Das Rheingold*), 14 August (*Die Walküre*), 16 August (*Siegfried*) and 17 August (*Götterdämmerung*). The audience included members of the German and international aristocracy, led by Kaiser Wilhelm I and his wife and by Dom Pedro II of Brazil. Among other notables were King Karl I of Württemberg, Grand Duke Carl Alexander of Saxe-Weimar, Grand Duke Friedrich Franz III of Mecklenburg-Schwerin and representatives of the Austro-Hungarian nobility. Also all present and correct were the composers Liszt, Saint-Saëns, Bruckner and Tchaikovsky and the painters Franz von Lenbach, Adolf von Menzel, Anton von Werner and Hans Makart, to say nothing of all the actors, poets, scientists and journalists. Among the old friends who came, of course, were the Schleinitzes, the Wesendoncks, the still unmarried Mathilde Maier and the ailing Friedrich Nietzsche.

Bayreuth was ill prepared for this onslaught. 'The little town offers, it is true, sufficient shelter to the strangers,' complained Tchaikovsky, 'but it is not able to feed all its guests. So it happened on the very day of my arrival, I learnt the meaning of the words "struggle for existence".' There was chaos in the guest houses, empty seats were fought over and the waiters were unable to cope. Generally the plates and dishes remained empty, too. 'Throughout the whole duration of the Festival,' Tchaikovsky went on, 'food forms the chief interest of the public; the artistic representations take a secondary place. Cutlets, baked potatoes, omelettes – all are discussed much more eagerly than Wagner's music.'[183] But Tchaikovsky's strictures did not apply to Wahnfried, where one reception followed hard on the heels of another, banquet giving way to banquet with luxurious regularity. But, as Lilli Lehmann recalled, 'Quite against Wagner's will, his house became the gathering place of the aristocracy and the influential patrons.' Nor can Wagner have been pleased that during the four weeks that Liszt spent in Wahnfried, he held regular court for his admirers. Wagner had no time for his father-in-law's ambitions to join the ranks of the Catholic clergy and had to stand by while the Abbé, seated at the piano, gathered around him all the beautiful women 'whom he ensnared and who enchained him in turn, while he kissed their hands, smiled at them and showered his love upon them in the form of the music that he played as one plays with children who did not understand him'. Liszt was by now sixty-four and yet in spite of his cassock he evidently still exuded an erotic appeal for the feminine sex. 'They all flirted with him and – shall I say it? – he with them.'[184]

Wagner too enjoyed a final fling during the summer of 1876, when, silently and in secret, he began an affair with Judith Gautier, who had likewise come to Bayreuth for the Festival. It may be recalled that Judith Gautier had been born in 1845 and had visited Wagner at Tribschen in 1869 and again in 1870 in the company of her then husband, Catulle Mendès. She revered and worshipped the composer, but at that date there could be no question of an affair. Not until they met again in 1876 had the situation changed, now that Judith was separated from her husband. 'I'm sad,' Wagner complained to his lover on 2 September 1876. 'There's another reception this evening, but I shan't be going down. I've been rereading a few pages from my life that I dictated to Cosima. She is sacrificing herself to her father's habits, alas! Did I embrace you for the last time this morning? No! – I shall see you again – I want to! because I love you! – Adieu – Be good to me!'[185] Judith left Bayreuth the next day, and throughout the months that followed, Wagner wrote numerous hot-blooded letters to his *petite amie* in Paris.

For a long time Cosima remained in the dark about the affair and it seems that it was not until February 1878 that she finally discovered the truth of the matter. It remains unclear if she confronted her husband and whether there was an argument between them. Cosima took her idolization of Wagner to the point where ideas and feelings that she would normally have confided to her intimate journal were censored. After all, the diary was intended for her children, who could not be allowed to find out about their father's bit on the side. Only the single guarded comment has come down to us:

The grief I was fearing has not passed me by; it has come upon me from outside. May God help me! . . . Oh, sorrow, my old companion, come back and dwell within me; we know each other well – how long will you stay with me this time, most loyal and dependable of friends? Purify me, make me worthy of you, I shall not flee from you – but when will you bring me your brother?[186]

And that is all.

Let us return to the summer of 1876. The first Bayreuth Festival came to an end and its visitors left for their various corners of the world, allowing a degree of normality to return to the town. Wagner was far from satisfied with the artistic side of the performances, many aspects of which had failed to reflect his vision of the work, while much had simply gone wrong. According to Cosima, 'R. says that his main feeling during the performances was, "Never again, never again!" '[187] He felt ill, complained about chest pains and was irritable and melancholic by turns. In mid-September the Wagners and their four youngest children (Daniela remained at boarding school) set off for Italy on a three-month holiday. They travelled via Munich and Verona, reaching Venice on 19 September. A few days later the bombshell exploded: 'Less pleasing letter from friend Feustel, who reports debts amounting to about 120,000 marks.'[188] Worse, the deficit continued to grow, eventually reaching 148,000 marks and effectively undermining all plans to revive the production in 1877. The Wagners continued their journey to Bologna and Naples and thence to Sorrento in the Bay of Naples, where they remained until early November. In spite of all their worries, they spent a harmonious few weeks here: Cosima taught her offspring during the morning, and during the afternoon they would bathe in the sea, take donkey rides and explore the surrounding area.

At the end of October, Nietzsche arrived in Sorrento with two of his friends. He had been ill for some time – he was suffering from severe headaches and a painful eye condition – and wanted to convalesce in Italy at the invitation of Malwida von Meysenbug, a mutual friend of both Wagner and himself. Cosima found him 'very run down and much concerned with his health'.[189] The Wagners spent the evening of All Souls' Day – 2 November – 'with our friends Malwida and Prof. Nietzsche'.[190] It was their last meeting: the Wagners did not see Nietzsche again.

The events surrounding this Thursday in Sorrento have long been the cause of wild speculations. Wagner and Nietzsche are said to have had a falling out during a walk along the cliffs at Sorrento, but this is only one of the stories put about by the philosopher's sister, Elisabeth Förster-Nietzsche. The truth of the matter is that the first Bayreuth Festival tolled the death knell of the men's friendship. In order to understand the reasons for this, we need to turn the clock back a few months. In early July, Nietzsche had published the fourth of his *Untimely Meditations* under the title 'Richard Wagner in Bayreuth'. At first sight the essay is an encomium glorifying the Bayreuth Festival, which Nietzsche described as 'the first circumnavigation of the world in the domain of art'. But on closer inspection the eulogy turns out to contain an insidious subtext. Ever since the beginning of 1874 Nietzsche had harboured doubts about the success of the Bayreuth venture, and throughout the later period his feelings veered between hope and recurrent scepticism. To that extent, 'Richard Wagner in Bayreuth' documents this uncertainty.

When Nietzsche arrived in Bayreuth on 23 July 1876 for the preliminary rehearsals of the *Ring*, he was already ill. A series of severe migraines made it impossible for him to follow events in the theatre, with the result that he was forced to leave Bayreuth even before the final dress rehearsals. He fled to the spa town of Klingenbrunn in the Bavarian Forest, but returned to Bayreuth on 12 August and remained there for two whole weeks, albeit in a wretchedly poor state of health. His experiences during this time must have left him profoundly shocked, for he found himself in a town that had almost literally lost its reason. Everywhere there were members of the establishment that he so excoriated – financially powerful and influential individuals, aristocrats and politicians, industrialists and socialites, all of whom described themselves as 'Wagnerians' but whose ranks he refused to join. He felt a stranger in Bayreuth, not least because the Wagners, otherwise engaged, had no time to worry about their young friend. 'I recognized nothing,' Nietzsche sighed many years later. 'I hardly recognized Wagner. . . . *What had happened?* – Wagner had been translated into German! The Wagnerian had become master of Wagner! – German art! The German master! German beer!' Even today we may still be amused by Nietzsche's mockery of the 'hair-raising crowd' of Wagnerians that he encountered in Bayreuth: 'Not an abortion was missing, not even the anti-Semite! – Poor Wagner! To what a pass had he come! – Better for him to have gone among swine! But among Germans!'[191]

Nietzsche had presumably travelled to Upper Franconia with unreasonably high hopes, expecting to see Wagner's artistic vision in unadulterated form, whereas what he found there was an embarrassing fairground atmosphere, with swimming Rhinedaughters, shaggy-haired Indian chieftains and absurdly comical dragons. He felt repelled by it all. But it is significant that he was either unable or unwilling to see that the composer, too, was disappointed and depressed at what had been achieved. It seems as if he believed that Wagner had betrayed the cultural ideal that the two men had propounded only a few years earlier, when Nietzsche had described himself as the composer's pupil. The 1876 Festival marked a turning point in their relationship, although the definitive breach did not come until Wagner had written the libretto of *Parsifal*. Nietzsche then felt personally insulted, regarding the composer's work on the score of his final music drama as an act of humiliating prostration before the Cross and also before the established Church.

But the truth of the matter is that Nietzsche's repudiation of Wagner was also an act of liberation. One contemporary expressed incredulity: 'For those who know Wahnfried, the problem about Wagner and Nietzsche is not why Nietzsche broke with Wagner but how he was able to tolerate such an association over such a long period of time.'[192] Only after their break was Nietzsche able to write such epoch-making works as *Human, All Too Human, The Gay Science, Thus Spake Zarathustra* and *The Antichrist*. And yet the subject of Wagner continued to obsess him. Between 1876 and the beginning of January 1889, when he lost all hold on reality (he died in August 1900), he used a whole series of polemical essays to wreak vengeance not only on his former idol but on Cosima Wagner, too. *Parsifal*, for example, was an act of tastelessness for which he held Cosima personally responsible: 'Frau Cosima Wagner is the only woman with any style whom I have ever got to know; but I blame her for corrupting Wagner. How did that come about? He had not "earned" such a wife: in gratitude he succumbed to her.'[193] Much of what Nietzsche noted down during the weeks and months leading up to his nervous breakdown amounts to little more than linguistic gymnastics that occasionally bears the signs of his impending madness. But was he really wrong to see in Cosima the true representative of the fanatical cult of Wagner that was growing increasingly strident? The answer is almost certainly not. In September 1888 there was a final flash of his razor-sharp intellect when in a draft letter to his former friend he wrote:

You know very well how much I know the influence that you have exerted on W[agner] – you know even more how much I despise that influence. . . . I turned my back on you and Wagner as soon as the fraud began. . . . Whenever Liszt's daughter attempts to meddle in matters relating to German culture and even religion, I am implacable.[194]

An Uncertain Future

The Wagners spent three months in Italy, returning to Bayreuth on 20 December 1876. Cosima recorded their homecoming in her diary: 'To start with, great trouble in the house, no servants, everything to be restored to order! Pleasure for me in the work, which prevents all looking ahead or behind. The children blissfully happy with the dogs.'[195] The lady of the house had her hands full preparing for her thirty-ninth birthday and Christmas: 'Shopping for Christmas tree, and then gilding and hanging the decorations, much hilarity with Daniella and Blandine.'[196]

The year, which had been as eventful as it had been strenuous, ended with a visit from Hans Richter and games with the children. One such game involved dropping pieces of molten lead into cold water and predicting the future on the basis of the shapes that emerged. History does not record the shapes of the Wagners' lead figures or how they interpreted them, but their future prospects were far from rosy. The deficit on the first Festival seemed to be a crippling burden, while more and more new bills were arriving that Feustel was unable to pay.

What should, and could, be done? Wagner seemed to lose all hope and for a time even thought of selling up completely. It was Feustel and the latter's thirty-one-year-old son-in-law, Adolf von Groß, a lawyer who later became Cosima's closest colleague, who kept their nerve and counselled calm. Feustel managed to persuade Ludwig's secretary, Lorenz von Düfflipp, to pay a visit to Bayreuth, but when the privy councillor arrived in the town on 21 January 1877, he had nothing to offer apart from friendly words for Wagner and a handful of civilities for Cosima. He admitted quite openly that he had no idea what His Majesty thought about the Festival or whether he wanted it to continue. But at least it was now clear that the king could no longer be counted on and that new sources of funding would have to be found. In February, Wagner received an invitation to conduct a series of concerts in London's Royal Albert Hall, which had been opened in 1871. The organizers promised a generous fee, and so Wagner was persuaded to accept the offer. Leaving their children behind, the Wagners left Bayreuth at six in the morning on 30 April 1877 and travelled via Ostend and Dover. In London, which the couple enjoyed as a city, Wagner conducted eight concerts between 7 and 29 May, dividing the duties between himself and Hans Richter. On 17 May he was accorded the signal honour of being invited to an audience with Queen Victoria and her youngest son, Prince Leopold, at Windsor Castle, but the queen, who had reigned since 1837, and the composer had little to say to each other. She did not attend any of his concerts, and so the conversation was limited to an exchange of polite banalities. Three years later, Wagner's frustration found expression in a tirade against the queen, whom he dismissed as a 'silly old frump for not abdicating, for she thereby condemns the Prince of W[ales] to an absurd life; in earlier times, he says, sons became their mothers' guardians once they came of age'.[197]

Wagner's London concerts proved an artistic success with their audiences, but the financial results fell short of expectations. The organizers had seriously miscalculated and for a time they even teetered on the brink of bankruptcy, so that the Wagners returned home on 4 June with only 700 pounds – a tenth of the Bayreuth deficit – in their pockets. By the following day they were in Bad Ems, where they were reunited with their children. Wagner spent the next four weeks in the resort, taking the waters in an attempt to recover from the exertions of the last few months. The Wagners then paid flying visits to Heidelberg, Mannheim, Lucerne, Munich, Eisenach and Weimar, where they spent some time with Liszt, before returning to Bayreuth in early August.

Wagner immediately threw himself into his work and made a start on the score of his final music drama, *Parsifal*. By 2 August, Cosima was already claiming to hear musical excerpts wafting down from Wagner's study. A week later he composed the melody of the Last Supper motif and on 26 September played through the whole of the first-act prelude from his initial orchestral draft. He made good work on the score during the following twelve months, completing the second act on 30 September 1878 and beginning the third act exactly a month later. On Christmas Day 1878 he marked Cosima's birthday in a very special way:

> Early in the morning I hear some rustling and think to myself that preparations are being made for the evening, since R. has promised me a party this evening, and last night they had to clear the presents away. Then Siegfried comes skipping into the room and says softly, 'Mama, Papa wants you to know that the Robber is playing something from *Parsifal*,' and then – the prelude begins, really begins, and is played to the end, while my heart reels in bliss!

The 'Robber' was none other than the famous Meiningen Court Orchestra, which Wagner had invited to Bayreuth and with which he had rehearsed the prelude in secret. After the run-through in the morning, there was a full-scale concert in the evening, when, under Wagner's direction, the Meiningen Orchestra played works by Beethoven and the *Siegfried Idyll* and repeated the *Parsifal* prelude. As Cosima wrote afterwards: 'There stands he who called forth these wonders, and he loves me. He loves me!'[198]

When Cosima returned home from a lunchtime visit on 25 April 1879, 'R. greets me with the news that *Parsifal* is finished, he has been working very strenuously!'[199] But Wagner did not want to raise people's hopes unduly and in mid-July announced that it would be 1881 at the earliest before the work could be performed. There were good reasons for this delay: he still had to orchestrate the draft, a task he began in August 1879 and finally completed on

13 January 1882. It was Cosima whom he had to thank for the fact that he was able to consider holding another festival at all. In January 1878 she had negotiated an interest-bearing loan of 100,000 marks from King Ludwig, thereby ensuring the Festival's future. The present credit, together with the one from 1874, was finally paid off by Wagner's heirs in 1906.

Although the future now looked more optimistic, Wagner's state of health worsened markedly during the second half of 1879, a decline reflected in the pages of Cosima's diary. Her husband was often bad-tempered, he complained about bouts of depression and additionally suffered from nightmares. But he was also increasingly plagued by physical ailments. Wagner and medicine is a chapter unto itself, a chapter than can now be reconstructed in only speculative, fragmentary form.[200] Medical diagnosis was still in its infancy at this date and effective therapies were often lacking, so that doctors were left with little alternative but to prescribe general remedies such as diet, rest or massage. Many doctors, moreover, held views that were coloured by mysticism or natural philosophy. Not until the second half of the nineteenth century did medicine acquire a solid scientific basis thanks to the work of the internationally renowned German pathologist and politician Rudolf Virchow. From all that we now know, it seems that Wagner had a lifelong allergy to certain woollen fabrics, hence his predilection for satin and silk. He was also afflicted by recurrent bouts of erysipelas, an inflammation of the skin caused by a streptococcus. There is additionally evidence of a chronic gastro-intestinal complaint that found expression in stomach ache, digestive disorders and flatulence, while his final years were marked by coronary insufficiency, an illness that meant that his heart was no longer able to provide the tissue with sufficient blood and, hence, enough oxygen.

Wagner's health fluctuated almost from one day to the next. In early November 1879 he had another attack of painful erysipelas, for which his local doctor, Carl Landgraf, prescribed inhalations of hibiscus, which initially seemed to help and brought some relief, only for Wagner to suffer a relapse on 5 December: 'R. wakes up in great concern,' Cosima noted in her diary. 'His nose is again swollen; he uses the steam bath, but it continues to swell, and it soon becomes evident that it is erysipelas!'[201] Wagner's poor state of health and the appalling autumn weather persuaded the Wagners to spend the greater part of the following year in Italy, and so they set off with all their belongings on New Year's Eve, spending the evening with friends at the Marienbad Hotel in Munich, before continuing their journey to Naples, where they arrived on 4 January and rented a luxury villa with a view of the famous bay. But however attractive his new surroundings, Wagner's health showed little sign of improving. He had only just arrived in the city when he caught a cold, so that, as Cosima wrote to Adolf von Groß, 'he feels increasingly unwell and today (Wednesday) he is in bed with erysipelas'.[202] A number of new acquaintances provided a welcome change for Wagner during this period. In mid-January the Wagners were introduced to the Russian painter Paul von Joukowsky, who had been an intimate of the American writer Henry James since 1875. The thirty-five-year-old Joukowsky invited James to meet Wagner, but James shied away from the encounter. The relationship between writer and painter was in fact already strained by this date, and so when James returned to England, Joukowsky threw in his lot with Wagner, who, undeterred by his homosexuality, was sufficiently impressed by his art to invite him to design the sets and costumes for *Parsifal*.

In early August, the Wagners decided to leave the Amalfi coast and travel to Siena, although the children had to remain behind in Naples with their governess and could not join their parents until later. Cosima's diary entry for Sunday 8 August reads: 'Breakfast at 12, after which we say goodbye to the children. In what circumstances shall we see one another again? Lusch, Boni, Eva in tears, Loldi and Fidi composed.'[203] The parents left by train, travelling via Pistoia and Florence and then spending a few days in the small Umbrian town of Perugia. Cosima found it difficult to be separated from her children and wrote to them every day. Her dependants, by contrast, were less reliable as correspondents. 'But, children,' Cosima complained to Isolde, 'I've received no letters, only two telegrams.' She went on to draw up a tally of letters sent and received as a way of encouraging her children to do better: 'Letters 5, postcards 3, telegrams 5, in other words 13 missives, whereas I've received only 2 telegrams from you!'[204] On 21 August the Wagners moved on to Siena, and it was here, on the twenty-third, that they were finally reunited with their children. They took out a lease on the Villa Fiorentina, where Pope Pius IV is said to have slept. The luxury estate was entirely to Wagner's liking. His bed was so large that one morning he told Cosima: 'In this bed there could have slept not only a pope, but the whole schism as well!'[205] But this stay, too, proved short-lived, and on 4 October the family moved on to Venice, where they remained until the end of the month. Their next port of call was Munich, where they stayed another two weeks. Here they met the painter Franz von Lenbach and attended one of his famous studio parties and were introduced to the writer Wilhelm Busch. On 12 November, following an afternoon rehearsal at the Court Theatre, Wagner conducted the *Parsifal* prelude for

King Ludwig. No sooner had the final notes died away than Ludwig demanded a repeat. Wagner duly obliged. But when the king then asked to hear the *Lohengrin* prelude by way of a comparison, the piqued composer handed over his baton to the court kapellmeister, Hermann Levi, and flounced out of the orchestra pit. This was his last encounter with Ludwig: the two men were never to see one another again.

On his return to Bayreuth, Wagner resumed work on the score of *Parsifal*. And as if in an attempt to put pressure on himself, he announced on 1 December 1880 that the next Bayreuth Festival would be held in 1882. Now there was no going back. And once again Wagner found that he needed help. In early January 1881 the twenty-six-year-old Engelbert Humperdinck arrived in Bayreuth to work as his musical assistant, and the months that followed witnessed a regular race to the finish between the composer and his copyist. The question as to who was to conduct the first performance of the new work was soon settled: it would be the forty-one-year-old Hermann Levi, who had been court kapellmeister in Munich since 1872 and who was by no means unknown to Wagner. The two men had got to know one another in the run-up to the 1876 *Ring* cycles and felt a mutual respect. During the intervening years Levi had repeatedly been acclaimed for his outstanding Wagner performances, so that there could be no doubt about his musical qualifications. In spite of this, Levi was hardly Wagner's dream candidate to unveil his final music drama. The composer's objections centred around his conductor's Jewish faith. How could the son of a rabbi from Gießen conduct so Christian a work? For a long time the very idea was intolerable, and yet in the end Wagner had no choice but to accept Levi after Ludwig agreed in October 1880 that he could have the use of his Munich orchestra and chorus for his 1882 Festival only on the condition that Levi was a part of the deal.

Far from sympathizing with Wagner's racist outlook, Ludwig supported Jewish emancipation. In October 1881, for example, we find him lecturing his favourite composer: 'That my beloved friend draws no distinction between Christians and Jews in performing his great and hallowed work is all to the good; nothing is more repellent and unedifying than such arguments; people are basically all brothers, in spite of their denominational differences.'[206] It was clear, then, that if Wagner were to accept Ludwig's generous offer, he could not avoid using Levi. And so it was that in January 1881 Levi was completely dumbfounded to discover that he was to be the first conductor of *Parsifal*.

Among Wagner's less attractive qualities was his insistence on repeatedly tormenting his new in-house conductor with anti-Semitic barbs. In late June

1881, when Levi was in Bayreuth to discuss preparations for the 1882 Festival, Wagner received a muddle-headed letter demanding that *Parsifal* should not be conducted by a Jew. The anonymous writer went on to accuse Levi of having an affair with Cosima. So nonsensical was this assertion that, as Cosima later recalled, the letter caused 'great mirth' in Wahnfried. But instead of simply tearing up and destroying the offending missive, Wagner waved it in front of the sensitive Levi's eyes: 'When the letter is shown to the poor conductor, he cannot master his feelings, it seems that such instances of baseness are new to him!'[207] Levi felt humiliated and the very next day left for Bamberg, from where he wrote to the composer, asking to be relieved of his duties. Wagner reacted with a charm offensive: 'For God's sake, come back at once and get to know us properly! Don't lose faith but take new heart. Perhaps this will be a great turning point in your life – but at all events, you are my *Parsifal* conductor!'[208] These lines were enough to persuade Levi to return, and by 2 July he was back in Bayreuth. As Cosima noted in her diary, 'At 1 o'clock return of our poor friend Levi as a result of R.'s splendid reply to his letter. Very relaxed, indeed even very cheerful mood at lunch. R. calls for *Hebrew* wine!' Once again Wagner could not resist the urge to indulge in anti-Jewish barbs: 'He indicates to Levi that he has been thinking of having him baptized and of accompanying him to Holy Communion.'[209] Levi was to attempt to flee from Wagner's influence on a number of subsequent occasions.

Mephisto Waltz

During the second half of 1881 Wagner began to complain increasingly about 'chest spasms', a condition that would now be diagnosed as angina but which was unrecognized at the time. Landgraf attributed the attacks either to a chill or to rheumatism, while the Master's health continued to deteriorate, a situation that suddenly grew much worse in late September, when Liszt arrived in Bayreuth for a two-week visit. The two men had known each other for decades, repeatedly drawing closer together, only to drive each other away again. Wagner had no sympathy with Liszt's lifestyle, not least when the gallant Abbé brought with him to Bayreuth a sense of French *savoir vivre* and an array of social customs that Wagner found deeply unattractive. The mere fact that Cosima and her father conversed in French was often enough to darken Wagner's mood to a dangerously sombre level.

On 24 September, Wagner held a formal dinner for his father-in-law, the other guests including Wagner's friends Heinrich Porges and Hans von

Wolzogen, who had been editor of the in-house *Bayreuther Blätter* since 1878 and whom we shall shortly be meeting again. It could have been a wonderful evening – the guests talked and played whist, while Liszt regaled the company with a performance of his masterly and bravura Mephisto Waltz. But the situation got out of hand:

> Then in the evening all sorts of things arise – our manservant drunk, for R. bad luck at cards, which he then abandons, but above all, I fear, the Mephisto Waltz, played by my father, along with a conversation with Porges while the rest of us are playing whist – quite an appalling atmosphere. He flares up, and everyone leaves in some alarm.[210]

Four days later Wagner was still complaining that 'everything, everything is a lie! He feels, for instance, that since my father played the waltz, the innocence of our relationships has vanished.'[211] It is not entirely clear what Wagner meant by this, but we may well be right in assuming that behind his emotional outburst lay common-or-garden jealousy. Yet Wagner's displeasure could just as easily be provoked by his inability 'to persuade my father to stay'.[212] Wagner certainly did not make life easy for his fellow creatures, not least when Cosima found herself caught in the crossfire between her husband and her father.

By October 1881 it was time for a change of scenery: 'We think of distant lands, of Palermo, he reads about it in Baedeker and then goes to his work with a kind of serene joviality.'[213] Once Wagner had completed the second act of *Parsifal*, the family set off from Bayreuth in early November, travelling by train via Munich, Bolzano and Verona to Naples and sailing from there to Palermo, where they took rooms at the Hôtel des Palmes. Here Wagner worked on the third act of *Parsifal* to the brink of physical exhaustion. Meanwhile, Josef Rubinstein, who had accompanied the Wagners to Italy, worked on the vocal score. 'I've nothing to report except that things are going tolerably well for us here beneath the palm trees,' Cosima wrote to Hans Richter on 7 January 1882. 'My husband will soon have completed his score, and Rubinstein is keeping pace with him with the vocal score. It's unclear how long we'll be staying here; the fact that we don't need to light a fire and in all likelihood shan't need to do so is a great blessing for my husband.'[214] A few days later Wagner completed his work on the full score of *Parsifal*. For the publishing rights to the finished work, Schott paid the unprecedented sum of 100,000 marks, approximately 800,000 euros at today's prices. Now Wagner could really begin his vacation. He made a number of new acquaintances, including one with the French painter Auguste Renoir, who asked for – and was granted – permission to paint the composer's portrait. The Wagners also made contact with various members of the Sicilian landed gentry.

It was at around this time that the barely nineteen-year-old Blandine got to know Count Biagio Gravina with whom she evidently soon fell in love. By mid-March the thirty-one-year-old count was already asking for her hand in marriage, a request that apparently left Boni 'very surprised'.[215] The Gravinas' family background and financial circumstances seem to have been not a little confused, so that Cosima was unsure of herself, but on the whole the count appeared to be a good match, and after a certain amount of hesitation his offer of marriage was accepted. The marriage was planned for that summer in Bayreuth. Wagner now began to grow bored in Palermo, and when he suffered another series of heart attacks in April the family decided to return home. They arrived back in Bayreuth on 1 May, and Wagner immediately threw himself into the preparations for the world premiere of *Parsifal*. Levi arrived in mid-June and, according to Cosima, stage rehearsals began on 2 July. Levi assumed control of the musical side of the production, Joukowsky was responsible for the sets, and the technical director was Fritz Brandt, replacing his father, Carl, who had died the previous December. But even family members were roped in, as Daniela reported to her father:

> Every other day we invite the singers to lunch in turn, followed by the prin-
> cipal members of the orchestra, and at the end we'll be arranging a great
> banquet for all the scrapers, blowers and singers. We spend the evenings on
> our own; after 7–8 hours' work every day we're all very tired, but never –
> thank God – bad-tempered. And yet there are problems aplenty: the bells,
> the choirs, the awkwardness of the onstage drapery, the heat and remarks by
> various individuals – but what's the point of listing them all?[216]

The curtain rose on the opening performance of *Parsifal* at four o'clock on the afternoon of Wednesday 26 July. The weather failed to oblige. Pouring rain meant that Festival-goers entered the theatre dripping wet, while Wagner took exception to the number of onlookers who lined the route to the theatre. Much else excited his ire:

> The first act goes more or less according to his wishes, it is just the large
> amount of 'play acting' he finds displeasing. When, after the second act,
> there is much noise and calling, R. comes to the balustrade, says that though

the applause is very welcome to his artists and to himself, they had agreed, in order not to impinge on the impression, not to take a bow, so that there would be no 'curtain calls'. After our meal R. and I are together in our box! Great emotion overwhelms us. But at the end R. is vexed by the silent audience, which has misunderstood him; he once again addresses it from the gallery, and when the applause then breaks out and there are continual calls, R. appears in front of the curtain and says that he tried to assemble his artists, but they were by now half undressed.[217]

In spite of this, the world premiere of *Parsifal* was an artistic triumph from start to finish. The world's press, too, responded enthusiastically, and the Festival ended with a handsome surplus of 140,000 marks. Between 26 July and 29 August there was a total of sixteen performances presented to an audience made up of faces both familiar and still unknown. Among those who attended were Franz Liszt, Anton Bruckner, Léo Delibes, Camille Saint-Saëns and Arthur Nikisch, Nietzsche's sister Elisabeth, Mathilde Wesendonck, Judith Gautier, Malwida von Meysenbug, a young theology student by the name of Lou Salomé and the eighteen-year-old Richard Strauss, who had only just left school. Old friends like Carl Tausig and Peter Cornelius were now dead, while others such as Nietzsche stayed away out of disenchantment. Another prominent figure from Wagner's past who was conspicuous by his absence was King Ludwig II, who, pleading illness, remained aloof.

Blandine and Count Gravina were married on 25 August, four days before the end of the Festival. Cosima described the event in her diary: 'At 11.30 the civil marriage ceremony at Wahnfried; around 11 o'clock the town councillors bring Blandine a pretty table centrepiece. The mayor's speech very dignified; at 12.30 lunch, 27 people at table.'[218] The church ceremony took place the following day, after which the couple left on their honeymoon. In the run-up to the nuptials it seems from a letter that Bülow wrote to his daughter that there had been a certain difference of opinion between him and Wahnfried:

What do you mean when you write that 'your plan to come to B[ayreuth] for the wedding seems to present Mama with certain difficulties'? . . . In spite of this I would urge you to let me know the ukase that is being insinuated here, at least to the extent that it is of relevance to me in my relationship (or, rather, non-relationship) with you and Blandine. . . . Be so kind as to clear up this matter for me without delay.[219]

Bülow was not welcome in Bayreuth, even if his sizeable dowry was. As a result, Blandine's wedding took place without her father – not that this prevented Cosima from asking her ex-husband to make a public announcement about the wedding. 'I have not the slightest reason to announce Blandine's wedding,' Bülow wrote, '*ni dans la forme, ni dans le fond*. Blandine's home is her stepfather's, because it is her mother's house. I am equally obliged to postpone a meeting with her and her husband to a later date and a better time, if such a time is at all possible for me!'[220]

Death in Venice

Wagner and his family left Bayreuth on 14 September 1882 and travelled to Venice, where they took a palatial suite of rooms in one of the finest examples of Venetian High Renaissance architecture, the Palazzo Vendramin-Calergi. Not to be confused with the Palazzo Vendramin on the Giudecca, the Palazzo Vendramin-Calergi lies on the Grand Canal and was extended in around 1614 with the addition of an Ala Bianca, a side wing in which Wagner and his entourage rented fifteen or so rooms. In addition to the members of his own family and various servants, accommodation also had to be found for visitors and friends. In the course of the following months, these included Siegfried's teacher Heinrich von Stein, Hermann Levi, Paul von Joukowsky, Josef Rubinstein, Engelbert Humperdinck, the art historian Henry Thode and Blandine and Biagio Gravina, all of whom came to pay their respects. As at Wahnfried, the assembled company ate, made music, read and held long discussions. Liszt arrived on 19 November and remained until the middle of January, a visit that seems to have taxed the sixty-nine-year-old Wagner's physical resources to their limits, leading to repeated outbursts of anger. On one occasion Wagner took exception to the fact that Liszt arrived late for supper and on another he objected to his piano playing. Or else he complained about his father-in-law's alleged lack of a sense of humour and frequently criticized his music. He felt only scorn and contempt for such masterly examples of Liszt's late ascetic style as *La lugubre gondola*. 'Late in the evening, when we are alone, R. talks about my father's latest compositions, which he finds completely meaningless, and he expresses his opinion sharply and in much detail.'[221] Wagner avoided any direct confrontation with Liszt, and so it was Cosima who generally felt the sharp edge of her husband's tongue.

On Christmas Eve Wagner rented the Teatro La Fenice and performed his early Symphony in C major with a local amateur orchestra. He had last conducted the piece half a century earlier. At the end of the concert, the musicians and all of the Wagners' friends who were present drank a toast to Cosima's forty-fifth birthday. 'Then R. murmurs in my father's ear, "Do you love your daughter?" My father looks startled. "Then sit down at the piano and play." My father does so at once, to everybody's cheering delight.'[222]

In early 1883 Wagner began work on his last major project, an essay headed 'On the Feminine in the Human', but he found it difficult to concentrate and was often ill-tempered. Suddenly he took against the Palazzo Vendramin-Calergi and complained about its domestic arrangements, claiming that the family had never had any luck in this regard. The bad weather in the form of driving rain and storms whipped up by the scirocco added to his depression: he seemed to have lost patience with Venice. 'Just think,' Daniela wrote to Adolf von Groß at the end of January, 'we're all looking forward to being back in Bayreuth and to the summer, which we imagine will be glorious. I also think that Papa's daily massages will strengthen and prepare him for all possible exertions.'[223] Hermann Levi arrived in Venice on 4 February. Although he stayed with Joukowsky, he spent most of his time with the Wagners at the Palazzo Vendramin-Calergi. In the evenings, they talked, or Wagner sat at the piano, playing improvisations on the old folksong *Harlequin, You Must Die*. At nine o'clock on the evening of Shrove Tuesday, the family set off for Saint Mark's Square, where they observed the lively comings and goings, admired the colourful masks and watched Prince Carnival being carried to his grave as Ash Wednesday dawned. It was during this period that Wagner and Levi discussed the cast for that summer's revival of *Parsifal*. There has been much speculation that it was on this occasion that the name of a certain Carrie Pringle was mentioned, a soprano who had sung one of the Flowermaidens in the 1882 performances. Wagner, it was rumoured, had been intimate with the twenty-three-year-old singer, and Levi had now been asked to invite her to Venice in order for her to audition for the Master and possibly perform other services besides. Commentators have even speculated that when Cosima found out about the planned visit, she and Wagner had a furious row on the morning of 13 February 1883. Within hours Wagner was dead.

It is an appalling thought that Wagner's fatal heart attack may have been caused by a fit of jealousy on Cosima's part. But this is not the end of the story, for it has also been claimed that shortly afterwards Carrie Pringle wrote to Cosima to apologize for causing the agitation that led to Wagner's death and that decades later Carrie's letter was destroyed by Wahnfried's archivist, Otto

Strobel.[224] The suggestion that a family row may have been to blame for Wagner's death can be traced back in the main to Wagner's doctor in Venice, Friedrich Keppler. Our search for evidence begins in the sumptuous Palazzo Barbarigo della Terrazza, where Keppler and his colleague Professor Paiusco ran a gynaecological clinic during the winter months. Keppler was evidently a society doctor, for in the summer he practised in the fashionable resort of Wildbad in the Black Forest. It is not entirely clear when and under what circumstances Wagner got to know him. He is first mentioned in Cosima's diaries in March 1882 – before the *Parsifal* performances in the July and August of that year – but his name does not occur again until 12 December 1882. The Wagners were evidently reluctant to place their complete trust in Keppler's skills as a physician, not least because his work as a gynaecologist hardly qualified him as an expert on coronary illnesses. Be that as it may, in the wake of the death of his prominent patient Keppler drew up a kind of medical report for the writer Henry Perl (the pen name of Henriette Perl) that was published as a foreword to her book *Richard Wagner in Venice*. Keppler hinted at all manner of 'emotional and psychological excitements' to which Wagner was allegedly exposed during his final months in Venice, before continuing, 'The actual attack that brought the Master's life to such an abrupt end *must* have had a similar cause, but I cannot become involved in speculations of this kind.'[225] This legend has proved exceptionally tenacious, but it has so far been impossible to show that there is any truth to it.[226] Conversely, there is considerable evidence that both supports and refutes these often conflicting assumptions. Let us attempt to disentangle the various strands in the argument.

Carrie Pringle was then living in Milan, where she was presumably continuing to take singing lessons, so that in terms of the actual distance, a visit to Venice is entirely conceivable. But with this we are again entering the realm of speculation, for it is doubtful if Levi would have invited the soprano to Venice. He thought that she had been over-parted the previous summer, and the two of them had clearly not seen eye to eye. Admittedly, the first evidence of this comes in a letter that Levi wrote to Adolf von Groß three weeks after Wagner's death. Whether he informed the composer about his reservations while he was in Venice must remain a matter of conjecture. The conductor is therefore ruled out as a witness, not least because between 9 February and his departure on the twelfth he 'spent most of his time in bed'.[227] Cosima's diary entries for this period are astonishingly vague. On 11 February, for example, she noted that Wagner had thought of all the women he had loved: 'He says, "All my women are now passing before my eyes." '[228] The unsuspecting Daniela added a note: 'One of his dreams during his last two nights was that he received letters from women – one of them Frau Wesendonck, another a woman whom both Papa and Mama had forgotten; he said he did not open these two, but set them on either side of the table, saying to himself, "What if Cosima is jealous?" '229 Was this imaginary second letter from Carrie Pringle? We do not know. But Wagner's dreams certainly suggest that petty jealousies hung in the air in Venice. Cosima hints as much in a previously unpublished letter to Heinrich von Stein: on 12 February – the eve of Wagner's death – she wrote: 'I should add that your letter did me a lot of good in my depressed and agitated mood.'230

But what happened in the Palazzo Vendramin-Calergi on 13 February 1883? The then twenty-two-year-old Daniela von Bülow summed up her recollections of that day in a kind of diary, a document that allows us to reconstruct much of the drama on the day of Wagner's death: 'On getting up, he said to Mama, "I must be careful today". He then had breakfast with her as usual, but that was the last time we saw him alive that day.' After breakfast, Cosima sent Daniela into town on various errands. When she returned to the palazzo at one, she found her mother completely distraught, sitting in the salon and playing Schubert's *Lob der Thränen* on the piano. It is unclear why she chose this singularly depressing song, a setting of a text by August Wilhelm Schlegel that dates from 1818, one of the most critical years in Schubert's life. It is by no means impossible that the mysterious row between Cosima and her husband took place during this period when Daniela was out of the building.

Wagner did not appear for lunch, to which Paul von Joukowsky had been invited. He told his servant Georg that he was not feeling well and so he remained at his desk in his study. One of his maids, Betty Bürkel, was positioned in the adjoining bedroom as a precaution. Suddenly she heard a violent groan: 'When B[etty] rushed in, he was in such pain that he was barely able to speak, but called out: "My wife and the doctor." ' Wagner had suffered a serious heart attack. Cosima rushed in, and Georg hastily undressed his master so that if necessary he could use the lavatory. Wagner's chest spasms continued to grow worse. Cosima handed him a medicine that had previously helped to alleviate his convulsions, but on this occasion it failed to work. With Georg's help Wagner was moved to the banquette in his dressing room, while Cosima held his head. When the servant inadvertently dropped Wagner's expensive watch while gathering up his scattered clothes, Wagner cried out: 'My watch.' They were his final words. Cosima kissed the dying man. In Daniela's words, 'With her kiss she received his final breath.'

By the time that Keppler arrived at the palazzo, he could do no more than confirm that Wagner had died at around three in the afternoon. What followed was a bizarre lament of positively Middle Eastern proportions. The body was laid out on a couch, where a kneeling Cosima clutched its knees. After more than an hour had passed, she allowed the children to file into the room, one at a time – first Siegfried, then Isolde, Daniela and finally Eva. 'She told me', Daniela recalled, 'that we could decide to do with her whatever we wanted, she would agree with all her heart, we shouldn't express the pain we all felt but should stick to the order of the day, she didn't want to see anyone apart from us, we were now her masters, her dear masters.' By the late evening, she was still lying at the foot of the couch. When Daniela begged her to go and lie down, Cosima retorted: 'If you want me to go to bed, I'll do so, but you must lay him next to me.' Inconceivable though it may seem to us now, the dead Wagner was carried to his bed by Georg and Joukowsky, after which Isolde and Daniela undressed their mother. Completely distraught, the two sisters had to stand by while Cosima 'bent over him fervently and at length, holding his head in her hands and bidding him good night'. Outside a storm of hurricane-like violence raged and torrential rain beat down, while Cosima nestled up to the corpse and rested her head on her late husband's shoulders. And so she remained all night.

The next morning Cosima still refused to abandon Wagner's deathbed. 'In response to my tearful request', wrote Daniela, 'she took two spoonfuls of broth, but would not move from Papa's side.' The body had in the meantime begun to decompose, the lips were colourless and the skin a greyish colour. The children kept coming into the room to ask their mother to leave, but in vain. To make matters worse, the sculptor Augusto Benvenuti had arrived and was waiting impatiently to take Wagner's death mask. Not until the afternoon of the fourteenth – a good twenty-four hours after Wagner's death – did Cosima finally let go of the body. Keppler literally had to prise her away from it. He then promised to call her as soon as he had begun to wash and embalm the body, after which he carried her to Daniela's bed. 'Mama was very quiet that evening.' Daniela recalled. 'Whenever we went in to see her, she would smile at us in an eerie manner and say a few tender words – she seemed only to be longing with feverish calm for daylight to come and for the moment when she could be reunited with the body.'

Adolf von Groß and his wife, Marie, arrived in Venice the next morning, the fifteenth. There was chaos inside the palazzo, the dead composer, his grief-stricken widow and four utterly confused children presenting a picture of absolute horror. He set about restoring some semblance of order to the proceedings and on Cosima's instructions ordered a coffin with a glass lid from Vienna, at the same time making arrangements for the body to be taken back to Bayreuth. During the afternoon, Keppler and Joukowsky secretly started work on preserving the body. Meanwhile Cosima asked her daughters to cut off all her hair, and Daniela, Isolde and Eva did as they were bidden, sewing the hair into a velvet cushion. Hans Richter now arrived from Vienna in order to assist the family in whatever ways he could. Liszt, too, planned to travel to Venice, but Cosima vehemently opposed the idea, so keen was she not to see her father. Keppler finished embalming the body that evening. The chemicals that he used were highly toxic, and so Cosima was able to sit with her dead husband for only a few minutes. She placed the velvet cushion containing her hair on his breast and knelt at his feet. Keppler then asked her to leave, but without success. Another six minutes passed, during which Cosima remained at Wagner's side, and it was only when Adolf von Groß insisted that she agreed to follow him into another room. To be on the safe side, Keppler locked both the main doors to the room but overlooked a third door, through which Cosima slipped back to the body. There was consider-able agitation when the children discovered that Cosima was no longer in her room, and it took them a while to find her back in the room with her husband's dead body.

The family returned to Bayreuth via Innsbruck and Kufstein on Friday 16 February. Journalists joined the train at each of its intermediary stops, and countless grieving onlookers left wreaths and flowers. The cortège reached Munich on the afternoon of 17 February. After a short break, during which an orchestra played part of Beethoven's 'Eroica' Symphony, the train continued its journey north. 'We could still hear the first trumpet call from Siegfried's Funeral March,' Daniela recalled.[231] The journey ended in Bayreuth shortly before midnight. The coffin remained at the station all night, with a guard of honour provided by local townspeople. The official service took place the next day on the station forecourt. Bayreuth was in mourning. Black flags hung from most of the houses, and the church bells tolled the death knell. Felix Mottl watched as the cortège passed: 'With tears in our eyes we followed the procession as it made its way to Wahnfried.'[232] Alongside old friends such as Heinrich von Stein, Hermann Levi and Hans von Wolzogen, others who had come to pay their last respects were representatives of King Ludwig of Bavaria, Grand Duke Carl Alexander of Saxe-Weimar and Duke Georg II of Meiningen.

But Cosima refused to see any of them. The burial took place late on the Sunday afternoon in the presence of only Wagner's immediate family and his most intimate friends. Accompanied by Wagner's dogs, the coffin was carried from the garden gate to the back of the villa by Adolf von Groß, Hermann Levi, Hans Richter, Hans von Wolzogen and others. Following the blessing, from which Cosima likewise absented herself, the mourners dispersed. Only then did she approach the open grave. 'Mama climbed down into it,' Daniela recalled, 'and for a long time lay on the coffin until Fidi went to fetch her and we brought her back inside. She then lay down, while we ourselves returned to our friends – and to our lives.'[233]

4

The First Lady of Bayreuth

(1883–1900)

Trials and Tribulations

In the days after Wagner was buried, Cosima was almost literally paralysed by grief. Now forty-five years old, she had spent only a relatively short period of her life with Wagner, and yet her initial reaction to his death was to regard it as the end of her own existence: life without Wagner seemed inconceivable to her. She refused to see people, spurned the food that was set before her and rejected all offers of medical help, with the result that friends of the house feared, not without good reason, that she was placing her own life at risk. 'I was once told by Wagner', Ludwig II wrote in some concern to his private secretary, Ludwig von Bürkel, on the night of 19/20 February 1883, 'that His wife would die a week after Him or at least that she would want to do so; I beg you to find some way of preventing this misfortune.'[1]

With hindsight we may question the extent to which Wagner's gloomy prophecy should be taken seriously, but Cosima's family and friends certainly believed that she was capable of suicide and were understandably afraid. Only at the end of that first week did they heave a sigh of relief when the deadline indicated by Wagner was safely past. 'I am writing to you today with a tremendous sense of relief,' Paul von Joukowsky told Malwida von Meysenbug on 22 February, 'because since yesterday we believe that we may hope that their mother has been saved for her children.' In spite of this, Joukowsky was convinced that he would never see Cosima again: 'She will remain in the upper rooms of the house, living entirely for his memory and for their children; all other life has ceased for her.' Cosima, he went on, striking a clairvoyant note, would 'eke out an existence uniquely suited to her nature, that of a nun who remains a heavenly, hourly comfort to her children'.[2]

Joukowsky's powers of prophecy were clearly considerable, for his comparison of Cosima to a nun certainly pointed the way ahead. During the years
that followed, she brought together the divisive band of Wagnerians and
turned it into a cohesive, quasi-religious congregation of Bayreuthians sharing
a common philosophical outlook. Cultivating a mixture of otherworldliness,
selfless piety and servile humility, she slipped into the role of the abbess of a
religious community, her true self gradually disappearing behind the image of
the 'Master's wife' who desired only to carry out what she claimed were
Wagner's last wishes. In promoting this stylized image of herself, she did not
shy away from even the most drastic measures, and Wagner had been in the
ground for only two weeks when she asked Daniela to write to Lilli Lehmann:
'I do not know if you have any letters in Mama's hand – but if this is the case,
you would be doing our mother a great favour by responding to her urgent
and oft-repeated entreaty to destroy everything in her hand.'[3] The soprano
had absolutely no intention of incinerating Cosima's letters, and they are now
among Lehmann's unpublished papers in Berlin. Malwida von Meysenbug
was another correspondent who declined Daniela's request, albeit with the
promise that 'on my death no misuse will be made of these letters, which I
have in my own safe keeping'.[4] Cosima can hardly have been afraid that these
letters would reveal embarrassing details about her past as they are far too
innocuous for that. Rather, she was keen to destroy all trace of an existence
independent of Wagner's: nothing was to remind the world of Cosima Wagner
as a person. In this way she sought to identify herself completely with
Wagner's life and works, so that it seemed as if the Master lived on in his
widow. Thus began the bizarre cult of Wagner that was to characterize the
ensuing decades.

Meanwhile, there was plenty going on behind Wahnfried's façade of
mourning during that crisis year of 1883 as alarming news arrived in the villa
from a variety of different quarters. An initial source of annoyance came from
Friedrich Keppler, whose attitude to his Hippocratic oath of silence was
nothing if not cavalier. He had taken it upon himself to feed the baying pack
of journalists with titbits of information gleaned from his visit to the Palazzo
Vendramin-Calergi on 13 February. During the weeks after Wagner's death
the papers were filled with sentimentalized accounts of the events in question
based on information that could have come only from Keppler. Whatever the
garrulous doctor may have known, it was enough to trigger the alarm bells in
Wahnfried, prompting Adolf von Groß, who already had his hands full
sorting out the chaos, to write a strongly worded letter:

A few days ago we read in all the newspapers what you find in the enclosed cutting. We hope that you will place me in a position of being able to deny this. Frau Wagner and the children ask that nothing be published along these lines. If you have written down your observations, I would ask you to send them to me in a sealed envelope. As the children's guardian, I shall hand over what has been entrusted to me to Siegfried when he comes of age.[5]

It remains unclear what indiscretion Keppler had committed, but Groß may have been referring to the medical bulletin drawn up for Henriette – Henry – Perl. Whatever the answer, Keppler was from now on *persona non grata* in Bayreuth, his reputation rubbished in Wahnfried's time-honoured tradition. The Festival's chorus master, Julius Kniese, for example, even complained that 'Wagner would still be alive today if he had not fallen victim to an acknowledged charlatan, Dr Keppler, in Venice'.[6] The way in which Keppler was treated suggests he had struck a raw nerve.

Keppler's lack of tact was undoubtedly tiresome, but a more pressing concern was the need to find a solution to a number of complex legal problems. At the time of his death, Wagner's finances had been in a bad way. He had left neither a will nor instructions on the future running of the Bayreuth Festival. As a result there was now a power vacuum, but it did not take Cosima long to realize that she needed to seize the initiative if she was to save the Festival. But who could inherit it? It was her administrator, Adolf von Groß, who dealt with this awkward question with foresight and sensitivity. At first sight the legal situation seemed exceptionally complicated. There was no question that, as Wagner's widow, Cosima was entitled to inherit. But what about the five children? Under one of the basic tenets of German law, 'pater est, quem nuptiae demonstrant'. In other words, in the eyes of the law the children of a married woman have only one father: the woman's husband. Daniela and Blandine were Bülow's children not only by birth but also by law; Isolde and Eva, although undoubtedly Wagner's children, had both been born while Cosima was still married to Bülow, and since Wagner had never acknowledged them as his own, they too were regarded as Bülow's. To add to the confusion, Isolde bore Bülow's name, whereas Eva described herself as a Wagner. Only in the case of Siegfried had Wagner claimed to be the child's father. He was legitimized in the wake of his parents' marriage in August 1870. All in all, then, only Wagner's widow and son were entitled to inherit his estate. No further clarification was necessary, and yet Cosima still sent Groß to see Bülow in Meiningen in order 'to torment him with the idea of changing his will', as Bülow's widow, Marie, recalled several decades later.[7]

Cosima wanted to play safe. In response to his ex-wife's urgent entreaty, Bülow made a formal declaration on 9 March 1883: 'I acknowledge that Siegfried, who was born on 6 June 1869 during the divorce proceedings between me and Frau Cosima née Liszt, later the wife of Herr Richard Wagner, is not my son.'[8] It was a clever move on Cosima's part, because it allowed her to establish the dynastic principle whereby the Master's widow stood at the head of the family and passed on the sceptre of power to the natural successor, the Master's son. This marked the start of a regular cult of the then thirteen-year-old Siegfried. 'You must now live for Siegfried,' Cosima urged her daughter Daniela. 'May all your thoughts be directed to this.' And again: 'Look after Siegfried; this is all that I ask of you; let your first thought on waking be for him, your first action of the day, your finest care.'[9] All four daughters were later lavishly provided for from the ever-increasing royalties, and yet Cosima's actions resembled nothing so much as a means by which to disinherit Isolde and Eva. Some thirty years later this circumstance was to play an important role in the Beidler affair.

One thing is certain, however: within weeks of Wagner's death, Cosima had decided to ensure that the Bayreuth Festival remained within the family. In this she was supported by friends of Wahnfried. 'Who could initiate Siegfried into so glorious a task in life as well as she can?' trilled Malwida von Meysenbug. 'Who could continue the work of Bayreuth in as true a spirit as she can, at least until such time as Siegfried can take it over?'[10] For 1883, twelve performances of *Parsifal* were scheduled, the plans having been drawn up by Wagner himself. As in 1882, the conductors were Hermann Levi and Franz Fischer, and the musical assistants were Julius Kniese and Heinrich Porges. All four men were familiar with every last detail of the composer's ideas for the work. There was everything to be said, therefore, for leaving Wagner's plans unaltered, and it was in this spirit that the rehearsals began in early July 1883. 'All the familiar preparations and excitements are already in full swing,' Daniela wrote to Malwida von Meysenbug in late June, 'but we are avoiding them and continuing to lead our quiet, solitary lives.'[11]

Cosima, too, continued to live the life of a total recluse in Wahnfried, and even Levi was unable to speak to her in person. 'Leave me the grave and my grief,' she is said to have told Adolf von Groß. 'His friends may assume the task of disseminating his fame, my husband thought along these lines, it is all the same to me.'[12] One is bound to ask if Wagner really said this. It certainly seems unlikely, because to judge from all that we know, he had no great regard for 'friends' such as Hans von Wolzogen, the editor in chief of the in-house *Bayreuther Blätter*. An entry in Cosima's diary of 9 February 1883 reads:

In the evening R. talks about his supporters – how they seem to be designed to make all the ideas he expresses look ridiculous. (He excepts Stein.) He tells Jouk. that he never expected the *Blätter* to last more than two years; he is considering what is to become of Wolz. And finally he loudly regrets having built Wahnfried, the festivals also seem to him absurd![13]

As the future was to demonstrate, Wagner's misgivings about his 'supporters' were to prove entirely justified. Many felt called, but few were chosen. Following the composer's death, those supporters showed their true colours as militant activists, with men like Wolzogen and Kniese attempting to 'rescue' the Festival by pursuing policies of their own. In early March 1883, for example, Wolzogen called on the directors of all the German theatres to mount benefit performances, the proceeds of which would accrue to the Bayreuth Festival. The response was modest, to say the least. The managers in question had plenty of words of encouragement, but Bayreuth's coffers remained worryingly depleted. Botho von Hülsen, the all-powerful general manager of all the royal theatres in Berlin, turned down the request out of hand. For decades the former soldier had resisted Wagner's works. Why should he now encourage them? Indeed, it seems more than likely that Wolzogen's naïve approach brought a smile to his lips. Outside Bayreuth, the editor in chief of the *Bayreuther Blätter* was regarded as a simpleton and nowhere taken seriously. The fact that not even Wagner himself thought the *Bayreuther Blätter* had a future surely speaks for itself.

The thirty-four-year-old Julius Kniese likewise felt called upon to save Bayreuth and to that end developed the boldest of plans: Liszt was to become the Festival's music director, while Bülow was to be appointed its principal conductor. The idea was simply grotesque. At the age of seventy-one, Liszt could have been no more than an interim appointment, while no one could seriously envisage Bülow in any kind of working relationship with Wahnfried. It comes as no surprise, therefore, to learn that both musicians politely declined the invitation. Kniese was a rabid anti-Semite, his main concern being to sideline Hermann Levi, for Munich's star conductor had committed a grievous error by failing to recognize the genius of his musical assistant. The emotions that were vented here were the envy of the loser and the wounded vanity of the mediocrity. Kniese's letters to his wife, Olga, are full of anti-Semitic tirades and base attacks: 'Levi often spends time with Wagner's children, playing the enthusiast and the self-sacrificial lamb, occasionally howling sentimentally and, in short, using all the means at his disposal to ensnare the girls, who have little understanding of human nature, and to enlist them for his own private interests.'[14] Elsewhere Kniese complains about Levi's 'pernicious Jewish influence', claiming that he is coarse, has the voice of a cattle-driver 'and stands before *Parsifal* as before something completely incomprehensible to him'.[15] But even if Kniese's hate campaign found a receptive audience with the Wagners, there could be no thought of dispensing with Levi's services: they needed him too much for that.

All in all, the standard of the 1883 performances fell short of the previous year's. There were also the individual problems and arguments mentioned earlier, so that to the outside world the Festival gave the impression of chaotic disorganization. At all events, it is striking that Cosima clearly played no part in the various deliberations on the Festival's future. No one thought that she would ever return to public life, still less that she would assume a leading role in running Bayreuth. But they were soon to be proven mistaken. True, she remained largely invisible during the summer of 1883, conveying messages to others via her children or Adolf von Groß, but all the time she was working away in the background, planning to take over the running of Bayreuth. 'Frau Wagner wants the Festival next year,' an incredulous Julius Kniese wrote to his wife, Olga, on 25 July.[16]

But Cosima did not stop there, for by the autumn of 1883 she was already drawing up plans for the Festival from 1884 to 1889 and providing a detailed account of the way in which she envisaged preserving Wagner's legacy for posterity. During the first year there would be only a revival of *Parsifal*, but from 1885 she hoped that other works would be staged in parallel with it: *Tristan und Isolde* in 1885, *Der fliegende Holländer* in 1886, *Lohengrin* in 1887, *Tannhäuser* in 1888 and *Die Meistersinger von Nürnberg* and the *Ring* in 1889. Although this plan was to be repeatedly revised, it was already sufficiently developed for Cosima to draw up provisional cast lists: 'The same team of singers – for Elisabeth, Elsa and Eva a virginal figure such as Fräulein Belce.'[17] For the present, however, Cosima operated in secret, a secrecy for which there were good reasons. In the first place, there was the lack of any legitimacy: Wagner had left no instructions conferring on Cosima the running of the Festival. Quite the opposite: in September 1882 he had written to Hans von Wolzogen, 'I am now seventy and cannot think of a single person who could say what I believe needs to be said to anyone involved in such a performance, be it the singers, the conductor, the director, the machinist, the set designer or the costume designer. Indeed, I barely know of anyone who would agree with me on judging what can be said to work and what does not work – there is practically no one on whose judgement I could rely.'[18] Presumably Wagner's wife was included in these strictures.

Cosima had a considerable knowledge of music. Of that there can be no doubt. But she had never appeared onstage as a performer and as a result she was not regarded as a professional. What was it, then, that marked out Wagner's forty-five-year-old widow as someone capable of taking up her husband's rightful inheritance? Her sole claim to legitimacy consisted in the fact that she had been married to Wagner, so that from now on her status as Wagner's widow was invested with a powerful emotional force, the love and respect that others felt for the dead composer now being projected on to her. By 1884 Cosima was ready to take a more active role in the practicalities of running the Festival. In spite of the devotion shown by Levi and other artists, she was no doubt aware that she was walking a tightrope. How would her intervention be interpreted? Would the artists accept her criticisms? Her whole approach was extremely clever: she made herself unassailable by remaining invisible within a black-curtained booth at the side of the stage. There she sat with a copy of the score, observing the proceedings through small slits in the walls of the booth. She said nothing, and no one was allowed to speak to her directly; her corrections, suggestions and instructions were written on scraps of paper passed on to the artists by her zealous assistants. One such note read: 'Perhaps it would not be taken amiss if you were asked yet again to ensure that tempi and themes are set forth more clearly from the outset.' On another occasion she complained about the Grail bells, 'which unfortunately are always feeble'. But she was also capable of praising the performers: 'The prelude went very well.'[19]

Cosima was effectively performing a play within a play, so that the whole set-up had a sense of mystery about it. Her booth resembled nothing so much as a confessional, while she herself acquired all the characteristics of a high priestess, praising, criticizing and pointing the way ahead. 'The fact that the performances this year were so perfect is due in no small way to the active intervention of Frau Wagner,' Hermann Levi wrote to his father, adding that 'after each performance, the director, Herr Fuchs, and I received detailed written criticisms, and her remarks were so pertinent and so perceptive and contained so much important information about the art of performing the work that in the space of these few days I learnt more than in twenty years of working as a conductor.'[20] This was certainly an extraordinary claim to make, but it affords impressive proof of the extent to which Cosima's plan was working. Henceforth people spoke in hushed, reverential tones of 'the task of saving Bayreuth', by which they meant Cosima's histrionic performance.

Cosima was able to win over her artists to her cause, but the same was not true of the Wagnerians who made up the Wagner Societies up and down the country. The first of these societies had been established in cities such as Mannheim, Leipzig, Munich, Dresden, Mainz, Berlin and Cologne in the years after 1871 with the aim of collecting money for the Bayreuth Festival, and it was they who now proved a source of considerable annoyance, leading to a dangerous trial of strength in July 1884, when the general assembly of the umbrella organization voted to set up an International Wagner Foundation. The Wagner Society felt that it had lost out under this new arrangement and demanded the right to vote on artistic and financial matters, while also agitating for a 'stylistically pure presentation of original German musical and musico-dramatic works of other composers too'.[21] Both demands were regarded as an open affront by Wahnfried, an attitude which the family felt able to adopt by appealing to Wagner's manifest rejection of the whole nature of the Society. More important, however, was an objection that they were unwilling to articulate in so many words: the Society's right to have a say in the matter would have undermined the family's power base. As they saw it, the individual societies were merely minions enacting orders transmitted from the headquarters in Wahnfried. Cosima preferred not to react in person to the resolution. 'Wahnfried itself found the draft profoundly embarrassing,' Adolf von Groß complained to Wagner's official biographer, Carl Friedrich Glasenapp. 'In consultation with Wahnfried, it should be possible for someone in Munich to express the request that the draft be withdrawn, relieving us of the need to provide a response to it.'[22]

There could hardly have been a clearer expression of Wahnfried's conviction that the various Wagner Societies did not operate on the same level as Wagner's heirs. As a result, this particular experiment ended ingloriously for the Universal Wagner Society: following an extraordinary general meeting in April 1885 there was talk only of continuing the Bayreuth Festival. Cosima had had her way and impressed upon the outside world the legitimacy of her claims to run the Festival. Although there was no festival in 1885, she took the opportunity to issue a circular in which she officially described herself as its new director: the transfer of power was complete.

Friends and Assistants

Cosima had seized power in Bayreuth but she now had to defend her position. Her initial concern was to safeguard the Festival's artistic and economic success as this was the yardstick by which she would be judged as the Festival's new director. And she was sufficiently astute as to bolster her power base by engaging a number of well-qualified advisers. 'At the end of this month I shall be going to Bayreuth for a meeting about the Festival,' Hermann Levi informed his father in a letter of early August 1885. 'Richter, Mottl and I will form a kind of artistic directorate.'[23] This was Levi's first meeting with Cosima since February 1883. It was she who had convened the session in an attempt to ensure a sense of artistic continuity, the engagements of Levi, Richter and Mottl being dictated by sheer common sense inasmuch as they would guarantee a high degree of professionalism, something that was particularly important in the case of a theatre that operated only during the summer months and had a limited rehearsal period. All three, moreover, could lay claim to Wagner's imprimatur, Richter and Mottl as Wagner's pupils, Levi as his designated *Parsifal* conductor. Their appearance in the orchestra pit gave audiences the reassuring feeling of true seriousness of purpose and the highest possible standards. At the same time, however, Cosima's relations with both Levi and Richter were not free from underlying tensions.

Let us begin with Richter. Cosima's letters to him are striking, first and foremost, for their polite and friendly tone. It is only when we read between the lines that the problems start to emerge. Cosima valued the forty-two-year-old conductor as a leading member of the first generation of Wagnerians and as a friend of the family, and yet she was afraid of his independence and authority. For his part, Richter respected Cosima as a friend, but he was unwilling to submit to her iron rule without further ado, and there is no doubt that on the podium in the sunken pit it was he who had the final say. Moreover, Richter was the only member of her staff who shared her intimate knowledge of the Tribschen years – the very period that Wagner's widow was least anxious to recall. In general, she could be implacable in her demands, but with Richter she was oddly insecure: 'Many thanks for your kindness in taking heed of my modest remarks' was one of her well-considered formulas designed to curry favour with the conductor.[24] Of course, there was no lack of gossip and malice – Mottl in particular eyed his older colleague with suspicion, insinuating more than once that Richter was lazy and lacked the discipline necessary to rehearse, quite apart from which his tempi were all wrong. But Cosima could not manage without Richter, who was an internationally sought-after conductor – he ran the Richter Concerts in London from 1879 and the Birmingham Triennial Festival from 1885 – so that Cosima could hardly show him the door. And, unlike Mottl, he refused a fee, an act of self-privation that Wahnfried welcomed with particular enthusiasm.

Hermann Levi was four years older than Richter and the grand old man among Bayreuth's conductors. He had been court kapellmeister in Munich since 1872, leaving his mark on the city's musical life in altogether exceptional ways. His vast musical experience and penetrating judgements made him an outstanding authority in the world of music. Not only was he Wagner's preferred *Parsifal* conductor, he also championed the music of other contemporaries such as Brahms, Cornelius, Berlioz, Bruckner and the young Richard Strauss. His translations of the texts of operas by Gluck, Gounod and Mozart were regarded as inspired and even today retain their importance. He was also a cultured writer and editor with a wide range of literary interests. He edited Goethe's short stories, published a selection of Goethe's *obiter dicta* and translated short stories by Anatole France, who in 1921 won the Nobel Prize for literature.

Levi's unconditional regard for Wagner's works, his brilliance as a conductor, his comprehensive erudition and his love of Goethe and Schiller were all qualities that attracted Cosima Wagner. Even in purely numerical terms, their correspondence is significant: Levi's unpublished papers include more than 250 letters from Cosima, while nearly 230 documents have survived from him to her. The exchange of letters between the administrative head of the Festival and her 'major', as she called him, covers not only concerns relating to its actual running and matters of interest to them in their daily lives but also questions of philosophy and literature. And yet their dealings were by no means free from tensions, a further, deeply offensive element maintaining a constant counterpoint to their sense of mutual respect. Time and again, their harmonious working relationship was undermined by the recurrent theme of Levi's 'birth defect' – his Jewish ancestry. Cosima never missed an opportunity to let Levi know that she did not trust Jews. For all that she valued him as an artist, as a Jew he was merely tolerated. 'Everyone dies a Christian,' she wrote on one occasion, 'for Christianity is a truth. Blessed are they who can be so in life!'[25] Elsewhere she described Levi's Jewishness as his demon: 'This darkly demonic element in you used to fill me with real anxiety, but it now speaks to me as a prayer for redemption.'[26] Levi was powerless in the face of such attacks. More than once his pride bridled at such sustained humiliation, and he would then be reduced to such a state of despair that he would beg to be released from his contract, but ultimately he was unable to escape from the hold exerted by Cosima and Bayreuth. On one such occasion, Cosima referred him to the 'Master's will', arguing that she was not justified in releasing him from an obligation that Wagner himself had imposed: 'I am completely serious when I say that we have to tolerate one another.'[27]

Among Cosima's less attractive qualities was her fondness for passing spiteful comment on Levi in her letters to non-Jewish friends such as Marie von Wolkenstein and Adolf von Groß. In one such letter she describes him as 'a Rabbi's son who became our *Parsifal* conductor only as the result of an inscrutable fate',[28] and in another she inveighs against 'our foreign brethren', by which she meant Levi and other Jews. For Cosima, it was clear that 'just as it is impossible for a woman to become a man, so a Jew cannot become a German – this is not a question of better or worse, but simply of two fundamentally different things'.[29]

When Levi died in Munich in May 1900, it was the notoriously anti-Semitic Houston Stewart Chamberlain whom Cosima asked to write an obituary for the *Bayreuther Blätter*. Chamberlain agreed to the request, whereupon Cosima proceeded to list a whole series of points that she felt he should make. She recalled Levi's 'high level of intellectual culture' and praised not only his 'conscientiousness in practical matters' but also the 'generosity that led him to reject all forms of remuneration'. Significantly, however, she did not mention the fact that he was a gifted musician and a great conductor. Instead, she went on to claim that 'what led to serious conflicts was the very quality that his race inherited as a curse: a lack of faith, even where he felt a sense of conviction, and a lack of devotion, even when he felt a sense of reverence'.[30] In Wahnfried's jaundiced eyes, Jewish ancestry ruled a person out of court as someone who could make an authentic artistic contribution to the Festival. Exactly the same was true of Mahler, with whom Cosima also corresponded, occasionally asking him for his help and soliciting his opinion. Mahler was widely regarded as one of the leading Wagner conductors of his day, and yet he was never invited to work in Bayreuth. 'Everyone tells me that he's very talented,' Felix Mottl wrote to Cosima, 'but unfortunately he is Jewish!'[31]

Mottl was born in 1856 and was the third conductor on Cosima's team of advisers. He had studied under Bruckner, among others, at the Vienna Conservatory and was only nineteen when he joined the music staff of the Vienna Court Opera as a *répétiteur*. From 1881 to 1903 he was court kapellmeister in Karlsruhe, and during that time he raised the musical standards of the company to a level that could stand comparison with any in the world. He was a Wagnerian down to his fingertips, while at the same time championing the music of French composers such as Berlioz, Chabrier and Chausson. His Bayreuth career began in 1876, when he worked as an assistant on the inaugural *Ring*. Ten years later he conducted the Festival's first production of *Tristan und Isolde* and from then on was regarded as one of the leading stars in the Wagnerian firmament. He was undoubtedly Cosima's favourite conductor – there was no other musician to whom she felt so close, no other who understood her so completely. Mottl had none of the 'shortcomings' that she felt compromised her dealings with Richter and Levi: he was neither immoderately idiosyncratic nor Jewish. Her pet name for him was 'Spielmann' (minstrel), though she also addressed him as 'my dear Felix' and even as 'sonny boy'.

There have been repeated rumours to the effect that Cosima and Mottl were lovers, but their surviving correspondence contains no evidence to confirm this claim. Mottl's colleagues such as Felix Weingartner accused him of adopting far too servile a response to Cosima's rod of iron. 'If Frau Wagner had ordered him to conduct a passage in 3/4-time in 4/4 – and her delight in giving orders rose in direct proportion to the degree of obedience that she received in return – he would have praised the inspired insight on her part and at the very least have pretended to follow her instructions.'[32] There is some truth to this reproach. Once, when Mottl was criticized over certain musical details, he wrote to Cosima: 'It was all a matter of complete indifference to me, because you had said that you yourself were satisfied!'[33] There is no doubt that Mottl knew how to handle Cosima. He was a cunning but likeable rogue who with his ingratiating Viennese accent flattered her need for homage and subservience. His previously unpublished diaries reveal a different side to his character as a man much given to grumbling. In July 1892, for example, we read simply: 'Frau Wagner mad.'[34]

No list of Cosima's friends and assistants would be complete without a mention of Adolf von Groß. Groß was born in 1845 and was one of the principal figures in Cosima's empire, and there is no doubt that without him the history of the Bayreuth Festival would have taken a very different turn. A wily financier, he was a partner in the banking firm run by his father-in-law, Friedrich Feustel, with the result that he had excellent contacts with the world of international finance. It was he who saw to the Festival's detailed financial and organizational arrangements, negotiating contracts, drawing up budgets, keeping the books and even helping to choose the singers and sorting out matters of an entirely trivial and personal import. But he also administered the Wagners' growing private fortune, a fortune from which the Festival's own finances were not always clearly differentiated. As a rule it was a matter of some indifference to Wahnfried's inhabitants where their money came from: they simply sent unpaid invoices to 'Uncle Adolf', who got on with the business of paying them. 'I wonder if Fidi [Siegfried] could let me know the state of his finances,' Groß wrote to Cosima in 1893, 'so that I can replenish them in good time.'[35]

Groß carried out all these tasks in a totally disinterested way, demanding no fee for his services. Like Richter and Levi, he regarded it as an honour to serve the Wagnerian cause. Cosima trusted her administrator unquestioningly and even discussed all her private concerns with him. He revered her with a directness that bordered on the obsequious: 'I think I know much of what is worrying you and have never wanted anything more than to be able to serve you, which I shall do for as long as you wish.'[36] It is arguably one of the less praiseworthy aspects of his character that he cultivated the spirit of the subaltern and played a not inconsiderable role in establishing a kind of courtly ceremonial and elaborate etiquette among members of the Wagner family.

Light and Shade

'I feel powerless to lay at Your Majesty's feet the expression of my thanks and put it into mere words.'[37] Thus Cosima began her last surviving letter to King Ludwig II of Bavaria. It was written in response to a letter from Ludwig dated 21 September 1885 in which he had declared his willingness to be patron of the 1886 Bayreuth Festival. Cosima thanked him in her own unique way: she had assembled a book of Wagner's draft projects, his thoughts and unfinished writings, and she now presented the ever-generous Ludwig with a copy of it.[38] But in order to avoid upsetting him, she had struck out all the potentially compromising passages. It is not possible to tell if Cosima knew the true state of the king's health at this time. He had long since lost interest in the affairs of state and was behaving in increasingly bizarre ways, avoiding human contact and growing more and more unreasonable. There was also the catastrophic state of the privy purse, which was millions of marks in debt as a result of Ludwig's building spree. At the end of January 1886 he threatened to take his own life if his creditors were to lay claim to his castles in settlement of the sums of money owing to them, prompting the government to act. On 8 June 1886 the neurologist Bernhard von Gudden signed a medical report in which he asserted that Ludwig was incapable of ruling – he was 'mentally disturbed' and incurably ill. By the next day the king had already been certified and stripped of his royal office. By the tenth of the month, one of his uncles, Luitpold of Bavaria, had been appointed regent. And by the thirteenth Ludwig and Gudden had been found dead in the waters of Lake Starnberg in circumstances that have yet to be fully explained. 'I assume that you are as upset and

shocked as I am,' Malwida von Meysenbug wrote to Daniela. 'Not for a very
long time have I been as moved by an event that had nothing to do with me
personally.'[39] The Wagners were certainly deeply saddened by the death of
their friend. 'It is difficult to express in words the feelings with which I
received news of the heroically magnificent death of our glorious king,' Eva
wrote to her sister Blandine. 'It seems almost an act of desecration to speak
about it!' But Bayreuth's façade of grief also concealed a sense of real uncertainty: what would happen to the Festival? And would the new prince regent
agree to the arrangements that had been made by his predecessor? Cosima
and Adolf von Groß travelled to Munich post-haste 'to secure the future of the
Festival', as Eva put it. 'They achieved their aim, so the Festival can start, as
planned, on 23 July and end on 20 August.'[40]

During these turbulent weeks a young man arrived in Bayreuth whom Eva
described in her letter to Blandine as 'a very nice kapellmeister' who 'has come
to rehearse the boys' choir. Herr Weingartner is from Danzig and is a great
favourite of Levi. He calls on us regularly every evening and plays to us quite
marvellously from the works or, as was the case yesterday, from Beethoven.
This is a great comfort, and we can never tear ourselves away.' With his
youthful charm, the twenty-three-year-old Austrian conductor conquered the
hearts of the women of the house, including that of Eva, who was evidently
infatuated with the dashing assistant. 'Herr Weingartner is coming for coffee
this afternoon. We are all very fond of him. He is extremely cultivated yet infinitely modest & kind.'[41] Weingartner had been only eighteen when he had
completed a course in music in Graz, after which he had moved to Leipzig to
study composition and the piano at the city's conservatory, subsequently
taking lessons with Liszt in Weimar. Weingartner felt very close to Liszt, just
as he did to Levi, whom he affectionately called 'Papa'. Many decades later he
published his memoirs, in which he left a detailed account of life in
Wahnfried, an account that is less than flattering to its occupants but which
confirms what we know from other witness statements, making it an important source of information about the Wagner household at this time.

Even after Cosima's return from Munich, the only topic of conversation in
Wahnfried continued to be Ludwig's last hours. As Weingartner recalled,
Cosima was convinced that the king had committed suicide. 'She could see
the king striding into the water, or so she said, her features suffused by a
visionary expression. At the same time she herself strode through the room.'[42]
Cosima's strange behaviour puzzled Weingartner. In general, there was something odd 'about this woman, who seemed almost larger than life in her black,

unpleated dress and nun-like widow's bonnet that completely covered her hair'.[43] He was particularly surprised at the flattery and the obsequiousness found in the Wagner household and also at the fact that she never mentioned her late husband by name. According to Weingartner,

> 'This was said' meant 'My husband said this'; and 'at the time that this act was instrumented' meant 'at the time that the Master instrumented this act'. The language used by his widow gave the impression that Wagner had never walked on earth in human form. Her children maintained this tone in her presence but otherwise they abandoned it. The girls would then speak simply of 'Papa', while Siegfried, adopting the somewhat melancholic tone that was so typical of him, generally referred to him as 'my father'.[44]

A few days after Weingartner arrived in Bayreuth, Cosima's eldest daughter, Daniela, returned home from Berlin, where she had been visiting her fiancé, Henry Thode, who edited an arts journal there. The couple were planning to marry in early July 1886. It was Daniela's second attempt at matrimony, although Wahnfried preferred to draw a veil over the fact that two years earlier, at Cosima's behest, she had become engaged to the Festival's technical director, Fritz Brandt. It was intended to be a useful union, but Daniela had little time for her husband-to-be and made no secret of that fact. When Brandt discovered by chance that the relationship was due only to Cosima's insistent urging, he was understandably angry and asked Bülow – a second father to him – for his advice. Bülow was beside himself with fury, expressing his anger in a previously unpublished letter of 3 August 1884: 'She doesn't deserve you – no more is her sister, with her heartless and mindless frivolity, worthy of that Sicilian wastrel, Count Zero.' His calumnies knew no bounds: 'What a mess! It's their grandfather's system all over again! . . . How this hollow society of the high nobility disgusts me! It wakens in me all the emotions associated with the revolutions of 1848 – I was a social democrat before you were born.' Bülow had such a low opinion of his daughter that he thought she was simply 'modelling herself on her own mother' – in other words, Cosima – and playing with Brandt in the cruellest possible way in an attempt to get even with Bülow. 'She knows how fond of you I've grown and is now punishing me for the fact that I want nothing more to do with the Parsifal Hebrews and the literary vegetarians. It's entirely possible.' His advice was clear: 'Fritz – if at all possible, withdraw. Otherwise you would be joining a family that is cursed on both sides. My own forebears were practically useless – and the immorality and brilliance of the ancestors of D.'s mother were likewise a cause for concern in more ways than one.'[45] Brandt followed Bülow's advice and gave Daniela her marching orders. 'I myself am inconsolable,' Bülow wrote to Brandt a week later. 'I no longer have a daughter. Folly – or – notoriety!' And, finally, 'You were the last remaining link between Bayreuth and me. Now it's all over.'[46]

Brandt now fell into disfavour and was banished from Bayreuth's Green Hill, but ultimately he may have counted himself lucky, especially when we recall the fate of his successor, Henry Thode. After her engagement with Brandt had been called off, Daniela withdrew to the Berlin home of Countess Marie von Schleinitz, and it was here that she met Henry Thode. Thode had been born in 1857 and hailed from a respected and extremely well-to-do family. His father, Robert, owned a bank in Dresden and was the American consul in the city. During the summer the family lived at Schloß Schoosdorf in Silesia, while in the winter they stayed in a vast mansion in an exclusive residential quarter of Dresden. Henry Thode studied art history in Vienna and, after holding posts in Bonn and Frankfurt, was appointed to a chair in art history at the University of Heidelberg in 1894.[47]

Thode was initially drawn to Blandine, but she was already married to Count Gravina, and so he transferred his affections to Daniela in the spring of 1885. Unsettled by the end of her relationship with Brandt, Daniela appealed to her mother for advice. Cosima's reply reads:

> If you find Dr Thode pleasant company and feel that you agree on all the main things and if his intentions are serious, then I think you can consent to this union if the conditions – the family and their circumstances – suit you and promise you a life free from care. (I have just asked Fidi, and after a moment's hesitation he answered with a slow, weak 'yes'. And 'Is Herr Thode rich?' he added after a while.)[48]

The eighteen-year-old Siegfried did not have to worry about the Thodes' financial circumstances. But Henry Thode's parents can hardly have welcomed his choice of bride. Robert Thode thought that his son was too young to marry, but this was presumably no more than a pretext, as it seems that they had taken an instant and instinctual dislike to Daniela, whose 'financial parity' with her husband-to-be was also in question. But after vacillating for several months, the parents agreed to the match. Weingartner reports on the two ceremonies on 3 and 4 July 1886, the first at the local registry office, the second in church:

As always, Frau Wagner was dressed in a long, flowing widow's dress, although today it was not black but pale grey. For a time a kind of wistful joy lit up her deep mourning. Here was a woman with a masterly understanding of what it took to create an impression. All who were present, myself included, admired the taste that she had shown in choosing these widow's weeds for a wedding and the way that she moved in them.[49]

Daniela's father, Hans von Bülow, did not attend his daughter's wedding: 'May God grant the third generation less grief in their domestic lives!'[50] But her grandfather, Liszt, travelled to Bayreuth for the occasion, leaving again after a few days. Mottl, too, was invited to the reception, commenting in his diary on a striking conversation between mother and daughter: '"I'm annoyed that my father [Liszt] has left. I hope you'll get more pleasure from your own father." "I very much doubt it," says Daniela.'[51]

Cosima was enchanted by her new son-in-law. The eloquent young man came from one of the best houses in Germany and was about to embark on a brilliant academic career. In short, he was what was called a good catch. At the same time, it was clear to Cosima that in Henry Thode she had found an apostle who would promulgate the Bayreuth creed or, rather, that she could turn him into such a prophet. When he was considered for the post of professor of art history at the University of Heidelberg in the summer of 1893, she activated her wide-ranging network of contacts. Her aim was simple: she wanted a family member to occupy a chair at one of Germany's leading universities. Thode's application was supported by various friends of Wahnfried, including Hugo von Tschudi, Reinhard Kekulé and the influential head of the cabinet of Grand Duke Friedrich von Baden, Richard von Chelius. Cosima's plan paid off, and Thode proved a suitably grateful son-in-law.

Prior to his appropriation by the Wagners, Thode had been interested chiefly in the Italian Renaissance, but under Cosima's influence he turned increasingly to German art history. Even during his first term in Heidelberg he added Wagner's writings to the syllabus. The dissemination of Bayreuth's ideas, he insisted, should have absolute priority: 'Everything else is a matter of indifference.'[52] In his work on Arnold Böcklin and Albrecht Dürer, he championed a narrow-minded national aesthetic that went too far for his professional colleagues and for artists of the eminence of Max Liebermann. 'It was very much to his misfortune that he married into the Wagner household,' complained the political scientist Adolf Grabowsky:

Since then he has regarded himself as the guardian of Bayreuth's golden hoard. And inasmuch as Bayreuth famously symbolizes Germany's intellectual resources, he also sees himself as the guardian of Germany. Every remark that Thode makes is an address to the German nation. But this coat is too large for the man. In order to fill it, he pads himself out with vacuous phrases. He's often right – but the way in which he says it![53]

However acrimoniously Thode was attacked, Cosima always stood by him. When her 'Heinz', as she called him, claimed to have discovered three previously unknown paintings by Dürer, two of which turned out to be misattributions, Cosima advised him to remain calm: 'It is possible that they don't share your views. But what of it?! Perhaps they think the Dürers aren't Dürers, you certainly won't hold that against them.'[54] By 1907 Thode had helped to found the Werdandi League, an obscure *völkisch* sect which in Harry Kessler's contemptuous phrase was intended 'to save German Art from "decadence" by appealing to Richard Wagner. The greatest decadent as an antidote to decadence – a comic recipe! . . . It is all supposed to come together in the "German mind", truly a concept for old maids'.[55]

From the outset the marriage of Henry and Daniela Thode was ill-starred, and it seems likely that the relationship foundered even on their wedding night. Whenever he approached her, she would suffer violent nervous convulsions, and when a doctor advised him to avoid sexual intercourse, Thode became sexually frustrated. The reasons for Daniela's behaviour lie in deep-seated emotional complexes subtly insinuated by Cosima. Daniela had been only three when her parents' marriage had fallen apart and Cosima and Wagner had become clandestine lovers. As the eldest of the children, she undoubtedly felt the trials and tribulations of the following period with particular intensity. As if this were not already complicated enough, Cosima then saddled her daughter with an altogether inhuman burden of responsibility: 'My dear, whenever you experience grief or mortification, you should think that you are atoning for me and with me for my guilt in life – this will give you strength and courage.'[56] Elsewhere she even wrote that Daniela had to 'be everything' for Hans von Bülow and 'make up for a cruel destiny'.[57] Incredibly, Cosima was determined that her daughter should shoulder her own burden of guilt as an adulteress. Or, to put it another way, Daniela had to rectify the wrong that her mother had wrought. There is also some evidence that Cosima unconsciously treated Bülow's children, Daniela and Blandine, differently from Wagner's. In a previously unpublished letter from Daniela to Isolde, the former complains about the many years that I spent sadly and unfairly, not understanding our mother any longer, feeling completely alien from her and not knowing why she had built a wall between you and me. You were both too young to understand and to sympathize with how I suffered, I started to become unjust in my feelings towards you both. . . . Our mother is a genius, there's no doubt about it, and she wants others to behave as geniuses towards her, which is wonderful of her but not always entirely easy for others![58]

Whatever may lie behind this mysterious hint, something was not quite right in the Wagner–Bülow household. Perhaps Daniela's attitude to Wagner's own children was profoundly ambivalent – great affection and sisterly love on the one hand but, on the other, jealousy resulting from the preferential treatment that they enjoyed, a jealousy that she was unwilling to acknowledge. Cosima evidently gave her eldest daughter the feeling that she was less than equal as a family member. Perhaps Daniela reminded her of her failed marriage, the painful ending of which was a source of perpetual self-reproach. The task of atoning for Cosima's guilt was one that Daniela could never hope to complete, and this, together with the unspoken assumption that she was of less importance than Isolde, Eva and Siegfried, left her with a tormenting sense of inferiority. Throughout her life she suffered from bouts of hysteria, paranoid self-doubt and severe depression. Blandine, too, seems to have been conscious of the fact that she was treated unfairly: 'Mama never showed any real concern for me,' she complained to an acquaintance years later, adding with a note of resignation: 'It is enough that I can tell my conscience that Mama never suffered on account of me.'[59]

At the same time, however, Cosima worshipped Siegfried to distraction, holding him up as a lofty and ultimately unattainable ideal. But this fixation on the 'Master's son and heir' also meant that Cosima was placing an enormous emotional burden on her daughters, with the result that Henry Thode, for example, viewed the relationship between his wife and his brother-in-law, Siegfried, with exceptionally critical eyes. By 1913 the Thodes' marriage was broken beyond repair, and yet Daniela refused even so much as to consider the idea of a legal separation but demanded to continue the relationship in order for the couple to be able to serve the Bayreuth cause and, with it, Siegfried. A bewildered and embittered Thode wrote a note to himself: 'And on top of everything the assumption that I'm living for her brother! Even now, in this situation, when she knows what pain I'm in, it is her brother who remains her main concern. I begrudge him nothing and wish him well. But even now: her brother above all else?' And he went on: 'I'm of secondary importance. She feels true pity for her brother – not for me.'[60]

Thode had already had a number of minor affairs with other women, including the dancer Isadora Duncan, but by the beginning of 1910 he was involved with a Danish violinist, Hertha Tegner, who was then only twenty-six. 'That Danish woman', as she was dismissively described by Wahnfried, gave him everything that he had lacked in recent decades, but when he demanded a divorce, the Wagners – especially Eva and Siegfried – went on the offensive, their attacks culminating in the reproach that his actions were threatening the very lives of Daniela and Cosima. After a whole series of painful confrontations, Thode and his wife were legally separated in January 1914. In one of his final letters to Daniela, he complained that 'ours was never a true marriage with roots in all that is natural. And it was not rooted in all that is natural because it was not love that drove you to offer me your hand and because you never reached the point of loving me other than as a friend – and because our union was never complete'. Their marriage had been a great mistake. They had married 'without feeling the force of reciprocal love'.[61]

But let us return to the summer of 1886. By July the preparations for that year's Festival were in full swing. The repertory included not only a revival of *Parsifal* but also the first performances in Bayreuth of *Tristan und Isolde* under Cosima's supervision. Richter was otherwise engaged in Vienna, and so the conducting duties were divided between Hermann Levi for *Parsifal* and Felix Mottl for *Tristan und Isolde*. Levi recalled the early rehearsals in a letter to his father:

> I collect Frau Wagner from Wahnfried at eight in the morning, and by half past we are driving up to the theatre together. The rehearsal lasts until one, after which we (Frau W., Mottl and a young friend of mine, Weingartner) have lunch in the restaurant, where we discuss all manner of things until three, I then sleep for an hour, more rehearsals from four till eight, I then go back into town and change, and by nine I am back at Wahnfried for supper.

Levi was clearly overjoyed that his friendly relations with the others appeared to be thriving. 'Mottl and I are like brothers', he assured his father. Frau Wagner, too, had 'boundless confidence' in him: 'In short, to work in this way, in such harmony and with such excellent prospects of success, is heaven on earth.'[62]

But was the sky over Bayreuth really so cloudless? And was the atmosphere in the theatre and at Wahnfried as untroubled as Levi insisted in his letters to his father? Rabbi Benedikt Levi was, to say the least, sceptical about 'the Wagner circus', and it is entirely possible that his son's letters were designed to place a positive gloss on the whole affair. For his part, Mottl had his suspicions. He was struck, for example by the fact that the Wagners 'quietly mocked their *Parsifal* conductor, an attitude barely concealed beneath the smiling mask of friendship'. And he was embarrassed by the conductor's subservience, describing Levi's attitude to the Wagners as 'a constant emotional and physical bowing and scraping'. When one of the children publicly criticized Levi ('Oh, Levi, you're talking complete rot'), Weingartner lost his temper, taking Levi to one side and upbraiding him in no uncertain terms: 'He looked at me with a sad expression, and in a voice breaking with emotion he muttered the words, "It's easy for you in this house, you're an Aryan!" '[63]

Weingartner was dismayed at the way in which the Wagners treated his idol. After one rehearsal the young conductor accompanied Cosima from the theatre to Wahnfried. Weingartner seized his chance and spoke up in support of Levi: 'She listened to me calmly and at the end remarked that there could be no bond between Aryan and Semitic blood.' But Weingartner refused to give ground. ' "I don't expect that we shall ever see eye to eye on this, my dear Weingartner," Frau Wagner retorted with chilling calm.'[64]

The preparations for the 1886 Bayreuth Festival gradually drew to an end, and the town's hotels and guest houses filled with Wagnerians from Germany and elsewhere. Adolf von Groß was relieved to note that ticket sales were gratifying, although not all the performances were sold out. For one performance of *Tristan und Isolde*, for example, it is said that only a dozen tickets had been sold in advance, resulting in much papering of the house. But this was very much the exception and in no way affected the artistic results. The opening night of *Parsifal* and the Bayreuth premiere of *Tristan und Isolde* were both enthusiastically received. But Bayreuth had now become an event in the social calendar, and many well-to-do visitors came to meet others like them, Cosima's elegant receptions proving particularly popular. Those who received an invitation to these events undoubtedly felt that they belonged to the crème de la crème: musicians, painters and writers were on the guest list, as were politicians, members of the aristocracy and high-ranking military officers. Not infrequently up to 200 guests were invited. 'Yesterday evening was the first great reception,' Eva reported to her sister in Italy. 'We'd made ourselves look very beautiful, Lulu in her fiancée's outfit and Loldi and I in our blue & white dresses respectively.' Cosima was on form, plying her guests with tea, coffee and champagne, while Eva arranged a buffet with all manner of dainties and delicacies. 'Princess Marie of Meiningen was there,' Eva recalled. 'Apart from her, there were also many society ladies from Berlin (I was less enraptured by them!), as well as Bruckner, who in kissing the back of my hand with a real smacker of a kiss nearly tore my mittens to shreds. Everyone was splendidly entertained, and it all passed off most excellently.'

The whole event was superbly stage-managed, Cosima gliding through the house with her regal demeanour and deigning to dispense tokens of her grace and favour, while exuding an aura of unapproachability. The ladies present maintained a respectful distance, while only the menfolk were allowed to kiss her hand. 'After they had regaled themselves on my buffet,' Eva continued, 'the music began.' A pupil of Liszt played one of his mentor's virtuoso piano pieces, *Saint Francis Walking on the Waves*, in honour of Henry Thode. For the performer, it was a particular honour to make music at Wahnfried on such an evening and, moreover, to play a piece dedicated to the mistress of the house. 'Finally there was ice cream,' Eva concluded her report, 'and with that the house slowly emptied.'[65]

Crocodile Tears

Liszt arrived in Bayreuth from Luxembourg on 21 July 1886. As on previous visits, he stayed in rooms placed at his disposal by the Frölich family immediately next to Wahnfried. 'He did not look at all well,' Weingartner recalled, 'but seemed tired and very frail.'[66] He had caught a chill while sitting in a draughty train compartment, and this continued to trouble him. Several of his former pupils, including August Göllerich, Bernhard Stavenhagen, Lina Schmalhausen, Alfred Reisenauer and Weingartner, looked after their ailing teacher and kept him company during games of whist, a pastime he particularly enjoyed. On the twenty-fifth, Weingartner even accompanied him to a performance of *Tristan und Isolde*, but on the following day his health deteriorated. There was phlegm in his lungs, and he was suffering from increasingly violent fits of coughing that wracked his whole body. His forehead would then turn a mottled red with the effort, and he found it almost impossible to breathe. There was no doubt about the seriousness of his condition. By now his chill had turned to pneumonia, and with that his fate seemed sealed. Such an illness in a man who had just turned seventy-five was essentially incurable. Penicillin would have helped, but this was not to be developed until 1938.

The events that unfolded under the Frölichs' roof in late July 1886 were undignified in the extreme. Throughout this period Lina Schmalhausen kept a diary that was highly critical of Cosima Wagner.[67] Cynical though it must sound, the death of her father came at a bad time for her. The 1886 Bayreuth Festival had opened just over a week earlier, and everything inevitably revolved around Wagner. Liszt's lingering death disrupted the smooth running of the Festival, with its succession of performances, lavish gala dinners and brilliant soirées, with the result that Cosima had neither the time nor the leisure to attend to her dying father. True, she arranged for meals to be sent over from Wahnfried, but Liszt was additionally suffering from problems with his teeth and was unable to chew on the steaks and cutlets in apricot sauce. Lina Schmalhausen made some clear broth for him in order to ensure that he ate something. 'If only I had fallen ill somewhere else,' Liszt is said to have complained in his despair. 'But to have to be ill right here, amid all this clamour, is really too stupid.'[68]

Cosima suddenly appeared at her father's bedside on the morning of the twenty-seventh, after he had spent the whole of the previous night hallucinating. Liszt's valet, Miska, could hardly believe his ears when she abruptly declared that from now on she herself would take care of her father, who was not to receive any visitors, and that included Lina Schmalhausen and her father's other pupils. Her intervention was to have disastrous results, for she was clearly too preoccupied with the Festival to be able to care for a patient as sick as her father. She arranged for a bed to be placed in the adjoining room in order for her to spend the nights there, but from now on there was effectively no one caring for Liszt. His landlady, Frau Frölich, told an anxious Lina Schmalhausen that he had spent the whole night groaning terribly but that Cosima had heard nothing as she had closed the door to her room.

Mottl said goodbye to Liszt on the afternoon of 30 July: 'With him again in the afternoon. Very weak & feeble. Groaning loudly. Poor beloved Master. "Are you tired?" Frau Wagner asked him in French. "I don't know!" were the last words I heard him speak.'[69] Things came to a head that night. Lina Schmalhausen hid in the bushes in the garden and was able to watch Cosima arrive at the Frölichs' house from the theatre at midnight. There she was met by the doctor, Carl Landgraf. After a brief exchange, she went straight to bed without looking in on her father. At two in the morning, Liszt suddenly shouted: 'Air! Air!' He was suffocating and in unspeakable pain. This attack lasted half an hour, Liszt's screams and groans being audible throughout the neighbourhood. He finally collapsed and sank into a coma. Landgraf eventually arrived ninety minutes after he had been summoned and initially thought that Liszt was already dead but then administered 'Hoffmann's drops' – a mixture of alcohol and ether – so that Liszt regained consciousness. His death throes continued.

Cosima now realized that she was completely out of her depth caring for a dying man, quite apart from which she had to prepare for a reception that evening at Wahnfried. On the morning after Liszt had fallen into a coma, she engaged the services of a nurse. Bernhard Schnappauf enjoyed her trust as he had worked as Wagner's valet. That evening Landgraf returned with his colleague, Dr Fleischer from Erlangen. Together they took the patient's pulse, while Schnappauf tried to relieve his suffering by wrapping his calves and chest in compresses. It was all that they could do. The hours passed. Back in her hiding place in the garden, Lina Schmalhausen claims that shortly after eleven o'clock Liszt received two injections in the region of the heart. These may have been camphor, which Schnappauf had obtained from the local chemist. The consequences were dramatic: Liszt's body rose up violently and was convulsed by violent spasms. At around a quarter past eleven, the groaning suddenly stopped – Liszt was dead. Cosima knelt beside the body, then lay across his legs, before finally sitting in a chair at the foot of the bed. Inconceivably, she then fell asleep, her head lolling from side to side. From time to time she would wake up, only to drift off to sleep again. Lina Schmalhausen was able to observe every detail of this remarkable scene. Thinking it absurd that Cosima had simply fallen asleep beside her dead father, she assumed – wrongly – that Liszt was still alive.[70]

'God! How comforting!' Eva reported to her sister, Blandine. 'In Mama's arms! With no one else with him, he fell asleep completely painlessly!'[71] Eva was evidently no stickler for the truth, for Cosima and her father had certainly not been alone. And in the light of all that we know, the claim that Liszt's death was painless and 'comforting' is open to serious doubt. Cosima further humiliated her dying father by denying him – an Abbé – the consolation of the Church. 'Herr Korzendorfer, the ecclesiastical councillor, expressed his surprise at the fact that the dead man was not given the last rites,' Schnappauf later recalled.[72]

But this was not the end of this squalid tragedy. Cosima refused to have the body under her roof, and so it was simply left at the Frölichs'. According to Schnappauf, 'Frau Frölich expressed her displeasure at the fact that the body was being laid out in her house without so much as a by your leave.' To make matters worse, the high temperatures caused the body to decompose very quickly, understandably alarming the Frölichs. When the stench made Isolde ill, Frölich finally lost his temper and demanded that the body be removed forthwith, otherwise he would get the police to take it away. 'I immediately hurried off to find Frau Cosima,' Schnappauf recalled. 'She was still in bed. I told her what had happened and was instructed to transfer the body to Wahnfried once it had been placed in a coffin and the coffin had been sealed.'[73] Liszt's mortal remains were finally collected in an ordinary handcart.

There was also an unseemly argument over the burial arrangements. Grand Duke Carl Alexander of Saxe-Weimar wanted his illustrious subject to be interred in Weimar, while powerful voices were raised demanding that the body be taken to Hungary. Among the leaders of this last-named group were Carolyne von Sayn-Wittgenstein and members of the Budapest Order of Saint Francis, to which Liszt had belonged in life. But Cosima successfully appealed to one of her father's instructions, according to which he wanted to be buried where he died: Bayreuth. Weingartner recalled that 'we, his last pupils and friends, acted as pall-bearers. Heavy clouds hung low in the sky, but the rain was only light.'[74] A memorial service was held the next day, 4 August, in the town's Catholic church. Here, too, it was Wagner who in an appalling display of poor taste was central to the proceedings. Not a note of Liszt's own music was heard. Instead, Bruckner played the organ, improvising on themes from *Parsifal*. According to Lina Ramann, a close friend of Liszt, Bruckner's playing was 'monotonous, endless and wearisome. When Liszt's pupils, unable to conceal their dismay, asked him why he had not based his improvisations on a theme from one of Liszt's own compositions, he replied that unfortunately he did not know any – they should have given him one.'[75] The local church choir also offered an indifferent rendition of a number of standard liturgical pieces, and three priests added their nasal singing to the discordant tones of the choir. All in all, the service could hardly have been more embarrassing. Weingartner and Liszt's other friends could hardly believe what they were witnessing: 'The Wagner family showed no outward sign of mourning. The daughters wore black dresses, but that was all.'[76]

Worse, Cosima refused to allow the flag on the theatre to fly at half mast. Nor was there a memorial concert. Quite the opposite in fact: on the very day of the funeral service, she again invited Festival-goers to join her for another elegant evening at Wahnfried. Even Mottl found such haste distinctly unseemly: 'Wahnfried. Food. In the entrance hall there was still the smell of mortality emanating from Liszt's dead body.'[77]

Cosima's apparently cold-hearted lack of concern is bewildering. As Weingartner suspected, 'Everything was made to look – as if on purpose – that Franz Liszt's passing was not of sufficient importance to dim the glory of the Festival even for a moment.'[78] His suspicions cannot be dismissed out of hand. For Cosima's thoughts and actions all revolved around the Bayreuth Festival, so that, at least from her own perspective, it was only logical that not even the death of her father should disrupt its smooth running and her theatrical response to the legacy that it was now her destiny to administer. And so life went on as usual in Bayreuth. According to Mottl's diary entry of 14 August 1886: 'In the evening to Wahnfried. Adagio from Beethoven's F sharp minor. C. kissed my hand afterwards.'[79] Those who felt unable to resume their former round turned away in dismay. Among this group was Felix Weingartner, who received a last-minute appeal from Ernst von Schuch in Dresden, requesting his assistance at the Court Opera. Weingartner asked Cosima to release him from his contract: 'She looked at me with her curiously veiled eyes and, with an ironic expression in her voice, she asked what I hoped to achieve in Dresden. "I hope to enrich my artistic experiences and perhaps find a further chance to get on in life." – "And you don't find that here?" – "No!" – "Then goodbye!" ' And that was the end of Weingartner's career in Bayreuth. 'Perhaps a word of subservience would have changed my destiny completely. But I said nothing and left with my head held high.'[80]

Princess Carolyne von Sayn-Wittgenstein survived Liszt by only seven months, dying in Rome on 8 March 1887. 'The death of the princess left a deep impression on me,' Cosima admitted in a letter to Adolf von Groß. 'During her lifetime, this woman caused me a great deal of suffering, but she also aroused great feelings in me & introduced me to the most unique experiences.'[81] As if triumphing one last time over her old rival, she wrote to Daniela: 'I genuinely think that the defeat that she suffered over the transfer of Grandpapa's remains dealt her a blow from which she was unable to recover. She had to submit, and with that she died.'[82]

A Change of Direction

From an artistic point of view, the 1886 Bayreuth Festival was a great success. Audiences had every reason to be grateful not only to Hermann Levi and Felix Mottl, to the singers and chorus and, indeed, to the music staff in general, but also to the Festival's new director, who had survived her ordeal by fire. The experimental idea of performing a second work alongside *Parsifal* had proved a triumph. Buoyed up by her success, Cosima declared that she would hold another festival in 1887 and that it would include new productions of either *Die Meistersinger von Nürnberg* or *Der fliegende Holländer*. If this were to be impossible, she would stick to *Parsifal* and *Tristan und Isolde*. This premature announcement led to a serious rift between her and her managing director, Adolf von Groß, who felt that his advice had been ignored and who pleaded for a year off. As a banker and businessman, he foresaw the enormous financial risks ahead, for it was by no means certain that the success of 1886 could be repeated in 1887. Perhaps Groß was also thinking of the performance of *Tristan und Isolde* for which only twelve tickets had been sold. But Cosima refused to listen: 'I felt only sorrow that day, and it was so profound that I had to tell myself that I would not be attending the next Festival.'[83] For the present the subject was dropped. 'My sad discussion took place last Tuesday,' Cosima told Daniela on 18 January 1887. 'Mottl was not present, and so I drove to Karlsruhe with Levi to inform them that Adolf continues to believe that a Festival is impossible this year.' Although Cosima thought differently, she agreed to the delay, albeit with a heavy heart: 'But now I'm as resolved as ever to do what I am doing & not doing, completely & without grumbling, & with joyful resolution I have asked the two conductors to put it about that the break is fully justified. That is all that I have to say about how I feel.'[84]

And so the year's break was decided on. In early February 1887 Cosima left to visit the Thodes in Bonn, where her son-in-law was teaching art history at the local university. The couple had moved to the small town on the Rhine in the summer of the previous year. After the events of the previous twelve months – the 1886 Bayreuth Festival, the death of her father and, finally, her arguments with Adolf von Groß – Cosima was pleased to be able to spend a few carefree days with her 'beloved children'. By the date of her return to Bayreuth, her mood was positively high-spirited. Here we encounter a very different Cosima: not the Master's widow or the strict and unapproachable grande dame but a woman with a sense of humour and a love of life, a woman, in short, who liked to gossip about others and who enjoyed the occasional tipple. 'But let me tell you about my return home,' she wrote to Daniela:

In Nuremberg I felt very tired as I'd finished off half a bottle of Boxbeutel in Würzburg &, as you can imagine, this, together with half a bottle of Marsala, was enough to make me doze off, so that I simply didn't notice Schilda & the children came looking for me in vain, even in third class. Finally Soldchen and Fidchen discovered me. And so I arrived in Ithaca more sleepy than anything & was compared with Noah.

Cosima had been aghast at Daniela's appearance. For a long time her eldest daughter had been suffering from insomnia, exhaustion and the nervous spasms to which we have already referred. In order for her to build up her reserves, Cosima recommended a very particular regime:

> Cocoa in the morning, at around eleven some raw ham & a glass of your wonderful Hochheimer, then your very nice lunch, but without black coffee afterwards, then, before you go out, in God's name, a glass of Schön's milk (though I'd prefer an egg), in the evening your supper, at nine a glass of beer, but no tea.[85]

Back in Bayreuth, Cosima resumed her life as head of the Festival. Even though there were no performances in 1887, she was still fully occupied, preparing for the following year. In an age when the telephone was not yet available as a means of mass communication and a century before the invention of the internet and email, the handwritten letter was still the medium of choice. Cosima corresponded with conductors, singers, orchestral musicians, artists, professors, politicians, princes and heads of ruling houses as well as with members of her far-flung family and also, of course, with family friends. And she was an extraordinarily industrious correspondent: 'Forgive my brevity,' she wrote on one occasion to Heinrich von Stein, 'but this is my twenty-sixth letter since yesterday.'[86] Elsewhere we find her complaining that 'we have counted around forty-three letters of this kind during the past week alone.'[87]

By the mid-eighties, Cosima's eyesight was growing perceptibly worse, and so most of her letters were dictated to Eva, who acted as her mother's private secretary. There has been much speculation about Cosima's mysterious eye disease, but it is not possible to say for certain exactly what she was suffering from. From 1886 onwards she was treated by the famous eye doctor from Erlangen, Oskar Eversbusch, who was widely regarded as one of the leading experts in the field of ophthalmology, but he was evidently unable to help. Perhaps the ultimate reason for Cosima's failing eyesight was altogether banal: decades later, her daughter-in-law, Winifred, declared that she was simply too vain to wear glasses. Again according to Winifred, she was never completely blind, as some writers have asserted. Whatever the facts of the matter, Eva was generally to be found at her mother's side. She also accompanied her on her frequent travels.

As the head of the family business, Cosima generally spent between two and three months every year away from Bayreuth. Visits to the more active

Wagner Societies in Hamburg, Dresden and Mannheim were obligatory stops on her journey, as were family visits to see her daughters Blandine and Daniela in Italy and Bonn respectively. Although there was no lack of amenities on these journeys – Cosima always stayed at the best hotels – such tours were none the less adventurous and very tiring. Then, as now, Bayreuth was not on the high-speed rail network, so that the already wearisome journey times were additionally extended by transfers and lengthy waits. The journey from Bayreuth to Berlin, for example, took around twelve hours to complete.

Although there was no Festival in 1887, Cosima paid several visits to Levi and Mottl. Both men were exceptionally busy, and so these meetings mostly took place in Munich or Karlsruhe. Just before her departure for Karlsruhe in early March we find Cosima writing to Daniela: 'I shall be staying there for two to three days, which I mention so that your father hears about it & doesn't plan a visit of his own with the Meiningen Orchestra.' Seventeen years after she had divorced Bülow and four years after Wagner's death, there could still be no question of a normal coexistence between the former couple: they simply kept out of each other's way. It seems in fact to have been Bülow who needed to keep his distance. For her part, Cosima respected her former husband as a brilliant musician and had boundless trust in his authority as a Wagnerian. Indeed, she could even imagine a closer association, as she explained to Daniela:

> If he talks to you about Bayreuth & if it can be done without causing him any agitation, you could tell him that I have often thought of turning to him on matters that need resolving. I do not think that such questions will arise very often, but if it is all right by him, I would turn to him not in the form of a letter but simply with the relevant question; but if it isn't all right by him, we can forget about it, as I am not unsure of myself, & where our own cause is concerned I have boundless trust in the power that protects that cause.[88]

Bülow evidently declined to have any direct contact with his former wife, and it was Daniela who had to act as go-between. We can only speculate on the reasons for his reserve. Perhaps the emotional wounds inflicted by so heart-rending a marital tragedy had not yet fully healed. Or perhaps he was simply unable to champion the cause of Bayreuth. One thing is certain: although he had been uniquely supportive of Wagner and of his music, he was – to put it mildly – sceptical about Cosima's fanatical cult of the composer, and in his frustration he noted how even his own daughter was guilty of the idolatry that tolerated no other gods but the Master. When he tried to interest Daniela in the music of Brahms, he encountered only scorn and incomprehension. And so we find him writing to his second wife, Marie, at the end of July 1887: 'This one-sided fanaticism is unshakeably deeply rooted in my daughter: she refuses to hear about the "Bear" [Brahms] and seems incapable of understanding even so much as an iota about him. It will take years for my daughter to see the light: I shall not live to see it. Everywhere there is only an armed peace!'[89] Within days he was writing again and complaining that

> there is absolutely no place for me in my children's hearts. I am really no more than a tiresome appendage: Bayreuth's idolatry always comes first: Wolzogen, Stein (who recently died in Berlin and who continues to be mourned) – Levi, Richter, Mottl – yes, even Seidl – – they are all far more important figures than the apostate, the man who reveres the 'arch-enemy' (!!!) Brahms, the so-called father whose damned obligation it should be to keep going down on bended knee before the founder of the new religion – for this is how the brilliant tone-poet is actually seen. This is the basic tone of every conversation – there is no theme that does not point to it at least indirectly and certainly in a way that makes me nervous – after all, I am well versed in reading between the lines. What emotional torment![90]

The Year of the Three Kaisers

In early August 1887 Cosima travelled to Munich for another of her meetings with her team of conductors. As always, she stayed at the elegant Marienbad Hotel between the Karlsplatz and the art galleries. Built in 1850, it was one of the most exclusive hotels in the city, its guests over the years including such famous names as Clara Schumann, Sigmund Freud, Hugo von Hofmannsthal, Jacob Burckhardt, Giacomo Puccini and Rainer Maria Rilke. Cosima particularly valued its central location: the main station was only a few hundred yards away, and the Botanic Garden was right outside the door, inviting hotel guests to stroll among its trees. At the top of the agenda were the preparations for the following year's Bayreuth Festival. Cosima initially wanted to stage *Die Meistersinger von Nürnberg* alongside *Parsifal* and *Tristan und Isolde*, but Levi, Mottl and Groß all felt that productions of three different works were logistically and financially impossible. More or less reluctantly, Cosima accepted the recommendation of her advisers and limited the repertory to a revival of *Parsifal* and a new production of *Die Meistersinger von Nürnberg*. It was also decided to start negotiations on installing electric lighting in the theatre, which until then had been lit by gas and carbon arc lamps.

Perhaps the most important invitation that Cosima extended at this time was an unofficial one. On 3 August 1887 she met Count Philipp zu Eulenburg-Hertefeld. 'After breakfast I went to see Cosima Wagner,' Eulenburg wrote the next day to his mother. 'She had sent me a telegram from Bayreuth, inviting me to an interview to discuss next year's performances. She was staying at the Marienbad and was enchantingly kind – she asked me in particular to thank you for being so good to her daughters.'[91] Cosima had known the forty-year-old count since her time in Berlin, when he had often listened to his mother playing piano duets from Wagner's operas with Frau von Bülow, so that it was almost inevitable that Eulenburg should go on to become a Wagnerian. Throughout his life he was drawn to the world of aesthetics: he wrote pseudo-medieval ballads as well as plays, poems and fairytales, and he also composed songs – his *Rosenlieder* were published by the highly respected firm of Bote & Bock in Berlin and were very popular in their day. There is no doubt that the sensitive count was a cultured individual with a fine sense of style and impeccable manners. His conversation was as intelligent as it was charming and witty, and never did his star shine more brightly than at the elegant dinner parties and soirées to which he was regularly invited. As the evening drew to an end he would sit down at the piano and sing his melancholic songs about bygone heroes in a silkily seductive voice. But nostalgia was not on the agenda at Cosima's meeting with Eulenburg, and it is unlikely that she had any real interest in his poems and compositions, at which she will merely have smiled in secret. Cosima had other plans for Eulenburg, and these plans were highly ambitious. Eulenburg was now a leading diplomat and had excellent connections with the worlds of the aristocracy and politics. Since the previous year he had been close and even intimate with the Prince Wilhelm, who was his junior by twelve years and who was later to become Kaiser Wilhelm II.

There has been much speculation about the homosexual goings-on among members of Wilhelm's entourage. Although both the prince and Eulenburg later married, the latter even fathering eight children, they evidently felt drawn to earthy male society, and it was presumably not just for the hunting that they met at Schloß Liebenberg, the Eulenburgs' family seat to the north of Berlin. A court favourite like the count had many enemies, and it comes as no surprise to discover that many of those who begrudged him his success muttered darkly about 'Philly's' sexual escapades. There was talk of erotic involvements in

Vienna, of affairs with Starnberg fishermen, blackmail, hush money and secret police files – all in all a fairly murky brew. A number of years later the then retired chancellor, Otto von Bismarck, added his twopenn'orth to the gossip, blaming Wilhelm II's courtiers for his fall from grace in March 1890. So keen was Bismarck to be avenged that his former protégé Eulenburg now came into his line of fire. He called him a 'kinaidos' – an effeminate rake – and, according to his personal physician, Ernst Schweninger, is said to have descended to the most offensive levels of personal vituperation whenever a visit from his erstwhile colleague was announced: 'Fingers up your arse! Eulenburg's coming.'[92] But Bismarck merely provided the ammunition, leaving the journalist Maximilian Harden to deliver the coup de grâce many years later. In November 1906 Harden unleashed a scandal that shook the Reich to its foundations and left Eulenburg a social pariah. But that is another story.[93]

For the present the sun shone down from a cloudless sky on Count Philipp zu Eulenburg-Hertefeld. Although the elderly kaiser, Wilhelm I, was still alive and no one could have foreseen that his son, Prince Friedrich, would rule for only ninety-nine days, Bayreuth none the less regarded Prince Wilhelm as the great white hope of the future. 'We are building entire palaces of hopes on Prince Wilhelm,' Levi wrote to his father.[94] This assessment pointed in the right direction, not least because Prince Wilhelm's liberal parents, Crown Prince Friedrich and his wife Viktoria, had little time for Wagnerism, a dismissive attitude for which Cosima blamed 'the calculating predators' – one of her terms for the Jews.[95] In making such early contact with Prince Wilhelm and pre-empting any possible dynastic emergency, Cosima revealed exceptional astuteness, her aim being not merely to ensure the patronage of the house of Hohenzollern and, with it, a rich vein of money, but above all to make sure that the 'cause' of Bayreuth became a national 'cause' as well.

Eulenburg assumed the role of go-between for Bayreuth, Cosima having pulled out all the stops in terms of her powers of diplomatic persuasion. The count was suitably impressed:

Liszt's famous daughter is starting to look more and more like her father. Her auburn hair, which was once so beautiful, hangs lank around her large, long face and has turned grey – almost as grey as her large eyes, in which her unusual intelligence shines in a way that is half good-natured and half coyly artful. She wears a long black lace veil picturesquely draped around her head and shoulders and a black wool dress with puffed sleeves that is modern and at the same time stylish.

In his diary Eulenburg also praised the 'acuity' of Cosima's 'intellect' and her knowledge of human nature: 'The Festival is in good hands as long as she remains alive; and she is concentrating on this task to such an extent that she speaks only to people whom she needs for the Festival, an approach that is bound to add greater strength to the enterprise.'[96]

Their next meeting took place in Bayreuth some six weeks later. Eulenburg's diary entry of 18 September 1887 reads:

> Remarkable though this woman is, she has set her sights far too high. A chair in Wagnerian literature and music at the University of Berlin, which she has mentioned on more than one occasion, is absurd. My own view is that the German element in Wagner's music, embodied in the existing Bayreuth Festival, can serve to reinforce the national consciousness, something that the German needs more than other nationalities. This means that it is important to safeguard the Festival not just from a political standpoint. To support it is also a German cultural challenge.

Even if Eulenburg could only smile at Cosima's idea of a university professorship in Wagner studies, for which she was presumably thinking of her son-in-law, Henry Thode, there was no doubt that Bayreuth was already well on its way to becoming a shrine to German nationalism. According to Eulenburg, Prince Wilhelm's enthusiasm for Wagner had by now reached 'boiling point' and there was no doubt in the diarist's mind that he would provide 'the greatest possible support for the Wagner cause'.[97] Cosima had won the day. Thanks to Eulenburg's intimacy with Prince Wilhelm, the rooms of the future German kaiser were now open to her and to Wahnfried. She returned to Munich at the end of January 1888, this time in the company of her daughters Eva and Isolde. Together with Levi, they called on Count Eulenburg, who shortly afterwards reported to Prince Wilhelm:

> A true miracle occurred a few days ago, when Frau Cosima Wagner, who was in Munich for the day, 'graciously agreed' to spend the evening with me. This was the first time since her husband's death that she had set foot in anyone else's home. We spoke a good deal about your Royal Highness and observed that in you alone lies the future of the Bayreuth cause.[98]

The year 1888 has gone down in German history as the year of the three emperors. Kaiser Wilhelm I died on 9 March at the age of ninety-one and was succeeded by his fifty-seven-year-old son, who was already gravely ill. Kaiser Friedrich III died on 15 June from cancer of the throat after a reign of only ninety-nine days. Next in line of succession was the twenty-nine-year-old Crown Prince Wilhelm. 'Philly's' friend was now the emperor of Germany and the king of Prussia. Within days Eulenburg was writing to Cosima: 'The idea of addressing yourself to His Majesty the Emperor seems entirely apt and I shall be glad to expedite this myself. I am sincerely sorry that the death of Kaiser Friedrich will prevent our present respected master from coming to Bayreuth – at least I assume that this will be the case.'[99] A visit to Bayreuth by the new kaiser was certainly unthinkable during the three-month period of official mourning: public opinion would have seen in it a lack of respect. 'I am delighted to hear that the Festival is passing off smoothly,' Wilhelm wrote to Cosima in late July 1888, 'and I wish you well for the continuing progress and prosperity of a creative venture that I have followed with lively interest. I see it as one of the loftiest tasks of the German kaiser to appoint himself its protector and patron.'[100] These were undoubtedly grand words, and they certainly caused the hearts of Wahnfried's inhabitants to flutter with expectation. Germany's ruler as the champion and patron of the Wagnerian cause? Such an idea galvanized Cosima, and in her delight she put out a series of press releases. 'It was with genuine jubilation', wrote an overjoyed Malwida von Meysenbug, 'that I saw from the newspapers that your success is more brilliant than ever & that the young Kaiser has promised his support for what he regards as a national cause. May he be blessed for showing such magnificent understanding.'[101]

But Cosima had even bigger ideas, so keen was she to exploit the goodwill of the country's new ruler and to seize the opportunity to ensure that friends and intimates of the Wagner household were moved into key positions in Berlin. Part of this plan involved endowing the aforementioned chair in Wagner studies. Next on the agenda was a shake-up in the senior management of the royal theatres: she hated their present intendant, Count Bolko von Hochberg, and was determined to see him toppled from power and replaced by Count Eulenburg. She also suggested appointing her favourite conductor, Felix Mottl, to a post in the capital. It should be mentioned in passing that Hochberg had had the temerity to criticize Mottl, who had conducted *Parsifal* at the 1888 Bayreuth Festival, taking over from an ailing Hermann Levi. Cosima's protégé had evidently had problems with the demanding score and had proved unequal to the challenge. Weingartner, too, was among Mottl's critics: 'This year's *Parsifal* was a caricature of the piece as a result of speeds that were dragged out to an unprecedented and incomprehensible extent by Mottl. The most offensive aspect of the whole affair was the way in which they tried to give this caricature a racial gloss and speak of a "Christian" *Parsifal* that had even been "redeemed".[102] Weingartner was even more outspoken in a letter to Levi: 'It was Frau Wagner's influence that brought this about, and that influence was pernicious. It is altogether sad that this great woman could not curb her own vanity and that in her attempt to achieve something great on her own initiative she violated the most sacred relic that she should have left inviolate in a spirit of awestruck reverence.'[103]

Bolko von Hochberg could have learnt from Weingartner how quickly one could fall out of favour in Wahnfried's eyes. But he failed to understand that Cosima could not take a joke where the Festival was concerned. Eulenburg repeatedly warned Hochberg not to cross swords with Cosima, but in vain. 'If they hail Mottl as their Messiah,' Hochberg defended himself, 'they are merely demonstrating that they understand nothing or that their fanaticism has made them both blind and deaf.' His fury at the Wagners knew no bounds, and in his rage he even spoke of a 'deceitful, mendacious, vulgar brimstone band headed by an old adulteress who was born to a whore and who has appointed a Jew boy her prophet. That's how it is! May the devil take her! It makes me sick just to think about it.'[104] But Hochberg's indignation came too late, and his critique, although justified, was seen in Bayreuth as a declaration of war. When Eulenburg attended the Festival in early August 1888, he discovered to his horror that Cosima already saw him as Hochberg's successor. 'She seems to be working very energetically against Hochberg in support of my own candidacy,' he noted in his diary. 'I find this extremely unpleasant and embarrassing on Hochberg's account, but I still don't believe in a position that has now been so undermined.'[105]

Eulenburg was to be proved right, and Hochberg kept his post until 1902 as Wilhelm was unable to bring himself to dismiss him. Indeed, Cosima failed to achieve any of her ambitious goals: not the endowment of a chair of Wagner studies nor Mottl's appointment nor even the patronage of the house of Hohenzollern. The reasons for her failure were closely bound up with the figure of the new kaiser: Wilhelm was an upstart who lacked experience, maturity, perceptiveness, patience and self-control, all of them qualities for which he compensated with pithy sayings, an air of arrogance and displays of garish ostentation. Cosima had committed the error of taking at face value the signals sent out by the new kaiser, not realizing that there was a yawning void between the claims that he made for himself and the actual reality of the situation and that as an ally of Wahnfried he was vocal but ultimately feeble. Only in this way can we explain Cosima's effusive reaction to Wilhelm's initial greeting. In her 'most humble report' she described the audience at Bayreuth as 'comparable to a congregation whose members feel drawn together by their contemplation of the ideal'. In the course of her letter, which is a masterpiece of diplomacy, Cosima flattered the kaiser, flirting with him and skilfully appealing to his vanity: 'Your Majesty's gracious words have filled my soul like a call from God and amid hot tears I thanked God for them in the profound loneliness in which I find myself and my work, praising Him for having sent us the help from on high that we so need.'[106]

Wilhelm would no doubt have been willing to accept the invitation to become Bayreuth's royal patron, but, together with Eulenburg and Cosima, he had reckoned without the imperial chancellor. Bismarck had never had any time for Wagner and his music or for the whole of the mythology bound up with Bayreuth – and that is putting it mildly. It is said that the old chancellor had even dismissed the dead Master as a 'monkey'. Moreover, Cosima was very friendly with Marie ('Mimi') Schleinitz, the widow of Alexander von Schleinitz, who had died in 1885. The Schleinitzes could number themselves among the many contemporaries for whom Bismarck felt only the most abject loathing. His hatred could be boundless, and Cosima's friendly dealings with the Schleinitzes automatically aligned them with 'the women hostile to my father', to quote his son, Herbert.[107]

Bismarck's lack of culture was legendary. According to Eulenburg, 'singing was banned in the Bismarck household and replaced by bouts of heavy drinking'.[108] Given his hostility and lack of interest in the arts, it comes as no surprise to learn that – as Eulenburg explained to Cosima – 'the imperial chancellor has spoken out empathically against His Majesty's becoming a patron of Bayreuth'. For a power-hungry tactician like Bismarck, Wilhelm's support of the Wagners represented a dangerous display of sentimentality. In particular, he was afraid that 'the sensitivities of the House of Wittelsbach would be offended by such a step'. In other words, Luitpold of Bavaria might feel that he had been passed over. 'I expect I shall have an opportunity to see the kaiser in the not too distant future', Eulenburg went on, 'and I shall no doubt discover more details on that occasion.'[109] Some three weeks later he reported on his conversation with Wilhelm: 'The Kaiser is most eager to see the performances next year. He told me: "The break would be too long if I were unable to see anything next summer either. If you write to Frau Wagner, please mention how much I want this." ' This sounded very positive, but who was to pay the piper? Only a few lines later, Cosima discovered the answer: 'The Kaiser was saddened at the political events that have kept him from becoming royal patron. His whole heart was in it!'[110] Adolf von Groß had already been sceptical about Hohenzollern patronage and immediately wrote to Cosima to say that it was now clear 'that the question of royal patronage has been decided in the negative'.[111]

Bismarck had got his way. Eulenburg was evidently so embarrassed by this turn of events that in one of his next letters to Cosima he sought refuge in some particularly bizarre phraseology: the Bayreuth Festival, he attempted to console her, would in future 'rise like a phoenix from all these unpleasantnesses – for all the tribulations, all the hostility of the gnomes will be burnt to ashes in the flames of true enthusiasm for our cause!'[112] The 'gnomes', we can only assume, were critical contemporaries like Prince Bismarck.

The attempt to enlist Wilhelm II as the Festival's royal patron foundered not least on the fact that he was a phoney and a blusterer who grew intoxicated on his own platitudes. Had he not described his patronage of Bayreuth as 'one of the loftiest tasks for the German kaiser'? Cosima had been taken in by his orotund oratory, but when she asked him for his support, he backed away. Adolf von Groß had foreseen this development. In lengthy and secret negotiations with Ludwig August von Müller, Munich's chief of police and later Bavarian minister of culture, he persuaded Luitpold to become royal patron, a move that evidently took a great weight off Wilhelm's mind. 'He hopes that the prince regent's patronage will bring only good to you and the cause,' Eulenburg informed Cosima, 'and it is this that he desires above all else.'[113]

During the first few weeks of 1889 countless letters passed between Liebenberg and Bayreuth, many of them discussing in detail the arrangements for that summer's Festival. 'The presence of the kaiser in Bayreuth together with the prince regent will turn out to be quite wonderful,' Eulenburg assured his correspondent. But, turning to Wilhelm's taste in music, 'I think that in this particular case it would be best to perform *Parsifal* and *Die Meistersinger*.'[114] This was a tactful way of saying that the kaiser's musical education left much to be desired: 'Unfortunately, rhythm always delights him more than melody.'[115] With regard to Wagner's music dramas, Eulenburg went on: 'He instinctively grasps the national side of this art, for in his delight at Wagner he has not yet realized that his musical sensibilities are less developed than his nationalism and that his enthusiasm might not have reached boiling point if Wagner had set only subjects like Rienzi.'[116] Cosima decided on

Parsifal, this time with Levi back on the podium, *Tristan und Isolde* under Mottl and *Die Meistersinger von Nürnberg*, this last-named a work which, entirely to Wilhelm's taste, was very much Hans Richter's party piece.

Rehearsals began at nine on the morning of 24 June 1889. In the course of the next twenty-five days there were daily rehearsals for the chorus, orchestra and soloists as well as stage rehearsals in the theatre. Although the burden of running the Festival was borne by many shoulders, it was Cosima who held all the threads, she who was ultimately responsible for deciding contentious questions, and so she attended all the rehearsals. As a rule, outsiders had no idea that this demanding rehearsal schedule sometimes left the fifty-one-year-old Cosima at the very brink of exhaustion. Even in 1887 Daniela had already complained that her mother was running herself into the ground: 'Her whole body needs looking after, above all her poor eyes, which are a source of genuine concern to me.'[117] But Cosima gave no indication of her infirmity to the outside world, demanding only that her colleagues should 'serve the work', a demand to which everything else, including her own health, was secondary.

'So far there have been no official announcements about the kaiser's visit,' Levi told his father in a letter dated 4 July, 'and Frau W. already doubts if he'll be coming at all. But public support will be tremendous; the opening performances are already sold out.'[118] The last of the rehearsals – the dress rehearsal of *Die Meistersinger von Nürnberg* – took place on 19 July, and two days later the Festival opened with the first night of *Parsifal*. 'I'm still completely elated by the magnificent performance! It was the best I've ever conducted,' Levi told his father. 'It was as if God's blessing lay upon every note.'[119]

For outsiders, the pseudo-religious aura that wafted down from the Green Hill was difficult to stomach. One of these outsiders was Brahms's pupil Elisabeth von Herzogenberg:

> People like that go to *Parsifal* just as Catholics visit graves on Good Friday, it has become a church service for them. The whole bunch of them are in an unnaturally heightened, hysterically enraptured state, like Ribera's saints, with their eyes raised aloft so that one can see only the whites of them, and under their shirts they all have carefully tended stigmata. I tell you, the whole thing has a really bad smell to it, like a church that has never been aired or like a butcher's display of meat in summer: a blood-thirstiness and musty smell of incense, a sultry sensuality with terribly serious gestures, a heaviness and a bombast otherwise unprecedented in art weighs down on one, its brooding intensity taking one's breath away.

What she found in Bayreuth was a 'bag of spiritual conjuring tricks' and an 'unhealthy ecstasy which, fired by the stigmata, is almost an emetic for stomachs accustomed to a diet of Bach'.[120]

However irreverent Elisabeth von Herzogenberg's comments, they none the less contain a grain of truth. Six years after Wagner's death, the esoteric and pseudo-religious features of the Festival were plain to see. In her letter to Wilhelm II, Cosima had compared Bayreuth audiences to a congregation: there was a sense of a play within a play, *Parsifal* constituting a sacred relic placed before a congregation of worshippers for only a few days each year. In terms of group psychology, this was extremely effective, for it allowed Cosima's congregation to define itself by virtue of its exclusive access to this fetish.

For his part, Kaiser Wilhelm made the pilgrimage to Bayreuth's Green Hill on Friday 16 August. Initially he kept a low profile and left the prince regent, Luitpold of Bavaria, to take the stage. There was no performance on this particular day, and so the artists organized a reception for their ruler in Bayreuth's Neues Schloß. It proved a lively occasion, attended, as it was, not only by the Wagners and the artists but also by local dignitaries and politicians. Wearing his Bavarian uniform, Hermann Levi conducted Weber's *Jubel-Ouvertüre* and received a gold baton from Luitpold in return. There was a celebratory mood disrupted only by Mottl's carping: 'Levi is a ghastly, fidgety Jew!' he complained, clearly envious of his older colleague's success. Not even Luitpold found favour in his eyes: 'The prince regent a dull-witted, uncouth animal in his whole attitude, appearance, gait and language. He says only stupid things.'[121] The kaiser and his wife, Auguste Viktoria, were officially welcomed to Bayreuth the following morning with a ceremony accompanied by all manner of pomp and circumstance. Mottl again described the event in his diary: 'Reception for the kaiser in the Neues Schloß. My hymn of welcome in B flat major. Kaisermarsch. He makes a splendid impression. The expression in his eyes is kind, bright and clear, and he has rid himself of all the stable manners that I had occasion to note as recently as 1886. Next to him, the prince regent looked like an arse beside a beautiful face.'[122]

The Bayreuth Circle

Kaiser Wilhelm's visit to Bayreuth was an undoubted triumph for the Festival and was assiduously promoted as such by Wahnfried. A whole year earlier Cosima had asked Count Eulenburg whether she could mention the kaiser's presence in her publicity. Permission was duly granted, and the Festival lost no opportunity to plume itself with imperial feathers, Hans von Wolzogen in particular revealing exceptional ingenuity in exploiting Wilhelm's flying visit. Since 1885 the Universal Richard Wagner Society had published an annual diary featuring Germanic names, Christian saints and all kinds of vaguely heroic sayings. The 1889 edition was adorned by a photograph of Wilhelm II, whose accession was celebrated in the foreword with an 'acclamatory greeting to his youthful Majesty'. The greatest hopes were pinned on the new ruler, who was to provide leadership 'in the universal struggle for the culture of the future! For it is towards this goal that we Bayreuthians are moving and pointing through time.'[123]

'We Bayreuthians'? The phrase is involuntarily comical as the foreword was signed 'Munich', which is where the publication's editorial offices were situated. In other words, the term can hardly have referred to the entire population of the little town in Upper Franconia. It is Cosima herself who provides an explanation of the expression. Writing to her daughter Daniela in April 1881, she explained that 'in order to turn a view of art into a world view, initiates are needed, and just as people used to talk about Pythagoreans, so we may speak of Bayreuthians'.[124] The following day she returned to her theme:

> As an opera composer your papa cannot be regarded as a party leader but, rather, he may be seen as the founder of Bayreuth and as a philosopher, and to that extent the term Wagnerian may be used to describe those people who everywhere follow him . . . That is why there can be Wagnerians because there is a Wagnerian idea that these people attempt to put into practice, whereas there can be no Lisztians as your grandpapa, although a great artist, did not implement any ideas any more than Beethoven and others did.[125]

It is true that Wagner had never wanted to be a 'party leader' and that he was essentially unsympathetic to the cosy camaraderie of clubs and societies in general. Although the Master demanded allegiance from his followers, he regarded with deep suspicion all personal allegiances and commitments. This explains why his views on the Bayreuth Festival, on the various Wagner Societies and on his comrades in general depended on the current situation and, not least, on his mood of the moment. Cosima's diaries are awash with remarks that support this interpretation: there were times when he would become depressed and announce his readiness to abandon everything, disciples such as Wolzogen causing him particular annoyance, and yet there were other occasions when he became positively euphoric and eager for action. At the very end of his life, finally, he expressed his contempt for his supporters, 'who seem to be designed to make all the ideas he expresses look ridiculous'.[126]

One has the impression that Wagner was only superficially interested in his followers. It is the famous sociologist Max Weber who provides us with the key to understanding this phenomenon: charisma. Weber defines charisma as

> a certain quality of an individual personality by virtue of which he is considered extraordinary and treated as endowed with supernatural, superhuman, or at least specifically exceptional powers or qualities. These are such as are not accessible to the ordinary person, but are regarded as of divine origin or as exemplary, and on the basis of them the individual concerned is treated as a 'leader'.[127]

According to Weber, it is a matter of some indifference whether or not these qualities are in fact present. What matters, rather, is how they are perceived and interpreted by that leader's followers. In other words, the term charisma describes an almost intimate interaction between the charismatic personality – Wagner – and his disciples. In Weber's words, there is 'no system of formal rules, of abstract legal principles, and hence no process of rational judicial decision oriented to them', but only the inspirations and revelations of the charismatic individual: 'It is written . . . but I say unto you.'[128] When Wagner died in 1883, the symbolic figure died with him, and the situation changed completely. His death marked the birth of the 'Bayreuth circle', an ideological group of men and women who saw themselves as the Wagnerian avant-garde. It would be wrong, however, to regard this community of like-minded individuals as any normal society that people could join or resign from at will and that held its drink-fuelled meetings in smoke-filled public houses, drawing up rules and handing out badges to its older members. True, this could be a description of many of the other Wagner Societies that for the most part pursued the cult of genius like any other educated middle-class association. But the operations of the Bayreuth circle were more complicated than this, for we are dealing here with an esoteric gathering of like-minded men and women, all of whom subscribed to the idea of developing, interpreting and promulgating Wagner's concept of culture along dogmatic lines. Or, rather, it would be more accurate to say that these fanatics promoted what they themselves understood to be Wagner's concept of culture. Today we would speak of a 'network', a modern form of organization in which at least two people or institutions are engaged in a constant exchange of information, while remaining largely independent of one another. The networkers of the Bayreuth circle saw Bayreuth not as an innovative theatre workshop but as a kind of substitute religion that humankind needed to embrace if it was to be saved. As a result, it was not always easy to draw a line between this and pseudo-religious sectarianism. 'But we should now remind ourselves', Carl Friedrich Glasenapp wrote to Ludwig Schemann shortly after Wagner's death, 'that it is our task to pass on what we have seen as the true apostles and evangelists of a new covenant and as its living witnesses.'[129] But such a gospel – to stick with Glasenapp's image – was far from being unambiguous. Wagner's views were not infrequently confused and self-contradictory: if his *obiter dicta* were to be turned into a coherent view of the world, then they would require exegesis and need to be invested with canonical status. The 'Bayreuthians' made skilful use of this lack of clarity, and the anti-authoritarian, revolutionary views that had formed the breeding ground for Wagner's creative *oeuvre* were successively eliminated and replaced by their very opposite. In his youth, Wagner had been fired by enthusiasm for the Polish War of Independence of 1830 and for the July Revolution that broke out in Paris that same year, but the radical liberalism of these early years was airbrushed out of existence in his disciples' picture of their hero. Or, to put it another way, Wagner was robbed of his own biography and brought into line. And all of this was done with constant appeals to the dead Master, who could no longer defend himself against such an act of wholesale misappropriation.

As for Cosima, she had effectively only a single card that she could play to legitimize her activities, and that was her widowhood, a quality to which she gave a positively theatrical dimension, leaving many with the impression that the Master lived on in her. Glasenapp ventured into the choppy seas of hagiographic hyperbole when claiming that 'to my mind' Wagner's life 'is continued in Her, his survivor, pure and untroubled and therefore uniquely authoritative.'[130] Cosima's authority was certainly decisive, for in Wahnfried many strands came together. 'Wahnfried' was not only the portentous name that Wagner had chosen for the home where he spent his final years, it was also synonymous with Cosima's sphere of influence. Among members of Wahnfried's inner circle were the writers Hans von Wolzogen and Ludwig Schemann, Wagner's early biographer Carl Friedrich Glasenapp, Cosima's youthful admirer Heinrich von Stein, her son-in-law Henry Thode and her future son-in-law Houston Stewart Chamberlain. With Cosima at their head and with Wahnfried as their command centre, these gentlemen were, so to speak, the Wagnerian politburo.

The community's journalistic mouthpiece was the *Bayreuther Blätter*, which Wolzogen edited from 1878 until his death in 1938. He was born in 1848 and was lured to Bayreuth in 1877, with the result that Wagner then felt the need to employ him. If the journal began life as a rag for the Bayreuth Patrons' Society, it developed over the years into a 'German Periodical in the Spirit of Richard Wagner', to quote its subsequent subtitle. Initially it was published every month, although by the end it was appearing only quarterly. Throughout its history it appealed to a distinctly heterogeneous readership: music lovers and cultured individuals interested in literature and the arts in general all found a forum here, as did German Nationals, supporters of Bismarck, opponents of democracy, guardians of public morals, fanatical vegetarians, teetotallers and even contemporaries opposed to 'scientific medicine'. However diverse these obscure groups may have been, they were linked from the outset by their shared anti-Semitism and narrow-minded nationalism. Many of the articles that appeared in the pages of the *Bayreuther Blätter* are now almost impossible to read, so linguistically turgid is their style, and so emotionally charged and half-baked their ideas. Among the journal's 400 or so contributors we find a number of eminent names, including those of the novelist Theodor Fontane, the French pacifist Romain Rolland and the composer Richard Strauss, although none of these writers contributed more than a single article. No doubt they withdrew instinctively as soon as they discovered the company they were being forced to keep. The vast majority of the writers were men like Constantin Frantz, who compared the Jews to tapeworms, and Arthur Seidl, who argued that Jesus was an Aryan. For enlightened and liberal contemporaries, Bayreuth's in-house journal was an unedifying gutter newspaper. Even people intimate with Wahnfried were eager to keep their distance. 'No member of the Society needs receive the *Bayreuther Blätter*,' Hermann Levi hastened to reassure his highly sceptical father, 'not even I myself would like to drum up publicity for it.'[131]

One is bound to ask if all this was really undertaken 'in the spirit of Richard Wagner'. And the answer is that this seems unlikely. In his disciples' hands, Wagner's ideas degenerated to the level of a muddy and vulgar ideology that hailed a chauvinistic art out of touch with the real world as if it were a substitute religion. All in all, the sixty-one volumes of the *Bayreuther Blätter* represent what Michael Karbaum has termed 'one of the darkest chapters in the history of German ideas'.[132]

Cosima appeared by name only very infrequently in the pages of the journal, and yet the importance of her role cannot be overstated. She busied herself in the background, taking all the final decisions on questions of ideological orthodoxy and judging, censoring and even initiating articles. 'Time and again Cosima provided her friend Wolzogen with the most valuable contributions,' Max Millenkovich-Morold wrote approvingly in his biography of Cosima, 'but for a long time readers did not know or guess that she was responsible for them.'[133] Elsewhere Millenkovich-Morold writes that 'the unnamed editor in chief was Cosima, who read through all the submissions and meticulously prepared each new issue with Wolzogen.'[134] Her own contributions appeared under the significant pseudonym of 'Wahnfried'. She was particularly drawn to the writings of Arthur de Gobineau, writer, diplomat and self-styled count. Largely ignored in his French homeland, Gobineau enjoyed almost cult status in Bayreuth, where his ideas seemed to Cosima to represent a gratifying confirmation of her own journey in life.

Gobineau's doctrine attests to the hatred of a pseudo-aristocratic snob for the post-Revolutionary France in which he had failed to make his mark. His racist tract, *Essay on the Inequality of the Human Races*, was inordinately praised in the pages of the *Bayreuther Blätter*. Between 1881 and 1937 no fewer than sixty-one often substantial articles were published on the subject of its controversial French author. In 1894 a number of influential members of the Bayreuth circle around Ludwig Schemann founded a no less influential Gobineau Society whose publications appeared as a supplement to the *Bayreuther Blätter*. As early as 1882 Cosima was already championing the idea of a German translation of Gobineau's *Essay*, which appeared in four volumes between 1898 and 1901. And when Gobineau died in Turin in October 1882, it was again Cosima who wrote an unctuous obituary of her former friend for the *Bayreuther Blätter*. In this context, it matters little that German writers on Gobineau adopted a highly idiosyncratic approach to his ideas: whereas Gobineau himself had propagated the idea of three 'primeval races', 'black', 'yellow' and 'white', his Bayreuth disciples assiduously applied the notion of the superiority of the 'white race' to the German nation to the exclusion of all others.

One cannot but be struck by Bayreuth's power of attraction for foreign eccentrics like Gobineau. To limit our discussion to the key figures in the Bayreuth circle, Cosima was, strictly speaking, of French and Hungarian parentage, while Glasenapp lived in the Latvian city of Riga, where he had been born in 1847. Chamberlain had a Scottish mother and an English father and had been brought up in France and England. Wolzogen, too, belongs in their company at least in a wider sense: his mother died two years after he was born, and the child was brought up by an aunt in Berlin in a house built by his maternal grandfather, the famous architect and designer Karl Friedrich Schinkel. Here he spent the formative years of his childhood as a 'rootless being'. He attended the Breslau Grammar School, which he described as 'a real "Jewish school" in which the German race was only sporadically represented'.[135] This circumstance, coupled with a visit to the multi-ethnic region of Galicia, left him feeling unsettled and finally led to his belief that 'a dogged German resistance to all that was foreign had been awoken in me'.[136]

One final example of this phenomenon was Cosima's daughter-in-law, Winifred Wagner, who married into the family in 1915, an English orphan who grew up in Germany and who, like the others, was a 'rootless being'. However different their lives, their indeterminate origins and the feeling that they were not at home in a country that was in any case difficult to define left them all suffering from alienation complexes that found expression in an aggressive ultra-nationalism, the intensity of their fanaticism conditioned by the degree of their uncertainty or, in Gobineau's case, the extent to which he saw himself as a failure. Politically motivated Wagnerism was not about music, opera and theatre: Wagner himself was only the name for something else, the 'spirit of Bayreuth', an aggressively Teutonic and Christian doctrine of salvation. Count Harry Kessler was surprised at the extent to which Wagner was misunderstood by his dogmatic followers: 'It throws a curious light on Wagner's admirers,' he commented, 'but also on Wagner himself, that one can enjoy him passionately without understanding him.'[137] There is no doubt that without Cosima and her accomplices, the occasionally bizarre cult of Wagner in Wilhelminian Germany might have petered out in the sands of insignificance, but instead they jointly succeeded in transforming the spirit of Bayreuth into a national and nationalist 'cause'. It was Cosima's charisma as the legitimate 'guardian of the Grail', her organizational skill and her ideological obstinacy that enabled Bayreuth to prove so disastrously effective as a political force in Germany.

Family Planning

After two extremely busy festivals, the doors of the theatre remained closed in 1890, Cosima using the break to prepare for the following season. In July she auditioned the singers, and in the autumn she travelled to Munich with Mottl for another of her conductors' conferences. Between them, Levi, Mottl and Cosima decided that in 1891 they would revive *Parsifal* and *Tristan und Isolde* and mount a new production of *Tannhäuser*.

It was at about this time that Siegfried Wagner moved to Berlin. He had completed his schooling in 1889 and then spent a year studying music with Engelbert Humperdinck in Mainz. Cosima would have preferred it if he had decided in favour of music from the very outset, but she agreed to allow him to pursue his interest in architecture and funded his studies at the Technical University in Charlottenburg, after which she would determine his subsequent course in life. It was with a heavy heart that she saw him go, and she evidently pined for her twenty-one-year-old son, because by January 1891 we find her writing to a friend in Berlin and announcing that she would be arriving with Eva and Isolde for a stay lasting several weeks: 'We need a salon, two bedrooms, one with two beds, also a servant's room. I don't know if there are guest-house prices for food at the Windsor Hotel; we prefer to eat on our own in our rooms.'[138] The recipient of these lines was Anna Kekulé, the wife of the archaeologist Reinhard Kekulé von Stradonitz, who also ran the department of antiquities at the Royal Museums in Berlin. Cosima had known the couple for many years and had become very friendly with Anna Kekulé. After her husband's death in 1911, Anna even spent a number of weeks each year in Bayreuth, where she saw to Cosima's needs and provided her with nursing care.

Back in 1891, Anna Kekulé was evidently able to help Cosima and her two daughters, reserving rooms for them at the elegant Hotel Hohenzollern. In Berlin, Cosima frequented the very best houses, seeing the Kekulés on frequent occasions and calling on the physicist Hermann von Helmholtz and his wife Anna, Liszt's pupil Karl Klindworth, the cabinet adviser Bodo von dem Knesebeck and the banker's wife Anna vom Rat. In addition to her numerous social obligations, Cosima also availed herself of the rapidly expanding city's cultural amenities. The art historian Hugo von Tschudi took her on a guided tour of the art gallery, and she also attended a performance of *Tannhäuser* in preparation for that summer's Bayreuth production, although the Berlin staging proved a disappointment, offering little that could provide a model for Bayreuth. Although she was impressed by the Elisabeth of the soprano Rosa Sucher, casting the main tenor role was causing Cosima some headaches, and when the Munich *Neueste Nachrichten* reported, prematurely, that she was engaging Max Alvary, she reacted with some asperity. 'This is more of Levi's tittle-tattle,' she wrote angrily to Adolf von Groß, 'it's impossible to tell him anything, but it has persuaded me not to write to him any more. He then has recourse to flattery, this lack of character on his part has become absolutely unbearable.' The conductor, she went on, 'has this appalling

Jewishness about him that makes all contact with him an embarrassment. He turns everything into gossip! Worry & grief & everything! Forgive me my ill humour, but I prefer a man to be a man.'[139] But, as Groß pointed out to Cosima, Levi was not in fact to blame for this indiscretion: 'In the present case, he is entirely innocent, the excellent Alvary, celebrating his triumphs in Munich, was unable to keep a secret.'[140] But it made no difference: Cosima was convinced that Jews were indiscreet and given to gossip.

Many of the more dyed-in-the-wool Wagnerians regarded Cosima's decision to introduce *Tannhäuser* to the Festival repertory as an act of blatant provocation, arguing that the work was 'unworthy of Bayreuth' inasmuch as it was too traditionally operatic and rooted in conventions described as 'alien to the spirit of Bayreuth'. Cosima boldly swept aside these misgivings and ignored the numerous protests that she received. It was Mottl on whom fell the dubious honour of conducting so controversial a piece. His assistant was the twenty-seven-year-old conductor and composer Richard Strauss, who had come to Bayreuth in 1889 with glowing testimonials from Hans von Bülow, no less. By 1891 Bayreuth was willing to entrust to him the task of conducting some of the rehearsals. He was 'fanatical, as only young people can be', Cosima wrote enthusiastically to Houston Stewart Chamberlain.[141] On another occasion she praised him as a 'rising star, armed for our cause from head to toe'.[142]

The correspondence between Cosima and her 'dear expression', as she affectionately called the young Strauss, attests to a sense of genuine sympathy and mutual respect. Strauss was talented and took idealism to the point of self-sacrifice. He was ready to learn from Cosima, whom he addressed as 'most highly respected and gracious Frau Wagner' and who encouraged him in turn with almost maternal solicitude. Nor was it long before their friendly dealings extended to Cosima's children: Strauss visited Blandine and her husband in Italy and spent time with the Thodes in Frankfurt, but it was his willingness to support Siegfried's earliest musical endeavours that gave her the greatest pleasure. The temptation to make Strauss a family member was clearly irresistible, and for a time Cosima toyed with the idea of pairing him off with Eva, his junior by three years. But Strauss turned her down, for he was already in love with his pupil, Pauline de Ahna, whom he married in 1894. This may have caused the first rift between Strauss and Wahnfried, but other factors lay behind the definitive breakdown of the relationship in 1894, when Strauss conducted *Tannhäuser* in Bayreuth and Cosima is said to have whispered in his ear: 'Well, well, so modern and yet you conduct *Tannhäuser* so well.'[143] It was the modern composer who was viewed with increasing mistrust by Wahnfried. His decision two years later to write a tone poem inspired by Nietzsche's *Thus Spake Zarathustra* amounted to an act of downright sacrilege in the Wagners' eyes. His modern musical language, the no less modern librettos of his operas and, not least, his success as a composer – none of this found favour in Wahnfried, and by the end of 1895 the correspondence between the two parties was growing more and more sporadic. By the end they spoke only ill of one another.

There is no doubt that envy played a part in this turn of events, the relatively unsuccessful Siegfried, in particular, resenting his contemporary's triumphs. Ultimately, the history of music was to prove Strauss right. But in 1891 the relationship between Strauss and the Wagners was still unclouded. Only Levi felt uncomfortable and excluded and had difficulty getting through that summer's Festival, so much did he feel that he had been insulted and badly treated by Cosima, Mottl and probably Strauss as well. At the end of the season, he wrote to Cosima, a letter that still has the power to touch us deeply:

> I have the clear feeling that my shoulders have grown too weak not only for what I have to do in Bayreuth but also for what I have to bear and endure; I am wounded and ill and I long for rest. And so I beg and entreat you to release me from this impasse!! You have said so often both in earnest and in jest that I am the cross that you would have to bear till the end. But when is the end? Why can it not be today?[144]

Cosima replied by return of post, beginning her letter by drawing Levi's attention to 'the Master's will' and roundly declaring that she was not in a position to release the conductor from his post. 'You say that you are wounded and ill. My God, who isn't? Have we not learnt to regard life as a wound for which only death or repentance can cure us?'[145]

It is hardly surprising that Cosima's markedly cool and businesslike reply did little to dispel Levi's doubts. He wrote again on 21 September and this time did not mince his words:

> The fact that I have failed to coax from you – I will not say a heartfelt note – at least a friendly acknowledgement of my efforts demonstrates a point that I have made to you so often and that you have always been kind enough to contest with equal frequency, namely, that it is not my actions, thoughts and remarks that offend you but that you regard my entire nature and my mere

existence as something hostile to you personally and disruptive to your whole circle.[146]

Levi touched on a sore point with Cosima by confronting her directly with her anti-Semitism. It was a clever move on his part. But Cosima's riposte proved just as clever. Indeed, one could even describe it as a diplomatic masterpiece. She began by linking Levi's fate to her own: 'If – which I hope is not the case – your physical strength were to prove insufficient, I am sure that you would prefer to perish with me in Bayreuth rather than eke out your living elsewhere.' And she went on:

> The qualities in you that offend me are part of your line, whereas all your good and admirable qualities are your own and cannot, therefore, be praised sufficiently highly. With me, the opposite is the case: I inherited my good qualities (assuming there is anything good about me), whereas the bad qualities, which I do not need to enumerate, are entirely my own.

Cosima confessed to her guilt and at the same time appealed to Levi's gallantry: 'Be more magnanimous towards me than I have been towards you, and let us try once again to see if we can make it work.'[147] Cosima's calculations paid off, and Levi withdrew his resignation, returning to Bayreuth to conduct *Parsifal* in 1892 and again in 1894. (There was no Festival in 1893.)

Oedipus Rex?

With the end of the 1891 season, Siegfried Wagner turned his back on Berlin and moved to Karlsruhe, where he pursued his interest in architecture at the city's polytechnic, while at the same time deepening his knowledge of music through his contacts with Felix Mottl, who was kapellmeister to the court of Baden. As Siegfried recalled many years later, Mottl's performances fired in him 'an increasingly powerful desire to embrace music as a profession'.[148] Cosima was overjoyed at this development as she had always hoped that Fidi would one day devote himself to music. By Christmas 1891 some of his earliest compositions were among the seasonal gifts presented to family members. 'For the children', Cosima wrote to inform Reinhard Kekulé

> we had Santa Claus and the infant Jesus as well as a beautiful chorale by Luther. As always, Siegfried had lots of little gifts for everyone, with his own

songs, a watercolour, things both practical & impractical, in short, the dear provider that God has given me. His plans are not yet entirely fixed. More on this in person, as I am very much looking forward to seeing you both very soon.[149]

Cosima's mysterious reference to Siegfried's plans leads us neatly on to the next section of this chapter. The young man had decided to undertake a world cruise with his friend Clement Harris, his junior by two years, whom he had got to know in Frankfurt. Harris was the son of a wealthy shipbuilder from London and was studying at the Hoch Conservatory in Frankfurt, where his piano teacher was none other than Clara Schumann, Robert Schumann's septuagenarian widow. Much has been written about the relationship between Siegfried and Clement Harris, and from all that we know from letters and diary entries, it seems that the two men were lovers. Harris was homosexual, and it appears that Siegfried, now in the process of discovering his own sexuality, was drawn to the sensitive, attractive and charismatic youth. It is doubtful if the Wagners even suspected what was going on. 'Very best wishes to dear little Clement,' he wrote on one occasion to his half-sister Daniela, 'during the few days that I'm there he should keep as far away from Parnassus as possible.'[150] Perhaps Daniela suspected. But Cosima, at least, appears to have harboured no suspicions, for we find her writing to Anna Kekulé:

> Clement Harris has invited him on board his father's ship, & no one, least of all myself, would understand it if I said no. They are sailing from London via Suez to India – under the most favourable circumstances imaginable, or so it is said. The trip lasts until June, when he starts work as music assistant at our Festival. He has recently already conducted a choir & it went very well.[151]

Cosima maintained her outward composure, and it was only Adolf von Groß who discovered what she was really feeling: Siegfried's departure in the middle of January and the prospect of hearing nothing from him for weeks on end had triggered what amounted to a panic attack. 'I am pursued by the most terrible thoughts,' she admitted to her financial adviser on Easter Day. 'They'll kill Fidi to get even with his father.' It is significant, perhaps, that Cosima was afraid that Siegfried might be the victim of a French assassination attempt: 'The French can be appalling. It was all I could think about last night.' Cosima was completely beside herself with worry and dangerously close to a breakdown. In order to spare Eva and Isolde from so pitiful a sight, she even thought of leaving Bayreuth under some pretext or other:

> Will you tell them that I have to go to Wiesbaden for a few days (because of Bahry) and that I'm setting off this evening (if I can't get away any sooner). How could I ever have allowed him to make this journey? It is as if I have sacrificed Fidi. And I do not know what can reassure me. Some good-for-nothing might attack him in an attempt to prove himself a hero.

So distressed was she that she started to entertain the most fantastical ideas: 'Do you think it may be possible to protect Fidi – perhaps through the German Embassy?'[152] Groß did all in his power to persuade Cosima that she need not worry, but it was in vain, as she found herself tormented by increasingly irrational fears, suddenly taking it into her head, for example, that Siegfried would be unable to tolerate the climate. 'You may be assured that Siegfried is well,' Groß sought to console her. 'Harris's father would certainly not allow his children to travel to places where there was a threat from the climate; Siegfried has already survived more than half the time that he will be away from you, and he'll be safely back with you in two months at the latest.'[153]

When Siegfried returned to Bayreuth in early July, the sense of delight was unbounded. He now informed his mother that he had finally decided in favour of a career in music. Cosima was overjoyed. In official accounts of Wahnfried, Siegfried's decision was hailed as a revelation promising true salvation. Richard Du Moulin Eckart, for example, wrote that 'While the world was rebelling against the Green Hill and its first lady, her future assistant was emerging in the person of her son.'[154] Siegfried's decision to devote himself to the Bayreuth Festival will not in fact have been quite as voluntary as Du Moulin Eckart's panegyric suggests. Perhaps Cosima suspected the bond that linked Siegfried and Clement Harris. According to Sven Friedrich, the world cruise that exacted this tribute was 'Fidi's honeymoon'.[155] Ultimately Siegfried could not escape from his mother's psychological conditioning, and he no doubt knew that his affair with Harris would have its price, a price that meant he would now have to join the family business.

Siegfried Wagner's name first appears in the list of musical assistants at the 1892 Bayreuth Festival, thereby marking the beginning of a bad tradition designed to extol and celebrate the young man. From the outset the fact that it was merely the circumstances of his birth that made him the head of a flourishing enterprise was a serious handicap for him. Even before he could develop his own identity, he was already 'the Master's son', on whose narrow shoulders rested the burden of a great inheritance.

Siegfried Wagner was undoubtedly talented. He first conducted the *Ring* in 1896, when he was only twenty-seven, and it is clear that he made a success of it. 'Siegfried conducted the *Rheingold* rehearsal outstandingly well,' Mottl noted in his diary on 1 July 1896.[156] Two days later we read: 'Siegfried is amazing.'[157] Although there are conflicting accounts of his conducting, contemporary witnesses agreed in praising his well-developed sense of the theatre. His principal gifts probably lay in the field of stage direction, where he could draw on his interest in architecture and the visual arts. But he could also write poetry and music, in keeping with his father's ideal and his mother's wishes. Under the influence of his teacher, Engelbert Humperdinck, whose *Hänsel und Gretel* received its first public performance in 1893, he discovered for himself the medium of the fairytale opera. His own contributions to the genre include *Herzog Wildfang*, *Der Kobold*, *Bruder Lustig*, *Sternengebot* and *Banadietrich*.

His first completed work for the stage, *Der Bärenhäuter*, was finished in 1898 and staged in Munich the following year. It tells the story of the soldier Hans Kraft, who gambles away the souls that have been entrusted to him and who by way of punishment is forced to wander the earth unwashed and wearing only a bearskin. Siegfried's librettos tend to be over-complex, the various strands in the narrative creating an often confusing impression. For Weingartner, Siegfried was the 'unfortunate Dauphin of Bayreuth', whose opera *Herzog Wildfang* was based on 'such a pitiful farrago of a libretto' that it was 'simply deplorable' that it was allowed to appear at all. It was plain to see, he went on, 'that we are dealing here simply with the exploitation of a father's great name in order that a microscopic talent might be blown up to apparent greatness and thereby ensure that the Festival has an "heir" '.[158] In his musical language, Siegfried remained a product of the nineteenth century, and however well crafted his works may have been, they leave one with the impression that the epoch-making music dramas of his father had never existed. Gustav Mahler, Siegfried's elder by only nine years, had forced open the door to the twentieth century, leaving Schoenberg, his junior by five years, to slip through. Siegfried, meanwhile, peered anxiously through the keyhole and, failing to understand what he saw, withdrew. Debussy identified the problem when he wrote that *Herzog Wildfang* was 'like a student exercise by a pupil of Richard Wagner, but not one in whom the master was very interested'.[159] In short, Siegfried was the 'worthy but mediocre son' of the great Richard Wagner.[160]

Cartoonists like William A. Wellner poured scorn and contumely on the young Wagner: 'Mama! Mama!' cried Siegfried, portrayed sitting at the piano, 'I've just had an idea – Papa's Redemption motif!'[161] Karl Kraus, too, poked fun at Siegfried's 'unnatural resemblance to his father' in the best tradition of *Die Fackel*, the satirical periodical that Kraus published in Vienna. 'Even though I can't compose, I can at least give the appearance of doing so,' was the annihilating mot that Kraus placed in Siegfried Wagner's mouth.[162]

Cosima simply refused to accept that her son's talent was limited at best. Like so much else in her life, her relationship with her son was invested with a certain degree of fanciful exaggeration and bombast. She pinned hopes on him that he was incapable of fulfilling, and any outsider who voiced the vaguest doubts about his genius immediately fell into disfavour. Attacks on Fidi she felt were directed at herself, and she took them very personally. In Wahnfried and its incense-laden environs, Siegfried's inviolability led to abject sycophancy and idolatry: 'It might have been possible to do something about the young man's often childlike helplessness if it hadn't been for the fact that a repulsive subservience had nestled at the little son's feet,' Weingartner noted at an early date.[163] Even close friends like the Kekulés parroted Cosima to the letter: 'It is wonderful that your Siegfried has set out on his career in so assured and triumphant a fashion.'[164] Elsewhere Kekulé even appealed to the dear Lord: 'I think I can understand all the memories, the humility, the pride and joy and the piety and love that must animate your heart on seeing your Siegfried striking out so triumphantly on the path in life that God has decreed for him.'[165] Not even the fickle Felix Mottl was immune from all this: 'Letter from Frau Wagner,' he noted in his diary in early April 1904. 'Enthusiastic about Siegfried's "Kobold". She writes that it is "one of life's unforgettable experiences".'[166] When he finally heard the opera, he had only one word for it: 'Talentless,' he wrote in his diary.[167]

Throughout his life Siegfried Wagner felt that he had been passed over and badly treated as a composer. Convinced of his own significance, he could not understand why the public at large took such a limited interest in his works. It was 'the others' who were to blame for this deplorable state of affairs, he believed, and by 'the others' he meant the Jews, the press, degenerate contemporary taste and so on. 'Siegfried makes it impossible to hold a natural, uninhibited conversation with him,' complained Count Harry Kessler,

as he has dogmatic views on every possible subject, views that he forcefully expresses with total contempt for those who think differently. Provincially narrow-minded, untouched by the breath of the great big world outside Bayreuth. It is unclear if Siegfried creates such a wooden impression because he has this mentality or whether he has this mentality because he is naturally so wooden. The character traits are impotence, narrow-mindedness and smugness.[168]

Within the Bayreuth congregation, there was also, of course, more than a little envy at work. Their jealousy was directed first and foremost at rival composers, who – wrongly, they believed – were smiled upon by fate. At the head of their list of detested rivals was Richard Strauss. Following the sensational success of *Salome* in 1905, Siegfried turned on his former friend and in the course of an interview compared him with a 'stock exchange speculator'. His inferiority complex was plain for all to see: 'The week is of interest only for *Salome* composers,' he reproached the music editor Alfred Holzblock.[169] He was even critical of *Der Rosenkavalier*, missing no opportunity, good or bad, to inveigh against the work. 'I defended Strauss very calmly,' recalled Kessler, 'whereupon Siegfried laughed out loud and said: "Well, my dear (he calls me 'his dear'!), I forbid you to come to my concert." He is a shapeless, ungainly individual, without any sense of refinement; but good-natured.'[170] The liberal press sided with Strauss, with the result that Siegfried was once again the butt of mocking barbs. In the *Neue Musik-Zeitung*, for example, Alexander Moszkowski dipped his pen in vitriol: 'One thing I'd like to remind you, and it's certainly worthy of mention: Strauss is the great son of minor forebears, not the other way round.'[171] The more Siegfried struggled to make headway against the prevailing wind, the more unshakeable was the idealized picture that Cosima formed of her son. In *Salome* she found only 'the most utter nonsense, coupled with unnatural sexual practices'.[172] The fact that Fidi's own morality would not have been considered anything to write home about was another of the truths that was never so much as mentioned in her presence. As we have already observed, it is not clear to what extent Cosima was aware of her son's private life. Contemporary attitudes viewed homosexuality as a perversion that was criminal in the eyes of the law. Under Paragraph 175 of the Reich's penal code, men found guilty of 'an unnatural sexual act' could be sent down for up to six months. Siegfried had no choice but to keep his sexual orientation a secret, not only in the case of the great love of his youth, Clement Harris, but also on his later visits to Berlin, where the anonymity of the big city offered him a certain degree of protection. Even as late as the early 1970s contemporaries could still recall rumours of sexual shenanigans in the municipal park in Bayreuth. At all events, Adolf von Groß had his hands full paying off blackmailers and freeloaders. On one occasion we even find Groß begging Cosima not to underestimate his work: 'There is much that is not so straightforward and that cannot be settled by the sale of tickets.'[173] But Groß evidently did not dare express himself any more clearly than this. For her part, Cosima brushed it aside, writing to Marie von Wolkenstein to ask if the daughter of the art historian Wilhelm Bode 'would not make a suitable wife for Fidi. But no doubt he'll find one for himself.'[174]

Siegfried Wagner was essentially a tragic figure. Cosima projected immoderately high hopes on him and in that way brought down on him what Sven Friedrich has called 'the curse of self-denial'. This yawning gulf between his family's expectations and his own private needs and orientation left its mark on the whole of his life. Many writers attest to his humour, good nature, his guileless directness and his winning ways in his dealings with others. But he was simply not cut out to be a hero. It was not in his nature to rescue and redeem an ideologically radicalized and esoterically transfigured Wagnerian community. In short, he did not have it in him to be 'the Master's son'.

La Grande Dame

The new production of *Tannhäuser* that was staged in 1891 was hailed as a milestone in the Festival's history by Wahnfried's official biographers. Cosima's disciples, including Houston Stewart Chamberlain, described it as a great and courageous artistic feat that had finally made it clear to its many admirers that the work 'belonged in Bayreuth, with the result that this year's Festival acquired the significance of a veritable turning point'.[175] Richard Du Moulin Eckart likewise added his voice to the chorus of celebration: Cosima's *Tannhäuser* had 'raised Bayreuth to the lofty heights at which it was to remain under the wonderful and ever more comprehensive guidance of this altogether unique woman'.[176] This 'unique', 'august' and 'noble' woman, the 'Master's widow', the 'first lady of Bayreuth': these were only some of the expressions of homage that were then in circulation. In the eyes of her apostles, Cosima achieved feats that could evidently no longer be judged by traditional standards. Absurd though many of these expressions of praise must seem to us today, they none the less make it clear that Cosima was firmly in control of the situation and had the Wagnerian community safely in hand. By the early 1890s many contemporaries were unable to tell the difference between the true facts and Cosima's self-serving interpretation of them. In this she was helped by her profoundly impressive appearance, an appearance that contributed greatly to the world's perception of her as a grande dame. Count Harry Kessler – man of letters, patron of the arts, diplomat and, last but not least, a keen-eyed observer – visited Wahnfried in July 1897: 'Cosima entirely in black, wearing a kind of hat and a black gauze veil stretching down as far as her eyebrows; beneath it the fabulously energetic face with its powerful bone structure; the cheek bones and nasal bone seem to be made of granite.' Kessler felt that 'outwardly, there was nothing at all feminine' about Cosima. 'Her bust by the door to the main salon looks like that of a young man, at least until one discovers the hair. . . . Among all her guests, men and women, she seems to belong to another race: all bones and willpower.'[177]

Philipp Eulenburg was another contemporary unable to escape from her spell, even if he seems to have been able to see beyond the façade of the myth: 'Frau Cosima's hair is now completely white,' he wrote knowingly to Wilhelm II,

> and she now looks more than ever like John the Baptist in the wilderness. Her daughter Evchen is still pretty but will soon have to get married. I am only afraid that the desired prince will not come. Evchen is in the unfortunate position of being the daughter of the 'cleverest woman' and the 'greatest man', so that she feels she has inherited intellectual traits that she simply does not have. . . . Frau Cosima seemed genuinely to have come from the wilderness, so much did she eat. Your Majesty must know slim people who eat a vast amount of food without ever putting on weight. God knows where it goes. With Frau Cosima the spirit presumably eats too, but in this case one knows where it goes – only the physical process remains a mystery. . . . Frau Cosima only ever says clever things. It does not matter what she is talking about. But such intellect is not edifying, for only a woman's profound kindness is edifying. By this I do not mean that a woman's lofty intellect is troublesome to me. But I could scream when there is only wit with one's coffee at breakfast, not cream, and if her thin arms embrace me amorously straight after the last roll has been eaten.[178]

One of the Wagners' harshest critics was the writer Maximilian Harden, and in his portrait of Wahnfried he mocked Cosima mercilessly as the 'dowager queen of Bayreuth':

> Its sensitivity made all the keener by scepticism, the ear soon notes that Master Richard is not much more than 'the dearly departed'. . . . Here is a

court whose mistress almost believes that her womb brought forth all that blossoms and blooms on this sod of earth, a belief that she is persuaded to hold because every breath and gesture on the part of her many courtiers counterfeits that conviction. . . . This Bayreuth is a brain-spun creation of hers, and she alone is its God. In the convent whose air is thick with incense and which forces even the most defiant of men to his knees, Nietzsche's shrill anger, sprung from disappointment, would have learnt how to laugh. Instead of contemptuously promising 'Redemption to the Redeemer', he would have called for some oaf to shatter the stained glass windows and allow the stale and stuffy convent air to be blown away by the springtime breeze of a cheerfully active existence.[179]

In spite of their caustic polemics, Harden's reproaches are not entirely unjust. As the 'dowager queen', Cosima cultivated a degree of courtly ceremonial that ensured that the Wagners became Bayreuth's unofficial royal family. According to Kessler, 'Bayreuth has all the appearance of a minor princely seat, with the Wagners as its tin-pot potentates.'[180] And the soprano Anna Bahr-Mildenburg recalled that 'at half-past eight in the morning, one could see Frau Wagner driving up to the theatre in her large landau, accompanied by her daughters and by Siegfried. She sat bolt upright in the carriage, and only a slight inclination of her head altered the lines of her proud bearing whenever she smiled and thanked passers-by for their greetings.'[181] Even in Berlin, Cosima remained a figure of tremendous authority as Kessler was able to observe: 'Socially speaking, Cosima rules the roost here; such a position is unique; princesses, ambassadors' wives and countesses – all of them tremble before her and blush with delight when Cosima deigns to address them.'[182] When Kessler expressed his surprise at such deference, an English acquaintance noted with genuine envy: 'Oh, but you know, she is a Queen.'[183]

If such obsequious acts allowed Cosima to carry on like a true grande dame, she was also capable of the most extraordinary pettiness. The narrow dividing line between *grandezza* and mortified small-mindedness is revealed by an act of thoughtlessness on Weingartner's part. Cosima bumped into him in Mannheim, where he had evidently forgotten to inform her of his change of address. Anyone else might have overlooked this minor inattentiveness, but not Cosima: 'You thought I would discover your address for myself. Of course, it would have given me pleasure to call on your wife after we'd met. That I did not do so you may put down to the fact that you both have the advantage of youth, whereas I have the enviable prerogative of old age.'[184]

There was something amounting to an unwritten code of conduct that Cosima insisted be strictly observed. This included not mentioning certain names in her presence. The composers Giuseppe Verdi and Ruggiero Leoncavallo enjoyed this dubious honour, as – at a much later date – did Cosima's own daughter, Isolde. Outsiders did not always find it easy to cope with these local customs, and when the famous tenor Leo Slezak turned up in Bayreuth and chose 'Vesti la giubba' from *Pagliacci* as his audition piece, Cosima was clearly piqued. 'There was general and undisguised dismay throughout the hall,' Slezak recalled,

> and the director of music, Herr Kniese, gasped. . . . Even the attendant who had ushered me in, tottered. Frau Wagner seemed taken aback, but after she had recovered from her astonishment, she rather coldly remarked that it might be better if I sang something by the Master – if I could sing anything besides *Pagliacci* – what Wagner arias did I know?

Once the assembled company had recovered from its sense of shock, Slezak sang Froh's arietta from the final scene of *Das Rheingold*: 'I was dismissed with the remark that my vocal accomplishments were still rather scanty.'[185]

In addition to her countless commitments as the Festival's general administrator, Cosima also had to run a large household. Although Blandine and Daniela were living with their husbands far from Bayreuth, neither Siegfried nor Cosima's two unmarried daughters, Eva and Isolde, had left home. And so we meet Cosima not only as the head of a major theatrical concern but also as a caring mother and housewife. Thanks to the royalties that were now flowing into the family coffers with gratifying regularity, the Wagners led affluent lives, and it went without saying that the lady of the house had neither to cook nor clean. To deal with her day-to-day chores, Cosima employed a female cook, a chambermaid and a gardener. And yet one cannot but be struck by the attention to detail that she lavished on even the most minor concerns. When having new covers made for three cushions, she asked Anna Kekulé to help her: 'I've searched in vain in all the main outlets in Munich, where such things can normally be found in relative abundance. My dear, would you be so kind as to look round for these three fabrics in Berlin? But please deal with this request only if you have time, if the weather makes it easier for you & if you happen to be passing one of the main stores.'[186] Anna Kekulé found what Cosima was looking for at a haberdashery store run by Valentin Mannheimer in the Hausvogteiplatz in Berlin. The anti-Semitic barb in Cosima's letter of thanks is significant: 'I was much amused to see your dear handwriting beneath Herr Mannheimer's label. We simply cannot get by without these "Heimers".'[187]

At the beginning of 1893 Dora Glaser entered Cosima's service as her new companion and lady-in-waiting. Between then and the 1930s she was an indispensable part of the Wagner household. She came from a simple background and had only the vaguest idea of what was going on in the theatre and in Wahnfried, but she respected her mistress all the more for that. For her part, Cosima trusted her housekeeper so much that whenever she was away from home, it was Dora Glaser who was placed in charge. 'Please give Cook the following instructions in my name, so that something is ready for the sixth,' she wrote on one occasion:

> First, buy a good shoulder of Prague ham from Heuberger: and look out for a good piece of beef from the butcher (neck or sirloin). Boeuf à la mode, show Cook the recipe in the cookery book, it's the one we're used to. Also look up asparagus sauce in the cookery book. And also, dear Dora, obtain three chickens from Kraus in Bamberg and tell Cook that we'd like them served as an Irish stew. Finally Cook might try to get hold of some trout.[188]

There was no Festival in 1893. The following year began with bad news on the family front when Hans von Bülow died on 12 February. His death was not unexpected. The severe headaches that had tormented him all his life had become unbearable during his final months. In his desperation he tried all manner of remedies and submitted to all kinds of medical experiments. Wilhelm Fließ, a colleague of Freud, diagnosed a 'nasal reflex neurosis', a fantasy ailment that he attempted to treat with positively medieval methods by removing a piece of his patient's nasal septum and cauterizing the nasal cavities with trichloroacetic acid. This treatment amounted to a form of torture and understandably did nothing to relieve Bülow's pain. Quite the opposite, in fact. Finally, in his despair, Bülow left with his wife for Egypt in early February 1894, a visit recommended by Richard Strauss. They hoped that the Egyptian climate might have a salutary effect, but it was too late, and by the time he arrived in Cairo, Bülow was already dying. His wife recalled his final hours: 'By the morning of the twelfth his face had turned dark, and when his doctor asked him how he was feeling, he could barely whisper the word "Bad". He said nothing more. Injections, doctors, consultations were all in vain.'[189] Cosima received the news of her first husband's death on 13 February, the eleventh anniversary of Wagner's passing. 'Our faith was powerfully shaken yesterday,' she wrote to Anna Kekulé on the fourteenth. 'We had to struggle to regain it.'[190] Cosima's words seem oddly cool and reserved. And yet it is clear from a poem that she penned in her first husband's memory that his death affected her deeply:

> From gentle shallows' many-coloured shores
> The ship strikes out to breast the storm-tossed main.
> The billows overwhelm its yawing mass,
> A single sound within these vasty wastes.
> Above it, clouds their rained-soaked burden bear
> As endless night enfolds both sea and sky.
> Alone and motionless in hallowed rest
> The hounded sailor ploughs life's dreadful sea.
> Behold, by Tristan's rock the setting sun
> Is glimpsed again before it sinks from sight.
> The sea and sky are turned a blood-red gold.
> It rises up and says: I come, I part
> And, parting, drive away the night-time host
> And banish gusty tempests' black-browed wrath.
> O lonely man, I'll keep you company!
> Arise, O weary one, and come to me.
> To you I sing my solemn threnody:
> All hail, O pure one, greeted by my rays!
> All hail, brave heart, my robe bears you aloft!
> All hail, my hero, swallowed by the sun!
> All hail, your mother gives you to the flames![191]

It was announced that Bülow's memorial service would be held in Saint Michael's Church in Hamburg on 29 March 1894, raising the delicate question in the Wagner household as to which of its members should attend the ceremony. 'The news has arrived,' Cosima wrote to Adolf von Groß, not knowing where to turn. 'Do you not think that we should send Fidi and Lulu? . . . Would it be possible for him to stay with your father? I feel that Siegfried should attend the service. Or do you think it should be Biagino? Or no one? Please let me have your views on the matter.'[192] Contemporary etiquette would certainly have looked askance if Bülow's former wife had turned up alongside his widow, and yet there is something strangely chilling about the fact that

Cosima toyed with the idea of sending no one at all to Hamburg to represent the family. In the event, Siegfried attended the service, together with Bülow's daughter Daniela and her husband.

Gone to the Dogs

The 1894 Festival featured a new production of *Lohengrin* alongside revivals of *Parsifal* and *Tannhäuser*. As so often, the preparations were overshadowed by a series of painful confrontations with Hermann Levi, which on this occasion were triggered by a sustained anti-Semitic campaign on the part of one of the music assistants, Oskar Merz. When Levi demanded that Cosima assert her authority and she failed to distance herself sufficiently forcefully from Merz, Levi asked yet again to be relieved of his duties: 'I am Jewish, and since it is now a dogma in and around Wahnfried that a Jew must look and think and act in such and such a way and above all because it is believed that a Jew is incapable of devoting himself to your cause with sufficient self-sacrificial dedication, everything that I say and do is judged from this one point of view.'[193] Although Cosima was able to persuade her 'major' to return to Bayreuth to conduct *Parsifal*, this new incident makes it appallingly clear how anti-Semitically charged the atmosphere in Bayreuth had become. It was not so much the occasional oafish comments and insults that wounded Levi but the constant sneers and countless barbs. In short, it was now considered de rigueur to adopt an anti-Jewish tone within the family circle. Even Adolf von Groß, who could hardly be numbered as one of the more fanatical members of Cosima's entourage, was guilty of anti-Semitism. In the wake of a visit to the fashionable spa of Marienbad, he complained about the 'masses' of Jews that he found there: 'It's almost impossible to describe what one sees in M. In this regard Carlsbad is much better, whereas if you go out walking in M. you meet only Jews for hours on end, but there, I am pleased to say, the opposite is true.'[194]

The artistic results of Cosima's staging of *Lohengrin* were evidently mixed. Although there was no lack of the usual gushing enthusiasm on the part of those journalists who toed the Wahnfried party line, critical contemporaries like Weingartner found it impossible to join in the chorus of praise: 'In many respects the staging was inept, while in others it simply flew in the face of Wagner's own directions.'[195] Even the sound of the orchestra under Mottl was a cause for some concern: 'The sound of the covered orchestra was dull and uninspiring. The "Bayreuth tempo" flourished as it had at that hapless *Parsifal* in 1888, endlessly spinning its viscous threads over the entire work like some monstrous spider fashioning its web, so that, for the first time in my experience, the piece seemed too long.'[196] Particularly controversial – not just in the minds of implacable critics like Weingartner – was Cosima's apparent predilection for singers with a less than adequate command of German: 'Throughout the whole evening,' Weingartner complained, 'there was little in the way of a correct pronunciation of the German language, since the only native Germans were the singers playing the King and the Herald. . . . Frau Wagner accorded the Elsa the honorary title of "Triumph des Auslandes", literally, the "triumph of foreign lands", thereby giving official recognition to the aim of the Festival management.'[197]

Weingartner was undoubtedly exaggerating here, for it is hardly likely that Cosima would have signed up the soprano Lillian Nordica simply on the strength of her American passport. Rather, she must have been impressed by her vocal abilities. But stars like Nordica also brought a cosmopolitan glamour to the sleepy town of Bayreuth, and this was undoubtedly important inasmuch as most of the tickets were sold to members of the international moneyed classes. One member of this group was the nineteen-year-old Helene Carol of Boston, who travelled to Bayreuth in the company of a number of female friends and a grand piano. Unable to find any suitable accommodation for herself and her staff worthy of the daughter of a millionaire, she rented the Fantaisie outside Bayreuth for six weeks at a total cost of 6,000 marks. Coaches and horses were also brought specially from Berlin, as the *Coburger Zeitung* reported at length:

> The horses and carriages are used to transport food from Schloß Fantaisie, where it has been specially prepared for the American ladies by their own kitchen staff, to the theatre, where it is served to them in the intervals. It is estimated that Miss Carol has some ten thousand marks at her disposal to meet her day-to-day needs.[198]

The combined cost of the tickets for each performance amounted to no more than 600 marks and was presumably the smallest item in the visitors' budget. If Cosima geared her casting policy to the expectations of immensely wealthy tourists, it was because, as a good businesswoman, she knew that internationally well-known singers would help to boost ticket sales. For Felix Weingartner, who regarded himself as a Wagnerian rather than as a Bayreuthian, these concessions represented a betrayal of Wagner's own ideas:

'Against this tenet Frau Wagner has grievously sinned. But she herself is not German and has no appreciation of the German character.'[199]

There is no doubt that Weingartner did not like Cosima. But was he wrong to dislike her? After all, Wagner's 'synthesis of the arts' was originally meant to appeal to the whole of society in all its richness and variety, whereas Cosima's Bayreuth had little in common with this concept any longer. The Green Hill had become the playground of the rich and powerful, audiences being made up of members of high society and the type of person to whom Cosima was naturally drawn: aristocrats and crowned heads of state, politicians, diplomats, high-ranking military men and, last but not least, the international plutocracy. During his life, Wagner himself had felt only contempt for the princely houses beloved of his second wife: 'They are all worse than just ghosts – they are the descendants of ghosts,' he told her in 1881.[200] At the same time, however, he feared that these 'ghosts' would one day take over Wahnfried: 'R. had a restless night,' Cosima reported in her diary on 8 September 1882. 'He dreamt of Wahnfried, which had been completely altered; everywhere arrangements for a reception, and when he was asked who he was, he loudly and angrily gave his name, and at the same time heard me laugh in a neighbouring room, then he woke up.'[201] Wagner's dream suggests that he would secretly have resisted this particular development. Whether he could have stopped it if he had lived we simply do not know.

The fact remains that by the mid-nineties Cosima had her 'Bayreuthians' firmly under her control. She was now at the very pinnacle of her power, although the courtly subservience that she exacted wherever she went often took curious forms. And in 1894 the family could also be counted on to produce headline-grabbing scandals. In the August of that year it was Cosima's Newfoundland that was the centre of media attention. The dog fell ill and needed an operation, but instead of consulting a vet, Cosima asked her own physician, Heinrich Landgraf, to operate on the animal in the municipal hospital. Unbelievably he agreed. For obvious reasons, the treatment of so unusual a patient could not be kept secret for long, and the situation soon escalated, the left-wing press in particular venting its bile and venom and complaining – with some justification – that simple workers were often denied medical care, while the Wagners were able to have their dog treated by the staff at the local hospital. One of the local papers, the *Bayreuther Abendzeitung*, even reported on a crowd of people gathering outside the building, before noting with a certain smug satisfaction that 'the outcome of the operation was far from favourable as the "patient" that had been treated in the operating theatre unfortunately gave up the ghost at ten o'clock that night. Next on the operating table is a human being, who we hope will fare rather better.'[202] In his desperation Landgraf tried to limit the damage caused by the whole affair by writing to the town council and claiming that the operation had been 'of great scientific interest' and that the procedure had, of course, been carried out 'according to all the rules of antisepsis.'[203] But his excuse was threadbare, and he duly received a reprimand for 'gross misuse of the hospital as a communal institution'.

As for Cosima, there is no doubt that there was great sympathy for animals in the Wagner household. 'So you've now become a vegetarian & quite right too,' she wrote to the soprano Lilli Lehmann. 'I'd like to be one myself but no doctor will allow it.'[204] But was she motivated merely by a sense of compassion for an ailing animal? 'There are few things that divide people more than their relationship with animals and their attitude to that relationship,' she told the local mayor, Theodor Muncker. 'In my own household I should like to describe this relationship as religious.' In the course of her letter she delved ever more deeply into her bag of rhetorical tricks in drawing attention to the 'honour and support' that Bayreuth had received from the Festival. 'That we thought that we could count on local sympathies is something that people will no doubt appreciate, but it was wrong of me to forget my initial point, namely, the essential difference in people's attitudes to animals. For this mistake, I sincerely beg my fellow citizens' indulgence.'[205] Far from apologizing, Cosima added fuel to the fire by accusing her critics of ingratitude. Effectively she was saying that as far as the Master's family was concerned, other standards applied.

Dogs in general were a popular topic of conversation in the correspondence that passed between Cosima and Houston Stewart Chamberlain, the latter attempting to introduce a note of lofty intellectuality by expatiating on 'true Newfoundlands', 'exceptional breeds' and 'cross-breeds': 'The breed that you describe as "true Newfoundlands" is undoubtedly the result of a cross and, indeed, most likely of repeated cross-breeding.'[206] Cosima was evidently impressed by Chamberlain's superficial understanding of biology: 'I subscribe to all that you say about dogs; I always knew that Newfoundlands were descended from Saint Bernards.'[207] Perhaps this was why Cosima had no scruples about having her four-legged friend treated in a hospital because, aided and abetted by Chamberlain's dubious opinions, she was convinced that racially speaking her beloved Newfoundland was a particularly valuable animal. Whatever the answer, the incident attests yet further to Cosima's unabashed delusions of grandeur.

After another year's closure, the Festival reopened in 1896, and on this occasion there was only one work on the programme, the *Ring*, which was being revived for the first time in Bayreuth since 1876. Five cycles were given in all, two conducted by Mottl and two by Richter, while Siegfried Wagner made his Bayreuth conducting debut with the fifth. 'The latest news is a conflict between our conductors,' Cosima reported in June 1896.[208] Arguments fuelled by petty jealousies had broken out between Mottl and Richter. 'Richter, the hypocrite,' Mottl fulminated in a diary entry. 'Frau Wagner gets involved. Amateur business onstage.'[209] Two weeks later we read: 'Supper at Wahnfried. Levi refreshing after Richter's philistinism.'[210] Cosima could only smile at such sparring: 'I think it will sort itself out.' Her pride and joy remained Siegfried: 'Calmly assured, he intervenes only when it is necessary, proving more and more by the day how much we need him. May God protect him!'[211]

Meanwhile, mysterious news was reaching Bayreuth about the 'Sicilians,' Blandine and Biagio Gravina, leaving Cosima distinctly unsettled. 'The loneliness that is not filled by love & the ordeals that cannot be understood in a religious sense are turning into an intolerable burden & I cannot deny that I am anxious.'[212] Elsewhere she was a little more explicit: 'Yesterday we received a letter from Blandine! It is bound to be a cause for sadness that their marriage has turned out to be so incurably unhappy and their relationship so complicated.'[213]

What had happened? There had clearly been problems with the Gravinas' marriage from the outset, at least if we may believe a letter from Isolde to Malwida von Meysenbug: 'Biagio married her from inclination, and even if marriage is not easy for her, we still believe that she can make it bearable & that this will contribute to the development of her finest qualities.'[214] To suggest that Blandine and Biagio Gravina married out of 'inclination' and that the marriage could become 'bearable' hardly sounds like a grand passion. After fourteen years it was all over. The reasons for the failure of their marriage are shrouded in mystery, but it seems clear that Gravina suffered from severe depression. He was a failure as a naval officer, and his elder brother had inherited the family fortune, adding to his financial difficulties. Time and again Cosima had had to come to the help of her destitute son-in-law, but when he continued to demand money from her, her patience finally gave out: 'I had written to him again & told him yet again how Blandine and I have been let down & that I had made it clear that from now on Blandine must finance her own and her children's existence,' Cosima told Adolf von Groß in October 1896.[215]

By September 1897 the pace of events had quickened. The count was ill, Groß wrote to tell Cosima. 'I am afraid that there is no longer any hope for him – his doctors, too, are in despair at his condition, except that they are unable to say when the end may come, it may be sudden or it could take weeks.'[216] Financially ruined and utterly desperate, Gravina shot himself through the head on 14 September 1897. Cosima immediately travelled to Italy in order to be with Blandine. A picture of horror met her in Palermo:

> I found Blandine in a pitiful state, her grief having been made far worse by the circumstances in which she found herself (mother-in-law and sisters-in-law vociferously superstitious, five doctors, all of whom treated him badly; if the patient were to have recovered, it would have been thanks to the Madonna, if not, then the doctor was to blame). I had the satisfaction of leaving her feeling far better than when I arrived.[217]

The thirty-four-year-old Blandine later left Sicily with her children and settled in Florence, bringing the family a little closer together. They were only a short distance from Daniela and Henry Thode's holiday home at Gardone on Lake Garda, and visits to Germany were now much easier, with the result that the 'Italians' often travelled to Bayreuth. 'We're holed up in Wahnfried,' Cosima wrote to Anna Kekulé in March 1898. 'First, I'm awaiting everything that croaks & bawls, and, second, Blandine and her four little children are coming for three months.'[218]

A new source of annoyance emerged when Cosima discovered that Marie von Bülow was planning to publish her late husband's correspondence. Wahnfried was inevitably concerned that their publication might mean embarrassing revelations as Bülow was well known as a candid correspondent with a notoriously acerbic style. Cosima was fully aware of this. But she was unable to challenge the publication on legal grounds – seven volumes were published between 1895 and 1908 – and so she had recourse to her practised skills as a diplomat:

> If I understand the matter aright, we represent two principles which as far as they affect this publication might be described as virtual opposites. If possible, you would like to retain all the intimate details in order to allow the personality to emerge in sharp focus as a living entity. My daughters, my son-in-law and I set out from the principle that nothing of an intimate nature should enter the public domain . . . and that in any correspondence

between two people there is enough of general interest to lend value to its publication, indeed that in a certain sense a life is exalted when random and sometimes regrettable things are excluded from it.[219]

But Cosima's objections were unavailing, and Bülow's widow went ahead with her plan to publish letters of both public and private import.

Two years later – in 1899 – the first volume of Liszt's correspondence with Carolyne von Sayn-Wittgenstein was published. This, too, met with Wahnfried's disapproval, encouraging Cosima to write to its editor, Marie Lipsius (better known under the pen name of 'La Mara'), and beg her to remove all the passages relating to herself and her siblings. Again her request was in vain. 'I wished it hadn't happened', she wrote subsequently to Anna Kekulé. 'It is not that a single word of my father's could ever be anything but elegant, but that these public displays of love & suffering are alien to my whole nature.'[220] Revelations and indiscretions of every kind were wholly repugnant to Cosima. On the eve of the new century she could hardly have foreseen that only a few years later her own children, Isolde and Siegfried, would provide the material for an unedifying mud bath and cause the family's reputation untold harm.

5

A New Era

(1900–14)

In 1899 Berliners marked New Year's Eve with particularly lavish celebrations. Crowds flocked in vast numbers to the Schloßplatz, where the memorial to Kaiser Wilhelm was floodlit and the guards' artillery regiment fired a twenty-one-gun salute at the stroke of midnight. In the euphoria of the moment, revellers forgot the arguments of the last few weeks over when the new century should in fact be ushered in: on the night of 31 December 1899 or not until twelve months later. 'It is true', ruminated the *Vossische Zeitung*'s editorial writer, 'that people have been arguing over the matter and that scholars, writers, poets and thinkers are continuing the battle over when the new century actually begins, but both the State and the Church authorities have decreed that according to our own calendar the start of the new century should be marked on 1 January 1900.'[1] The paper even reported that Kaiser Wilhelm II had personally intervened and ended the argument with his official ukase.

Cosima Wagner was deeply unimpressed by all this and spent the final day of 1899 getting on with her correspondence. 'These dates mean little to me,' she told Bodo von dem Knesebeck, 'so it is a matter of complete indifference to me when people wish to start the new century.' But she sympathized with her correspondent's predicament because, as cabinet secretary to the Empress Auguste Viktoria, he had to attend the festivities in the imperial capital: 'I shall be thinking of you this evening and shall imagine you surrounded by all that magnificence – it means a lot to me to be able to imagine someone who, in the midst of all this empty hullabaloo, can see through the veil of deception. That is something positive.'[2]

Although Cosima had continued to maintain a firm grip on her Bayreuth flock, the new century began with all manner of major and minor annoyances. In general the following years were to witness the gradual but wholesale breakdown of Wahnfried's carefully managed power structure. The emergence of a rival Wagnerian enterprise in Munich and the end of the debate over Bayreuth's exclusive right to perform *Parsifal* – a debate that ended badly from Wahnfried's point of view – affected the family deeply. Moreover, Cosima's decision to retire as the head of the Festival in 1907 left a dangerous power vacuum that her son-in-law Houston Stewart Chamberlain was quick to exploit. Last but not least, there was the 'Beidler case', the embarrassing implosion of a family that kept an avid public in a state of extreme suspense in the weeks leading up to the outbreak of the First World War and that ended in the physical and mental breakdown of Wagner's favourite daughter, Isolde. But one thing at a time.

Parsifal *Mania*

'Evil tricks threaten us', Cosima wrote to Carl Friedrich Glasenapp on 3 January 1900, quoting from Hans Sachs's speech at the end of *Die Meistersinger von Nürnberg*. 'Let's hope that the sacred spirit of Germany will protect us.'[3] Only a few days earlier it had been announced that Prince Regent Luitpold of Bavaria had agreed to build a new theatre in Munich, an idea due in the main to the actor and director Ernst von Possart, who had been running the city's Court Theatre since 1893 and making something of a name for himself with his Wagner productions. Work on the theatre – later to be known as the Prinzregententheater – began in April 1900 and was undertaken by the firm of Heilmann & Littmann, which specialized in theatres and other monumental buildings. The architect, Max Littmann, based his designs on those of the theatre in Bayreuth, fomenting the fear that Possart was planning to open a second Wagner theatre. Wahnfried had followed developments in Munich with intense interest, but the news that work on the building was about to begin left Cosima and her intimates more agitated than ever. In haste she cobbled together a 'riposte' in which she explained in detail why Wagner had chosen to build his theatre in Bayreuth, not Munich, pulling out all the stops in declaring that the new theatre 'flies in the face of the Master's intentions' and was even 'diametrically opposed to them'.[4]

Ever since Wagner's death Cosima had functioned as the leading expert on 'the Master's wishes', but on this occasion her appeal to those alleged intentions was of no avail. The prince regent sought to reassure her that he was concerned to ensure that Bayreuth and Munich worked well together, but the outcome inevitably proved very different. Possart stuck unerringly to his resolve, an attitude that struck Cosima as tantamount to an act of blatant provocation.

After all, the combative intendant was ultimately questioning Wahnfried's claim to be Wagner's sole representative on earth. It was still unclear, moreover, to what extent Possart's theatre, with its amphitheatre-shaped auditorium that could seat 1,050, would affect visitor numbers in Bayreuth.

In spite of everything, the 'Munich Richard Wagner Festival Theatre', as it was initially called, opened on 21 August 1901 with a performance of *Die Meistersinger von Nürnberg*. That the Wagners were pleased to receive the not inconsiderable royalties from the performances is another story. Profits and morals were two very different sides of the same coin. But the business with Possart made Wahnfried aware of its own limitations. Although the 'Master's wishes', as expounded by Cosima, were viewed as legally binding among the Bayreuthians, their legislative impact outside that coterie was modest in the extreme. Against this background, it is odd that Cosima should have chosen this very moment to launch an initiative that once again claimed to be based on Wagner's 'will'. On this occasion, however, her objective was rather different.

Since the autumn of 1898 there had been ongoing discussions about a revision to the existing copyright law. Cosima hoped that when parliament debated the issue there would be a majority in favour of extending the term from thirty to fifty years from the date of the artist's death. For Wagner's heirs an early re-examination of this arrangement was important, otherwise the copyright on his works would expire in 1913. There were also rumours that the ever-enterprising Ernst von Possart was planning to stage *Parsifal* in Munich, a plan that left the Bayreuthians horror-struck. After all, the Master had decreed that his *Bühnenweihfestspiel* could be performed only on Bayreuth's Green Hill, any alternative being tantamount to an act of desecration. In this, Wahnfried was able to quote from a letter that Wagner had written to Ludwig II in September 1880: 'I must now try to consecrate a stage for it [*Parsifal*], and this can only be my Festival theatre in Bayreuth, which stands here all alone. There, and there alone, may *Parsifal* be presented now and always: never shall *Parsifal* be offered in any other theatre as a mere amusement for its audience.'[5]

Armed with this argument, Cosima began her own diplomatic offensive. 'Many thanks for your efforts with regard to the term of copyright protection,' she wrote to Richard von Chelius on 18 June 1900. 'I have already spoken to a number of members of both the Centre Party and the Conservative Party. I expect most from the Centre Party as its members are used to championing ideas.'[6] Initially, it looked as if those in favour of extending the period of copyright protection would get their way, not least because there was no lack of support among publishers and the Cooperative of German Composers. 'If the draft bill goes through,' Cosima told Knesebeck on 10 January 1901, 'then *Parsifal*, at least, will be protected for the foreseeable future, and one of the main dangers of Munich's speculative dealings over its new theatre will have been successfully averted.'

But the initial negotiations in the Reichstag on 8 and 9 January 1901 failed to provide the desired breakthrough. 'Of course we did everything possible,' Cosima went on in her letter to Knesebeck. 'Adolf Groß called on the gentlemen at the Ministry of Justice, I myself wrote to the then chancellor, Prince Hohenlohe, and we were assured in various quarters that our prospects were good.' But she was also aware of the difficulties of her plan: 'If we are to have any chance of success in the Reichstag, we cannot say that the creator of *Parsifal* intended this work for Bayreuth alone and that the sacred mysteries of Christianity should never be abandoned to ordinary theatres.' In Cosima's view, it would have been enough for an 'act of princely grace and favour or for the enthusiastic claim of a civilized nation' to safeguard *Parsifal* for Bayreuth, but electoral law militated against such a course of action:

> It seems to me that this universal suffrage is like an ulcer on the body politic, a boil that contains all manner of noxious fluids. Who will be the bold surgeon who conducts an operation that now seems necessary to every sensible person? How strange it is that it was Bismarck who left us this feature of French demagogy, a feature that means that we shall never be able to hear the voice of the German nation.[7]

At the end of their opening session, the country's elected representatives decided to set up a committee to discuss the proposal further. Wahnfried could be satisfied with the work of this committee as the majority of its members had already expressed their support for an extension to the period of copyright protection. Within weeks the draft proposal had been brought back to the Reichstag for further discussion. But at the session on 19 April 1901, Eugen Richter, a member of the Liberal People's Party who had been sitting in the Reichstag since 1867, delivered himself of an inflammatory speech that tipped the mood in his favour. Long regarded as an acerbic orator, he was feared as much by the government as by the Social Democrats, who were the party of opposition. Drawing on powerful arguments, he defended his decision not to support an extension and even proposed shortening the period of copyright protection, although this, of course, was no more than a tactical manoeuvre. He ended his speech with an anecdote:

> Someone who was otherwise completely remote from the matter recently expostulated in my presence: 'What? Is Wagner's *Parsifal* to be performed for decades to come only in Bayreuth because his heirs allow it to be staged only there, whereas they don't even allow it to be performed in Munich?' In my own view, this right is not intrinsically justified but has merely an industrial basis that it is in Bayreuth's interest to maintain, but they now want to extend this right artificially by another such regulation.[8]

Richter was not alone in his criticisms. Only a few minutes later Heinrich Dietz, a member of the German Socialist Party, added fuel to the fire by claiming that 'a well-known family in Germany' had tried to influence the legislative process:

> In the final analysis one cannot hold it against the family in question for wanting to legitimize a situation that works to its own advantage. Every citizen is free to petition the government. . . . Why shouldn't the aforementioned family say: 'Yes, my honoured nation, the late Richard Wagner wrote so many exceptionally beautiful and fine works, we would ask you to be good enough to ensure that we, his family, receive the income from those works for another twenty years'? If this law is passed, it will be tantamount to a gift of around one million marks to the Wagner family; and I do not think that the Reichstag can put its name to this.[9]

The permanent secretary at the Ministry of Justice, Rudolf Nieberding, was sufficiently stung by Dietz's attack to issue a formal announcement to the effect that he was not personally acquainted with the Wagner family and had exerted no pressure on the parliamentary process. The second of these claims, at least, was a barefaced lie, as Adolf von Groß had most definitely met 'gentlemen from the Ministry of Justice' for secret talks on the subject. But his intervention made no difference: thanks to the rhetorical pyrotechnics of Richter and Dietz, there was now a widespread suspicion that the planned extension to the period of copyright protection amounted to a 'Lex Cosima' and, as such, was a handsome gift to Wagner's heirs. When Otto Arendt of the Conservative Party entered the debate and spoke out in all seriousness in favour of a special law 'for the preservation of the Wagner theatre in Bayreuth' in an effort to ensure 'that *Parsifal* and, with it, the viability of the Wagner theatre be preserved in the longer term',[10] it was a step too far even for the most well-meaning parliamentarians. Arendt's speech effectively tolled the death knell of all attempts to extend the period of copyright protection, and the move was rejected by 123 votes to 107.[11]

Among those who were disappointed by this development was Richard Strauss, who had followed the negotiations closely. 'The government is weak and spineless,' he wrote to his parents. 'They simply lack a man like Bismarck to shout down so skilful a parliamentarian. Herr von Nieberding was power-less against Richter, who is far cleverer and far more experienced as a speaker. The whole affair is very sad for us: but for the time being there's nothing that we can do to change it.'[12] Strauss was no doubt right to complain that the permanent secretary could do little in the face of Richter's skills as a polemi-cist, but it was no less true that Wahnfried's undercover diplomacy had clearly gone too far. However sophisticated the methods used to conceal its attempts to influence the situation – and those attempts are well documented by Cosima's letters to Knesebeck and Chelius – they were bound to be rejected by self-confident representatives of the people such as Eugen Richter and Heinrich Dietz.

At the very last minute Cosima drafted a detailed memorandum that was sent to all the members of the Reichstag. In it she attempted to deal with 'factual errors' and take the wind out of her critics' sails. In the process she left no rhetorical trick untried, insisting, for example, that Wahnfried had in no way wished to influence the parliamentary process. 'There has been some confusion here between influence and information,' she explained. Her aim, she went on, had only ever been to elucidate Wagner's wishes and to point out that 'his theatre stands on the hill at Bayreuth alone and that only there is his Sacred Stage Festival Drama *Parsifal* performed. This is his legacy to the German nation.' She hoped that the members of the upper house would 'put right the wrong that has been done and honour the greatest of all composers by carrying out his final wishes.'[13] The equation of personal interests with those of the 'German nation' was all too transparent a move, and the members of the Reichstag no doubt recognized this when by a clear majority they preferred not to react to her emotionally charged appeal.

Once attempts to have the period of copyright protection extended had failed in the Reichstag in the middle of April 1901, Bayreuth pinned its last remaining hopes to the banner of public opinion. In mobilizing the masses in this way, Cosima certainly had some unusual allegiances in mind. Writing to a pastor in Barmen, for example, she noted how happy she would be 'if the clergy could be persuaded to take an interest in ensuring that the Sacred Stage Festival Drama *Parsifal* were protected and its sublime and sacred object not abandoned to ordinary theatres'.[14] Writing in the *Bayreuther Blätter*, Hans von Wolzogen sought to ensure that the nation was primed with suitable propaganda, while dyed-in-the-wool Bayreuthians struck a note that was downright hysterical, a note that inevitably called forth mockery and condemnation in the columns of liberal newspapers such as Friedrich Naumann's *Die Zeit*. The music critic Paul Zschorlich used the term '*Parsifal* mania' to describe the 'false enthusiasm that thinks it can honour Wagner by defending Bayreuth. . . . *Parsifal* mania is the term I give to the idée fixe that Wagner and Bayreuth must forever form one and the selfsame concept'.[15]

Meanwhile, Cosima was seeking to enlist the support of influential contemporaries, and she even reprinted the text of her Reichstag submission as a kind of pamphlet, describing it in a letter to Princess Feodora von Schleswig-Holstein, the youngest sister of the Empress Auguste Viktoria, as 'containing everything that constitutes our tale of woe'.[16] Kaiser Wilhelm's close friend, Philipp zu Eulenburg-Hertefeld, was likewise contacted by Bayreuth: 'It is a matter of supreme importance to me that H. M. the Emperor, our most gracious lord, should deign to take note of my letter'.[17] Cosima was clearly staking everything on the kaiser's intervention. At the end of October 1901 Wilhelm sent word via Houston Stewart Chamberlain that it was his 'most emphatic and irrefutable desire never to allow *Parsifal* to be performed in any other theatre'. Above all, the kaiser held out the prospect of 'measures' that 'would be effective in this regard even beyond Germany's frontiers'.[18] Cosima met the kaiser at a dinner held by the chancellor, Bernhard von Bülow, in Berlin on 6 February 1902. 'The kaiser himself was charming', she wrote soon afterwards to her friend Countess Wolkenstein. 'He greeted me & Eva most cordially, adding that it was a long time since he had last seen us. I used the opportunity to prostrate myself at his feet and thank him for his kindness in the matter of copyright protection. He then spoke about Munich and about his worries with regard to Bayreuth.' Wilhelm's jovial manner impressed Cosima. 'It was half past twelve by the time that he got to his feet, saying: "Frau Wagner should have been in bed long ago." We were completely taken with him, including his whole appearance, his firm gaze and the way he gestures with his hands'.[19]

But, as was so often the case, there was a vast gulf between what Kaiser Wilhelm II said and what he was actually capable of achieving. His sound-bite references to his 'most emphatic and irrefutable desire' and his flamboyant manner were a clever way of covering up his own powerlessness and probably also his lack of interest in the affair. Cosima should have known better, for the truth of the matter is that for all his vocal support, Wilhelm was an ineffectual ally. Although he could convene the Reichstag and the Bundesrat, which represented the individual states, appointing and dismissing civil servants, and, together with his chancellor, determine political guidelines, he had no right of veto when it came to the laws of the lower and upper houses, with the result that ultimately he had no choice but to sign the new law as it affected the copyright in works of literature and music.

Many contemporaries regarded Wilhelm as an upstart, lacking in self-control, full of himself and ignorant. He was 'an out and out amateur in the field of art', Bernhard von Bülow commented laconically in his memoirs, 'and, as we know, the essence of the amateur consists in the fact that he has no clear idea about the difficulties and seriousness of art.' When Bülow asked Cosima for her opinion of Wilhelm following her supper with him, she answered diplomatically: 'As a person, the kaiser is someone I find very sympathetic, but in order to explain even the basics of art to him I'd need to spend at least three years alone with him on a desert island.'[20] The suspicion that Wilhelm's cultural interests were nothing to write home about also emerges from between the lines of a letter from Chamberlain to Cosima: 'He told me quite candidly that to philosophy he brings neither knowledge nor interest, and I expect that the same is true of the philosophy of natural science.'[21] Many years later, Du Moulin Eckart complained about Wilhelm's 'lack of culture, with which he involuntarily infected everyone around him', concluding that 'with regard to Bayreuth and its first lady, it must be said that things went on without him and, indeed, in spite of him'.[22]

The question of Bayreuth's exclusive right to perform *Parsifal* continued to exercise the Wagners. As we shall later have occasion to note, they returned to the attack in 1913, when they again attempted to have the term of copyright protection extended. But before that could happen, Heinrich Conried had mounted a spectacular coup, or 'Gralsraub' – literally, a 'rape of the Grail' – and in that way ensured the obloquy of the Bayreuth faithful. Conried, whose real name was Heinrich Cohn, hailed from Bielitz in Silesia and had begun his career as an actor in the Austrian provinces. If he enjoyed scant success in this field, he made up for it by being a wily and highly successful businessman, becoming managing director of New York's Metropolitan Opera in February 1903 and immediately announcing his aim of staging *Parsifal* before the year was out.

In Bayreuth the news came as a bolt from the blue. 'There is no doubt in my own mind', Cosima wrote to Felix Mottl, 'that the idea of staging *Parsifal* in New York came from Possart. He has his reasons, but it stymies our plans for a law to protect the work, and a number of our main singers will be lost.'[23] Possart and Conried undoubtedly shared the same interests: the Met's new manager wanted to cause a stir with a spectacular opening gambit, while Possart was able to seize his chance to deal a further blow to Bayreuth's claims to have a monopoly of the work by supporting the New York venture in every way that he could. Once again Cosima appealed to 'the Master's wishes': 'Not only was I expecting our Bayreuth artists to refuse to take part, I also thought that every artist would know how to honour the Master's wishes.'[24] Her hopes were misplaced, and in her desperation she even thought of asking President Theodore Roosevelt for his help. 'Do you know through whom I could reach Rosevelt [*sic*]?' she asked her friend, Countess Wolkenstein. 'And, more generally, do you think that Rosevelt can express himself on such a matter with any prospect of exerting his influence?'[25]

But it was all to no avail, and Conried even managed to persuade such an experienced man of the theatre as the Munich designer Carl Lautenschläger to work as his technical director. But Cosima was particularly hurt by the fact that Conried's 'rape of the Grail' was aided and abetted by singers such as Milka Ternina, Anton Van Rooy, Alois Burgstaller and Anton Fuchs, all of whom had worked at Bayreuth, in some cases for many years. Another artist who travelled to America at this time was Felix Mottl. Although Mottl had ensured that there was a clause in his contract exempting him from any involvement in the *Parsifal* production, the engagement of Cosima's favourite conductor as music director at the Met for the 1903/4 season was undoubtedly Conried's greatest coup.

Mottl had been court kapellmeister in Karlsruhe since 1881 and after more than twenty years had grown tired of local conditions. At the same time, his marriage to the singer Henriette Mottl-Standthartner was heading for disaster: Frau Mottl was universally regarded as hysterical, unpredictable and chronically extravagant. On several occasions she had threatened to kill herself or her husband. An entry in Mottl's diary for 14 April 1905, for example, reads: ' "I've hated you for ten years," Frau Mottl said to me today. "If I had a razor, I'd cut your throat." '[26] Mottl was keen to escape from this impasse, and in Conried's offer he thought he could see a way out of his dilemma. And yet he also feared that – to put it mildly – Bayreuth would be unsympathetic to his decision. In several letters to Cosima he sought to justify his actions and assure her that he would take no part in the 'rape of the Grail'. Adolf von Groß, with whom Mottl was friendly, likewise declared his position: 'I'll stand by you,' he promised Mottl, 'and do what I can to ensure that your step is properly understood. I'm sure that it won't come to a break.'[27]

For the present, the situation seemed under control, and it was with Cosima's blessing that Mottl set off for New York in October 1903. But within weeks of his departure it was learnt that in 1904 he would be moving to Munich as general music director and that he would therefore be working with the hated figure of Ernst von Possart. With that, Cosima's patience was at an end. If she had been able to forgive Mottl his brief flirtation with New York, the same was certainly not true of his defection to the camp of her anathematized arch-enemy. 'Why', she chided him in a letter of 15 December 1903, 'did you have to go to America in the very year in which *Parsifal* was desecrated there? And how has it come about that you found yourself working for the very person who committed this crime? And why did it have to be Munich that you moved to after Karlsruhe? And if you have already put up with so much there, why couldn't you put up with Karlsruhe any longer?' Mottl presumably realized at this point that Cosima was resolved to sever all links with him, and yet she still offered him a way out of his present predicament: 'If you were successful in preventing the Prinzregententheater from becoming a festival theatre,' she ended her letter, 'and if you were able to ensure that it was used for some other purpose, I would welcome your Munich appointment as the intervention of divine fate.'[28] Mottl was unable, of course, to accept this 'offer' as Cosima's suggestion amounted to an act of sabotage and would have meant disowning Possart, his future superior.

'I know all about the lies that are currently circulating about me in Wahnfried,' Mottl complained to Countess Christiane Thun-Salm. He was particularly critical of Siegfried Wagner: 'Siegfried was in Karlsruhe and told them there that in recent years I've let everything go to seed in Bayreuth and no longer made any effort!' Siegfried was evidently using his former mentor's precarious position to rid himself of his rival. 'But it makes no sense to play hide-and-seek and then to be offended, & I've absolutely no intention of putting up with it any longer! Frau W. can ask of me whatever she wants, but these grotesques should be nice & quiet & modest, for that alone befits them.'[29]

Mottl was under enormous pressure to explain himself. Even Cosima's daughter Blandine, who was far from being one of the more fanatical members of the family, clearly had doubts about the conductor's probity. 'I had nothing whatever to do with it,' he assured her, 'I swear by all that's holy! . . . Like Kleist's Arminius with the Romans, I was firmly resolved to use lies and deception and every form of falsehood in serving our cause. I failed comprehensively.'[30] Blandine was evidently unsure what to make of this letter and so she showed it to her twenty-one-year-old son, Manfredi, whose laconic comment is revealing: 'I believe him,' he noted in the margin of the letter. 'It's curious only that he wanted to emulate Arminius and the Romans.' Ultimately scepticism gained the upper hand. Although Mottl returned to Bayreuth in 1906 to conduct *Tristan und Isolde*, a breach was unavoidable in the longer term, now that he had refused to knuckle under to Cosima. This, at least, is how the official Wahnfried biographers depict the situation, showering Cosima's erstwhile favourite conductor with contempt and contumely. Cosima too added her voice to their chorus of disapproval and in the wake of Mottl's death in 1911 even spoke of a 'sense of liberation, for our poor friend was worn out as an artist and compromised as a human being'.[31]

But let us return to the autumn of 1903. In September the family tried to institute proceedings against Conried and the Met, but the attempt was bound to fail because America had not signed the Berne Convention. Wagner's works were not protected in North America, and so the only question that the New York circuit court had to settle was how Conried could have come into possession of the performing material. It quickly emerged that in 1902 a guileless Siegfried Wagner had allowed Schott to publish a miniature orchestral score. Wagner's publisher, Ludwig Strecker, recalled that 'the full-size scores were sold by the publisher only in return for a "declaration" that was intended to guard against misuse'. But this did not apply to the miniature scores, which were 'everywhere obtainable without a declaration and could be used to prepare a copy suitable for the purposes of conducting the piece'.[32] With characteristic astuteness, Conried had had the performing material prepared by copyists, with the result that Cosima's case was ultimately thrown out by the court.

If she had initially hoped that her case would find a sympathetic ear among American audiences, she was to be bitterly disappointed. American newspapers – especially the German-language papers that were published on the East Coast – printed countless malicious articles whose *Schadenfreude* was plain for all to see. The local *Morgen-Journal* wrote mockingly of Cosima as the 'dowager queen of Bayreuth' and complained that her charge against Conried was full of 'sentimental drivel'.[33] 'Young Siegfried', too, came into the paper's line of fire: 'Even if Saint Cosima is unable to prevent the wicked Conried from performing *Parsifal* here, she may still wreak terrible revenge by sending her son here and having him perform his operas for American audiences.'[34] Suddenly there were rumours that Cosima herself would cross the Atlantic and stage *Parsifal* in person. 'Let us hope that the report is untrue,' opined the leader writer of the *Morgen-Journal* in late August 1903, dipping his pen in vitriol, 'otherwise we shall have the whole story of *Parsifal* in a nutshell: the sanctity of the Master's intentions will remain inviolate if American dollars flow into the Villa Wahnfried's coffers; but if the money remains in this country, it is merely a dirty trick on the part of grasping Americans.'[35]

Cosima was certainly thinking of making the journey to New York, but only to take her stand in the witness box. 'I'm afraid, however, that it will be no more than an empty gesture,' she complained to Adolf von Groß, adding that she was 'not at all well versed in contractual matters and a very poor businesswoman to boot'. Here she was merely fishing for compliments, for Cosima was anything but a 'poor businesswoman'. 'Only you, my one and only Adolf, would be a much more significant presence because you can advise them on everything.'[36] Her attempts to cajole Groß into going to New York were in vain, and he gratefully declined the invitation to take part in what would have been a juridical suicide mission.

The Met production of *Parsifal* opened on 24 December 1903. Thanks to Mottl's diary we are well informed about the rehearsals and the performances. In early December he noted in his typically whimsical way:

> Kapellmeister Herz, who has been dealt a doubly grievous blow by fate – first with a club foot and second with the musical direction of the New York *Parsifal* – has shown astonishing zeal at the rehearsals. He is for ever to be seen hobbling along the corridors of the theatre with the help of a walking stick that lends him ape-like agility, commandeering Flowermaidens, Esquires, Knights and bell-ringers for extra rehearsals. While the solemn sounds of the Grail can be heard coming from one of the rehearsal rooms, a chorus from *Cavalleria rusticana* or from *Tosca* is clearly audible in another corner of the building. These combined goings-on are an act of absolute sacrilege against the Holy Ghost. A bishop by the name of Burgess has been inveighing from his pulpit against the production of *Parsifal*. Unfortunately, what he has to say about the work itself is so silly that it is impossible to agree with him.[37]

For obvious reasons Mottl did not attend the actual performance but turned up at the opera house in time to hear 'the A flat from the top of the dome sung a quarter of a tone flat. . . . All in all, one does not need to be a fanatical supporter of Wahnfried to feel that this staging is morally wrong and artistically unfinished.'[38]

The Grail, then, had been ravished. Eighteen months later, on 20 June 1905, the lawyer and conductor Henri Viotta mounted a production of *Parsifal* in his native Amsterdam. Here, too, Bayreuth had to stand by, unable to intervene, as the Netherlands did not sign the Berne Convention until shortly after the performances. The Richard Wagner Society for Germanic Art and Culture that was formed in Berlin at this time was to some extent a reaction to events in New York and Amsterdam, its self-declared aim being to 'combat inartistic and anti-cultural endeavours.'[39] The Society's chairman was Josef Kohler, an old friend of Wahnfried. A respected legal historian, he had drawn up a secret report for Cosima the previous year, pointing out the hopelessness of any legal steps to give *Parsifal* special status.

But was '*Parsifal* mania' really only about money, as the chorus of Bayreuth's critics repeatedly claimed? Or was Cosima in fact fighting for something else? The financial aspect of Bayreuth's attempts to impose a ban on other productions was easy to see, of course, but the royalties were only one side of the coin, and many commentators overlooked the fact that this coin had a second, even less attractive side. The battle over *Parsifal* and the attempt to extend the period of copyright protection was also a battle for Wahnfried's claim to be seen as the sole representative of the 'Master's wishes'. This concept provides a useful starting point for a glance at a study published in 1912 by the Austrian writer Hermann Bahr. Bahr was a Wagnerian, albeit far from fanatical in his beliefs, but he undoubtedly knew the workings of Bayreuth better than most because his wife, the singer Anna von Mildenburg, had first appeared at the Festival in 1897. He describes a typical interval on the Green Hill:

> The main interval came after the second act of *Parsifal*. At one table sat the Queen of Württemberg and her ladies, beside them a lively gaggle of picturesque German women, here Schweninger and his followers . . . over there the German-eyed Ludwig von Hofmann, alongside the tall Nordic figure of the bellicose Michael Georg Conrad, the reverent-featured, John-the-Baptist-like Hans von Wolzogen, Chamberlain, questioningly taciturn in his expression, Frau von Heyking, Bettina's granddaughter, Crown Prince Hohenlohe, Countess Wydenbruck gossiping with Jesko von Puttkamer . . . Thode's ecclesiastically Roman profile, Johannes Müller's weather-beaten,

battle-tempered, strong-willed countenance and, beside him, Artur Bonus looking as if he has stepped straight out of a play by Ibsen translated into the Italian, and, next to him, the tall figure of Prince Max von Baden.[40]

And so Bahr goes on for another one and a half pages. In short, representatives of the Bayreuth establishment such as Wolzogen, Thode, Schweninger and Chamberlain rubbed shoulders with politicians such as Jesko von Puttkamer and members of the plutocracy. But *Parsifal* also cast a particular spell on Protestant theologians such as Johannes Müller and Arthur Bonus, the latter the spokesman of a radically Germanicized Christianity.

Whatever their underlying differences, these men and women all represented a reactionary stratum of upper-class society that met in Bayreuth once a year to seek what Bahr described as their 'redemption': 'Common to them all is their need to admit that what they have experienced here is something wholly unique, something that cannot be compared with anything else in the world and that they could not have experienced elsewhere. . . . They undergo a profound inner transformation and experience the union of the receiving congregation and the spirit of creation.'[41] It is clear from Bahr's language that *Parsifal* was a kind of monstrance, a holy relic that could be taken from its tabernacle on only a few days every year, when it was placed before its congregation to be worshipped. Cosima's Bayreuthians defined themselves by reference to their exclusive access to this fetish. Armed to their ideological teeth, they believed that it was their duty to prevent the rape of the Grail for only in that way could they preserve the exclusive character of their community.

Iconoclasm

'In order to keep a community together,' observed Franz Wilhelm Beidler, 'one needs unbelievers. Cosima always sought to maintain that view and even convinced herself that there were enemies all around her.'[42] It is debatable whether some of the enemies whom Cosima identified as such actually warranted that title. Rather, one has the impression that her battle served in the main to curb separatist ambitions within the Wagnerian community.

In 1903 the world celebrated the ninetieth anniversary of Wagner's birth and the twentieth of his death, prompting the suggestion that a memorial to the composer be established in Berlin. All too soon it became painfully clear to the organizers that it was unwise to cross swords with the house of Wagner. The idea of a monument to Wagner – the first such memorial in Germany – was first mooted in 1898, when a committee had been formed to discuss the question of financing and erecting it. The driving force behind the scheme was Johann Ludwig Leichner, an eminent local businessman who had been born in Mainz in 1836 and who had trained as an opera singer in Vienna before taking up engagements in Cologne, Königsberg, Magdeburg, Würzburg and Stettin, where he sang the role of Hans Sachs to Wagner's great satisfaction. While working as a singer, Leichner also studied pharmacy and succeeded in inventing a lead-free greasepaint make-up in the laboratories at the Friedrich Wilhelm University in Berlin, an invention that proved the starting point of his career in business. He retired from the stage in 1876 and built a factory producing perfume and powder that proved immensely successful. Much of the money that he earned in this way was used to promote the arts. With Leichner's backing, the plans to establish a Wagner memorial in Berlin seemed initially as if they would prosper, not least when the well-known sculptor Gustav Eberlein was commissioned to work on the monument.[43] Even Wilhelm II, who was required to sanction the project, contributed to it by submitting a number of sketches of his own and suggesting a handful of changes. Finally, Hans Richter, Felix Mottl and other leading Wagnerians had all agreed to sit on the committee and assured the organizers of their active involvement.

Plans for the official unveiling of the monument began at the end of 1902. The ceremony itself was due to take place on 1 October 1903 in the presence of the imperial family and numerous guests of honour from home and abroad, while two or three 'historical concerts' were also planned for the four-day festivities, their programmes including music by Wagner's contemporaries. The composer and conductor Fritz Volbach was commissioned to write a celebratory cantata for chorus and large wind band. A gala concert in the Reichstag and a banquet in the Winter Gardens were designed to appeal to polite society, while a musicological conference was aimed, rather, at an academic audience. At more or less the same time, however, opposition to these plans began to grow more vocal, rapidly escalating and ending in an unseemly squabble. 'It has come to my notice', Cosima wrote to Knesebeck on 28 November 1902, 'that Mascagni and Massenet are to represent Italy and France with their works, I also hear that a make-up manufacturer is arranging the whole thing because he has the financial means to do so.'[44]

It is striking that Wahnfried claims to have heard about these plans only at this point, a good four years after the committee was first set up to discuss the project. Bayreuth's mayor, Theodor Muncker, had in fact received a formal 'appeal' for a Wagner memorial in Berlin as early as 1898, but he appears not to have forwarded it to Wahnfried. It remains a mystery why Leichner and his colleagues did not contact the family directly. Whatever the reason, Cosima was deeply troubled by this turn of events, the news that such hated composers as Mascagni and Massenet might be involved in the celebrations causing outright indignation. She lost no time in drawing up a programme of her own, which her son-in-law Henry Thode expounded to an audience in Berlin's Philharmonic Hall on 13 February 1903, the twentieth anniversary of her late husband's death: 'How is Richard Wagner to be celebrated by the German people?'[45]

Thode began by offering a detailed account of the historical development of the music drama from Greek tragedy to Bayreuth. According to him, the programme at the celebrations surrounding the unveiling of the monument should reflect this process as closely as possible. As a result, Wagner should be honoured not only with performances of his own works but also by works that he held in high regard and that had served to inspire him. Among such works, Thode listed Gluck's *Iphigénie en Aulide*, Mozart's *Die Zauberflöte*, Weber's *Der Freischütz*, a Beethoven symphony and a Bach motet. In the field of drama he suggested Lessing's *Minna von Barnhelm*, Schiller's *Die Jungfrau von Orleans* and Kleist's *Der Prinz von Homburg*. Other European countries were to be represented by works by Shakespeare, Cherubini and Méhul. Conversely, the Netherlands, Sweden and Denmark had failed to produce any artists whom Wagner respected, in spite of their 'Germanic roots', and so these countries had to make do with folksongs and country dances. The unveiling ceremony was to be accompanied, finally, by speeches by Wolzogen, Chamberlain and Thode. There was no longer any mention of Leichner and his committee, which had effectively been stripped of its power. Cosima wrote to Thode to thank him for his efforts: 'My aim has been achieved, namely, to ensure that the first public word on this celebration is spoken as you alone can speak it. The game of hide-and-seek that these people have been playing until now has been ruined for them.'[46] The response to Thode's speech in the press was mixed. While the Wagnerian community hailed it as a triumph, outsiders criticized the speaker's ostentatious advocacy of Germanic virtue, even the Catholic daily *Germania* describing his comments as 'highly debatable inasmuch as the lecturer adopted a somewhat exaggerated tone in stressing the Germanic character of Wagner's art according to the pan-German model'.[47]

Leichner and his colleagues were understandably annoyed at this uncalled-for interference. But worse was to come. As early as 16 January 1903 Cosima had written to Hans Richter: 'Could I ask you to write an open letter to the committee and remind these people who is being celebrated? Please ask

which musician can trust himself today to write music for an unveiling ceremony of this nature. And tell them that only the greatest masters of music and
poetry are capable of adding lustre to such an event.'[48] Richter did as he was
told and even resigned from the committee, writing to the *Deutsche Zeitung*
and explaining in an open letter dated 6 May 1903 that 'We all know that
Richard Wagner needs no memorial but that he built his own memorial with
his Festival theatre in Bayreuth, which it is the task of the German nation to
enlarge at some future date and turn into a monumental edifice.'[49] Leichner's
reply appeared in the same edition of the paper:

> We believe that we are just as capable of understanding Wagner's spirit as
> you are and we shall organize the celebrations in such a way as to ensure that
> they are truly popular – far from evaporating in impractical phantasmago-
> rias, each and every one of their parts will allow the German nation to
> achieve a true understanding of this great composer. . . . It is this that we are
> fighting for, not for particular family interests. We are fighting for the
> Richard Wagner who no longer belongs to Bayreuth and to art historians but
> to the German people and, indeed, to the entire world.[50]

This was unequivocal. In particular, it was Leichner's sideswipes at
Wagnerians such as Thode ('art historians') that excited the ire of journals
loyal to Wahnfried. The Munich *Neueste Nachrichten*, for example, revealed a
particularly superior streak in stating that 'the letter is not even written in
entirely accurate German', before going on: 'There was no reason to implicate
the Wagner family in the argument, an involvement that can only be
described as demonstrating a lamentable lack of tact.'[51] Leichner's contribution was admittedly highly undiplomatic, but at least the two sides in the
argument had now declared hostilities, and Cosima's friends spent the weeks
and months leading up to the unveiling ceremony taking up their positions,
eminent musicians such as Karl Klindworth and Engelbert Humperdinck
generating much publicity by announcing that they would no longer be
working with Leichner. Even Mottl declared his opposition to the monument,
claiming that the whole project was 'thoroughly alien' to him and, in an open
letter to Leichner of 8 May 1903, asking for his name to be 'removed from the
list of committee members'.[52] Leichner replied by return of post:

> We can certainly comply with your request to remove your name from the
> list of committee members, but what we cannot do is destroy the printed

matter in which your name and photograph appear as these were produced at a cost of almost ten thousand marks. The only alternative would be for you yourself to assume responsibility for these costs, in which case we would reprint the material, omitting your name.[53]

Mottl was reluctant to agree to this. Indeed, his reply is significant for its vacillating tone: 'You should not misconstrue me,' he wrote on 9 May. 'It is a sense of entirely personal modesty that prompted me to make this request. So please leave things as they are, I certainly do not insist on superficialities.'[54]

Mottl's manoeuvring was clear. Once his colleague Hans Richter – a rival for Cosima's approval – had announced that he was resigning from the committee, he was obliged to follow suit. Whatever his attitude to Leichner's plans, he was determined not to give ground to Richter on any point concerning Wahnfried. Fritz Volbach, too, discovered what it meant to cross swords with the Wagners when Cosima informed him that he would find himself in an 'unfortunate position' if he did not withdraw the cantata that he had written for the celebrations: 'I should like to spare you this & that is why I am advising you to forgo a performance of your work.'[55] Volbach did as he was instructed.

Meanwhile the brouhaha surrounding the unveiling ceremony was providing the general public with much ribald – and free – entertainment. The Viennese translator Hans Liebstoeckl, for example, commented caustically that

The house of Wahnfried is fighting back. A phoney war has broken out. Preachers up and down the land are warning German idealists about Leichner's grease powder and at the same time helpfully drawing attention to Bayreuth, where the high ticket prices already prove that the supreme goals of art have still not been achieved, however handsome the royalties. We find ourselves, therefore, in the midst of a holy war in the world of culture. The businessman is the enemy.[56]

The Wagner Monument was unveiled, as planned, on 1 October 1903. Predictably, Wagner's direct descendants demonstratively stayed away, prompting the New York *Morgen-Journal* to strike a note of mockery: 'Even Kaiser Wilhelm has had to learn for himself that to get on the wrong side of Wahnfried is no fun. The kaiser no longer has a good word to say about his minister of culture, Konrad von Studt, after the latter persuaded him to become a patron of the celebrations attending the unveiling of the monument in Berlin.'[57] Wilhelm had long supported the project, but in the end he too withdrew his backing, retiring to his hunting lodge in Rominten in East Prussia and leaving his second son, Eitel Friedrich, to represent him at the ceremony.

Was Leichner really the 'enemy'? And why should the Wagner family object to a monument to its famous forebear? Leichner's critics reproached him for pursuing the project only as a way of drumming up publicity for his own make-up factory. He was also said to be vain and hoping for public recognition and the title of 'Privy Councillor'. While there is no doubt that he stood to gain a good deal of prestige from the project, it seems unlikely that his only interest was his personal standing and wounded vanity. A contemporary newspaper article throws some light on the matter. According to *Die Post*,

> there are now many experts in the field of music who no longer see Bayreuth as the sole source of their salvation but who have come to the conclusion that Frau Cosima and Siegfried Wagner have wandered far from the tradition and paths of the Master. This band of heretics – for as such they appear to the neo-Bayreuthians – has even had the temerity to believe that Wagner's music dramas are now being performed at least as well, if not better, in other artistic institutions in Germany than in the Franconian backwater that is the home of the composer of *Der Bärenhäuter*. . . . On those occasions when the Wagner family has first say, there are some people who do not wish to follow them, and if one does not respect the neo-Bayreuthians' views, others believe that they must withdraw their support.[58]

Central to the arguments – just as it had been during the debate about *Parsifal* – was Wahnfried's monopoly of Wagner. Cosima felt that a monument to her late husband was superfluous as long as Bayreuth was run as a family business. In order to maintain her grip on her flock, she needed 'non-believers' such as Possart, Conried and Leichner. Her plan worked, so much so that throughout the land her disciples could be heard repeating the mantra that Bayreuth was 'the living monument to Richard Wagner', a view perpetuated by Kurt Mey in the *Wartburgstimmen*, for example: Bayreuth was 'a memorial to the victorious and triumphant Master – and in his attempts to safeguard our most sacred German art may the true German God long continue to maintain it, in spite of our venomous enemies and biliously base calumniators'.[59]

Regime Change

'Mama ill. Could you come to Bayreuth on your way home and put up at Wahnfried – Eva Wagner.'[60] The recipient of this telegram was Cosima's personal physician, Ernst Schweninger, a distinguished doctor and teacher who had numbered Cosima among his patients since the early 1890s but who remained controversial as a general practitioner. Some observers thought him hopelessly overrated as a physician, even dismissing him as a charlatan, while others saw him as making an important contribution to developments in the art of medicine.

Schweninger was born in 1850 and was only thirty-two when he became Bismarck's personal physician. The Iron Chancellor had boundless trust in his abilities: 'Without him I would have died sooner,' the old man is reported to have said.[61] There is no doubt that Schweninger's career benefited from the aura that surrounded him as a result of Bismarck's patronage, yet his professional colleagues had a lower opinion of the abilities of so ambitious and fashionable a physician. It was against the wishes of the medical faculty of the University of Berlin that Schweninger was installed as professor of dermatology and head of the Charité Dermatological Clinic in October 1884. In 1900 he additionally took over as head of the new district hospital in Groß-Lichterfelde near Berlin, building it up into a centre of homeopathy until he retired to Munich in July 1906. In Lichterfelde he based his treatment on the simple things in life: a balanced diet, fresh air, steam baths, gymnastics and exercises and the curative powers of water. Particularly important were ingenious diets, the so-called 'Schweninger cure' becoming proverbial. Experienced academic doctors, conversely, mocked Schweninger for his approach, although it seems likely that envy played a part in their reaction because under his direction his clinic on the outskirts of the imperial capital soon became a magnet for polite and well-to-do society. If we may believe contemporary eyewitnesses, the controversial doctor was an exceptionally charismatic figure, a charcoal-black beard and very dark eyes giving his appearance a vaguely demonic aspect.

Schweninger knew how to handle fastidiously demanding female patients like Cosima Wagner. He had her room furnished with valuable rugs, cushions and covers so that she and her entourage – she was usually accompanied by the unmarried Eva – could feel at home. 'The physician is an artist,' Schweninger declared in a controversial book. 'The practice of medicine is the practice of an art, not of a science.'[62] He dismissed 'scientific medicine' and stressed the role of the doctor. Central to the success of any treatment was the doctor–patient relationship: 'To be a doctor means being the stronger of two people.'[63] Schweninger could be as strict as he was forbearing, as jovial as he was unyielding. He left his eminent patient in no doubt that the profession of a general practitioner was a princely calling – Schweninger himself used the term *Herrenberuf*, implying that he saw himself both as a gentleman and as a masterly superior.[64]

Cosima seems to have enjoyed this apportionment of roles, and in the course of the thirty years during which she saw Schweninger professionally she clearly allowed him to get very close to her. 'We are still under the impression of your visit,' she wrote to him in 1894. 'I can't remember the last time that I was in such an impetuous mood. There is no doubt in my mind that you have at least one advantage over your rivals – you show your patients how to live!'[65] Cosima consulted Schweninger in Berlin, Lichterfelde, Bayreuth and Munich, trusting him blindly in all things: 'My daughter and I have been following your instructions to the letter,' she reported on a course of treatment in Lichterfelde in 1902. 'The only liberty that I have allowed myself is a glass of white wine at midday, and also the occasional glass of beer.'[66] In emergencies he even visited his patient on the French or Italian Riviera, providing full-time care for which he ensured that he was handsomely paid, Adolf von Groß being left with the task of picking up the bills and silently meeting the doctor's demands.

On 19 February 1906 the thirty-nine-year-old Eva and her sixty-eight-year-old mother moved into rooms in the Groß-Lichterfelde District Hospital. As in previous years they had planned to remain there for four weeks. 'Schweninger turned up on Tuesday morning,' Cosima wrote to inform Groß shortly after arriving at the hospital. 'Eva & I were thoroughly examined & are now being most carefully looked after. There is no praise high enough for the concern & kindness that we've been shown.' Schweninger prescribed a strict diet for his patients: 'no meat at all, no alcohol, not even any vegetables; only if this regime is consistently applied does he expect to lift the state of lethargy. I am also to have plenty of rest, to receive few visitors & write as few letters as possible. Needless to add, we are following his instructions to the letter & now all we can do is to wait.'[67]

On her return to Bayreuth, Cosima threw herself into her work. The last Festival had taken place in 1904, and now it was a question of preparing for the 1906 Festival, with its total of twenty performances. Siegfried Wagner and Hans Richter were to conduct the *Ring*, while Franz Beidler and Karl Muck were entrusted with *Parsifal* and Mottl with *Tristan und Isolde*. A sixth conductor, Michael Balling, was responsible for the remaining performances of both *Parsifal* and *Tristan*. This was Mottl's final season in Bayreuth after a four-year break. Whenever Cosima was not preoccupied with the preparations in Bayreuth, she would travel to Dresden to rehearse the leading roles in *Tristan und Isolde* with Alfred von Bary and Marie Wittich. By the end of the 1906 Festival she could look back on an impressive record. In the course of the preceding twenty-three years, there had been fifteen Festivals under her management, during which time a total of 274 performances had been given. No one could have predicted, however, that this would be her last season in charge of the Festival. In spite of occasional health problems, she was still able to shoulder an impressive workload. Mottl alone seems to have foreseen the changes that were to take place. When he met Cosima again after an absence of several years, he was shocked by what he saw: 'Meal at Wahnfried,' he noted in his diary. 'Frau Wagner looking much older.'[68]

Initially, the 1906 Bayreuth Festival ran according to plan. Marked by the usual mummery, the opening was attended by the cream of European society, even Kaiser Wilhelm II cabling 'the heartiest and most sincere good wishes' from his annual visit to Scandinavia.[69] But in early August an incident took place which, unimportant in itself, served as a catalyst and tested the family's resilience to breaking point, culminating only a few years later in an acrimonious court case. Franz Beidler, by this time Isolde's husband, had conducted the *Ring* at the 1904 Festival, evidently to Cosima's satisfaction. Two years later he was due to conduct two performances of *Parsifal*, but committed the error of demanding a third, a demand that Cosima evidently found quite shameless. At all events, her reaction was exceptionally unforgiving: she wrote to her son-in-law, saying that she would be advising Isolde 'to break' with him 'as she is being drawn down into a world that is bound to destroy her great nature'. It was, moreover, dishonourable for a man 'to live off his wife's money and do nothing but allow his debts to be discharged by people whom he treats as you have treated us'. Cosima demanded that he should undergo a complete psychological change: 'Until this rebirth, which must find expression in actions, not words, we shall go our separate ways.'[70] Beidler's insistence on conducting a third performance was in fact no more than the final straw in a long-running argument. To understand the background to this development, we need to examine its prehistory in greater detail.

Franz Beidler was born in 1872 in the small Swiss town of Kaiserstuhl on the banks of the Rhine and first worked at Bayreuth as a musical assistant in 1896. It must have been at this time that he was introduced to his future wife, Isolde. Cosima would have preferred her Loldi to marry her favourite conductor, Felix Mottl and, indeed, it appears from the latter's diary that there was a brief flirtation between the two of them. But Mottl went on to fall in love with the soprano Henriette Standthartner, whom he married in December 1892. Isolde was certainly not the sort of woman to be forced into marriage by social convention. Not only was she regarded by common consent as the prettiest of Cosima's four daughters, she was also exceptionally self-assured. Whereas her eldest sister, Daniela, was much given to sullen brooding and to a feeling of inferiority, Isolde seems to have been the exact opposite, an attractive and open young woman with a pronounced love of life and at peace with herself. Such openness will have appealed to Beidler, a highly musical, good-looking and eloquent young man who was likewise not lacking in self-confidence. They soon fell in love with one another. 'My future son-in-law is a proficient young musician who has already proved himself here with us over a number of years and in whom I hope to find a proficient prop.'[71] Thus we find Cosima writing enthusiastically to Gustav Mahler in November 1900.

Beidler and Isolde were married in Bayreuth the following month – 20 December 1900. In a town as small as Bayreuth, the marriage of one of Wagner's daughters was a social event of the first importance. At the wedding breakfast at Wahnfried both the local preacher and the mayor spoke 'warmly about our house', Cosima noted with some satisfaction in a letter to Marie von Wolkenstein. Toasts were offered by Henry Thode and Siegfried Wagner, and Hans von Wolzogen declaimed one of his unctuous poems in a voice 'that resembled that of a Grail knight proclaiming a message from Montsalvat'. The couple then drove through the town, Isolde 'graciously greeting the dense crowd of onlookers to the left and to the right of her carriage'.[72] The parties then returned to normality.

'Since it is the husband on whom devolves the task of running the household,' Cosima insisted in a letter to her son-in-law, 'you will receive eight hundred marks a month from Adolf von Groß, Loldi's allowance & your salary combined.' She also had clear ideas on the future course of Beidler's career: 'You will increase your income initially by teaching & later by means of a fixed appointment. . . . I regard as honourable all types of work, for honour accrues to us not from without, and so I am pleased that you are already rehearsing the choir for the *Missa solemnis* & that your pupils are reporting for duty.'[73] However understandable Cosima's maternal concern for the well-being of the newlywed couple, this first semi-official letter already carried within it the seeds of later discord, Cosima having gone over Beidler's head and defined his position in the Bayreuth enterprise without consulting him. She was entitled to do so as the head not only of the family but also of the Festival, but her whole approach must have struck a strong-willed and self-confident young musician as frustrating in the extreme, for the role that Cosima planned for Beidler was not at all to his liking. She was pleased, she told Isolde on one occasion, 'that Franz too is now one of the representatives of our cause, that he will support Fidi, has a purpose in life & enjoys the inestimable good fortune of serving a cause & of being consumed by it.'[74] Elsewhere she even described it as 'a sign of providence that there is another man in our house besides Fidi who serves our cause!'[75]

From the outset Cosima left observers in no doubt that her beloved Fidi would one day take over the running of the Festival and that he was the undisputed heir apparent. It was a dynastic principle that she spent decades seeking to legitimize in the eyes of her congregation. For his part, Beidler was unquestionably keen to 'serve' the cause of Bayreuth, but certainly not as a musical assistant working in the shadow of Siegfried, so that an important cause of the later conflict may be found in the allocation of their respective roles as formulated by Cosima.

During the early years of their marriage, the Beidlers lived in harmony with the Wagners. On the day after they were married, they moved into a mid-seventeenth-century country house in the neighbouring village of Colmdorf. (Since 1939 the commune has been a part of Bayreuth.) The property remains an impressive residence. According to Cosima, 'It is altogether delightful there, and the two of them are happy. Loldi keeps saying that she has found the only thing she ever wanted.'[76] Cosima alone seems not to have believed that the peace would last. When Isolde became pregnant, Cosima had only words of mockery for her new son-in-law, telling her friend Marie von Wolkenstein that 'I was so struck by your inspired opinion on the insignificance of the father that I altered Siegfried's words to suit my own view of the situation – "I expect you made me without a father" – & placed them in the mouth of the future scion.'[77] Cosima's fifth grandchild saw the light of day on 16 October 1901, and her delight at Isolde's successful accouchement was understandably immense. 'I don't think one can imagine a more beautiful or a more loving mother,' Cosima told Marie von Wolkenstein. 'She refuses to be parted from the child, feeds it herself & says she can't describe the pleasure she feels when the child takes her breast in its mouth.'[78] Messages of congratulation arrived from every quarter, even Daniela Thode contributing a note, albeit one couched in her typically melancholic tone, conjuring up the spirit of her late stepfather: 'May all the blessings of his dead forebear rest on him and protect him throughout his life.'[79] Until the birth of Wieland Wagner in 1917, Franz Wilhelm Beidler was Wagner's only male grandchild.

Within a month the first major argument between the Beidlers and the Wagners had broken out following an intervention from Julius Kniese, who had gone running to Cosima to complain at Beidler's allegedly supercilious attitude and his refusal to help him to rehearse a choral work. Cosima read the Riot Act to her son-in-law, prompting Beidler's mother to leap to her son's defence. She complained that Isolde did not love Beidler sufficiently, that she was financially irresponsible and that she failed to take proper account of her husband's wishes. This was clearly nonsense, but Cosima lost no time in giving as good as she got, complaining that Beidler had committed a number of mistakes that were the result of a misconceived concept of freedom and 'excessive independence'. In short, Beidler had been badly brought up. Cosima also accused her of 'conducting a secret correspondence' with Beidler: 'Do not further insult my daughter by sealing your letters.'[80]

No doubt both parties were unduly sensitive, but Cosima was clearly convinced that Beidler was a disruptive influence on the family. Indeed, it is significant that in her letters to Marie von Wolkenstein she spoke only of 'the Colmdorf presence'. A new challenge to her authority arose in 1902, when Beidler received a prestigious invitation to conduct *Die Walküre, Siegfried, Lohengrin* and *Tannhäuser* in the presence of the tsar and tsarina in Moscow. 'This adventure is all that the Colmdorf presence needed,' Cosima complained to her correspondent.[81] A few days later she returned to the attack: 'Our Muscovites left yesterday. Loldi was sad to abandon the little one. I visited him this morning & was delighted to find how strong he is.'[82] Beidler's visit to Moscow was so successful that he was invited to become imperial music director in both Moscow and Saint Petersburg. 'This change in Franz's life affects me too,' Cosima wrote to Isolde. 'And the excellent qualities that we have always recognized in him are now joined by a flightier temperament.'[83] For the present, however, the couple returned to Bayreuth.

Eva Wagner, who dealt with her mother's correspondence and who exerted a certain influence on her, increasingly interfered in the arguments between the two sides of the family. In June 1902 she accused Beidler of faking a coronary disease in order to avoid the rehearsals for that year's Festival. Heinrich Landmann, the senior consultant at Bayreuth's District Hospital, had diagnosed the early signs of a fatty degeneration of the heart, but Eva refused to believe her brother-in-law. 'It is curious', she wrote to Adolf von Groß, 'that an illness has set in here at the most convenient moment.'[84] Beidler embarked on a course of treatment but evidently omitted to inform Cosima, so that it was Isolde who felt the full force of her mother's anger: 'Everything has gone to his head (in good ways as in bad), he no longer knows what he's doing. . . . I've gone as far as I can in terms of the freedom that I've given him, but to run off without even thinking for a moment that it was worth telling me what he was doing – – – that's simply not on.'[85]

Although there was no Festival in 1905, this did not mean a cessation of hostilities. Julius Kniese, Bayreuth's chorus master and, as such, one of Cosima's closest assistants, died on 22 April. 'I felt great bitterness', Cosima wrote to Adolf von Groß the following month, 'at not receiving a single word of condolence from Colmdorf, while the most touching messages poured in from far and wide, all of them recognizing Kniese's merits and saying how much they felt his loss. . . . Believe me, my dear Adolf, the obstacle here is Loldi! With Franz we'd get on famously, & it is this that depresses me most of all.'[86]

In spite of her grief, a successor had to be appointed as soon as possible, and it was Beidler whom Cosima considered as Kniese's replacement: 'I have a question for you, my dear: will you serve me & our cause by taking on Kniese's position? There may be aspects of this appointment that are not entirely to your liking, yet I believe that it would afford you a great deal of satisfaction.'[87] But Beidler turned down his mother-in-law's generous offer. He was not interested in working with an opera chorus in a theatre but wanted to concentrate entirely on conducting. In spite of this, Cosima still invited him to conduct *Parsifal* at the 1906 Festival, albeit not without wagging an admonishing finger: 'For our cause, which survives in spite of great difficulties, I consider it important that your name & competence are acknowledged & that you are not simply seen here as my son-in-law.' However well disguised, Cosima's criticism was unambiguous: Beidler lacked 'competence'. A further reproach followed a few lines later: 'We expect no thanks, because such thanks would diminish our delight in this feeling. But we hope both for your sake & for our own that you are kind enough to recognize & believe in the strength of our sincerity.'[88]

Cosima was indirectly accusing the Beidlers of ingratitude, and with that she appears to have crossed a line, setting herself, Siegfried and Eva on a collision course with the Colmdorfers. But the Beidlers were financially dependent on Cosima, adding to the complexities of an already awkward situation. Beidler's income from his conducting engagements in Moscow and Bayreuth, together with Isolde's allowance from her mother, had to be offset by debts and an expensive lifestyle – in Colmdorf, Beidler kept an aviary with over 100 exotic birds that he had brought back with him from Russia, an eccentric hobby that left Cosima distinctly unimpressed, as she made clear in a letter to Adolf von Groß: 'If, when doing him this service, you were to add a note to him to the effect that as long as one has debts, then one should not permit oneself such unnecessary expenses as an aviary and aviculture, you would be doing him a great moral service.'[89] Far from considering this intervention an expression of her maternal concern, Cosima's 'dear children' regarded it as a tiresome and unwarranted attempt to meddle in their lives.

In the course of time the relationship between Cosima and the Beidlers acquired all the characteristics of an eternal triangle, and it was Isolde who played the key role in all the arguments that arose between her mother and her husband. And yet it must be questioned if she was really in a position to intervene in any way that was remotely conciliatory. After all, she herself was part of the problem, her temperamental, irascible character an obstacle on the road to any successful compromise. Both sides grew increasingly touchy, and when Isolde complained in November 1905 that Cosima was discriminating against her husband, Cosima's patience ran out. In her response to her 'poor child', she insisted that 'I believe that I have conferred great honour on Franz, yes, a very great honour, indeed, by entrusting two performances of *Parsifal* to him. And now I have to sit back and listen to my own child telling me how ungratefully this has been received.' In order to avoid the charge that she was favouring members of her own family, she went on, she had not been able to offer Beidler more than two performances:

> If you are unable to understand my regulations, we should go our separate ways, for the unworthiness of your behaviour at the last Festival & the unworthiness of our present dispute is something I will not tolerate, from you above all. God has much – far too much – to forgive me for, but my conscience could not be clearer with regard to all that I have done for you and all that I have put up with. . . . But you are not in your right mind, & this excuses you, even for the fact that you have accused your own mother. But you'll come to your senses, regret your injustice towards me & beg me to destroy your unsympathetic lines as an example of the childishness that we have to tolerate in all our staff.[90]

It is clear, then, that the row between Cosima and the Beidlers in the summer of 1906 was merely the culmination of a long-running dispute. In both camps there were disappointed hopes, wounded vanities and more than a little suspicion. The 'psychological rebirth' that Cosima demanded in her letter of

11 August 1906 had to start with Beidler, who, in Cosima's eyes, had been guilty of a serious crime by violating the Bayreuth code. Cosima demanded unconditional commitment to the task in hand and expected that Beidler would selflessly take his subordinate place in Bayreuth's hierarchy. In short, she was demanding more than a mere admission of guilt: 'Until this rebirth, which must find expression in actions, not words, we shall go our separate ways.'[91] The discord in the Wagner family weighed heavily on all concerned. 'With all my heart I hope that a favourable outcome can be found,' Daniela Thode wrote to Adolf von Groß at the end of October 1906. 'I know no one as magnanimous in forgiveness as our mother.'[92] The opposing faction had a rather different perception of the affair, the Beidlers accusing Cosima of trying to wreck their marriage. 'If anyone can demonstrate that Eva, Siegfried and I have taken even so much as a single step in this direction,' Cosima assured Adolf von Groß, 'I shall regard all other wrongs as rights.' Cosima evidently did not expect a speedy solution to the conflict but believed, rather, that 'the consequences will be immeasurable'.[93] She was to be proved right.

On 5 December Cosima arrived at Schloß Langenburg near Schwäbisch Hall as guest of the castle's owners, Crown Prince Ernst zu Hohenlohe-Langenburg and his wife, Alexandra. Her visit was scheduled to last some weeks and began idyllically enough: 'This morning wrote some letters & spent time with Frau Wagner,' the prince noted in his diary on the sixth. 'Went for a walk with her before lunch. In the afternoon drove out and went walking in the forest with Frau Wagner. Read to her after tea.'[94]

Two days later, on the eighth, events took a dramatic turn, as Daniela Thode explained in a letter to Adolf von Groß:

> Mama woke up suddenly feeling very tired on the morning of the eighth, though there had previously been no sign of a chill – a strange cough-like groaning alarmed Dora [Cosima's maid], so much so that she called for the crown prince – when he and his wife arrived, they found Mama semi-conscious, with blood on her mouth – the doctor who was summoned and who was very competent, friendly and conscientious attributed her alarming state to a cardiac collapse – four heart spasms followed in quick succession.

The condition of the sixty-eight-year-old Cosima was life-threatening, and she kept drifting in and out of consciousness. According to Daniela, 'We were all prepared for the worst at any given moment.' The rest of the family was hurriedly summoned to Schloß Langenburg, but by the time they arrived that

Saturday evening the situation had improved. Cosima was 'mentally alert and even cheerful, taking an interest in everything but unaware of all that had happened to her the day before'.[95] Ernst Schweninger, too, hurried to her sickbed the very next day. The news that Cosima had collapsed spread like wildfire and even Kaiser Wilhelm II asked his commander in Berlin, Count Kuno Moltke, to keep him informed: 'Having taken a sincere interest in Frau Cosima Wagner's illness, His Majesty the Kaiser has deigned to ask me to request news of her condition today'.[96]

But the news was not good, convulsive spasms repeatedly following periods of slight improvement. On 12 December Cosima and her entourage returned home, and the press duly reported on their arrival back at Wahnfried: '12 December, 11.10 at night, Frau Cosima Wagner has just arrived back with Professor Schweninger, her son Siegfried and her daughter Frau Thode. She alighted from her compartment unaided and walked across the platform to the waiting carriage. She looked very pale. Frau Wagner spoke animatedly to the people around her'.[97] After a few weeks in Bayreuth, Cosima moved on to Cannes, Schweninger having decided that she should spend the cold winter months in a milder climate on the French Riviera. Unable to devote all his time to a single patient, however prominent, Schweninger engaged the services of the Berlin-based physician William Klette to accompany Cosima to Cannes. Born in 1869, Klette had made a name for himself by publishing books and articles on the origins and treatment of heart diseases and was also fully conversant with Schweninger's treatment methods.

Cosima led a reclusive existence on the Côte d'Azur. Schweninger had issued strict instructions that she should avoid all social contact and even all forms of exercise – especially the dictation of letters – and Eva, Dora Glaser and Klette ensured that his orders were obeyed. The prescribed period of rest proved effective, and by the time Cosima set off back to Bayreuth in the middle of May 1907, her health had improved markedly. In spite of these positive developments, however, there was no doubt that Cosima was in declining health. In future she would need to take greater care of herself, and there was no longer any question of her continuing to run the Festival. 'I'm still not allowed to do any work,' she complained to Hugo von Tschudi in the middle of June. 'My music is now the duet for the cuckoo and the cricket, as heard in the meadow at the edge of the forest'.[98]

The people around Cosima – and especially the influential Eva Wagner – were all convinced that it was her altercations with Franz Beidler that had provoked her physical breakdown, so that while a culprit was quickly found, the real cause of her mysterious illness remained unresolved. From all that we now know about her medical history, it seems that in December 1906 Cosima suffered an Adams-Stokes attack. Named after two Dublin physicians, Robert Adams and William Stokes, such attacks involve a brief period of unconsciousness caused when the heart temporarily stops beating. Such attacks are generally characterized by the fact that the victims, who are otherwise in excellent health, suddenly lose consciousness, often injuring themselves in the process. According to several reports, Cosima was found with blood on her mouth, suggesting that she may have bitten herself. Once the heart's normal rhythm has been restored, the person involved wakes up again very quickly, with no memory of the moment when he or she was unconscious.

Clearly the constant wranglings with the Beidlers must have undermined Cosima's health, but the family feud can have had nothing to do with an illness as serious as Adams-Stokes syndrome, which is the result of an organic disease of the heart. Nowadays such attacks can be prevented by fitting a permanent pacemaker, but a century ago the prospects for the patient's recovery were poor. Such attacks could recur at any time, and there was no real treatment to deal with them. Leaving aside the question of whether or not Eva should have known better, we can say only that for her it was beyond doubt that Beidler would have to leave Bayreuth. With the active support of Adolf von Groß and Hans Richter, she attempted to find an appointment for her unloved brother-in-law well away from the town. 'I very much believe,' Groß wrote to his 'angelic little Eva', 'that in finding an alternative post for Franz we shall have greatly helped your dear Mama.'[99] Elsewhere he described Beidler's departure as a 'release for our dear Mama'.[100] Among the posts considered were ones in Karlsruhe or, with Hans Richter, in Manchester.

As for Isolde, Cosima reported to Marie von Wolkenstein that 'Loldi is visiting us from time to time. Her health fluctuates, but I think her mind is more settled; she reminds me of a woman who has lost her way and who is afraid to turn round and retrace her steps on the path on which she has set out in error. Instead, she gropes her way forward, while plunging ever more deeply into the undergrowth. Her guardian angels will help her!'[101] Eva evidently exerted her baleful influence, for Cosima too blamed Beidler for her wretched state of health. 'Your husband's violation of our cause & of this most hallowed place', she wrote to Isolde, 'was an ordeal for us all. I see it as a sentence passed down on us by fate. It robbed me of my health and, with it, my happiness, which consisted of quietly getting on with our work.' Once again Cosima complained that Beidler 'had no word of remorse for me' and that the 'rebirth' that she had demanded had still not taken place. 'Once this has been achieved,' she went on, 'it may be possible for our family to work together again in the spirit of a healthy and friendly collaboration, which in my own view can still take place, but away from any involvement in the Festival for you yourselves have abandoned us and made all further participation impossible.'[102] Cosima's letter was unambiguous, and it was to have fatal consequences. She was laying down the conditions for a reconciliation, while at the same time making it plain that such a reconciliation could never be complete and that they could never go back to the status quo. Under such conditions it is difficult to imagine how friendly dealings with the Beidlers could ever be restored. A woman as proud as Isolde and a man as prone to overestimating his own abilities as Beidler could hardly accept Cosima's offer, which they no doubt regarded as a poisoned chalice. As a result, the conflict continued to boil away beneath the surface, Cosima's letter having made any reconciliation more difficult than ever. Worse was to come in the form of the Beidler case, when the family's private life was exposed to the scrutiny of the courts.

Cosima's illness brought to the fore the question of her succession. There was no doubt, of course, that Siegfried was the heir apparent. Not only had he been hopelessly spoilt by Cosima, who had indulged his every whim, but for decades he had been brought up as the Festival's future director. When he finally took over from his mother at the beginning of 1907, he could prepare for the next Festival in a relatively relaxed frame of mind, as it was not due to take place until the summer of 1908. For the present he avoided any public announcements on the subject, and it was not until October 1908, by which date his first season was already over, that he wrote to the soprano Lilli Lehmann: 'Tell everyone that I can now relieve her [Cosima] of all the vexation, annoyance, disappointments etc. over our so-called "artists". . . . This last summer has given my mother the delightful assurance that her work will live on and thrive worthily in my hands, and that is the best possible conclusion for her. Her heart (admittedly, you once claimed that she didn't have one!) is in reasonable order.'[103] The change of leadership passed off smoothly, and yet it soon became clear that the new director was either unwilling or unable to assume the role of the Wagner community's ideological head. The power vacuum created by Cosima's retirement was to be filled by another man – with disastrous consequences.

Rabble

'Thank God, I've good news of Mama,' Eva assured her Berlin correspondent, Anna Kekulé, in the middle of October 1908. 'Blandine's visit brought her a great deal of pleasure & an eight-day visit from Chamberlain provided her with a genuine, noble stimulus marked by good old-fashioned cordiality.'[104] Siegfried had met Chamberlain in Vienna and had invited him to return to Bayreuth after a seven-year absence to attend his – Siegfried's – first Festival. As Chamberlain later acknowledged, he had 'followed a sound instinct' in accepting the invitation.[105]

His instinct did not let him down. In the course of his summer in Bayreuth, the fifty-three-year-old writer was drawn closer to Eva, his junior by twelve years. As befitted members of polite society, their rapprochement took place during long walks, over tea and, above all, through the exchange of numerous letters. Within the space of a mere four months, Eva had sent some 240 letters, postcards and telegrams to Chamberlain, who proved no less assiduous a correspondent. It has not previously been known that Eva was not the first of Cosima's daughters to attract Chamberlain's attention, for as early as 1896 he had already courted Blandine: 'Earlier – when I was still a virtual stranger in Wahnfried – there were evenings when I had eyes for you alone.' He had showered Blandine with compliments and written ardent letters to her: 'Would you take it amiss if I were to write out an extremely passionate love poem for you?'[106] Interestingly enough, Blandine was already married at this time, though her husband was now in poor health, a situation that makes one wonder whether Chamberlain was trying to advance his claims to be considered Gravina's successor? Whatever the answer, he then turned his attentions to Isolde. Here, too, he was out of luck, and she brusquely rebuffed his advances. In Bayreuth it was recalled decades later that she had dismissed his sweaty approaches with the uncharitable comment that 'I can't bear to see his fishlike staring eyes any longer.'[107]

By August 1908 it was Eva's turn, and this time Chamberlain planned his operation more carefully, making a meticulous note in his diary of the various stages in this campaign. 'By 8 Aug. this intermediary stage was over,' we read in one entry.[108] By the time Chamberlain left Bayreuth on 28 August he was assured of victory and had resolved to ask for Eva's hand in marriage. In the letter that he wrote to Cosima on 1 September, he described himself as a 'lonely individual' who thought that he must 'find a home in Wahnfried'. This scarcely sounded like a lover's infatuation, but he asked his prospective mother-in-law to 'read between the lines'.[109] Cosima presumably understood what her 'dear friend' was trying to say.

Cosima should perhaps have taken a closer look at her future son-in-law and his remarkable earlier career. He had divorced his wife Anna in October

1906. (The couple had been married since 1878.) The Viennese judges had no difficulty resolving the matter as Chamberlain had not exactly been a faithful husband. For ten years he had been seeing a prostitute by the name of Josefine Schinner, who had even called on him at least once a week at his own home for what Chamberlain himself described as a 'manicure'.[110] But the Wagners, of course, had no idea of these infidelities, not least because to the outside world Chamberlain was a model of moral rectitude.

Houston Stewart Chamberlain and Eva Wagner were married in Bayreuth on 26 December 1908. 'Sweet little Eva in her bridal dress and veil,' the groom noted in his diary; 'spent the last half hour waiting at her Mama's; S[iegfried] fetches us at 12.04; all assembled; Mayor Preu conducts the civil ceremony in the salon, during which he gives a brief and pertinent speech; it's all over in ten minutes.'[111] There was no question of a church wedding in Bayreuth as the consistory of the Protestant church refused to give the couple its blessing, Chamberlain having emerged from his divorce as the guilty party. Eva tried to enlist the services of the influential theologian Adolf von Harnack, but not even he could help, with the result that immediately after the civil ceremony the newlyweds hastened to Zurich, where a church wedding took place the following day: Switzerland evidently had a more liberal attitude to such matters.

But who was this man who in December 1908 joined the Wagner family and who within months had become its spiritual leader? The son of a distinguished English admiral, he grew up in Versailles following his mother's early death. As a native Englishman in France and a French socialite in England – during the first few decades of his life he generally spoke French – he clearly felt a certain rootlessness during his youth. He studied the natural sciences in Geneva, but his university career ended in a nervous breakdown, after which he retired to Dresden. Convinced, as he was, that his health made him unsuited to a life based on regular work, he began a course of private study. He first made the pilgrimage to Bayreuth in 1882, when he attended the world premiere of *Parsifal* and experienced his very own epiphany, seeing in Wagner the founder of a new religion and in the composer's writings the embodiment of a new world view. In Bayreuth his fears and complexes were swept away, as was his sense of being lost: Wagnerism gave him a missionary sense of purpose in life. His name came to Cosima's attention through the numerous articles on Wagner that he published, mainly in the *Revue wagnérienne* that he helped to set up in Paris in 1885. The barely thirty-three-year-old Chamberlain first met Cosima in Dresden in June 1888, when it is said that he announced himself as a Bayreuthian, not as a Wagnerian. Cosima's response was apparently one of unbridled delight. His first contribution to the *Bayreuther Blätter* was published four years later, followed in 1895 by an illustrated study of the composer's life and works that went through several editions in the course of the following decades. The book is typical of its author's whole approach: subjective, contentious and often in contradiction with the facts, it is essentially the work of a linguistically gifted amateur. But Chamberlain's stilted writings were widely disseminated for they flattered their readers' vanity and gave the impression of being erudite without being boring. A subtle psychological profiling of the subject went hand in hand with quotations culled from an impressive range of literary sources and with scientific half-truths and a liberal dose of pseudo-philosophy, allowing the average reader to feel that they were cleverer than they had imagined. According to Hermann Keyserling, who had known Chamberlain during his days in Vienna, the writer used a clever trick to ensnare his audience: 'Chamberlain literally lived off sayings that were articles of faith to him; he would quote from the writings of others where any other writer would personally have examined the matter, drawing rational conclusions and demonstrating the validity of his argument. He showed an astonishing lack of the gift necessary for exact analysis and accurate discrimination.'[112] Keyserling was convinced that Chamberlain had very few ideas of his own. 'But when he got up on the ladder in his library in the morning and leafed through his books, he was always struck by the quotations that later became his principal modus operandi.'[113]

Chamberlain used history as a quarry, shoring up his own position by means of abstruse comparisons. This is certainly true of his next work, *The Foundations of the Nineteenth Century*, which first appeared in 1899, a substantial two-volume publication that made Chamberlain famous as the exponent of an ostensibly 'scientific' theory of race. In orotund phrases he praised the 'Aryan race' that had, he claimed, been harmed by Jewish influence, and he advocated the 'purity of Aryan blood' and 'selective breeding'. His claim to scientific respectability was absurd, and today's readers will find it hard to believe that the author of *The Foundations of the Nineteenth Century* enjoyed such a high reputation as a religious thinker, philosopher and even as a scientist. His explanations were marked not by empirically verifiable findings but by skilfully packaged assumptions and emotionally charged assertions, the tome's value as a propagandist tool resting on its unconscious, emotive power rather than on its reader's conscious perception of its content. Chamberlain appealed less to his readers' intellect than to their feelings, which he manipulated subtly but shamelessly, fomenting fears, activating psychological complexes and, under the cover of an educated middle-class erudition, preaching the doctrine of an aggressive anti-Semitism. It was a dangerous and highly effective brew. Chamberlain's *Foundations* became a best-seller, and by the outbreak of the First World War some 87,000 copies had been sold. A cheap edition that appeared in 1906 sold out within days. By 1941 the work had been reprinted more than thirty times.

Chamberlain's anti-Semitism was psychopathological in character, and there were several occasions when paranoid conspiracy theories pursued him even into the world of his dreams. 'You really are possessed by an anti-Jewish demon,' the theologian Adolf von Harnack told him in November 1912.[114] Chamberlain's answer was unequivocally clear: 'You won't change your opinion any more than I shall change mine.' For him, the Jews represented all that was 'bad, shameful and vulgar'. 'I hate them and I hate them and I hate them with all the resources of my soul,' he concluded.[115] Visibly proud of his dubious achievement, he claimed elsewhere that 'there is no man alive whom the Jews hate as much as they hate me'.[116]

A man like Chamberlain was very much to the liking of Kaiser Wilhelm II: he was a 'reformed' Englishman who wanted to be more German than the Germans and who had a pseudo-scientific answer to the burning social and political questions of the *fin de siècle*, an answer that boiled down to the sentence 'the Jews are to blame'. Years later, the Empress Hermine, writing in a previously unpublished letter to Cosima's daughter, Daniela, recalled that Wilhelm had been 'Chamberlain's most loyal and appreciative admirer'.[117] It was an unholy alliance that brought the kaiser and the writer together. Chamberlain's ingratiating letters bolstered Wilhelm's chauvinistic self-confidence, while the latter's praise confirmed Chamberlain in his 'German mission'. In point of fact, Chamberlain's image of Germany had little in common with reality but was rather a blank canvas on which he could project his own ideas. 'Far too often he clung to an idealized image,' recalled Keyserling, 'an image in which he could believe all the more sincerely in that it bore no relation to anything that could be found in the German character.'[118]

Chamberlain was evidently under no illusions about the society he would be mixing with when he married Eva Wagner, for in March 1904 we find him writing to Keyserling: 'As for the W. family, you really must make an exception of Frau Cosima. I can't believe that she was being dishonest with you, whereas the others . . . are a thoroughly dishonest lot.'[119] The harshness of his verdict was almost certainly due to the breakdown of his relations with Henry Thode, for the future brothers-in-law could not abide one another. With Cosima's backing,

Thode had publicly accused his rival of plagiarism in March 1900, claiming that Chamberlain had copied whole passages from Wagner's prose works when writing his *Foundations of the Nineteenth Century*, while failing to acknowledge that debt in his foreword. With that, Chamberlain's hitherto cordial relations with Wahnfried were seriously compromised. All the more remarkable, then, was the turn of events that took place in the summer of 1908. The union between Chamberlain and Eva Wagner was no love match in the classical sense, although this does not mean that the couple felt no affection for one another. Rather, the marriage between Wagner's daughter and one of the composer's most fanatical admirers seems to have been the product of a complicated set of circumstances, involving practical interests, personal vanities and great hopes for the future. Bride and bridegroom as well as Siegfried and, not least, Cosima Wagner all thought that they could profit from the liaison.

First to profit was Siegfried Wagner, who, now thirty-nine, was still unmarried and who must have felt that the pressure to find a wife exerted on him by his family and especially by Eva was growing increasingly intolerable. With the marriage of his influential sister, he no doubt hoped that he would no longer be the focus of such relentless attention. Ever since her father's death, Eva had devoted herself to her mother to the exclusion of all else – she was Cosima's travelling companion, secretary, assistant, reader and nurse all rolled into one. Not least as a result of these commitments she had scarcely had a private life to call her own. She celebrated her forty-first birthday in February 1908 and yet she was still single, a state of affairs that at this time was regarded as a serious shortcoming in polite society. To put it bluntly, her marriage to Chamberlain was a way out of this unfortunate situation. But there may also have been a second factor at work. Of the other members of the family, Biagio Gravina – Blandine's husband – had died in 1897; the marriage between Daniela and Henry Thode was far from happy, the two parties paralysed by discontent; and the relationship between Isolde and Franz Beidler was causing Cosima considerable anxiety. If we read Eva's letters and diary entries against this background, then it is impossible to avoid the impression that she was keen to put things right in her mother's eyes, for in spite of the many years that she had devoted to Cosima, she had never been her mother's favourite daughter: that was a position that had hitherto been occupied by Isolde. Eva clearly wanted to usurp that role by proving herself her sister's superior and marrying the 'perfect' husband. Until the very end of her mother's life, Eva continued to keep a meticulous record of Cosima's *obiter dicta*, making a particular point of recording her comments on Chamberlain. 'Your happiness with Houston is so uplifting for me,' was one such remark. Another was: 'How delighted your Papa would have been with Houston!'[120]

There is no question that Cosima was overjoyed at Eva's choice. The letters that passed between Cosima and Chamberlain are like so many antiphonal hymns that express the profound emotional affinity between the two correspondents. Cosima also recognized that her son-in-law represented a new and more modern type of writer who would help to disseminate Bayreuth's ideas. Where the writers of the older generation, including the mystically otherworldly Hans von Wolzogen and the much-derided Carl Friedrich Glasenapp, remained firmly rooted in the nineteenth century and were barely noticed outside Bayreuth, Chamberlain was able to contribute towards the formation of a nationalist camp with his journalistic writings. In 1899, for example, the print run of the *Bayreuther Blätter* can hardly have exceeded 400 copies, whereas Chamberlain was reaching an audience of tens of thousands with his *Foundations of the Nineteenth Century*. What was so 'modern' about Chamberlain's writings was his ability to create a universal ideology out of racist and nationalist ideas fuelled by a more general despair in the direction that civilization had taken. No less 'modern' was his concept of race, which differed radically from that of a writer like Gobineau. Whereas Gobineau and his Bayreuth disciples believed that all forms of miscegenation led irrevocably to the downfall of the human race, Chamberlain was fundamentally convinced that the opposite was the case. He stressed the concept of 'racial breeding': only through intermarriage could a race be 'bred' that would have any value or merit. But for Chamberlain 'breeding' meant 'selection', as is clear from his comment that 'the exposure of weak infants . . . was one of the most beneficial laws of the Greeks, Romans and Teutonic peoples'.[121] The National Socialists' exterminatory racial theories found an ideological precursor in Chamberlain.

'The first point that I should like to emphasize', Cosima wrote approvingly of Chamberlain's *Foundations*, 'is the thoughtful and convincing treatment of the question of race,'[122] while elsewhere her praise was even more fulsome: 'Your book will survive, you can be certain of that, and it will prove a milestone. You are the first writer to have had the temerity to speak the truth, namely, that the Jew is an essential factor in our civilization and so it is necessary to examine exactly who he is.'[123] Cosima was not only in agreement with Chamberlain on his 'treatment of the question of race', she also realized that Chamberlain's marriage to Eva gave her the chance to turn the writer into Wahnfried's prophet and spokesman. Central to her concerns was the idea of developing Wagnerism along contemporary lines, a development 'in which a particular role would be allotted to the man who had married into the family'.[124]

Chamberlain was evidently happy to accept his new role as household bard and as the family's ideological head. Keyserling was appalled when he visited his friend in Bayreuth only a few months after his marriage, for Chamberlain now resembled a 'harem wife' who had been 'completely subjugated and tamed':

> He left a depressing impression on me when I visited him in Wahnfried in 1909 and saw him, almost submissively, reading aloud from Plutarch to Siegfried Wagner, who sat there in his dressing gown on a kind of throne. He even pretended to be enthusiastic about being honoured with duties of this nature. But there is no doubt that he was happy, far happier than he had ever been as a free man. And once he had admitted that he had been defeated by the Wagners, the family naturally left him to do as he liked and encouraged him in all his special projects.[125]

For Chamberlain, marriage to Eva Wagner, the daughter 'of the Master of all masters', marked the end of a lifelong search. 'After some difficult years,' he wrote to Kaiser Wilhelm II, 'my ship of life is now gliding into more friendly waters. . . . The fact that we were destined for one another – this presentiment lay, half-conscious, at the bottom of our hearts for many years; the hour of sun-drenched consciousness has now dawned. Her noble mother has blessed this union in the kindness of her heart.'[126] Eva was still needed to look after her mother, and so Chamberlain moved from Vienna to Bayreuth. Up to May 1916 the newlyweds lived in Wahnfried, before moving into a house of their own at 1 Wahnfriedstraße. Until then Chamberlain used the new house merely as a refuge where he could work, even having a small observatory added beneath the roof in order to pursue his amateur interest in astronomy. Money was clearly no object.

As Keyserling acerbically noted, Chamberlain soon adapted to the Wagners' regime. During the daytime he would work on his latest venture, a biography of Goethe, but in the evening he joined the other members of the family to talk and make music or read. Nor was it long before he was helping to take important family decisions. With Adolf von Groß he maintained a particularly lively exchange. In October 1908, before his marriage to Eva, he had formally asked Groß for her hand, a request that must strike the modern reader as remarkably old-fashioned – Eva, after all, was already forty-one. But it should not be forgotten that as the children's legal guardian, Groß was more or less a member of the family. Be that as it may, Groß will have been pleased to have been asked, as Chamberlain never stinted on fine-sounding compliments. He spoke of the 'profound respect that I have felt for you for twenty-five years' and hailed Groß as 'the secretly beating heart not only of the Festival but of the family that has been entrusted to your care'. He even raised his relationship with Eva to pseudo-religious heights when referring to 'the salvation of Bayreuth' and philosophizing about his 'duties in the eyes of God'.[127]

Now sixty-three, Groß was particularly susceptible to Chamberlain's flattery, not least because he had clear misgivings about Siegfried's ability to run the Festival as a viable business concern. However much he may have admired Siegfried as a musician and director, the latter's private life and his guileless attitude to money must have been a thorn in the flesh to an experienced banker like Groß. In this regard, Chamberlain evinced great skill, for in his very first letter to Groß we find him insisting that it was 'a common courtesy to explain something about my own financial situation to you, the guardian of the Wagner family's material interests'. And his bank balance was certainly impressive, for, as he coquettishly explained, he was a 'desirable match from a financial point of view'.[128] With this and similar moves, he wormed his way into Groß's confidence.

For Bayreuth, Chamberlain's attractiveness was due in no small part to his character: after all, he embodied all the qualities that Siegfried appeared to lack – seriousness of purpose, tenacity, strength of character and steadfastness, combined with a certain degree of ruthlessness. From now on, many of the actions that Siegfried, hesitant and reserved by nature, was unable or unwilling to undertake bore Chamberlain's imprint, with the result that it was Chamberlain and Eva who formed the family's new centre of power. Eva shadowed Cosima, deciding who should be admitted to her mother's presence, who should accompany her on her daily walks and what information she could be given. As her mother's private secretary, she also controlled all lines of communication to her, and there was no getting round her. Groß routinely discussed legal and financial problems with the couple, including even the annual royalty statements. And Chamberlain's opinion was sought even on more intimate matters. When, for example, Mottl's estate was to be sold in the aftermath of his death in July 1911, there was a danger that Cosima's letters to the conductor might fall into the wrong hands, so that on Chamberlain's advice Groß bought up the papers for the not inconsiderable sum of 12,500 marks. 'The letters will remain locked away', Groß informed Chamberlain after the transaction was completed, 'and I shall place them in your possession on 18 October.'[129] In the event, Cosima's letters were not at all compromising, as had been feared, but no one could have known this in advance. The only thing that mattered was Chamberlain's success in preventing Cosima from being exposed to public humiliation. That he was unscrupulous in the means that he used and could even be brutally calculating is another story. 'Why should a worthy individual waste time on an inferior opponent?' he once asked Keyserling. 'Murder is the only correct response here.'[130]

Escalation

'Ah, how glad I would be to speak to you,' Daniela Thode wrote to Groß on 28 October 1908. 'There are many things that fill me with genuine anxiety – my most recent conversation with Loldi (Eva doesn't know about it) brought to light such strange things that we are bound to be worried about the course that events may take in the future.'[131] At the date in question it was still unclear what 'strange things' were going on in Bayreuth, but the sensitive Eva evidently had a sixth sense in this regard. The 'Beidler conflict' had been smouldering since the falling out with Franz Beidler in 1906, and by 1909 it had become uncontainable.

The year began with a vacation, Cosima and her entourage – her maidservant Dora Glaser and Eva Chamberlain – heading south in early January. They travelled via Bolzano, Trent and Milan to Santa Margherita Ligure, where, at Schweninger's suggestion, they were to spend the next few months. Here they were joined by Chamberlain, who had been visiting Switzerland. The agreeable ambiance of the Ligurian town and the mild temperatures had a beneficial effect on Cosima's health. The family spent the days taking long walks through magnificent gardens of palm trees, where even in winter the flowers filled the air with their heady perfumes, or else they visited the beautiful bay. In the evenings they generally read to each other.

This Mediterranean idyll was rudely interrupted in mid-March 1909, when Cosima suffered another particularly severe Adams-Stokes attack. The news of this latest illness proved a minor sensation, and newspapers such as the *Berliner Börsen Courier* printed detailed accounts of this dramatic turn of events:

> The health of Frau Cosima Wagner, who is currently staying on the Riviera, was causing some concern to the people around her, and in their understandable anxiety they summoned Professor Schweninger from Munich to

her bedside. In keeping with existing arrangements, Siegfried Wagner has travelled south to be with his family. Frau Wagner's much-weakened state is bound to give rise to a certain concern, but it is to be hoped that any more serious fears are groundless.[132]

Schweninger was evidently prevented from leaving Munich at such short notice, and so his instructions for treating his patient arrived by post a few days later: 'As far as Frau Wagner is concerned, it seems to me that if there were any more obvious signs of sleepless nights, mental hyperactivity, a greater need for alcohol (Asti and champagne) & a tired & drawn appearance, you would be fully justified in wanting to reduce the number of her visitors and to curtail her movements and mental stimuli.'[133]

Schweninger's long-distance decision to discourage his patient from undertaking anything that might make her agitated was understandable, of course, but his ban on intellectual activity and even on all forms of physical movement was to have a disastrous effect on Cosima's constitution, for a woman who had been used to actively organizing her life, conducting an extensive correspondence, receiving visitors and taking a lively interest in current affairs was condemned to a state of total passivity. Eva and her husband now shielded her from the world and on their return to Bayreuth even forbade her to renew contact with close friends and members of the family. The events that unfolded during the summer and autumn of 1909 were a prelude to the unfortunate court case that hit the headlines less than five years later. Until now, they have been shrouded in obscurity, but with the help of newly discovered documents among the unpublished papers of Siegfried Dispeker (Isolde Beidler's lawyer), Ernst Schweninger and Houston Stewart Chamberlain, these events can now be reconstructed in considerable detail.

The trail of evidence begins with a letter that Cosima addressed to Isolde in August 1909: 'Dear child, since my most recent attack I have been quite frail. Each meeting with you leaves me more agitated than I can say. We need to be patient for a little while longer; as soon as I feel strong enough I shall call you. In spirit we are united in the midst of folly and grief. Mama.'[134] Isolde evidently gained the impression that the Chamberlains were to blame for her cancelling a planned meeting and that they were trying to prevent mother and daughter from seeing each other again. There is no proof that Isolde's supposition was correct but, as the future was to demonstrate, her suspicions were by no means wide of the mark. Also worth bearing in mind is the fact that as Cosima's secretary, Eva could make barely perceptible changes to her correspondence. On 21 August, Siegfried Wagner sent a mysterious note to Isolde. It sounds like a warning, advising her, as it did, not to disturb the family peace: 'Dear Sister – I believe in my guardian angel! I believe in the guardian angel who protects our Festival theatre! Don't thrust aside your own angel! Your brother, Siegfried.'[135] It seems that tensions were mounting between Isolde and Franz Beidler on the one hand and Siegfried Wagner on the other.

The next document is dated 14 September and is a previously unpublished letter from Chamberlain to Adolf von Groß. According to Chamberlain, Isolde was planning to slander her brother and 'destroy the born upholder of the Bayreuth enterprise'. She was sick, he went on, and was being exploited by a 'villain' – Beidler. She belonged 'in the care of a psychiatric institution'. Chamberlain had no hesitation in speaking of 'manifestations of abnormality' and of 'the work of the devil':

Mama expects all the friends of Wahnfried to know how to behave in the present situation. They are faced by a simple either–or. It is quite impossible to serve two masters at once; one cannot be both for something and against it. However honourable the mood that misled people into this situation, any ambiguity in relations between Wahnfried and Colmdorf is henceforth impossible. Anyone who cultivates the company of Mama and the other members of Wahnfried proves that they no longer have any dealings with those wretches.[136]

It is highly unlikely that Cosima had any idea of what was being done in her name. Outside his own four walls, Chamberlain's bull of excommunication provoked absolute horror. Groß, for example, felt so offended by Chamberlain's presumptuous lecture that the latter was forced to apologize.[137] Thode, too, added his voice to the argument: 'The manifesto drawn up by my brother-in-law and sent to our friends did not have our approval in the form in which it was sent out, and we much regret the extremely serious and wounding consequences that it inevitably caused,' he wrote to Schweninger. 'The result is that three weeks ago my poor wife suffered another complete breakdown.'[138] At this date, then, the Thodes, Groß and Wolzogen were still siding with Isolde. True, she and her husband had committed a series of significant errors, but it was generally felt that the conflict could still be amicably resolved. Chamberlain had a different view of the matter: 'Many Colmdorf projects,'[139] he noted in his diary on 16 September, by which he presumably meant his next offensive. Having failed to have his sister-in-law and her husband excommunicated, he tried to enlist Schweninger's help as his accomplice, claiming that Cosima had told him that

> if she could find two people willing to go and beat that fellow [Beidler] to within an inch of his life, she'd give each of them 1,000 marks! So, what do you think, privy councillor? You and I? 1,000 marks isn't to be sneezed at – and the pleasure would in itself be worth a further 2,000 marks. But joking apart: I need your help, O miracle-working magus! Something must be done as quickly as possible: these people must leave Colmdorf and Bayreuth.

It seems unlikely that Cosima would ever have said this even in jest: after all, this was not her style in terms of its content or its formulation. But Chamberlain's hostility knew no bounds, and he now began a hate campaign against 'sissies' like Henry Thode, who were to be punished for their level-headed and, in his view, effeminate behaviour: 'No one knew who was wearing the skirts and who the trousers.' Chamberlain demanded that Schweninger should intervene as a doctor:

> You must write to my wife or to Herr von Groß and in your capacity as a doctor demand that this opportunity be used to remove this constant threat to your patient. You should be as serious and as peremptory in this matter as you generally are when issuing orders. Please do not say or do anything that is cursory, conditional or hedged about with qualifying clauses.[140]

Chamberlain was driven by hatred and, it seems, bent on revenge after he had lusted in vain for Isolde Beidler over a period of many years. But there was a second reason for his actions: if he depicted the Beidlers as 'manifestations of abnormality' who were not even worthy of being a part of the Wagner family, then his own star as the husband of Wagner's only remaining daughter would shine all the more brightly. As he told Schweninger, he would no more lose sight of his goal 'than a decent bulldog releases its grip on the neck of the bull that it has seized'.[141] Chamberlain's brutal language lays bare his twisted nature.

As for Isolde, she was in no doubt as to who her enemy was, complaining to Daniela Thode that 'a great deal of their misery is being caused by Ch[amberlain]'.[142] She repeatedly tried to make contact with Cosima in order to discuss the matter with her. On 5 November 1911, for example, she wrote: 'Let us now, O mother, build a bridge over all that separates us & allow our kind God to judge all right & wrong. Accept back your child, who is not lost, do so with love & believe her when she calls out to you in utter conviction that she deserves this act of love.'[143]

Beidler too picked up his pen that Sunday in November 1911 and begged his 'revered mother-in-law' for her forgiveness:

> I don't want you to think that I don't believe I've done wrong. No, I know that I have & gladly acknowledge my mistakes at all times. I willingly admit that as a result of the agitation caused by the circumstances in which I found myself, I went too far in the matter of *Parsifal*. . . . But what prompted me to withdraw and to become so irreconcilable was the letter that you wrote to me afterwards. It was this letter that made it impossible for me to ask you to forgive me for this action, something I would otherwise happily have done as I am always pleased to make good a wrong, even when that wrong seems understandable.[144]

The Beidlers' attempts at a rapprochement were all in vain and, indeed, they were bound to remain so as Cosima never saw their letters. As a precaution, Siegfried intercepted them, leaving Chamberlain to dismiss the Beidlers' démarche as a 'comedy of ostensible remorse'.[145] But Beidler now made the mistake of attacking Siegfried Wagner, claiming that he had assembled 'material' about his brother-in-law that he could produce if necessary. We can no longer be certain what these documents were. Perhaps Beidler was merely bluffing and the material never existed. Whatever the answer, there is no doubt that Beidler was referring to Siegfried's homosexuality. 'Come what may,' Siegfried retorted, 'I am afraid of nothing & of no one.'[146]

A further week passed during which Isolde was not admitted to her mother's presence. In her desperation she wrote a threatening letter to Siegfried: 'My husband has hinted at the severity of the charges against you, charges that have repeatedly come to my attention. I consider it my duty & even now am convinced that we had no alternative but to warn you.'[147] For the present Siegfried reacted with studied calm: 'Don't worry,' he reassured his sister. 'People spoke ill of the greatest king of all time, Frederick the Great, and Prussia became great and strong through him! So, don't worry! I shan't desecrate the theatre!'[148]

Siegfried can hardly have been as relaxed about the situation as he implied in his letter to Isolde, for the 'charges' were serious – and not just from a legal point of view. Only a few years earlier the journalist Maximilian Harden had accused Kaiser Wilhelm's confidant, Count Eulenburg, together with his general lieutenant Count Kuno Moltke and a number of others, of homosexuality, and the

'Eulenburg affair' had quickly escalated into the greatest scandal in the history of Wilhelm's Reich. Salacious details had come to light in a whole series of sensational court cases, destroying the reputations of the men implicated in the affair. Homosexuality was not just a criminal offence, it was also regarded as unmanly and repellent. Even though Eulenburg and Moltke were not sentenced, their careers were over. The press returned to the subject again and again, lubricious jokes about the kaiser's 'court camarilla' circulating in the streets and squares of the country as a whole. Siegfried Wagner would be threatened by a similar fate if Isolde and Franz Beidler were to go public with what they knew about the head of the Festival's sexual preferences. It did not bear thinking about: the son of 'the most German of all artists' would be no more than a figure of ridicule, unworthy of his forebears. For the present, however, his in-laws shied away from taking such a step.

Cosima was not allowed to find out about all this. Siegfried and the Chamberlains placed an even more rigorous cordon sanitaire around her and prevented her from having any contact with the Beidlers. 'Above all, beware of paying any surprise visits,' was the unmistakable warning that Isolde received. 'This is no joke!'[149] Siegfried demanded that his sister undergo a spiritual cleansing process: Beidler had poisoned her 'true nature' and now she had to 'spit out' the poison.[150] Reconciliation was impossible and, as was only to be expected, Isolde sided with her husband: 'You should finally get it into your heads that I shall always remain faithful to this kind & exceptional man, to whom God has entrusted me & to whom I owe a wonderful child.'[151]

The way in which Isolde defended her husband and lovingly stressed his qualities is touching in the extreme. In spite of this, their ten-year marriage had by now descended to the level of a low farce, Isolde refusing to admit that since 1908 her husband had been having an affair with the soprano Emmy Zimmermann. Their child, Eva Senta Elisabeth, was born on 22 May 1909 – by an odd coincidence, Wagner's ninety-sixth birthday. Eva later married the famous actor Ernst Busch, while also making a name for herself as a cabaret artiste. Beidler was not exactly a faithful husband. Years later he began an affair with one of his employees, Walburga Rass, whom he married after Isolde's death. This liaison produced two children. Beidler's extramarital affairs were the talk of Munich. In February 1911 Mottl reported that Beidler had 'opened up his heart' to him and revealed that he was 'in a passionate relationship with an (extremely bad or at least insignificant) opera singer, at which Isolde is said to have been crying & pining away day & night'.[152] Isolde's tragedy lay in the fact that, already ill and with her nerves in shreds, she did not have the strength to divorce her husband. To have done so would have meant giving in to Siegfried and the Chamberlains and buckling under the weight of family pressures. When Daniela asked her if she was planning to stick by Beidler in spite of everything, she replied: 'Yes, he is my husband, and I have a child by him.'[153]

The battle lines were now drawn up: on the one side were Isolde and Franz Beidler, while on the other were Siegfried Wagner and Eva and Houston Stewart Chamberlain. Only Blandine Gravina and Daniela Thode refused to take sides but tried, rather, to mediate between the two parties. But over the years the conflict had built up its own momentum, so that the actual cause of the family row had long since been forgotten. At stake was no longer the 'Parsifal affair' of August 1906 or Beidler's shameless behaviour or his alleged idleness or whatever other reproaches were levelled at him. By the end of 1909 it was the dynastic principle itself that was the subject of the feud. Who would rule over the Bayreuth Festival? Ultimately, then, Cosima Wagner's legacy was at stake. As Michael Karbaum aptly summed up the situation, it was a question of 'power without possessions for the Chamberlains and possessions without power for Siegfried Wagner'.[154]

A snapshot of the situation at the beginning of the new decade shows how hopeless things had become and that it boded no good for the future. Remarkably enough, there was for a time an unreal peace. In January 1910, Cosima returned to Santa Margherita Ligure in the company of her son, the Thodes and the Chamberlains and put up in a suite of spacious rooms at the Hôtel Continental. Built six years earlier, the five-star hotel had soon become fashionable. All who stayed here evidently set great store by sheer luxury, good service and total discretion. Guests felt at ease among people of their own kind and were determined that it should remain so. No less exclusive was the hotel's situation in the middle of a park planted with magnificent palm trees on a cliff overlooking the Ligurian Sea. From their windows guests had an unimpeded, breathtaking view of the Mediterranean. 'We had a wonderful day today,' Cosima told Adolf von Groß in the middle of March. 'While the Houstons undertook a successful ascent of the heights & Fidi & Heinz worked at home, I went with Lulu to the Villa Spinola, which the marchese had placed entirely at our disposal. We spent one of the most beautiful mornings in its magic garden.'[155] Among the few visitors whom Cosima received during her stay were the journalist Friedrich Dernburg and Gerhart and Margarete Hauptmann.

Cosima and her entourage returned to Bayreuth at the beginning of May, travelling via Milan, Zurich and Munich, where she broke her journey to consult Ernst Schweninger who, following his departure from Groß-Lichterfelde in 1906, had settled in the Munich area. She also saw Schweninger's colleague, Oskar Eversbusch, one of the leading ophthalmologists of his day, who had been treating Cosima for over two decades. They arrived back in Bayreuth on 14 May, and on the very next day Siegfried resumed his daily round and began planning the following year's Festival. After nearly five months in Italy, Cosima felt exceptionally well. 'Daily excursions, generally very refreshing,' Chamberlain wrote to inform Schweninger. 'In the evening she often comes down at around nine and remains until half past, engaging in lively and cheerful conversation – if she is tired, she goes to bed earlier.'[156]

At the end of this turbulent decade, Cosima was especially privileged to receive an honorary doctorate from Berlin's Friedrich Wilhelm University, which was celebrating its centenary in 1910, encouraging its Faculty of Philosophy to confer doctorates on a number of distinguished contemporaries. Among them were the founder of AEG, Emil Rathenau; General Alfred von Schlieffen, the president of the Reichstag; Count Hans von Schwerin-Löwitz; and Cosima. When we recall that it was only two years earlier that women had first been permitted to study at Berlin's alma mater, Cosima's doctorate seems exceptional. The prime movers were the archaeologist Reinhard Kekulé and the musicologist Hermann Kretzschmar, both of them long-standing friends of Wahnfried and undoubtedly keen to pay personal tribute to Cosima. The invitation was normally a mere formality: the University dean, Gustav Roethe, would send round a circular to members of the teaching staff, their unanimous consent a foregone conclusion. This was certainly the case with Rathenau, Schlieffen and the other candidates, but it was not so with Cosima. Out of the forty-one members of staff entitled to vote, eight abstained. An outright 'no' was out of the question as this would have meant a snub to Kekulé and Kretzschmar, but the abstentions were still an embarrassment. Nor was the protest confined to a particular faculty, for the eight naysayers were Heinrich Gustav Engler and Simon Schwendener (botany), Adolf Erman (Egyptology), Otto Hintze (history), Otto Hirschfeld (ancient history), Albrecht Penck (geography), Franz Eilhard Schulze (zoology) and Karl Stumpf (philosophy).[157]

We can only speculate on the reasons for this rejection as there was no discussion and no attempt to justify it. Perhaps it was simply that Cosima was a woman, but the dissidents may also have been disturbed by the fact that she was receiving the award as a reward for her lifetime's commitment to the

Bayreuth Festival. Whatever the answer, the outcome caused a minor scandal. In her letter of thanks, the newly elevated Dr Wagner revealed exceptional pride, striking an almost defiant attitude when adding that 'I understand the rare nature of the announcement and know that it is directed at the hallowed place of art to which I belong, and so I feel moved, uplifted and fortunate in the worthiest sense of the term'.[158]

Meanwhile the Beidlers had decided to leave Colmdorf and settle in Munich. 'I've informed Fidi but have said nothing to his dear Mama,' Groß told Chamberlain. 'Loldi wants to discuss some business matters with me tomorrow, I shall do nothing to make their move more difficult.'[159] Plainly relieved, Groß proved generous in victory, paying for the move and attempting to ensure that the departure of the alleged troublemakers passed off as quickly and as smoothly as possible. The Beidlers moved into a large apartment on the third floor of a luxurious corner house on the Prinzregentenplatz in the fashionable quarter of Bogenhausen. The throbbing life of a metropolis lay on their very doorstep, and the Prinzregententheater, where Felix Mottl was principal conductor, lay only a stone's throw away. It is an irony of history that only a few years later, Adolf Hitler, then a member of the National Socialist Workers' Party of Germany, took rooms in the same building, wealthy patrons having enabled him to afford such seigneurial accommodation. But the obsessively Wagnerian Hitler and Wagner's favourite daughter never met: by the time that Hitler moved into his suite of nine rooms in 1929, Isolde Beidler had been dead for ten years.

The Beidlers' move to Munich was overshadowed by serious illness, Isolde's doctors in Bayreuth having ascertained in early October that she was suffering from a persistent pulmonary infection. 'She doesn't look well,' Daniela Thode remarked, adding that Isolde was suffering from chronic insomnia, had had 'no real digestion for the past half year' and was extremely highly strung.[160] Her separation from Cosima was also a cause of great worry. In utter desperation at not being able to see her mother, she asked Hans von Wolzogen to intercede, appealing to his 'lofty friendship' and intimating that he alone could help: 'I am talking about my final farewell from my mother.'[161] But it was to no avail. Drawing attention to Cosima's current state of health, Wolzogen insisted that 'You will be taking the finest farewell that a child can take by forgoing that pleasure and not exposing her to any risk.'[162] But Cosima's thoughts, too, kept returning to the family tragedy, and it is clear that the feud affected her so deeply that she occasionally drank rather more than was good for her. 'Last night Mama drank an entire half bottle of champagne,'

Chamberlain complained, 'another act of insubordination. I am to ask you what you say to this. I would simply pour away half the bottle, for such a truly heroic nature will always continue to drink as long as there is a drop left in the bottle.'[163] A few weeks later we read: 'Her need for alcohol is powerful and causing us a good deal of worry.'[164]

Even in Santa Margherita, where Cosima again spent the early months of 1911, it was impossible for her to forget about her row with the Beidlers. If we may believe Eva's diary jottings, it was Beidler in particular who exercised Cosima's thoughts. 'How can she continue to live with that man?' she is reported to have said. 'As long as she remains with him, I want no further contact with her.'[165] Whether Cosima really said this must remain open to dispute, but it is at least called into question by a remark recorded by Mottl, who offers a different perspective on the case. It was, he heard from an acquaintance, 'a matter close to Frau Wagner's heart that she should be reconciled with Isolde before her end. But her children – headed, of course, by the loathsome Siegfried – will not permit this! Poor Loldi seems to have a lot to put up with. . . . It is a crying shame to see what has become of the Wahnfried family.'[166] Presumably the truth lies somewhere in the middle: as long as Isolde stood by her husband and as long as Cosima remained under the thumb of Siegfried and the Chamberlains, there could be no question of any reconciliation.

Dusk Falls on the Royalties

In 1913 there were celebrations to mark the centenary of Wagner's birth and the thirtieth anniversary of his death. Wagnerians all over the world remembered the great composer. In Leipzig, where he had been born in 1813, a street and a square were named after him. Elsewhere, he entered the pantheon of German civilization when a bust of him was unveiled in the marble hall at Walhalla near Regensburg, while Bayreuth honoured his son by giving him the keys to the city. Everything could have turned out well, except that the Wagners were in no mood for celebrations, which also explains why there was no Festival in 1913.

Wagner was now at the very peak of his popularity as the most widely performed opera composer of the day, but the expiry of copyright protection at the end of 1913 meant that this particular source of income was about to come to a sudden end. The ghost of royalties past haunted the halls of Wahnfried. If it was impossible to extend the period of copyright protection for Wagner's works, and the experiences of 1901 had suggested that they would again fail in this endeavour, the family at least hoped to revive last-minute interest in a *Lex Parsifal*. As a result, the previous year, 1912, was marked by feverish activity as Wolzogen, Chamberlain, the composers Richard Strauss, Max von Schillings and Hans Pfitzner and the writer on music Arthur Seidl, to name but a few, all sought in their various ways to champion the right of *Parsifal* to be treated as a special case. The thirty-eight-year-old journalist August Püringer proved particularly enterprising in this regard, founding a committee for the protection of *Parsifal* and initiating a petition that had soon been signed by more than 18,000 'German citizens'.

A glance at Püringer's circulars and at his articles in the Dresden *Neueste Nachrichten* suggests that he was the typical simple-minded fanatic. He sent out thousands of consent forms, reply slips and other business letters, all of them printed in vast numbers at his own expense, and he inevitably ended up bankrupt.[167] More than once he importuned the clearly embarrassed Wolzogen for his financial help. The Berlin, Dresden and Leipzig subcommittees not infrequently got in each others' way. The Berliners, for example, made their own independent efforts to raise money for the campaign, only to antagonize Gerhart Freiesleben, the chairman of the Leipzig faction, who wrote to Wolzogen to express his fears that 'the Jewish press' would 'immediately claim it was Wahnfried that was behind the movement and effectively pulling the strings'.[168]

The family had learnt its lesson from the events of eleven years earlier and at least externally maintained a prim reserve, anxious at all costs to avoid the impression that they were again exerting political influence. This thankless task was taken on by Reinhard Mumm, who had been initiated into the affair by his father-in-law, Adolf Stoecker. A Protestant clergyman and a member of the Christian Socialist Party, he even raised the matter in the upper house in late November 1912 but, as was inevitable, his intervention failed to make any difference, the legal position having remained the same. All in all, the campaign left the impression, at least on an organizational level, of desperation and a more or less total lack of coordination. That was one side of the coin. The other reflected the political force of the campaign, and this was certainly considerable. In the years that had elapsed since the last attempt to have *Parsifal* exempted from the country's copyright laws, the Bayreuth community had assumed a *völkisch*, nationalistic hue. Among its spokesmen were Chamberlain and, more especially, the Munich writer Michael Georg Conrad, for whom there had been only one question in 1906:

Do we Germans, as a nation reborn, want to rule the world with an iron will through Wagner's spirit and art and implement the moral principles of our national representatives? This is the first and last question bound up with the events that are taking place with terrifying clarity in our court case relating to the rape of the Grail. To put it at its most succinct: Are you for Bayreuth or against it? There is no middle ground. May the Master's will and work remain sacrosanct: Long live Bayreuth![169]

Conrad's writings aptly illustrate the extent to which Wagner's Bayreuth had moved away from the world of art and culture and entered the realm of politics. In retrospect, it is unsurprising to discover that only a few years later Conrad was one of the people responsible for introducing Hitler to Wahnfried. It is clear, then, that this second campaign was aimed at far more than merely achieving protected status for *Parsifal*. Central to it were political ideas that were to be communicated through Wagner's works. One such aim was 'national education by means of Wagner's art',[170] to quote the title of a book from this period. Another was the 'Germanicization of religion',[171] which was the subject of a study by Wahnfried's resident ideologue, Hans von Wolzogen. In 1914, the year in which the First World War broke out, Wolzogen hailed Bayreuth as a 'place of refuge' and a 'power station for the spirit of that inner world that we may summarize as idealism'.[172] The Vienna-based Indologist Leopold von Schroeder went even further: 'Through Wagner, Bayreuth has become the ideal centre for all Aryan nations,' he declared in his best-selling *Die Vollendung des arischen Mysteriums in Bayreuth* (The Consummation of the Aryan Mystery in Bayreuth).[173] Cosima typically thanked its author by inviting him to a lengthy private audience.[174] The role that Wagner's fanatical followers allotted to their hero in the centenary year of 1913 emerges from Carl Siegmund Benedict's edition of a selection of Wagner's letters, the front of which depicts the swan from *Lohengrin*, while the spine features a swastika in a circle of gold surrounded by a sunburst.

Bayreuth's hallowed temple to Wagner's music was a meeting place for a reactionary social elite that demanded special status for *Parsifal* while in reality wanting to abolish parliamentary democracy. It spoke effusively of the 'purity of the work', while demanding the expulsion of the Jews. Thirty years after Wagner's death, Wagnerism had become the vehicle for a *völkisch*, anti-progressive and anti-Semitic, all-embracing ideology, albeit one that did not go unchallenged: 'Bayreuth' was not a word to be bandied lightly in the presence of intellectuals such as Schoenberg, Walther Rathenau and Paul

Bekker. Schoenberg was quite right to observe that the Green Hill was now peopled 'almost exclusively' by 'the artistic snobs of all nations, plus the arrested developers, the old Wagnerians, who are inimical to the art of their own day'.[175] In Bekker's eyes, the Festival was often no more than an aesthetic backdrop and an artistic pretext. The music editor of the liberal *Frankfurter Zeitung*, Bekker mocked Wahnfried's 'emotionally charged ability to reinter- pret every special interest on Bayreuth's part as a national, ethical or religious demand in an attempt to make it seem more plausible'.[176] His caustic critique went straight to the heart of the matter: Bayreuth appealed to the nation and conjured up the notion of patriotic duty, whereas all that really mattered was the Wagners' coffers and the political ambitions of a reactionary clique.

The politically motivated cult of Wagner that emerged during the early years of the twentieth century left its mark on the period as a whole. Or was it, rather, political conditions that appropriated Wagner for their own ends? Presumably both suggestions are true. Walther Rathenau made fun of the Teutonic postur- ings of Wagner's characters, claiming that 'they were the expression of a kind of theatrical pomp associated with the most barbaric virtue'.[177] Foreign visitors such as John Maynard Keynes likewise found that the boundaries between Wagnerism and the politics of the kaiser's Germany were fluid: 'One can believe sometimes that no greater responsibility for the war lies on any one man than on Wagner,' he wrote in regard to the First World War. 'Evidently the Kaiser's conception of himself was so moulded. And what was Hindenburg but the bass and Ludendorff but the fat tenor of third-rate Wagnerian opera?'[178]

Tutte le Corde

By the middle of 1913 the family row within the Wagner household had entered its final and most critical phase, the calm of the last few months having proved altogether deceptive. If we may believe Eva Chamberlain, Cosima was still insisting that the Beidlers should separate. 'I want to forget and have forgotten, but the condition of this is their separation; and so the sticking point remains this separation, which has been imposed upon us!'[179] In the event Isolde evidently did not receive this message from her mother. 'Not posted at Fidi's request,' states Eva's note on the envelope – they presum- ably wanted to spare the feelings of their ailing sister who, since the July of the previous year, had been under constant medical care. Florenz Wigger's nursing home in Partenkirchen in Bavaria was the first station on her *via crucis*. Others were to follow.

Isolde's case notes have not previously been examined and in many ways make depressing reading. Florenz Wigger, who ran the sanatorium, diagnosed tuberculosis in both lungs, a diagnosis that was annihilating, as tuberculosis, or consumption as it was more commonly called, was a chronic infection that could not be adequately treated at this time. For patients, such findings meant a total change in their lifestyle: generally they had to spend years in a sanatorium, hoping that their serious illness would be cured by clean mountain air. Arosa was a famous health resort; another, Davos, was immortalized in Thomas Mann's *Magic Mountain*.

Isolde's condition seems to have caused real concern. According to Wigger,

> Given the patient's somewhat difficult nature, a regular, strict course of treatment has so far proved impossible. When the doctor prescribes treatment that requires the patient to remain lying down, he none the less has to reckon on her doing something very rash such as undertaking long excursions in bad weather, drinking excessive amounts of alcohol and so on. . . . The patient's exceedingly disagreeable domestic arrangements are also having a highly disruptive effect on the whole course of her treatment (and also on the patient's behaviour), often producing the most severe agitation.

The doctor declared himself powerless: 'For a full recovery Frau Beidler needs at least another one to two years, and it would be best if she were permanently placed in a suitable sanatorium, if possible far removed from her husband and his family.'[180] But Isolde was not prepared to submit to such a regime. Instead, she travelled restlessly between Partenkirchen and Munich, then spent a few weeks in Davos, before moving on to stay with her sister Daniela on Lake Garda, then finally returning to Munich. In the circumstances, there could be no thought of any recovery.

It was in this condition – physically debilitated and with her nerves in shreds – that in the middle of June 1913 Isolde Beidler received word from Adolf von Groß's brother Max that the Wagners were planning to cut her annual allowance and pay her only the statutory minimum. Isolde was understandably outraged and in a letter to Eva Chamberlain declared that in no circumstances was she prepared to renounce her rights as Wagner's eldest daughter. It was immaterial, she insisted, whether she was born 'under Bülow's roof or in Tribschen'.[181] To non-lawyers, the question was indeed irrelevant, for there could really be no doubt that Isolde was Wagner's natural daughter. But the legal situation was rather different, because in the eyes of the law Isolde was Bülow's daughter: she had been born during Cosima's marriage to the conductor, and Wagner had left no testamentary disposition to sort out his estate. Moreover, Isolde evidently did not know that in March 1883 Cosima had persuaded her divorced husband to legitimize Isolde and Eva as his own children. As a result, Siegfried alone was acknowledged as Wagner's child. Thirty years later Wahnfried's motives became abundantly plain: instead of a legal entitlement, Isolde could expect only 'voluntary subsidies' and was dependent on the goodwill of Siegfried Wagner and the Chamberlains.

It was all about money, of course. In 1909 Cosima and Siegfried appeared in a Who's Who of German millionaires,[182] and by the beginning of 1913 the family fortune had risen to the dizzying heights of 6 million marks.[183] Two sets of figures make it clear just how wealthy the family was. In 1913 the average annual income of a public employee was some 1,200 marks, so that 6 million marks represents around 5,000 annual incomes. At today's prices, this amounts to some 27 million euros.[184] In spite of all this, it was clear that by the end of the year the lavish income enjoyed by the Wagners would suddenly dry up and that from then on the family would have to live off their capital. To a certain extent Isolde was therefore a victim of circumstances. But she was also concerned about the position and the legal rights of her now twelve-year-old son, Franz Wilhelm, who was still Wagner's only grandson.

By June 1913 Siegfried had broken off all contact with his sister, leaving Adolf von Groß and Eva Chamberlain to deal with any correspondence. When Isolde wrote to him and asked him to address her concerns in person, rather than delegating them to Groß, it was Eva who replied, claiming that Siegfried did not have the time to trouble himself with points of detail but had 'asked Wahnfried's legal representative, Dr Franz Troll in Munich, to take charge of their implementation'.[185] As a result, Isolde was now obliged to deal with Troll, whose enlistment was largely Chamberlain's work. The two men had known each other for years, and Troll had often represented the maverick writer. Troll's opposite number was Siegfried Dispeker, a Munich lawyer from a well-respected Jewish family. He knew who he was dealing with and that the negotiations would not be easy. As he noted in his unpublished memoirs, Troll was 'as clever as he is knowledgeable, an opponent who knows all the tricks'.[186]

Isolde's lawyer was evidently motivated by the moral desire to prevent her from being disinherited. Vanity, too, may have played a part, for he was dealing, of course, with the family of Richard Wagner. But as an experienced lawyer, he must have known that his client had a poor case. 'Pater est quem nuptiae demonstrant': as we have already noted, under Bavarian law, the children of a married woman were deemed to be the children of the mother's husband, which in Isolde's case meant Bülow. True, the Codex Maximilianeus Bavaricus explicitly allowed for the possibility that the husband's paternity could be challenged, but this would have meant Cosima proving that she had not slept with her husband during the time when Isolde was conceived. How could Isolde have answered this delicate question nineteen years after Bülow's death? Dispeker's conduct throughout this affair also throws up a number of other questions. Did he not inform his client that her case was hopeless? Or was Isolde's threat of legal action no more than the helpless response of a profoundly desperate woman who had been forced into a corner? There is something to be said for the second alternative. Isolde evidently hoped that her family would shy away from an embarrassing court case and agree to an out-of-court settlement.

Isolde appealed to her mother one last time on 2 September 1913: 'You should know that neither for myself nor for my son will I allow my brother Siegfried to deny my descent from Richard Wagner.' As a precaution, she included with her letter a note from Dispeker, 'according to which I am justified in taking legal steps to assert my own and my son's rights, rights that have been contested in the most frivolous manner imaginable'.[187] Isolde's letter was viewed by Wahnfried for what it was: a clear threat. Cosima waited eleven days before replying:

> My child, I have received your letter & its enclosure. You have created a situation that only a lawyer can take any further. As a result, I have forwarded your letter & the enclosure from your lawyer to our own lawyer & asked him to deal with the same. Your mother, Cosima Wagner.[188]

A court case was now unavoidable, and in early February 1914 Dispeker instituted proceedings in the Bayreuth District Court. 'Although one could have been prepared for this indescribable act on Isolde's part,' Groß wrote to Chamberlain, 'I am none the less most painfully affected by it.'[189]

Although Troll was convinced that Isolde's case had no merit, Wahnfried was suddenly beset by self-doubt. Nerves were frayed, not least because Isolde had let it be known that she had in her possession a document in Wagner's hand stating that she was his child. Was it a bluff? 'We must be prepared for everything,' Groß wrote, 'and so I am informing you of this development and asking if you can make any sense of this gossip.'[190] The sixty-nine-year-old

Groß had to bear all the responsibility as Cosima and the rest of the Bayreuthians were all in the Italian resort of Bordighera until May. On top of his usual burden of administrative work – a Festival was due to take place later that year – he also had to prepare the case and travel to Munich to discuss the matter with Troll. He was keen to do all in his power to avoid a trial that was bound to be embarrassing for all the parties concerned. At the very last moment, however, he invited Josef Kohler to draw up a report which, as was to be expected, concluded by favouring Wahnfried and for which the professor received the handsome sum of 1,500 marks. Troll then made it available to the court. But none of this helped to avert the inevitable, and on 6 March 1914 the case of 'Frau Isolde Beidler versus Frau Dr Cosima Wagner' began in the Bayreuth District Court.

If Groß had initially hoped to exclude the general public, those hopes were dashed when the judge agreed to Dispeker's request to lift reporting restrictions. Journalists had a field day as more and more sensational reports found their way into the international media, and the general public, its appetite for gossip suitably whetted, lapped up everything it was fed. Chamberlain attempted to make a virtue of a necessity and to win over the representatives of the ring-wing press, the country's liberal newspapers being on the side of the plaintiff. An ally was found in the figure of the forty-five-year-old Berlin journalist Josef Stolzing-Cerny, who ran a news agency that provided articles for various German dailies. Chamberlain cunningly complained that 'not a single person has asked who in fact are the people who have conjured up this case and what reasons they may have had for doing so.'[191] Stolzing-Cerny took up the story, and it was not long before names had been named: 'Let us assume that we were dealing with a disagreeable feud in a well-known Jewish family, in which case a whole army of Jewish luminaries would already have been mobilized in their defence.'[192] Significantly, Stolzing-Cerny was one of the people who later introduced Hitler to Wahnfried. He became a member of the NSDAP old guard and worked for the *Völkischer Beobachter*. One of his favourite topics was 'Richard Wagner the National Socialist'.

Chamberlain found a second accomplice in the Munich journalist Josef M. Jurinek, who wrote for Hugo Bruckmann's *München-Augsburger Abendzeitung* and who launched a frontal assault on 23 May 1914, following it up with further salvos on the twenty-fourth and twenty-fifth. Emblazoned on the title page was the sensationalist heading to the whole series: 'Wahnfried's Honour'. His back was covered by his editor in chief, Hugo Bruckmann, Bruckmann and his wife Elsa having been friends of Chamberlain's for many years. It was Bruckmann, too, who published Chamberlain's books. Years later they transferred that friendship to Hitler, offering him financial support. Jurinek's articles were written to order: he discussed their content with Chamberlain and also sent them to Troll, who vetted them from a legal point of view and suggested various changes. Isolde was to be depicted as an avaricious and ungrateful daughter – the black sheep of the family. Finally, on 26 May, Jurinek published an interview with Siegfried Wagner, in which the head of the Bayreuth Festival repeated the usual clichés before ending with a minor sensation: he and Cosima had decided to transfer all the family's possessions, including its buildings and objects of value, to a 'Richard Wagner Foundation for the German Nation'.

The announcement proved to be an extremely clever move. Not only did it take the wind out of the sails of those critics who had described Wahnfried as Fafner's lair, it also came to the aid of Adolf von Groß, who had for some time been envisaging an emergency plan in case the court decided against Cosima Wagner, for it was hoped that a national foundation would undermine Isolde's claims. Jurinek's and Chamberlain's concerted action naturally found many critics, and newspapers such as the *Vossische Zeitung* and the *Frankfurter Zeitung* published vicious pieces claiming that the plans to establish a national foundation were nothing more than a bluff. Franz Beidler, too, issued a statement, declaring, superciliously, in the *Münchner Neueste Nachrichten* that 'in the interests of Siegfried's and Wahnfried's honour' he had no wish to go into any more detail about his dealings with Siegfried Wagner.[193]

Although the press campaign was waged with unrestrained acrimony by both sides, there could be no escaping from the fact that in spite of the support and declarations of sympathy received by Isolde, the case was not going well for her. At the eleventh hour the well-known sculptor Heinrich Wadere submitted a sworn statement, insisting 'that the family resemblance between Richard Wagner and Frau Isolde Beidler is so striking that one cannot possibly hold an alternative view'.[194] And Dispeker also received a visit from Chamberlain's first wife, Anna, who had come to express her outrage at her former husband's mendacious machinations and to report openly on his years of erotic escapades with Fräulein Josefine Schinner. As Dispeker recalled in his unpublished reminiscences, 'in order to characterize this man, Frau Chamberlain handed me the Viennese judgement on her divorce, saying that I could make whatever use of it I wanted and adding with a sarcastic smile: "There you have a fine example of the difference between theory and practice." '[195]

Dispeker no doubt foresaw that his client's case would fail. On 12 June he delivered a brilliant summing up and even demanded that Cosima should take the stand, but the court's decision, which was announced on 19 June, came as no surprise. The charge was rejected, and Isolde was ordered to pay the costs of bringing the action. We do not know how the parties reacted to the outcome, but no one can have been in any mood for celebrations. Now that Isolde had been disinherited, Siegfried Wagner and Chamberlain were able to make their own positions within the Bayreuth power structure unassailable, Siegfried as the administrative head of the Festival, Chamberlain as Cosima's son-in-law. And yet Wahnfried paid a high price for this pyrrhic victory: the family of the 'Master of all masters' had been exposed to public ridicule and struck outsiders as mendacious and profoundly unsympathetic. The now elderly Cosima also emerged as a loser, now that – for better or worse – her private life had been dragged into the limelight. The cult of Wagner had culminated in the repudiation of Isolde and had been revealed in all its hollowness. The dynastic principle that had been artificially maintained for decades had finally been enforced, but only at the cost of the family's integrity. Many contemporaries will have been reminded of Wellgunde's words in the opening scene of *Das Rheingold*: 'Du klügste Schwester! / Verklag'st du uns wohl? / Weißt du denn nicht, / wem nur allein / das Gold zu schmieden vergönnt?'[196] (Wisest of sisters, why complain? Do you not know to whom alone it is given to forge the gold?)

Wahnfried's break with the Beidlers was virtually total, only Daniela Thode remaining in contact with her sister, who had so fallen out of favour that her name could no longer be mentioned in Cosima's presence. Isolde had died before her time. Such an attitude seems heartless, and yet we should remember that for Cosima a mother's love weighed far less than the 'duty to the work in hand' that she constantly demanded. Everything had to be subordinated to Wagner and his legacy. 'Mama has never cared about me,' Blandine Gravina wrote in this context to Ernst Schweninger, adding with a note of manifest resignation: 'It is enough that I can tell my conscience that Mama never suffered on account of me.'[197]

As for Isolde, her rift with her mother continued to obsess her in spite of her defeat in court, and in numerous letters to Dispeker we find her complaining about her family's 'baseness' and providing more and more information about the injustice that she had suffered. But the case was not reopened, and there was no appeal. Isolde felt hounded: 'I am again at the end of my tether through constant sleeplessness & powerful soporifics,' she told Dispeker. 'I can no longer pull myself together and get on with my life.'[198] And, as if that were not already bad enough, her tuberculosis had also grown worse.

According to a doctor's report in early 1915, 'given the age of the patient and the appearance of mucous congestion, the prognosis is not good'.[199] At the Schweizerhof private sanatorium at Davos, her doctors were soon unable to help her as she insisted on flouting all their orders. She was addicted to pills and drank too much, while her consumption was leaving her increasingly frail. By the end she was no more than a shadow of her former self. When she felt that she was dying, she returned to Munich and in July 1918 sent an emotional telegram to Daniela:

> My dearest sister, try to come at once as my hours, nay, my minutes are numbered. Remarkably enough, the people around me haven't noticed. It would be tremendously comforting to have you with me at my end. But don't delay, things are very serious. I must look into your eyes once more. I also have too much weighing on my heart that you alone must know. And so I hope that I'll see you again, for the last time. Your faithful sister Isolde.[200]

Isolde's heart-rending cry for help left Wahnfried at a loss. 'But if she dies,' Eva Chamberlain wrote to Schweninger,

> what should we tell Mama? That the news will be a profound shock for her is beyond doubt. Is it possible or permissible to keep it from her? She has not mentioned this wretched daughter of hers for ages, not even to Adolf von Groß, a point he confirmed to us today. The last time I heard her say anything on the subject, it was: 'Just think, it is as if my feelings in this regard have died.'[201]

Eva's language is significant, as Isolde's fate was no longer at stake. Her terminally ill sister was no more than a 'wretched daughter' and, worse, an abstract 'subject' for discussion. Her death throes lasted seven long months. She must have suffered unspeakably and received high doses of morphine in an attempt to make the pain more bearable. Daniela travelled to Munich in early February 1919: 'We exchanged only a few words, she affectionately called out my name from time to time, but groans and complaints predominated.'[202] Isolde Beidler died at four o'clock in the afternoon on 7 February 1919 in her apartment on the Prinzregentenplatz. She was fifty-three years old.[203] At the burial three days later in Munich's Waldfriedhof, the family was represented only by Daniela Thode, Franz Beidler and the Beidlers' son, Franz Wilhelm, who was then seventeen years old. According to Daniela, 'Excerpts from *Parsifal* could just be heard coming from the cemetery chapel in the distance.'[204]

For the present, news of Isolde's death was withheld from Cosima in an attempt to spare her feelings, and it was not until May 1929 that she discovered from a remark by Blandine Gravina that her daughter was dead. 'Where's Loldi?' she had asked. 'In Davos.' 'So Loldi is dead,' Cosima had concluded. 'Yes, Mama,' replied Blandine, 'she was released long ago.'[205]

Back in 1914, barely a week had passed since the devastating trial when the Wagners were again in the headlines. On 27 June 1914, at the height of preparations for that year's Bayreuth Festival, the journalist Maximilian Harden published a long article in his own periodical, *Die Zukunft*, that appeared under the mystifying title 'Tutte le corde'. In it Harden used the outcome of the Beidler case to settle old scores with the 'nobs who inhabit Wahnfried, filling it with their festive, incense-laden rites'.[206] Harden's article amounted to a public execution. In meticulous detail he analysed Cosima's self-appointed role in the years after Wagner's death. It was, he wrote, as if she herself had

created Tristan and Sachs, the Dutchman and the Knight Templar. She accepted it all as if it had to be so, as if there could be no alternative, as if a decree on the part of the divine world order demanded that men of the calibre of Mahler and Humperdinck, Levi and Mottl should look up to her in a spirit of fearful reverence. . . . What did not smell sweet to her was not allowed to penetrate the ambit of her desires; and the only thing that smelt sweet to her was the incense burnt in the service of Wahnfried.[207]

Turning to Isolde Beidler and her fate, Harden spoke of 'dynastic delusions of grandeur'. And he summed up Cosima's and Siegfried's calculations as follows: 'We decide who belongs to us and whom we shall cut off from our household if as they were some rotten branch. We are like gods, boundlessly free to punish and to reward.'[208] Worse was to follow: 'Little Siegfried', as Harden contemptuously dismissed the head of the Bayreuth Festival, was 'a Saviour of a different hue, who cannot want to be all too visible to the naked eye'.[209] Readers immediately understood what was meant by these coded remarks. Although Harden has always been seen as a writer keen to hunt down and expose homosexuals, the individual's sexual orientation was in fact a matter of indifference to him. Rather, he was fanatically obsessed with what he perceived as the truth and hated people who lied or who had double moral standards. He felt a fundamental need to enlighten his readers and in the process not infrequently transgressed the bounds of campaign journalism.

Harden's oblique reference to Siegfried's homosexuality left Wahnfried horrified beyond words, although one reader, at least, was delighted by the exposé: 'Having taken a closer look at your article "Tutte le corde",' Franz Beidler wrote to Harden on 1 July, 'I feel impelled to write & express my extreme admiration & humble thanks.' Wahnfried's fear that he, Beidler, might tell the world about 'Siegfried's morality' was the real reason for the row, he insisted. 'I take the liberty of telling you this because I assume that it will interest you after you have shown such great concern for the whole business.'[210]

Beidler's ominous allusions came too late, for interest in the goings-on in Bayreuth had already faded. On 28 June 1914 – the day after the publication of 'Tutte le corde' – the heir to the Austro-Hungarian throne, Archduke Franz Ferdinand, and his wife were shot by a Serbian student while visiting the Bosnian capital, Sarajevo. Europe was now on the brink of the abyss, and people had other concerns.

6

The Long End

(1914–30)

World Conflagration

The twenty-second Bayreuth Festival opened on the evening of Wednesday 22 July 1914 with Siegfried Wagner's new production of *Der fliegende Holländer*. At first glance everything was just as usual: bunting fluttered from the buildings in the town, the hotels and guest houses were all fully booked and the streets and restaurants were teeming with well-dressed patrons. And yet many visitors felt that the mood was apocalyptic.

Less than a month had elapsed since the events in Sarajevo, a period that seemed in retrospect to be the calm before the storm. In spite of the fact that his nephew and heir had just been assassinated, the Austrian emperor Franz Joseph had chosen to take his vacation as always at Bad Ischl, while Wilhelm II had set off as usual on his visit to Scandinavia. But appearances were deceptive. Throughout these weeks of high summer, politicians, army officers and diplomats were working away behind the scenes in their attempts to turn the archduke's assassination to their own advantage. The balance of power in Europe had long been disturbed, extreme nationalism having combined with aggressive militarism to produce an explosive mixture that could be ignited with a single spark. War might already have broken out in the wake of the Morocco Crisis of 1905/6, and indeed such a course of action had been suggested by the chief of the general staff, Count Alfred von Schlieffen. But at that date the German authorities wanted no such course of action. Nine years later the country's position was far less favourable, France, Britain and Russia having in the meantime formed their Triple Entente and isolated the German Reich – the very development that Bismarck had feared most of all. Germany's only allies were now Austro-Hungary and Italy, a triple alliance that was in fact highly unstable as Italy was secretly steering a neutral course, before later preparing to declare war on its partners.

By the end all that was left was the unhappy alliance between Berlin and Vienna. In both capitals there were many who believed that a preventative war would liberate them at a stroke, with the result that the assassination of the unpopular heir to the Habsburg throne was by no means unwelcome. Wilhelm II had no qualms about writing a blank cheque to the Austrians, declaring his unconditional allegiance, an action that proved to be catastrophic in terms of his country's foreign policy. On 23 July – the day after *Der fliegende Holländer* opened in Bayreuth – Austro-Hungary delivered a sharply worded ultimatum to the Serbian government, even though it had not been proved that Serbia had had a hand in the assassination. The ultimatum expired two days later, at which point Austria mobilized its troops, declaring war on Serbia on 28 July. Germany declared war on Russia on 1 August and on France on the third, followed by England's declaration of war on Germany on the fourth. The whole world was now ablaze. In the circumstances, it was inconceivable that the Bayreuth Festival would run its natural course, and its countless visitors, headed by the foreigners who were now regarded as enemy aliens, fled the town, even many of the musicians returning home. The season ended with *Parsifal* on 1 August after a total of only eight performances.

The outbreak of war plunged the whole country into a state of hysteria. 'I no longer know any parties,' Wilhelm II appealed to his subjects, 'I know only Germans.' Volunteers flocked to enlist, everyone wanting to play a part, while those who remained behind were regarded as traitors and cowards: unfitness for military service thus became a failing. The population as a whole cheered as the troops reported for duty. In Berlin thousands of civilians lined the streets, the men waving their hats, while women and children presented flowers to the departing soldiers. There was no doubt that Germany was in the grip of a state of frenzy in anticipation of the coming hostilities.

Wahnfried naturally struck a nationalistic, patriotic note. 'How wonderful to see Austria and Germany united,' Siegfried Wagner wrote enthusiastically to the Viennese journalist Ludwig Karpath. 'How gladly one grants your emperor this experience after all he has suffered!'[1] The now forty-five-year-old Siegfried was one of those soldiers who fought on the home front, writing a choral work, *Fahnenschwur*, for male-voice chorus and large orchestra during the early weeks of the war and dedicating it 'to the German army and its leaders in enthusiastic gratitude'. Not one of Siegfried's better works, it received its first performance in Berlin in October 1914. The elderly Cosima was equally enthusiastic about the prospect of war: 'I took the liberty of congratulating

Herr von Hindenburg on his birthday', she informed Prince Hohenlohe-Langenburg. At the end of August, Paul von Hindenburg had defeated the Russian army at the Battle of Tannenberg and was now regarded as a national hero. He wrote to thank Cosima, sending her a card that she kept 'as a precious souvenir with a picture of the hero'. 'War', she went on, 'seems to suit us Germans far better than peace, when all that was un-German was rife'.[2]

But patriotic enthusiasm also opened the floodgates to false suspicions, malicious gossip and spying on one's neighbours. In small towns like Bayreuth there was a widespread tendency to snoop and pry into others' political allegiances, and even Chamberlain was drawn into the crossfire when at the end of August it was suddenly rumoured that he was transmitting secret signals to his fellow Englishmen from the small observatory at the top of his house. 'Without further ado, I am now, if not accused, then at least suspected, of betrayal of my adoptive homeland, where I enjoy the country's hospitality – in other words, I'm accused of the blackest and most shameful crime known to man.' He was clearly even afraid that he would be attacked: 'Today I don't even dare to go out into the street'.[3]

In spite of all the support that he received from Bayreuth's mayor, Leopold Casselmann, Chamberlain had to agree to close down his observatory as a precaution, and both Casselmann and Groß advised him at least in the shorter term to abandon his plan to apply for German nationality, arguing that people would not believe an 'enemy alien' capable of such a step. As a result it was not until August 1916 that Chamberlain was naturalized. In the event, these admittedly unedifying accusations merely confirmed Chamberlain in his 'German mission'. In his numerous 'war essays', which sold in enormous numbers, he adopted a stridently fanatical tone in inveighing against the Triple Entente, returning time and again to Great Britain's alleged treachery. In one article he even looked forward to the total defeat of his native country, which he described as 'rotten to the core'.[4] He also dismissed King George V as a 'traitor', which even Chamberlain's brother, Basil, thought excessive: 'There are certain decencies against which well-educated men never transgress, even in the greatest indignation. That you could do this shows merely that this wretched war has more or less demoralized us all'.[5]

Paradoxically enough, the premature end of the 1914 Bayreuth Festival was in fact not unwelcome to the Wagners, the outbreak of war diverting attention away from a family business that was beginning to show its age and that in the eyes of many observers had already outlived its usefulness. At least in a figurative sense the plaster was peeling off Wahnfried's walls, while the

Festival theatre was seen as the centre of an old-fashioned and even tedious performance style. And then there had been the numerous scandals and arguments that had done nothing to improve the family's standing in the eyes of the wider world. Cosima, now seventy-six, bore all this with her typical dignity and fortitude. 'What a model of the most sublime willpower our Mama is, even to the point of unapproachability!', wrote Eva.[6] And yet even close friends often did not know what was going on in Cosima's mind. After all, her life's maxims had always been to keep one's composure, not to let oneself go and on no account to reveal one's ignorance.

Now that Isolde had lost her legal entitlement to the family name, Siegfried Wagner could consolidate his position as head of the household, but at the same time there was mounting pressure on him to find a wife and continue the Wagner line. After all, one of the consequences of the Beidler case was that Isolde's son – and Wagner's first grandson, Franz Wilhelm – was now officially deemed a descendant of Hans von Bülow. Eva Chamberlain was forty-seven and could no longer be expected to produce an heir, and so it was left to Siegfried to ensure the dynasty's survival. In contemporary photographs the Master's son looks like an ageing dandy who had never voluntarily been a-courting. His clothes – knickerbockers, white tennis shoes and stand-up collars – were always the height of fashion, but perhaps just a little too elegant, lending him the air of a character from the world of operetta.

Siegfried knew there was a price to be paid for repudiating Isolde and that his bachelor days were over. The search began for a young woman of child-bearing age, with musical interests and, ideally, from the same circles as those that Wahnfried frequented. As chance would have it, just such a young woman turned up in Bayreuth in late July 1914. Winifred Williams, a seventeen-year-old orphan from England, was attending the Festival with her foster father, Karl Klindworth. The now elderly Klindworth and his wife had taken in the sickly child in Berlin and given her a thorough schooling, including a knowledge of housekeeping, baby care and a sense of civic respon-sibility. Arguably her most important asset was her familiarity with the world of music in general and Bayreuth in particular, a familiarity that she owed to Klindworth, who had been a friend of Wagner and a pupil of Liszt. She found herself standing before Siegfried for the first time during one of the hour-long intervals: 'For me this meeting with Siegfried meant love at first sight,' Winifred reminisced in 1969. 'It was his lovely warm voice that most impressed me, his whole appearance, his wonderful blue eyes captivated me. . . . For me, Siegfried was the unattainable ideal of my dreams.'[7] Flattered by such idolatry, Siegfried, too, felt a certain fondness for the 'little child', as Winifred was known by her foster parents.

They met again in Berlin that October, while Siegfried was in the city to conduct his cantata, *Fahnenschwur*. On this occasion, too, Winifred found Siegfried 'very sweet'. In the green room after the performance 'we looked at each other in silence for at least 1½ minutes'.[8] There followed a visit to the Klindworths, contacts grew closer, and Siegfried was evidently inclined to sue for Winifred's hand. But it was Eva Chamberlain who provided the decisive inducement: when her brother returned to Berlin in June 1915, she gave him a long letter to read on the journey. Headed 'Reflections for Your Journey from Your Nearly Fifty-Year-Old Sister', it contained neither a salutation nor a signature but constituted a clear demand: 'Take as long as you need to find the young woman that you, Wahnfried and our cause require,' Eva nagged him. Their mother, she went on, was nearly seventy-eight: 'What a joy and a consolation it would be for her to know that Wahnfried's future was assured!' Her own husband, she added, would soon turn sixty and she wanted to spend more time with him, 'so that some young and powerful support is desirable in the family'. And Eva ended by pulling out all the stops: 'Don't let Isolde's eerily triumphant words "Fidi will never marry" come true!' This sentence in particular must have rankled with Siegfried as it stirred memories of his painful confrontations with his sister. But behind Eva's well-meaning words lay a clear warning: as long as Siegfried was incapable of sorting out his private life and getting married, he remained vulnerable. Maximilian Harden's frontal attacks had been lost sight of in the fog of war. But what if a new assault were to be launched? It was unthinkable. 'And so you must find your Katherlieschen,' wrote Eva, 'and bring new life to our dear Wahnfried! It is high time!'[9]

Events now moved swiftly. Siegfried proposed to Winifred and asked her foster father for her hand in marriage. 'It should be you,' Winifred told her fiancé. 'I can scarcely believe my own happiness!'[10] Cosima, too, was delighted: 'Mama got Stassen to describe the sweet creature to her in great detail & was beside herself with pleasure at his artistic portrayal!'[11] In anticipation of the wedding, Cosima sent Daniela to Berlin to help the bride buy her trousseau. 'We're finally having a break from shopping as I'm already half dead,' Winifred wrote to one of her female friends. Daniela evidently felt very strongly that the future Frau Wagner should dress in keeping with her social standing and paid little heed to Winifred's own taste in clothes. 'I look so funny in very long skirts and hats with veils,' Winifred complained.[12]

By 22 September 1915, the 'young couple' – he was forty-six, she eighteen – had tied the knot. Because it was wartime, the civil and church services both took place in the reception room at Wahnfried in the presence of only the tiniest group of people. One of the witnesses was Siegfried's friend, Franz Stassen, who later recalled that 'Frau Cosima was seated in an armchair in a grey silk dress, her hands raised and clasped . . . the bride was in plain white with a long, full veil.'[13] Eva Chamberlain was understandably relieved to see her brother finally piloted into the dry dock of holy matrimony, assuring her friend Anna Kekulé that 'we can't thank God enough for having granted Siegfried this blissful happiness!'[14] To her sister Blandine she simply wrote that 'It really was high time!'[15] Cosima, too, added her voice to the chorus of celebration and spoke of her great happiness, 'for which I thank heaven every day'.[16]

Life During the First World War

'We spent the holiday quietly but filled with feelings of great solemnity', Winifred Wagner wrote to her sister-in-law Blandine Gravina on 2 January 1916. The last few days had in fact been unusually exciting for her: married life, her new surroundings, Christmas in the bosom of a large family and, finally, Cosima's seventy-eighth birthday were all a novel experience for her.

> The tree was lit at around seven in the evening – Mama sat in the entrance to the salon, Houston, Eva and Fidi were grouped around her, the servants had taken up their positions in the corner, and I sat at the piano. To begin the proceedings, Evchen read out a poem by Wolzogen – Christ in Wartime – after which I played the old Lutheran hymn *Vom Himmel hoch, da komm ich her*, to which Evchen read out the words, just to be on the safe side, in order to spare Mama the singing of the Bavarian dumpling throats.[17]

The young Frau Wagner had some difficulty adapting to Wahnfried's antiquated rules and regulations. Not only were there certain individuals such as Isolde who could never be mentioned in Cosima's presence, but Wahnfried was piled high with pieces of furniture and musical instruments that no one was permitted to touch. Hallowed by the Master's hand, these objects were like sacred relics. No one was allowed to sit in Wagner's favourite armchair, and so no one had sat in it for thirty-two years. One can imagine the cry of horror that echoed through Wahnfried's high-ceilinged halls when Cosima's new daughter-in-law chose to sit in precisely that seat. As Winifred remonstrated, 'No one had told me anything about it being a sacred chair.'[18] Siegfried generally burst out laughing whenever his uninhibited wife transgressed against family protocol, a reaction not shared by her sisters-in-law. Eva Chamberlain and Daniela Thode viewed the newcomer with deep suspicion. Thanks to whole armies of servants neither woman had ever had to do a decent day's work, not that this prevented them from giving instructions to Winifred, the latter's diploma in domestic science notwithstanding. As Winifred later observed: 'I was convinced that I knew more about housekeeping than my sister-in-law, who couldn't even thread a needle.'[19]

The daily routine in Wahnfried was strictly regulated and geared to the needs of Cosima and Siegfried. After breakfast, Winifred would read to her husband and discuss the concerns of the day before dealing with his correspondence, while Cosima reclined on a large sofa in the main salon:

> Throughout that time she generally kept calling me over, insisting that a young woman must be fully occupied. It was then that she gave me French lessons. I had to write to her daughters in French and I also read to her a lot – mostly in French. Then came her morning constitutional, which generally took her into the town through the Hofgarten. She had a habit of going into individual shops in order to rest there. And so every shop owner was always delighted when she came and sat down in his shop. She would then buy a few trifles, and once I was in the house, she generally brought something back for me, too: very small trifles such as a brooch or a paperweight or something similar. At midday she was helped back into bed, and then in the afternoon she was generally allowed to receive friends. Before or after tea my mother-in-law would then go out again for at least half an hour. But on this occasion we would take a car and drive out into the surrounding area and get out. The car would then be sent on ahead of us and we would follow it on foot. In the evening she would be read to for another hour, but I wasn't the only one to read to her. One or other of her daughters – Eva or Daniela – would also do so, and although it was still very early she would then be taken up to her room and put to bed.[20]

Of all these periods when members of the family read to Cosima, Sunday mornings took pride of place, for it was then that Chamberlain would read one of Luther's sermons, 'to which we invariably owe both strength & edification.'[21]

We should not imagine the elderly Cosima as a humourless and crotchety termagant, for Winifred recalls her mother-in-law often laughing out loud.

Even in old age, however, aristocratic manners were still extremely important to her, and woe betide all who failed to display them. 'As a child, I was always shy of Grandmama,' recalled Blandine's daughter, Maria. 'I tried to keep up, but I always did everything wrong. On one occasion, when I was on holiday from boarding school, Grandmama sneezed, and, like any well-behaved child, I said: "Bless you, Grandmama!" ' To which Cosima replied: 'How tasteless!' On another occasion, the young girl asked how her grandmother had slept, only to be told: 'I wouldn't ask such foolish questions!' Then there was the time when Cosima happened to find a bottle of bitters in her granddaughter's pocket: 'She took out the bottle and asked what it was – "Llliqqqueur," I stammered.' Cosima's reply was devastating. ' "Oh!" was all that she said between then and the next time I saw her – nothing else. And this brief, annihilating "Oh" left me as humble and as humiliated as any saint – and explanations were not allowed.'[22]

According to Eva, Cosima's French lessons were both edifying and serious 'for all that we read Beaumarchais' *Figaro*.'[23] Winifred tried to see the funny side of things. 'I hope the letter isn't full of crass mistakes.'[24] Cosima's love of lecturing her entourage was not without its comic side, even her servant of many years' standing, Dora Glaser, finding herself the dubious beneficiary of such didacticism – sometimes even in the middle of the night. Blandine's daughter, Maria, recalled that

> Grandmama's hearing has grown rather weak, and whenever she asks Dora something and Dora answers rather quietly, she doesn't hear the answer properly, and, conscious of her splendid former hearing, she blames Dora's poor pronunciation and makes her practise s and z sounds and clear word endings!!! It's amazing! And Dora, seeing the funny side of the situation, says finally: 'There, madam, that's enough for today, it's already late!'[25]

In the Wagner household, everything had been reduced to the level of a hallowed ritual – even Cosima's bedtime routine had acquired a certain set form:

> She had a parrot in the next room, and the parrot had noticed exactly what went on, I mean the ceremony of going to bed, and she always had an extra bottle of beer in bed to help her to sleep, and the parrot imitated this beer-gulping sound. And when she had finished her beer the parrot always said good night, good night, to which my mother-in-law responded with good night cock-a-doodle, good night cock-a-doodle.[26]

Clearly observant, the parrot could also imitate Eva Chamberlain, even though – as Winifred recalled – the bird could not abide her, so that whenever Eva, who was evidently prone to belching, came into the room, the parrot would mimic this sound too.

There is no doubt that Winifred had little say over her life, and the strict division of her daily round seems strange: 'Fidi is bringing her up magnificently and fully respecting Madame Patersi's rules,' Eva wrote to Blandine.[27] For all that this sounds authoritarian, it reflects the sort of distribution of roles that was entirely normal at this period. The wife had to see to her husband's well-being and back him up: 'He needed me constantly,' Winifred recalled, 'not just to read to him but also as a secretary and as a lightning conductor. Everything that he found disagreeable – receiving people whom he didn't want to see and whom he may not have liked –: that was where I came in. I organized all his trips and worked out all the timetables and booked all the hotels. So I was effectively his employer.'[28]

When Eva and Houston Stewart Chamberlain finally left Wahnfried on 1 May 1916 and moved into a nearby house of their own, Winifred's situation suddenly improved, for although Eva returned to the villa several times a day in order to tend to Cosima, deal with her correspondence or read to her, it was now left to Winifred to run the household, and she left her sister-in-law in no doubt as to who was now in charge. The young Frau Wagner proved to be a highly skilled employer, successfully organizing hearth and home for her demanding family. Even during the austerity of the war years, the Wagners lived like lords, refusing to cut back on the number of their staff. A cook and a scullery maid saw to their physical well-being, while Siegfried had his own personal valet, who also doubled as a chauffeur. Two chambermaids kept the vast house in order, and a gardener and his assistant tended the surrounding gardens. Cosima's only servant was Dora Glaser, who saw to all her needs and who had been working for her since 1893. 'Gradually she too became an invalid and needed help herself,' recalled Winifred. 'And so there were two older women who looked after my mother-in-law.' All told, there were nine servants to look after the three permanent residents, Cosima, Siegfried and Winifred.

'During the First World War,' Winifred recalled decades later, 'our homeland was effectively spared the ravishes of war, and with the exception of an increasing shortage of food, daily life really went on as normal – above all in Wahnfried.' Cosima's daughter-in-law was nothing if not resourceful in dealing with food shortages. She had no hesitation in turning Wahnfried's lawns into vegetable patches. 'Here, where I found peace from delusion, they are now planting potatoes in the gardens,' one enraged Wagnerian wrote to her, wilfully misquoting the Wahnfried sgraffito. But, as Winifred explained, 'It was important to fill the family's stomachs.'[29]

In April 1916 Winifred realized that she was pregnant. Two years after Franz Wilhelm Beidler – Isolde's son and Wagner's first grandson – had lost his claim to the family name, the continuation of the dynastic line seemed to be assured. Her pregnancy was largely unproblematic, and the nineteen-year-old mother-to-be generally felt exceptionally well. The two childless aunts, Eva Chamberlain and Daniela Thode, were not slow in offering well-meaning advice on how expectant mothers should behave, but Winifred preferred to place her trust in Ernst Schweninger. 'In a book by Dr Ammon, *The First Duties of a Mother*,' she wrote to Schweninger, 'I read that in the last two to three months a mother should take particular care of her breasts in order to ensure that they are capable of breast-feeding the child. So I wanted to ask you if you could give me any necessary rules of conduct.'[30] Schweninger was able to help his patient both in this and other eventualities. When it seemed as if the authorities might requisition Wahnfried's store of pickled eggs, Winifred lost no time in appealing to the famous physician in Munich: 'We're planning to submit a petition, asking that we be allowed to keep our pickled eggs, and intend to give Mama's invalid diet as the reason. . . . Would you be so kind as to provide medical confirmation of our need to be allotted several eggs a week for Mama?'[31] The plan worked.

Winifred's first child, Wieland Adolf Gottfried Wagner, was born in the Bayreuth General Hospital on Friday 5 January 1917. Cosima marked the event by sitting at Wagner's Steinway piano and playing a few bars from the *Siegfried Idyll*, which her husband had once written for their son.[32] She had not touched the instrument since Wagner's death. Now seventy-nine, she must have been deeply affected by the day's events to make such an exception after more than thirty years. Siegfried, too, was overjoyed:

Wieland Gottfried is thriving and snatching at his mother's breast like a little frog snatching at a fly. And little Winnie has milk in abundance to offer. She'd barely recovered from her labour pains when she said to me: 'Next year, Goldschniggelchen, we'll have another child so that the boy has company and doesn't get bored!' She's Katherlieschen incarnate. You can imagine how happy Mama is! Yes, heaven itself sent little Winnie to me![33]

Mother and son left hospital just over a week later, on 13 January. As was only to be expected with the Wagner family, their arrival back at Wahnfried was positively operatic in its extravagance. A family friend played 'Es gibt ein Glück, das ohne Reu' (There is a happiness without remorse) from *Lohengrin* as Winifred entered the building with the newborn infant. 'I walked through the reception room as if in a dream,' Winifred recalled. 'Approaching Mama, who was sitting at the entrance to the salon in sublime beauty, I brought her the future heir, my heart heavy with emotion!'[34] The couple's daughter Friedelind was born in early March 1918, followed in August 1919 by Wolfgang and in December 1920 by Verena.

Times were hard. Although the family was better off than the majority of Germans, the war-torn economy meant that for them, too, everything was in short supply, especially butter, sugar, milk and, of course, coal. Since Wahnfried could no longer be properly heated, Siegfried, Winifred and the children moved into Siegfried's former bachelor flat, leaving Cosima and Dora Glaser on their own in the rambling villa. When there was no longer sufficient coal to heat even the stove in Cosima's room, the two women wrapped themselves in thick woollen blankets. And yet these adverse conditions did nothing to undermine the Wagners' enthusiasm for the war. Quite the opposite, in fact. With its resumption of unrestricted submarine warfare in February 1917, the German Reich provoked the United States of America into declaring hostilities two months later, thereby bringing to an end any immediate prospect of peace. But Siegfried was euphoric: 'Finally, thank God! A year too late!'[35]

Cosima, too, was enthusiastic about the war. At the start of hostilities, a large map had been hung in the main salon in Wahnfried, allowing Cosima and Chamberlain to follow troop movements. 'I hardly need tell you,' she wrote to Prince Hohenlohe-Langenburg, 'with what interest I have been following all that you have described to me! From the desolate stretches of Poland and Galicia, with their sinister Jews who will always remain alien to us, to the pretty, civilized city of Lemberg.' During her daily walks through Bayreuth, Cosima would occasionally speak to some of the wounded soldiers who were now a regular feature of street life in the town. 'I recently stopped to talk to a man with a mutilated arm, who muttered darkly about his condition. "But you should tell yourself", I remarked to him, "that you have helped to ward off the French." ' But the man had other worries and grumbled that the French were a matter of total indifference to him. For Cosima, this was an instant sign that 'a certain lassitude is now noticeable'.[36]

The 'lassitude' that was Cosima's way of referring to Germany's war weariness increased as the fighting dragged on. In the wake of the exceptionally cold
winter of 1916/17 – a period that has gone down in German history as the
'turnip winter' and that led to countless deaths from the cold and an ever-
worsening food situation among the civilian population – a new sense of
hopelessness gripped the country. On the home front, there were signs of a
general breakdown in law and order as mass strikes caused mounting disrup-
tion: in Berlin alone more than 200,000 workers downed tools in April 1917.
In mid-July the Reichstag accepted a 'peace resolution' supported by the
Socialist Party, the Centre Party and the Progressive People's Party, demanding
'peace through understanding and lasting reconciliation among nations'. For
the political right this was tantamount to an act of treason. And in early
August, finally, sailors on the *Prinzregent Luitpold* attempted to mutiny in
Wilhelmshaven, an act that throws significant light on the desperate state of
the navy. At the same time the German Fatherland Party formed a powerful
countermovement. Founded by Admiral Alfred von Tirpitz, who had proved
himself to be a military failure, and by the director general of the East Prussian
Agricultural Credit Bank, Wolfgang Kapp, the organization was a rallying
point for rabid nationalists and chauvinists. By July 1918 it had 1.25 million
members in 2,500 local branches, its aims being to undermine the peace
process, to annex lands to the east and west of Germany and, indeed, to expand
'to the Pacific Ocean and the gates of India'.[37]

Demands such as these were not just absurd but in crass contrast to the
country's disastrous military situation. Wahnfried, too, shut its eyes to the truth.
'We have become enthusiastic members of the Fatherland Party,' Cosima wrote
to inform Prince Hohenlohe-Langenburg. 'The two appeals and Tirpitz's great
speech struck me as quite wonderful. On reading them, my son-in-law
Chamberlain exclaimed: "At last, the language of a German statesman!" '[38]
Chamberlain even dedicated one of his war essays to the Fatherland Party,
which he hailed as the patron saint of Germany: 'This party must and will
triumph over the other parties and will then reign supreme until there are no
longer any parties left in the German Reich. Amen to that!'[39] It was the hubris
of the swastika that finds embryonic expression here, just as, more generally,
Kapp's and Tirpitz's association paved the way, both ideologically and organiza-
tionally, for the later NSDAP, the famous historian Friedrich Meinecke seeing in
their movement 'an accurate prelude to the rise of Hitler'.[40]

It was during this turbulent period that Cosima celebrated her eightieth
birthday on 24 December 1917. 'I received many tokens of support from far and

near,' she proudly reported, 'and I found this particularly gratifying in that it showed me how significant the number of the supporters of our cause has now become. Even the German kaiser was kind enough to remember me.'[41] But Wilhelm's star was already waning and he was now little more than a puppet in the hands of his generals Hindenburg and Ludendorff, for all that Chamberlain was still mustering support for the kaiser and his war with undiminished intensity. In 1917 he published his essay 'Democracy and Freedom', dedicating it to 'The longed-for "Man with the Lion's Heart" in a sombre hour, in our faith in Germany's destiny'. The following year saw the publication of an entire collection of essays, *The Will to Victory*. Chamberlain's fanaticism was further fuelled by serious illness. In March 1918, for example, we find him writing to Gerhart Hauptmann to report that he had been 'struck down by a mysterious nervous and muscular disorder' and had 'left the ranks of those who lead independent, active lives and am now entirely dependent on the assistance of loving souls'.[42] According to the official version of events, England's declaration of war had so shocked Chamberlain as to undermine his health.

From a medical standpoint, this made no sense, of course. We cannot say with absolute certainty what mysterious illness Chamberlain was suffering from, although it may have been syphilis, caught during one of his countless erotic escapades decades earlier in Vienna's red-light district. The fourth and final stage of syphilis – neurosyphilis – involves severe neurological problems and paralysis, a diagnosis supported by the fact that Wahnfried spoke only evasively and euphemistically about Chamberlain's illness. After all, it would have been embarrassing if it had been known that such a fanatical racist was suffering from a common sexually transmitted disease. Whatever the truth of the matter, Chamberlain was confined first to a wheelchair and later to bed. By the end, he was completely paralysed. From the middle of 1917 onwards, he would dictate everything to his wife, and when his voice failed him some years later, she learnt to lip-read. Cosima remained one of his most fanatical readers – 'his essay on the Fatherland Party gave me particular pleasure'[43] – and she noted with pride the dizzyingly high sales figures for his war essays. When the German army began its final offensive in the west in March 1918, Cosima thought that she was living through 'a poem about legendary heroes, Hindenburg appearing to us like a demigod'.[44] This 'Michael Offensive' collapsed in the middle of July, allowing the Allies' counter-offensive to begin on various fronts.

Defeat was inevitable. On 9 November, Friedrich Ebert of the German Socialist Party replaced Prince Max as chancellor, and a few hours later his colleague Philipp Scheidemann proclaimed the German Republic from one of the windows of the Reichstag. The Reich was no more. That same day Wilhelm II abdicated and fled to the Netherlands to begin a life of exile. With the signing of the armistice between Germany and the Allies at Compiègne, the First World War finally came to an end on 11 November 1918. Many Germans refused to accept this outcome, giving rise to the legend of a 'stab in the back': motivated by self-interest and cowardice, democrats, revolutionaries, pacifists and, above all, the Jews were said to have destroyed a German army that was 'invincible in the field'. Cosima added her twopenn'orth: 'It seems to me that we Germans lack patriotism. With us a man without a fatherland is allowed to prevent our field marshal from speaking out, and every philistine in his cups finds fault with the strategy of Hindenburg and Ludendorff.'45

The Wagners viewed political events in Germany with uncomprehending dismay. As with so many other Germans, 'Bolshevism' was their bête noire, a catch-all condemnation for left-wing politicians, pacifists, the enlightened press, Jews and, in general, everyone who could be blamed for Germany's recent defeat. But 'Bolshevism' also concealed a deep-seated fear of the new world, fear of a society without a monarchy and ultimately fear of democracy. And the term was also used to stigmatize new trends in art and music. 'If Heracles had been commanded by King Euryatheus [sic] to cleanse the stables of German art,' complained Siegfried Wagner, 'he would no doubt have lost heart!! There isn't enough pesticide to complete this delousing process! Our little boy often says "dada", but I very much hope that he won't become a Dadaist!'46

Virulent anti-Semitism and Siegfried's continuing lack of success as a composer produced a poisonous brew. It was always 'the others' – the Jews – who were to blame for his failures. 'Well, I'm not a Jew,' he inveighed many years later, 'I'm no half-breed and I'm not married to a Jewess. There's no room for such people! – And I'm inspired to write real tunes! Which is forbidden! It's a pleasure to be a German! Ugh!'47 In particular, it was the Kroll Opera in Berlin, founded in 1927 as a centre of the avant-garde, that excited the hatred of Bayreuth, not least because the house, situated on the Platz der Republik, was in the hands of Otto Klemperer, who was not only Jewish but who also conducted a provocatively radical production of *Der fliegende Holländer*. As Franz Wilhelm Beidler later recalled, 'Given its whole outlook, it was inevitable that Wahnfried would reject the Kroll experiment. It is fairly certain that Siegfried Wagner stupidly applied Herr Goebbels's famous comment to this production and dismissed it as "cultural Bolshevism".'48

Developments in the theatre during the years of the Weimar Republic passed the Wagners by. They failed to understand that art was no longer interested in mere ostentation but that it also sought to present a critique of reality. As a result, the post-war period, with its numerous artistic and social developments, was regarded first and foremost as a threat. Berlin, not Bayreuth, was seen as the epicentre of modern art: here there were three major opera houses, more than forty theatres and several concert halls. Political satire thrived, while the great variety theatres showed a good deal of naked flesh. The palatial cinemas and smoke-filled cafés on the Kurfürstendamm and the Friederichstraße were famous all over the world. Museums such as the former Kronprinzenpalais, where Wilhelm II had been born, displayed the work of George Grosz, Oskar Kokoschka and Otto Dix. 'The city had a jewel-like sparkle, especially at night,' recalled the American dancer and singer Josephine Baker. 'The vast cafés reminded me of ocean liners powered by the rhythms of their orchestras. There was music everywhere.'[49] The city inspired a rather different response in Daniela Thode, Cosima's eldest daughter, for whom the capital of the unloved Republic was no more than a hotbed of sin. Following a visit to the city in 1930 she waxed indignant: 'The night-time goings-on in the immediate vicinity of the Kaiser Wilhelm Memorial Church, these insane orgies of lights, the vulgar hoardings, these repulsive advertisements tempting you to buy things, this raging unrest – I had the feeling that I was at one of Satan's fairgrounds and that people were dancing shamelessly on the very edge of Hell.'[50]

Throughout the war and afterwards, the daily round at Wahnfried was marked by casual anti-Semitism. At Christmas 1918 Siegfried sent a friend, Rosa Eidam, a poem of his own composition with the significant title 'Two Rosas': 'I know one Rosa and avoid the other,' this clumsy piece of poetastry begins, implying an obvious antithesis between Rosa Eidam and the Marxist politician Rosa Luxemburg:

> *Die Eine die ist in Ansbach geboren,*
> *Hat Kunst und Glauben zum Banner erkoren;*
> *Die andere ist ein wüstes Weib,*
> *Wühlen und Hetzen ihr Zeitvertreib.*
> *Die Eine die singt mit frommer Kehl'*
> *Allsonntäglich mindestens zehn Choräl'!*
> *Die andere, die aus Israel,*
> *Weckt Sonntags Zank und Volks-Krakehl!*[51]

[One of them was born in Ansbach and has pinned her colours to the mast of
art and faith; the other is a dissolute wench whose pastime is stirring people
up. One of them sings devoutly at least ten chorales each Sunday! The other
is from Israel and causes squabbling and popular scribbling every Sunday!]

The assassination of Rosa Luxemburg and Karl Liebknecht on 15 January
1919 was welcomed in many quarters, while the murder of the Wagners'
bogeyman, the Bavarian Prime Minister, Kurt Eisner of the Independent
Social Democratic Party, by Count Anton von Arco-Valley was greeted by
Cosima with unbridled glee: 'I've just been interrupted by the tolling of bells
for the Galician Semite. In my eyes Count Arco is a martyr.'[52]

An Austrian in Bayreuth

'I've been granted another grandchild,' Cosima wrote to Ernst zu Hohenlohe-
Langenburg in September 1919. 'He is to be called Wolfgang Manfred Martin
and will therefore have Goethe, the Hohenstaufen emperor and Luther as his
patron saints; it is with deep emotion that I observe this little mite, whose
development I shall not live to see, and yet – of this I am certain! – he will feel
my blessing in a solemn hour.'[53] Winifred's three children, Wieland,
Friedelind and Wolfgang, were Cosima's pride and joy. She liked spending
time with them and felt carefree and at ease in their company. As Winifred
later recalled, she also put up with a lot from them: 'The children were
allowed into her part of the building as soon as they were able to crawl, and
God knows what she endured at their hands. They even tried to clean her
teeth and comb her hair. She was very touching with the children.'[54]

For her grandchildren, Cosima's room had something mysterious about it:
the many relics that had once belonged to Grandfather Wagner and
Great-Grandfather Liszt, the plush armchairs into which the children sank
almost from sight, the unwieldy pieces of furniture that invited them to play
hide-and-seek and the old paintings on the walls all conspired to create the
impression of a magical fairytale. 'We climbed about on the sacred chairs,'
Friedelind recalled, 'played with the Master's souvenirs, even put on his
spectacles, to the delight of my father and the shocked disapproval of his sisters
who were divided between horror at the desecration wrought by our baby
fingers and pride in the vigour of the new Wagners.'[55]

But how idyllic was this family picture? 'The relationship between my
mother-in-law and me and between me and my mother-in-law was altogether

delightful,' insisted Winifred. 'We never had any misunderstandings.'[56] But Winifred was being less than wholly honest here. After 1919 there were more and more arguments between the two women. Superficially, at least, these were typical of the ritualized rows between daughters and their mothers-in-law, for all that both parties had recourse to tricks of the most devious kind. When daughter-in-law and mother-in-law refused to see eye to eye, Ernst Schweninger was asked to mediate between them. Winifred wrote to him:

> On behalf of my sister-in-law Eva I wanted to ask you to write a letter to Mama telling her not to call on people while she is out walking and, indeed, to end all such visits. She is now so agitated that not a day passes without her calling in on someone or other during her daily walks. She rushes up the steps, talks in the most animated fashion, then rushes away again, without stopping to catch her breath. In spite of all our reproaches, it is impossible to convince her that this is not what you have in mind for her, and so we'd be most grateful if you would spell out this point once again in a letter to her.[57]

Cosima was by no means bedridden but felt that her wings had been clipped by what she regarded as her family's excessive concern and that she was condemned to a life of total passivity. This was not the life for Cosima and, given her reserves of strength, it could only end badly. At the end of September, she wrote a cunningly worded letter to Schweninger:

> When I wanted my grandson, Gilbert Gravina, to play me a Mozart sonata today, my son intervened & said that this was forbidden. May I ask if I am to be prevented from hearing every single note of music now and for evermore or whether I may permit myself this pleasure now & again, at least in moderation? If I am to be permitted this pleasure, please write to my son to that effect, but if I am to be prevented, then I would ask you to write to *me* c/o Fräulein Dora Glaser at Wahnfried.[58]

When Winifred heard about Cosima's letter, she wrote in turn to Schweninger: 'Would you please reply to Mama's enquiry of yesterday's date to the effect that she may listen to music only as a source of pleasure, not as if she were teaching it, because it always leaves her terribly agitated. She beats time like a woman possessed.'[59] Siegfried, Eva and Winifred were undoubtedly being over-cautious. 'Almost everything she wants has to be refused her,' Blandine complained to Ernst zu Hohenlohe-Langenburg.[60] Fearful that

Cosima might suffer another Adams-Stokes attack, they forbade her to carry out even the most mundane activities, even though such activities would scarcely have posed a threat to her health. The parties seemed to have reached an impasse: if Cosima suffered such an attack, her children would feel that their rigid rules had been vindicated, whereas Cosima herself rebelled against all such rules.

In spite of these problems with her health, the octogenarian Cosima played a touching role in family life. 'I left Mama astonishingly well, thank God,' Blandine reported after visiting Wahnfried in September 1919. 'The way she came to congratulate Chamberlain on his birthday yesterday, in full dress, was like a picture from her great past.'[61] Cosima also took an interest in current affairs in Germany, although she felt only contempt for the political figures of the still young Republic, admiring only military officers from the old Reich such as Ludendorff and Hindenburg. When the country's president, Friedrich Ebert, died in late February 1925 and was succeeded two months later by the now elderly Hindenburg, Cosima was jubilant: 'The latest truly historic event filled both her and us with heartfelt enthusiasm – one really stands or, rather, kneels before it like some miracle and repeats the humble historic words: what a turn of events we owe to divine providence!'[62] Elsewhere Eva reports that 'each time he calls, Mama asks Adolf [von Groß] why Ludendorff doesn't become our dictator. She really can't imagine the whole situation in Germany, unarmed and defenceless as the country is.'[63] When Benito Mussolini came to power in October 1922 in the wake of his 'March on Rome', Cosima recognized in him a 'statesman-like figure: what one hears about him suggests a real power, and there is no doubt that he will remember what Germany has done for Italy'.[64]

Wahnfried's call for a 'Duce', a 'man with the heart of a lion', for whom Chamberlain had prayed in 1917, was soon to be answered. In late September 1923 Bayreuth's National Socialists organized a 'German Day' at which the main speaker was to be an as yet largely unknown Austrian politician by the name of Adolf Hitler. 'Preparations for the German Day bring the house to life,' Chamberlain noted in his diary on Saturday 29 September. 'Wheelchair ride through the flag-strewn town gave me a good deal of pleasure.'[65]

Hitler arrived in Bayreuth shortly before midnight that day and put up at the Anchor Hotel. Wahnfried looked forward with keen anticipation to this flying visit, for Hitler's name was already familiar to the Wagners and to the Chamberlains, the journalist Josef Stolzing-Cerny, who had already helped the family at the time of the Beidler affair, having acted as intermediary. The next day's events began with a march past by some 6,000 Brownshirts, a procession that made its way past Wahnfried and the Chamberlains' villa to an open-air service outside the town. Chamberlain was galvanized: 'German Day with Hitler! Much activity from dawn till dusk.' From his open ground-floor window, he waved at the passing troops. And he was not alone, for Cosima was sitting beside him, her presence, hitherto unknown, attested by Chamberlain's diary: 'Processions a.m. and p.m. watched from window and terrace, Mama present!'[66] One can easily imagine the elderly Cosima and her wheelchair-bound son-in-law reviewing Hitler's parade.

That Sunday evening Hitler gave a speech in the town's packed Reithalle, a hall formerly used for indoor equestrian events. In the course of his tirade he fulminated against parliamentary democracy, the Weimar Republic and every-thing deemed to be 'un-German'. Immediately afterwards, Hitler called on the ailing Chamberlain and received the blessing of the idol of his Viennese youth. He is even said to have knelt before Chamberlain and reverently kissed his hand. Whatever the truth of the matter, Chamberlain was delighted by the visit: 'In the evening from 9.30 to 10.30 visit from Hitler, uplifting!'[67] The two men met again at Wahnfried the very next day: '10.30 outside, waiting for Hitler in my wheelchair, moving welcome to Wahnfried: "May God be with you!" '[68] This time Siegfried and Winifred were also present. They took their guest on a tour of the house, although it is unclear whether Cosima was intro-duced to Hitler on this occasion. Chamberlain's diary makes no mention of such an encounter, although a meeting is by no means ruled out. After Hitler had left, Chamberlain wrote him a long letter:

My faith in all things German has never wavered for a moment, and yet I must confess that my hopes had reached a low ebb. At a single stroke you have transformed my state of mind. The fact that Germany can produce a Hitler in its hour of greatest need shows that it is still alive and kicking.[69]

From now on Siegfried and Winifred, too, were under Hitler's spell. 'Thank God there are still German men,' Siegfried exulted. 'Hitler is a splendid person, the true soul of the German people. He's got to bring it off!'[70] Decades later, Winifred was still effusively enthusiastic about Hitler as an individual: 'Above all, his eyes were tremendously alluring, entirely blue, large and expressive.'[71]

Contacts between the two parties grew closer, and when Hitler's attempted putsch in Munich failed on 9 November 1923, there was acute disappoint-ment in Wahnfried. As Chamberlain noted in his diary, 'Our thoughts are filled with worrying questions. Tired & weak!'[72] The leaders of the putsch were arrested, Hitler himself condemned to five years' imprisonment, although in the event he was already a free man again by the end of 1924. Throughout his time in Landsberg, the Bayreuthians continued to stand by their fallen hero. Chamberlain wrote hymns in praise of the prisoner that were published in nationalist newspapers. Winifred, too, put pen to paper in her unbridled enthusiasm. At the end of 1923 she collected care packages among Bayreuth's National Socialists and ensured that they reached Hitler in prison. According to Siegfried, 'My wife is fighting like a lion for Hitler! Magnificent!'[73] Winifred's championship of Hitler was remarkable. When the thirty-four-year-old dictator entered her life, she often felt lonely, empty and isolated within her family. Moreover, Siegfried's sexual interest in her seems to have waned with the birth of their children, leading to a resumption of his former relationships with men. There could be no question, therefore, of any erotic tension or sexual fulfilment in Winifred's life. In short, the Wagners' marriage was in crisis. Joseph Goebbels noticed this very clearly when he visited Bayreuth in early May 1926 and noted in his diary: 'She tells me her troubles. Siegfried is so feeble. Ugh! The Master should make him feel ashamed of himself. Siegfried too is there. Feminine. Good-natured. A bit decadent. Something of a cowardly artist. . . . A young woman crying because the son is not what the Master was.'[74]

Winifred had grown up without a father and knew only the elderly Karl Klindworth as her foster father. This lack of any male point of reference in her life clearly left her feeling a secret predilection for strong, passionate and ruthless men. Frustrated in so many ways, Winifred now met Hitler, who, radiating masculinity, struck her as the exact opposite of her husband. There has been much talk of an affair between Winifred and Hitler, but there has never been any proof of this. On the strength of all that we know, however, we may assume that at least on Winifred's side there was an erotic, sexual attraction.

A Living Monument

The post-war period brought financial problems for the Wagners as their fortune shrank. According to Winifred, 'The years of inflation that followed the war were even harder than the war itself as millions became a thousand millions, and a thousand millions became billions.'[75] This rapid devaluation was at its worst in 1923 and seemed unstoppable. In the May of that year one United States dollar was worth 47,670 marks on the Berlin Stock Exchange, whereas by October it was trading at 25,260,000,000 marks.[76] By the end of October, a hundredweight of briquettes cost several thousand million marks, begging the question of how people would survive the coming winter. Meanwhile, Siegfried Wagner was being urged by family friends to resume the Bayreuth Festival, prompting him to write to the journalist Alfred Holzblock in 1920: 'A housing shortage, lack of coal, wretched nutritional conditions (outside Bayreuth people are of the erroneous view that we are living in the lap of luxury here, whereas exactly the opposite is the case!) are all crucial. . . . In a word, the very idea of organizing a Festival in the next few years would entitle the local doctors to lock me up in an asylum.'[77]

It was not until the introduction of the rentenmark in the middle of November 1923 that inflation was brought to an end, enabling Siegfried to announce the reopening of the Festival theatre the very next summer. On the programme were *Die Meistersinger von Nürnberg*, the *Ring* and Wagner's final stage work, *Parsifal*. After a ten-year closure, the financial risks of such a move were enormous. Siegfried reckoned that it would cost between 6 and 8 million marks to stage these performances, a sum that the family, crippled by inflation, could not possibly raise on its own. The Wagners therefore needed allies or, rather, donors. As early as 1921 a German Festival Foundation had been set up with this aim in mind, its organizers handing out patrons' certificates and appealing in particular to a nationalist audience, which they hoped to lure to Bayreuth with their tub-thumpingly hyper-German views.

The political thrust of the movement was clear: the young Weimar Republic was a disease that had to be combated. 'All who love Germany and who want to contribute to its health and to its future as a civilized nation must come to the aid of Bayreuth,' read one such appeal.[78] Once again Wahnfried was adept at combining its own interests with those of Germany as a whole. And the strategy was successful, for by the end of 1925 the Foundation was said to have raised 8 million marks.[79] Even the exiled Wilhelm II supported the cause, signing a patron's certificate worth 1,000 marks in October 1921. A further source of income opened up when Siegfried Wagner was invited to undertake an extended concert tour of the United States of America. 'Mama mustn't know about it,' Daniela Thode insisted, 'we'll tell her that it's a tour of Scandinavia and that he won't be sending us any news about it because of the rising prices.'[80] The tour lasted from mid-January to late March 1924 and found Siegfried conducting concerts in Detroit, Baltimore, Chicago, New York and a number of other large cities.

The American press's description of Siegfried as 'his father's son' was involuntarily comical, while at the same time striking at the heart of his emotional complexes. Music lovers were interested in Siegfried only to the extent that he was Wagner's son and had little time for his own compositions. But Siegfried's behaviour was also deeply undiplomatic: most potential donors were Jewish, and yet it was precisely these people whom Siegfried antagonized with his all too public anti-Semitic tirades. A reporter from the liberal *Berliner Tageblatt* could hardly believe his ears when Siegfried, attending a banquet in New York, began to rail at the Weimar Republic and its head of state, Friedrich Ebert, and to revile Jewish artists such as the conductor Bruno Walter. The wallets of most of America's patrons remained resolutely closed thereafter, and what had started as a skilfully orchestrated campaign designed to raise funds for Bayreuth ended in financial disaster. In the end the American tour raised only a little over 9,000 dollars.

In spite of this financial shortfall, rehearsals with the singers began at Wahnfried some six weeks after the Wagners' return from America. The Danish tenor, Lauritz Melchior, recalled that 'there was a small hall with a gallery. And up above us sat a woman dressed all in white, like a ghost. She was pale; wan and with a veil. . . . Whenever Siegfried and I were working down below, we heard coughing and rustling above us. Siegfried immediately went up to the gallery. When he returned, he would say, "Mama wants . . .". And they were by no means unhelpful suggestions.' The Festival opened with *Die Meistersinger* on 22 July, and the following night Melchior made his Bayreuth debut as Parsifal. Cosima had already attended the dress rehearsal of *Parsifal*, following the opening act of the opera from her box. According to Melchior, 'She wanted to see me onstage. She wanted to check to see that I'd not forgotten anything.'[81]

For liberal politicians the 1924 Festival was unedifying in the extreme, and neither the chancellor, Wilhelm Marx, nor members of his government nor the country's president, Friedrich Ebert, made the journey to Bayreuth. And presumably they would not have been welcome, for the wooden seats of the Festival theatre were occupied by those who had declared war on the Weimar Republic. Ludendorff had turned up as early as the dress rehearsals, prompting Siegfried to fly the Reich's old black, white and red flag in his honour. And there were also sightings of Prince August Wilhelm of Prussia alongside high-ranking military men and wealthy industrialists. The writer, physician and conductor Kurt Singer described the scene in the pages of the Social Democrat *Vorwärts*: 'The stalls – festive, spruced up, dress suits and long dresses, national and conservative right down to the last swastika, uncritical in their acclaim (even during the fiasco that was *Das Rheingold*), reading and studying during the intervals. In other words, not the audience that Wagner wanted. There were not ten non-Aryans in the whole house.'[82] This 'magnificent, lovely Aryan audience', to quote Siegfried Wagner, stood up at the end of *Die Meistersinger* and launched into a frenetic rendition of all three verses of the German national anthem, turning an opera performance into a statement of political allegiance. Afraid of protests in the liberal press, Siegfried distributed leaflets, asking audiences to refrain from further displays of their own vocal accomplishments. In spite of this, the mood on the Green Hill remained highly charged, and old-school Wagnerians such as Richard Sternfeld were spat on and jostled – there was no longer any room for Jews in Bayreuth. Hypocritical to the last, the Wagners roundly declared that the Festival had never had anything to do with politics, a fantasy still being peddled by Winifred as late as 1975, when she simpered her memories into Syberberg's microphone. The opposite was the case, for the 1924 performances revealed with unprecedented clarity the way in which Wagner's works had been traduced.

A mere glance at the 'Official Bayreuth Festival Guide for 1924' is sufficient to refute the claim that Bayreuth was apolitical. As Karl Holl noted at the time in the columns of the *Frankfurter Zeitung*, the guide 'proclaims the total politicization of Bayreuth. Artistic and civic Byzantinism, nationalism and anti-Semitism have all joined hands here in a splendid show of solidarity.'[83] The book was no introduction to the world of Wagner's operas but a vade mecum in the fight against democracy, a liberal Germany, the Jews and all that was held to be 'un-German'. Wolzogen and Chamberlain both gave the enterprise their blessing, the former prefacing the 1924 volume of his *Bayreuther Blätter* with a quotation from Hitler, 'The outer struggle must be preceded by the inner one', while Chamberlain published essays in praise of the Fascist leader, making him seem interesting in the eyes of readers who were otherwise unreceptive to his rabble-rousing anti-Semitism. The relationship between Hitler and the Wagners became ever closer. Following his release from prison, he attended the 1925 Festival as a guest of the piano maker Edwin Bechstein and his wife. According to Winifred,

At the time we were roundly attacked for this visit by Hitler. He told us straight afterwards that he wanted to spare us these insults and attacks and that he would return to Bayreuth only when he could help the Festival, rather than harm it. And he was true to his word, difficult though that was for him – he didn't return to Bayreuth until 1933.[84]

After 1925 the meetings took place in secret, but their number was by no means reduced. Generally Hitler would turn up at Wahnfried after dark, Friedelind Wagner recalling that 'late as it was, he never failed to come into the nursery and tell us gruesome tales of his adventures. We all sat up among the pillows in the half-light and listened while he made our flesh creep.'[85] Chamberlain, too, could scarcely wait for Hitler's flying visits: 'Visit by A. H. highly enjoyable & enthralling, eyes wide open & directed at him.'[86]

It is no surprise, therefore, to find that Winifred Wagner, the Chamberlains and Daniela Thode joined the National Socialist German Workers' Party in January 1926. Siegfried, conversely, shied away from such a move: as director of the Bayreuth Festival, he wanted to seem to be independent, at least to the outside world. Joseph Goebbels – at that date the head of the Nazi party in Berlin – paid his first visit to Bayreuth in the May of that year and wasted no time in calling on Chamberlain, recalling the meeting afterwards in his diary in his typically auto-suggestive style:

> Chamberlain on a couch. Broken, mumbling with tears in his eyes. He holds my hand and will not let it go. His big eyes burn like fire. Greetings to you spiritual father. Trail-blazer, pioneer! I am deeply upset. Leave-taking, he mumbles, wants to speak, can't – and then weeps like a child! Farewell! You stand by us when we are near despair.[87]

One wonders if the meeting was really so emotionally charged. Chamberlain's diary reads simply: 'Dr Goebbels, interesting acquaintanceship.'[88] Only a few months later, on 9 January 1927, a figure described by Georg Schott as 'the seer of the Third Reich' died from the consequences of the nervous disorder that had plagued him for years. The local branch of the NSDAP paid tribute to the dead man in an obituary which, adorned with a swastika, spoke of him as its 'greatest and finest member' and as a ruthless fighter against 'all murderers of the German soul, first and foremost against the Jews.'[89]

As a freeman of Bayreuth, Chamberlain was accorded a lavish send-off. Black flags hung from the town hall, and horses draped in black drew the hearse from the dead man's house in the Wahnfriedstraße to the station, from where the cortège made its way to Coburg for the body to be cremated. According to the *Fränkische Volkstribüne*, 'It is impossible to imagine a more unworthy spectacle than the present funeral procession.' Brown-shirted SA troops wearing their typical storm troopers' caps escorted the coffin through the town. A huge wreath sporting an equally large swastika was followed by a contingent of troops wearing their regulation windproof jackets. Only then could the chairman and other members of the town council take their place in the hierarchy. 'It was undoubtedly deeply depressing and shaming for the representatives of the municipal authorities to have to trudge along behind the Nazis in their dirty-brown shirts.'[90] The ceremony in Coburg was attended not only by Chamberlain's family but also by ex-King Ferdinand of Bulgaria, Prince August Wilhelm of Prussia (significantly in his general's uniform, with an impressive row of medals on his breast) and Hitler. The *Coburger Volksblatt* reported that 'among those who came from outside the town, the "great" denizen of Braunau was noticed, his appearance eliciting muted cries of "Heil" among a handful of hysterical women, who fell silent, however, when they were made aware of the inappropriateness of their behaviour.'[91]

The news of Chamberlain's death was withheld from Cosima. 'Mama suspects nothing and must be told nothing,' wrote Daniela.[92] Her health had deteriorated rapidly from 1925 onwards as she suffered more and more of the attacks that the family so feared. She would still occasionally walk in the garden at Wahnfried, but most of the time she spent on a couch in her room.

Cosima seemed to be the last surviving representative of an age that had long disappeared. Her mother, Marie d'Agoult, her father, Franz Liszt, and her two husbands, Hans von Bülow and Richard Wagner, had been dead for decades. She had also outlived close friends and acquaintances such as Marie von Wolkenstein, Malwida von Meysenbug, Carl Friedrich Glasenapp, Felix Mottl and Hans Richter. Cosima was like a relic from a bygone age, and even members of her own family behaved 'as if they were standing before a shrine'.[93] When the Wagnerian soprano Emmy Krüger was accorded the rare honour of setting foot in Cosima's room, she thought she was attending an *auto sacramental*: 'During the intense and witty conversation between mother, son and daughter, the old woman allowed her fan to drop, and now, completely overwhelmed by the impression, I found myself sitting in the presence of this towering figure, who had almost become a legend in her own lifetime.'[94] Cosima lived in a world of her own imagination. According to Eva, 'Her fantasies pursue an almost alarming course as a result of her vivid & restless imagination & are often of a magnificently enthralling kind, always involving artistic work, she generally rehearses the role of Kundry & puts a conductor in his place!'[95]

Finale Lamentoso

When Cosima celebrated her ninetieth birthday on 24 December 1927, more than 200 letters of congratulation flooded in from Germany and the wider world. The Allgemeiner Deutscher Musikverein hailed her as the representative of a 'great and glorious period in German art',[96] a point stressed by the organization's chairman, Siegmund von Hausegger. Berlin's mayor, Gustav Böß, offered the city's thanks 'for all that her blessed life has given to the nation and to the world'.[97] And Hans Schemm, the head of the Bayreuth branch of the NSDAP, killed two birds with one stone, combining his good wishes with a political message: 'The works of the great Master that form the artistic basis of our own view of the world will fire us to ensure that our labours are increasingly earnest, profound and true'.[98]

Some of the good wishes that arrived in Wahnfried were nothing if not unusual. The Rostock writer and old-guard Wagnerian, Wolfgang Golther, sent in 'an heirloom from the possession of my late mother-in-law', a bottle of wine from 1783![99] For his part, Hugo Patermann, who owned a pharmaceutical firm in Teltow near Berlin, used the opportunity for more down-to-earth, self-promotional ends: 'Permit me to send you on your ninetieth birthday a small token of my esteem in the form of a few jars of Biomalt with lecithin, which for the last twenty years has been a well-known, tried and tested tonic'.[100] Bayreuth's city fathers, knowing Cosima's love of liquor, sent her ninety miniature bottles of champagne, adding that in her honour they had renamed the Hofgartenstraße, which would henceforth be known as Cosima Wagnerstraße.[101] But Cosima saw none of these letters, tributes and gifts, the family having decided to avoid all forms of agitation by concealing from her the fact that it was her birthday.

A year later we find Eva Chamberlain referring to her mother's 'all too familiar attacks – another one very recently, this time followed by fairly wild ramblings'.[102] By now Cosima could rarely leave her bed. During her final years Eva Chamberlain and Daniela Thode took it in turns to look after their mother and kept a note of all that she said. 'Mama's final words' is a mixture of banal memories and other remarks that border on the delirious. Now and again, however, we find profound aphorisms that recall recurrent themes in her life. Among notable examples are: 'The humble woman is something wonderful'; 'Throughout my life I have turned music into a religion'; 'Taking things seriously is what matters'; and 'If the style is there, the battle is won'.[103]

In early March 1930 Siegfried Wagner travelled to Milan to stage and conduct the *Ring* at La Scala. Winifred followed a few weeks later. 'Unfortunately the news that she brought about Mama's health was not so good,'[104] wrote Blandine, who was also in Milan. Winifred avoided telling her husband just how seriously ill her mother-in-law was as she thought that he should concentrate entirely on the performances. Her death was not unexpected. During her final days she often spoke about her parents, Franz Liszt and Marie d'Agoult. 'Do you know where Grandpapa is?' she asked Daniela on 27 March 1930. 'Is he in Pest?' 'Mama,' Daniela replied, 'he is no longer alive, he passed away long ago, he is resting here in our graveyard.' 'Oh, how happy I am that he's with us,' Cosima answered. 'Where's my grandmother?' She rambled on and was evidently in pain. Groans and scraps of sentences spoken in her delirium merged with one another: 'If God wills it so – wonderful.'[105] Significantly enough, her final words were directed at Hans von Bülow: 'Forgive!'[106] She died at ten o'clock in the morning on 1 April 1930 at the age of ninety-two.

Epilogue

'For us, the death could not have been foreseen,' Verena Wagner – nine at the time of her grandmother's death – now recalls. 'As always, we were at school – it was the first of April, after all, and when we got home, our nurse-maid, Emma, came out to meet us and told us that Grandma had died. Our first response was "April Fool". We didn't believe her.'[1] When Verena's parents returned to Wahnfried twenty-four hours later, they found the dead woman laid out in the salon at Wahnfried. The news of Cosima's death had spread very quickly, and within days some 1,300 letters of condolence had arrived from all over the world. Many prominent contemporaries wrote to express their sympathy: the composer Richard Strauss, the country's former kaiser, Wilhelm II, and the Viennese socialite Alma Mahler-Werfel were only a few of those who paid warm tribute to Bayreuth's grande dame.

The funeral service took place at Wahnfried on 3 April. Cosima had wanted a simple ceremony.[2] The coffin stood in the salon beneath a laurel tree and in front of a portrait of Wagner. Here the mourners took up their positions: members of the family, friends such as Groß and Wolzogen, the servants and the chairman and members of the town council. The blessing was spoken by the local dean and was framed by two of Bach's chorales sung by the municipal choir. The mourners then provided a guard of honour for the coffin as it was carried to the hearse. Horses draped in black drew the catafalque past the parish church to Saint George's. The whole of Bayreuth was in mourning and countless townspeople joined the procession. When it reached Saint George's a choir from the town's vocal academy sang the Lutheran hymn *Ach bleib mit Deiner Gnade*, after which the coffin was lifted into a car and, to the sounds of 'Heilig, heilig' from Schubert's *Deutsche Messe*, it drove slowly up to the theatre, where it stopped briefly, before continuing its journey to Coburg, where Cosima's remains were cremated.

In the wake of Wagner's death, Cosima had wanted nothing more than to follow her husband into the afterlife and to be reunited with him for all time. Not until forty-seven years later was her prayer to be answered, when her urn was buried at the head of Wagner's grave in the garden at Wahnfried. For Daniela, now seventy, and her half-sister Eva, who was her junior by seven years and who, together with Daniela, had tended her mother day and night over a period of many years, her death meant the end of a wearisome task. Only Siegfried was more deeply affected than he was willing to admit. 'My husband was as pale as a corpse,' said Winifred, recalling the funeral service. 'He was in such an agitated state that even at that point I was afraid that he might not be able to hold out. I very much have the impression that the death of his mother had such an impact on him that it made his existing heart condition much worse.'[3]

Winifred was to be proved right. During the dress rehearsal for *Götterdämmerung* on 18 July 1930, Siegfried suffered a heart attack and was taken at once to the town's General Hospital but failed to recover. He survived his mother by only 126 days. The son of the Master, Cosima's idolized Fidi, died in the arms of his wife on 4 August 1930 at the age of sixty-one. Within twenty-four hours Winifred had assumed control of the Festival. In the course of the years that followed, the family remained adept at regaling the outside world with all manner of intrigues, squabbles and titbits of gossip. On one point alone was there initially agreement: Adolf Hitler was the great white hope of the future. And the Führer could depend on the Wagners. On 30 January 1933 – the day on which the Nazis seized power – Eva Chamberlain wrote to Paul and Toni Pretzsch: 'My dear friends, would the two of you do me the pleasure of taking tea with me tomorrow, Tuesday, at four? The Strobels will also be coming. The mood of elation demands a heartfelt tête-à-tête among a group of like-minded souls! Heil! Yours, Eva Chamberlain.'[4] But that is another story.

Acknowledgements

In the course of my work I have received a great deal of help, for which I should like to express my heartfelt thanks. In particular, I am grateful to the staff of the various archives and collections that I have visited. Among these, pride of place goes to Sven Friedrich, Gudrun Föttinger and Kristina Unger at the National Archives of the Richard Wagner Foundation in Bayreuth.

In reminiscing about her grandmother, Verena Lafferentz granted me interesting glimpses behind the scenes. I am no less grateful to Neill Thornborrow for our rewarding and stimulating conversations and for making available previously unpublished material from Friedelind Wagner's estate.

I should also like to thank Thomas Rathnow and Tobias Winstel of Siedler Verlag in Munich, my Hamburg copy-editor, Hermann Gieselbusch, and my designer, Ditta Ahmadi, in Berlin, whose eye for aesthetic detail benefited both text and illustrations.

Further help was provided by Barbara Wenner, Karin Graf, Rebekka Göpfert and the staff of the Graf Agency. Susanne Dornau, Simone Kinateder and Antje Korsmeier prepared translations of the many French-language originals. Dirk Mühlenhaus helped me – not for the first time – in deciphering almost illegible manuscripts. I am immensely grateful to them all.

My especial thanks go to Hildegard Baumgart and her Baumgart Foundation, which she established in Munich in 2006. Without her generous support I should never have been able to realize my aim of writing the first scholarly biography of Cosima.

Other individuals whom I should like to thank for their help are Dagny Beidler, Dieter Borchmeyer, Charles F. Dupêchez, Wolf-Dieter Gewande, Serge Gut, Brigitte Hamann, Klára Hamburger, Ilona and Wilfried Hilmes,

Eva Jaeggi, Peter Jungblut, Michael Karbaum, Maximilian Lautenschläger, Simone Claudia Müller, André Schmitz and Alan Walker. Finally, I must thank all who read through my burgeoning typescript. Above all, I am grateful to Peter Franzek for his particularly constructive and encouraging suggestions at various stages of my work.

Notes

Abbreviations (see also Unpublished Sources)
AEM   Archiv des Erzbistums München und Freising
BAB   Bundesarchiv Berlin/Koblenz
BHA   Bayerisches Hauptstaatsarchiv
BNF   Bibliothèque nationale de France
BSB   Bayerische Staatsbibliothek München
HUB   Humboldt Universität Berlin
HZA   Hohenlohe-Zentralarchiv
MSB   Münchner Stadtbibliothek
NAB   Nationalarchiv der Richard-Wagner-Stiftung, Bayreuth
NTH   Neill Thornborrow Private Archives
ÖNB   Österreichische Nationalbibliothek Wien, Handschriftenabteilung
SAB   Staatsarchiv Bamberg
SAM   Stadtarchiv München
SBB   Staatsbibliothek zu Berlin, Preußischer Kulturbesitz, Musikabteilung
SBM   Wissenschaftliche Stadtbibliothek Mainz
SHB   Katholisches Dompfarramt St. Hedwig Berlin
STB   Stadtarchiv Bayreuth

Prologue

1. Cosima Wagner, *Die Tagebücher*, ed. Martin Gregor-Dellin and Dietrich Mack, 2 vols (Munich and Zurich 1976–7), i.21; trans. Geoffrey Skelton as *Cosima Wagner's Diaries*, 2 vols (London 1978–80), i.27 (entry of 1 Jan. 1869).
2. Harry Kessler, *Das Tagebuch*, 9 vols (Stuttgart 2004–10), iii.291 (entry of 15 March 1900).
3. Maximilian Harden, *Köpfe*, 4 vols (Berlin 1923–4), iv.305.
4. Françoise Giroud, *Cosima la sublime* (Paris 1996), 13.
5. Giroud, *Cosima la sublime* (note 4), 267.

1. A Childhood Without Parents (1837–55)

1. Franz Girard, *Como und der Comersee mit Umgebung* (Munich 1910), 7.
2. Girard, *Como und der Comersee* (note 1), 28.
3. Charles F. Dupêchez (ed.), *Mémoires, souvenirs et journaux de la Comtesse d'Agoult (Daniel Stern)*, 2 vols (Paris 1990), ii.142.
4. Dupêchez, *Mémoires de la Comtesse d'Agoult* (note 3), ii.147.
5. Klára Hamburger (ed.), *Franz Liszt: Briefwechsel mit seiner Mutter* (Eisenstadt 2000), 115 (letter from Franz Liszt to Anna Liszt, *c.* 22 Oct. 1837).

6. Dupêchez, *Mémoires de la Comtesse d'Agoult* (note 3), ii.151.
7. See Alan Walker, *Franz Liszt: The Virtuoso Years 1811–1847* (London 1983), 248.
8. Dupêchez, *Mémoires de la Comtesse d'Agoult* (note 3), i.299–301.
9. Dupêchez, *Mémoires de la Comtesse d'Agoult* (note 3), i.294.
10. Jacques Vier, *Marie d'Agoult, son mari, ses amis: Documents inédits* (Paris 1950), 22–3.
11. See Walker, *Franz Liszt: The Virtuoso Years* (note 7), 214.
12. See Walker, *Franz Liszt: The Virtuoso Years* (note 7), 273 and 285.
13. Dupêchez, *Mémoires de la Comtesse d'Agoult* (note 3), ii.178 and 180–1 (entries of 10 and 19 July 1838).
14. Dupêchez, *Mémoires de la Comtesse d'Agoult* (note 3), ii.252.
15. Serge Gut and Jacqueline Bellas (eds), *Franz Liszt – Marie d'Agoult: Correspondance* (Paris 2001), 383 (letter from Marie d'Agoult to Franz Liszt, 23 Oct. 1839).
16. Dupêchez, *Mémoires de la Comtesse d'Agoult* (note 3), ii.13.
17. Marcel Herwegh (ed.), *Au printemps des dieux: Correspondance inédite de la Comtesse Marie d'Agoult et du poète Georges Herwegh* (Paris 1929), 64.
18. Hamburger, *Franz Liszt: Briefwechsel mit seiner Mutter* (note 5), 142 (letter from Franz Liszt to Anna Liszt, Aug. 1839).
19. Gut and Bellas, *Correspondance* (note 15), 413 (letter from Marie d'Agoult to Franz Liszt, 19 Nov. 1839).
20. Gut and Bellas, *Correspondance* (note 15), 425 (letter from Franz Liszt to Marie d'Agoult, 24 Nov. 1839).
21. Gut and Bellas, *Correspondance* (note 15), 754 (letter from Marie d'Agoult to Franz Liszt, 18 Jan. 1841).
22. Gut and Bellas, *Correspondance* (note 15), 430 (letter from Marie d'Agoult to Franz Liszt, 27 Nov. 1839).
23. Gut and Bellas, *Correspondance* (note 15), 490–1 (letter from Franz Liszt to Marie d'Agoult, 31 Jan. 1840).
24. Gut and Bellas, *Correspondance* (note 15), 530 (letter from Marie d'Agoult to Franz Liszt, 21 Feb. 1840).
25. Gut and Bellas, *Correspondance* (note 15), 542 (letter from Marie d'Agoult to Franz Liszt, 28 Feb. 1840).
26. Gut and Bellas, *Correspondance* (note 15), 518 (letter from Marie d'Agoult to Franz Liszt, 10 Feb. 1842). (The ellipsis represents a passage physically removed from the autograph.)
27. Dupêchez, *Mémoires de la Comtesse d'Agoult* (note 3), ii.32.
28. Dupêchez, *Mémoires de la Comtesse d'Agoult* (note 3), ii.34–5.
29. Hamburger, *Franz Liszt: Briefwechsel mit seiner Mutter* (note 5), 151 (letter from Franz Liszt to Anna Liszt, 9 Aug. 1844).
30. Hamburger, *Franz Liszt: Briefwechsel mit seiner Mutter* (note 5), 388 (undated letter from Anna Liszt to Franz Liszt, [April 1844]).
31. Hamburger, *Franz Liszt: Briefwechsel mit seiner Mutter* (note 5), 151 (letter from Franz Liszt to Anna Liszt, 9 Aug. 1844).
32. Hamburger, *Franz Liszt: Briefwechsel mit seiner Mutter* (note 5), 154 (letter from Franz Liszt to Anna Liszt, 26 Aug. 1844).
33. Gut and Bellas, *Correspondance* (note 15), 1099 (undated letter from Franz Liszt to Marie d'Agoult, [April 1844]).
34. Gut and Bellas, *Correspondance* (note 15), 1113 (letter from Marie d'Agoult to Franz Liszt, 3 June 1845).
35. Hamburger, *Franz Liszt: Briefwechsel mit seiner Mutter* (note 5), 175 (letter from Franz Liszt to Anna Liszt, 3 May 1845).
36. Hamburger, *Franz Liszt: Briefwechsel mit seiner Mutter* (note 5), 390 (letter from Anna Liszt to Franz Liszt, 5 Sept. 1846).

37. Hamburger, *Franz Liszt: Briefwechsel mit seiner Mutter* (note 5), 199 (letter from Franz Liszt to Anna Liszt, 22 Oct. 1846).
38. Hamburger, *Franz Liszt: Briefwechsel mit seiner Mutter* (note 5), 207 (letter from Franz Liszt to Anna Liszt, 10 Feb. 1847).
39. Max Freiherr von Waldberg (ed.), *Cosima Wagners Briefe an ihre Tochter Daniela von Bülow 1866-1885* (Stuttgart 1933), 111 (letter from Cosima Wagner to Daniela von Bülow, 10 Jan. 1881).
40. Paul Pretzsch (ed.), *Cosima Wagner und Houston Stewart Chamberlain im Briefwechsel 1888-1908* (Leipzig 1934), 99 (letter from Cosima Wagner to Houston Stewart Chamberlain, 17 April 1889).
41. NAB (letter from Cosima Liszt to Franz Liszt, 14 June 1846).
42. NAB (letter from Cosima Liszt to Franz Liszt, 14 Nov. 1847).
43. NAB (undated letter from Cosima Liszt to Franz Liszt).
44. See Alan Walker, *Franz Liszt: The Weimar Years 1848-1861* (London 1993), 26-9.
45. Hamburger, *Franz Liszt: Briefwechsel mit seiner Mutter* (note 5), 408 (letter from Anna Liszt to Franz Liszt, 9 Dec. 1847).
46. Marie von Bülow (ed.), *Hans von Bülow: Briefe*, 7 vols (Leipzig 1895-1908), i.235-6 (letter from Hans von Bülow to Franziska von Bülow, 2 Sept. 1850).
47. Hamburger, *Franz Liszt: Briefwechsel mit seiner Mutter* (note 5), 227 (letter from Franz Liszt to Anna Liszt, 21 Sept. 1848).
48. Daniel Ollivier (ed.), *Correspondance de Liszt et de sa fille Madame Émile Ollivier 1842-1862* (Paris 1936), 42 (letter from Blandine Liszt to Franz Liszt, Feb. 1850).
49. Ollivier, *Correspondance de Liszt et de sa fille* (note 48), 43-5 (letter from Franz Liszt to Blandine Liszt, 28 Feb. 1850).
50. Hamburger, *Franz Liszt: Briefwechsel mit seiner Mutter* (note 5), 241 (letter from Franz Liszt to Anna Liszt, 5 Oct. 1850).
51. NAB (letter from Cosima Liszt to Franz Liszt, 16 Jan. 1853).
52. Ollivier, *Correspondance de Liszt et de sa fille* (note 48), 72 (letter from Blandine Liszt to Franz Liszt, 4 April 1851).
53. NAB (letter from Cosima Liszt to Franz Liszt, 15 July 1851).
54. NAB (undated letter from Blandine Liszt to Franz Liszt, [between 18 Aug. and 17 Sept. 1853]).
55. NAB (letter from Cosima Liszt to Franz Liszt, 15 June 1852).
56. BNF (NAF 25191, 383-8): 'Scène de la vie intime' (20 March 1855).
57. Ollivier, *Correspondance de Liszt et de sa fille* (note 48), 89 (letter from Blandine Liszt to Franz Liszt, 6 June 1853).
58. NAB (letter from Cosima Liszt to Franz Liszt, 25 Dec. 1851).
59. Ollivier, *Correspondance de Liszt et de sa fille* (note 48), 83 (letter from Blandine Liszt to Franz Liszt, 3 July 1852).
60. Ollivier, *Correspondance de Liszt et de sa fille* (note 48), 55 (letter from Franz Liszt to Blandine Liszt, 5 Nov. 1850).
61. NAB (letter from Cosima Liszt to Franz Liszt, 20 Oct. 1851).
62. NAB (letter from Cosima and Blandine Liszt to Carolyne von Sayn-Wittgenstein, 3 April 1853).
63. NAB (letter from Cosima Liszt to Franz Liszt, 18 April 1853).
64. Ollivier, *Correspondance de Liszt et de sa fille* (note 48), 65 (letter from Franz Liszt to Blandine Liszt, 17 Jan. 1851).
65. Waldberg, *Cosima Wagners Briefe an ihre Tochter* (note 39), 111-12 (letter from Cosima Wagner to Daniela von Bülow, 10 Jan. 1881).
66. Cosima Wagner, *Die Tagebücher*, ed. Martin Gregor-Dellin and Dietrich Mack, 2 vols (Munich and Zurich 1976-7), ii.102; trans. by Geoffrey Skelton as *Cosima Wagner's Diaries*, 2 vols (London 1978-80), ii.27 (entry of 12 Feb. 1878).

67. Waldberg, *Cosima Wagners Briefe an ihre Tochter* (note 39), 233 (letter from Cosima Wagner to Daniela von Bülow, 26 Oct. 1881).
68. Richard Wagner, *Mein Leben*, ed. Martin Gregor-Dellin (Munich 1976), 516; trans. Andrew Gray as *My Life* (Cambridge 1983), 503.
69. Marie Fürstin zu Hohenlohe, *Erinnerungen an Richard Wagner* (Weimar 1938), 13–14.
70. NAB (letter from Cosima Wagner to Marie von Schleinitz, 10/11 Oct. 1875).
71. Hohenlohe, *Erinnerungen* (note 69), 14.
72. Wagner, *Mein Leben* (note 68), 516; Engl. trans. 504.
73. NAB (letter from Cosima Liszt to Franz Liszt, 20 June 1854).
74. La Mara (ed.), *Franz Liszt's Briefe: Briefe an die Fürstin Carolyne Sayn-Wittgenstein*, 4 vols (iv–vii) (Leipzig 1899–1902), iv.206 (letter from Franz Liszt to Carolyne von Sayn-Wittgenstein, 20 July 1854).
75. Pretzsch, *Cosima Wagner und Houston Stewart Chamberlain im Briefwechsel* (note 40), 229 (letter from Cosima Wagner to Houston Stewart Chamberlain, 24 May 1891).
76. NAB (letter from Blandine Liszt to Carolyne von Sayn-Wittgenstein, 1 Dec. 1854).
77. NAB (letter from Blandine Liszt to Carolyne von Sayn-Wittgenstein, 4 Dec. 1854).
78. NAB (letter from Blandine Liszt to Carolyne von Sayn-Wittgenstein, 9 Dec. 1854).
79. NAB (letter from Blandine Liszt to Carolyne von Sayn-Wittgenstein, 2 June 1855).
80. NAB (letter from Blandine Liszt to Carolyne von Sayn-Wittgenstein, 11 June 1855).
81. Hamburger, *Franz Liszt: Briefwechsel mit seiner Mutter* (note 5), 269 (letter from Franz Liszt to Anna Liszt, 13 Aug. 1855).
82. Hamburger, *Franz Liszt: Briefwechsel mit seiner Mutter* (note 5), 429 (letter from Anna Liszt to Franz Liszt, 18 Aug. 1855).
83. Hamburger, *Franz Liszt: Briefwechsel mit seiner Mutter* (note 5), 431–2 (letter from Anna Liszt to Franz Liszt, 3 Sept. 1855).
84. Hamburger, *Franz Liszt: Briefwechsel mit seiner Mutter* (note 5), 435 (letter from Anna Liszt to Franz Liszt, 25 Sept. 1855).
85. Ollivier, *Correspondance de Liszt et de sa fille* (note 48), 142 (letter from Franz Liszt to Blandine Liszt, 18 Sept. 1855).

2. A Marriage of Convenience (1855–64)

1. See Wolf-Dieter Gewande, *Hans von Bülow: Eine biographisch-dokumentarische Würdigung aus Anlass seines 175. Geburtstages* (Lilienthal 2004).
2. Marie von Bülow (ed.), *Hans von Bülow: Briefe und Schriften,* 8 vols (Leipzig 1895–1908), i.298 (letter from Hans von Bülow to Marie Isidore von Bülow, 26 Jan. 1851).
3. Quoted by Frithjof Haas, *Hans von Bülow: Leben und Wirken. Wegbereiter für Wagner, Liszt und Brahms* (Wilhelmshaven 2002), 21.
4. Quoted by Marie von Bülow, *Hans von Bülow in Leben und Wort* (Stuttgart 1925), 281.
5. Quoted by Marie von Bülow, *Hans von Bülow in Leben und Wort* (note 4), 280.
6. Quoted by Marie von Bülow, *Bülow: Briefe* (note 2), vii.379–80.
7. Edith Stargardt-Wolff, *Wegbereiter großer Musiker* (Berlin 1954), 71.
8. See Isolde Vetter, 'Hans von Bülows Irrfahrt durch die Medizin: Mit Briefen und anderen unveröffentlichten Zeugnissen aus seinem letzten Lebensjahr', *Südthüringer Forschungen 28: Beiträge zum Kolloquium Hans von Bülow, Leben, Wirken und Vermächtnis* (Meiningen 1994), 100–18.
9. La Mara (ed.), *Briefwechsel zwischen Franz Liszt und Hans von Bülow* (Leipzig 1898), 143 (letter from Franz Liszt to Hans von Bülow, 1 Sept. 1855).
10. La Mara, *Briefwechsel zwischen Liszt und Bülow* (note 9), 152–3 (letter from Hans von Bülow to Franz Liszt, 30 Sept. 1855).
11. Marie von Bülow, *Bülow: Briefe* (note 2), iii.48–9 (letter from Hans von Bülow to Jessie Laussot, 13 June 1856).

12. La Mara (ed.), *Franz Liszt's Briefe: Briefe an die Fürstin Carolyne Sayn-Wittgenstein*, 4 vols (iv–vii) (Leipzig 1899–1902), v.195 (letter from Franz Liszt to Carolyne von Sayn-Wittgenstein, 29 June 1861).

13. Daniel Ollivier (ed.), *Correspondance de Liszt et de sa fille Madame Émile Ollivier 1842–1862* (Paris 1936), 147 (letter from Cosima and Blandine Liszt to Franz Liszt, 21 Oct. 1855).

14. La Mara, *Franz Liszt's Briefe: Briefe an die Fürstin Carolyne Sayn-Wittgenstein* (note 12), iv.277 (letter from Franz Liszt to Carolyne von Sayn-Wittgenstein, 25 Nov. 1855).

15. Cosima Wagner, *Die Tagebücher*, ed. Martin Gregor-Dellin and Dietrich Mack, 2 vols (Munich and Zurich 1976–7), i.301; trans. by Geoffrey Skelton as *Cosima Wagner's Diaries*, 2 vols (London 1978–80), i.285 (entry of 19 Oct. 1870).

16. Marie von Bülow, *Hans von Bülow in Leben und Wort* (note 4), 65.

17. La Mara, *Franz Liszt's Briefe: Briefe an die Fürstin Carolyne Sayn-Wittgenstein* (note 12), iv.233 (letter from Franz Liszt to Carolyne von Sayn-Wittgenstein, 23 July 1855).

18. Marie von Bülow, *Hans von Bülow in Leben und Wort* (note 4), 67–8.

19. Marie von Bülow, *Bülow: Briefe* (note 2), iii.41 (letter from Franziska von Bülow to Marie Isidore von Bülow, 18 May 1856).

20. See Alan Walker, *Franz Liszt, Vol. 2: The Weimar Years 1848–1861* (London 1989), 458.

21. Max Freiherr von Waldberg (ed.), *Cosima Wagners Briefe an ihre Tochter Daniela von Bulow 1866–1885 (Stuttgart 1933)*, 176 (letter from Cosima Wagner to Daniela von Bülow, 23 March 1881).

22. Cosima Wagner, *Die Tagebücher* (note 15), i.28; Engl. trans. i.33 (entry of 8 Jan. 1869).

23. Carl Maria Cornelius (ed.), *Peter Cornelius: Ausgewählte Briefe nebst Tagebuchblättern und Gelegenheitsgedichten*, 4 vols (Leipzig 1904–5), ii.382 (undated letter from Peter Cornelius to his fiancée [early June 1866]).

24. Marie von Bülow, *Bülow: Briefe* (note 2), iii.107 (letter from Hans von Bülow to Richard Pohl, 17 Aug. 1857).

25. Hans Jürgen Syberberg, *Winifred Wagner und die Geschichte des Hauses Wahnfried 1914–1975* (video interview with Winifred Wagner released by Alexander Verlag of Berlin in 1975 and again in 1993 with IBSN 3-923854-85-4).

26. SHB (entry in marriage register no. 259/1857).

27. NAB (wedding announcement of Hans and Cosima von Bülow).

28. Richard Wagner, *Sämtliche Briefe*, ed. Gertrud Strobel, Werner Wolf, Werner Breig and others (Leipzig 1967–2000 and Wiesbaden 1999–), viii.295 (letter from Richard Wagner to Hans von Bülow, 1 April 1857).

29. Marie von Bülow, *Bülow: Briefe* (note 2), iii.110 (letter from Hans von Bülow to Franz Brendel, 7 Sept. 1857).

30. Marie von Bülow, *Bülow: Briefe* (note 2), iii.113 (letter from Hans von Bülow to Franziska von Bülow, 18 Sept. 1857).

31. Marie von Bülow, *Bülow: Briefe* (note 2), iii.115 (letter from Hans von Bülow to Julius Stern, 19 Sept. 1857).

32. See Robert Bory (ed.), *Liszt et ses enfants Blandine, Cosima & Daniel* (Paris 1936), 165 (letter from Cosima von Bülow to Marie von Sayn-Wittgenstein, April 1858).

33. Marcel Herwegh (ed.), *Au printemps des dieux: Correspondance inédite de la Comtesse Marie d'Agoult et du poète Georges Herwegh* (Paris 1929), 219 (letter from Cosima von Bülow to Emma Herwegh, 9 April 1858).

34. Bory, *Liszt et ses enfants* (note 32), 171–2 (letter from Cosima von Bülow to Marie von Sayn-Wittgenstein, July 1858).

35. Wagner, *Sämtliche Briefe* (note 28), ix.349 (letter from Richard Wagner to Hans von Bülow, 20 July 1858).

36. Quoted in Julius Kapp, *Richard Wagner und die Frauen* (Berlin 1951), 152.

37. Cosima Wagner, *Die Tagebücher* (note 15), i.28; Engl. trans. i.33 (entry of 8 Jan. 1869).

38. Marie Fürstin zu Hohenlohe, *Erinnerungen an Richard Wagner* (Weimar 1938), 14–20.

39. Wagner, *Sämtliche Briefe* (note 28), ix.186 (letter from Richard Wagner to Hans von Bülow, 10 Feb. 1858).

40. Wagner, *Sämtliche Briefe* (note 28), xiii.98 (letter from Richard Wagner to Hans von Bülow, 4 April 1861).

41. Jules Laforgue, *Berlin: Der Hof und die Stadt 1887* (Frankfurt am Main 1970), 10-11.

42. Herwegh, *Au printemps des dieux* (note 33), 214 (letter from Cosima von Bülow to Georg and Emma Herwegh, 21 Nov. 1857).

43. Herwegh, *Au printemps des dieux* (note 33), 217 (letter from Cosima von Bülow to Georg and Emma Herwegh, 11 Feb. 1858).

44. Laforgue, *Berlin* (note 41), 60.

45. See Ilse Stempel, 'Deutschland in der "Revue Germanique" von Dollfus und Nefftzer 1858-1865' (dissertation, University of Bonn, 1967).

46. Paul Pretzsch (ed.), *Cosima Wagner und Houston Stewart Chamberlain im Brief-wechsel 1888-1908* (Leipzig 1934), 88 (letter from Cosima Wagner to Houston Stewart Chamberlain, 28 March 1889).

47. See René Martin, 'Une femme de lettres françaises à Berlin (1857-1865): Mme Cosima de Bülow', *Revue de littérature comparée*, xi (1931), 686-710, esp. 697.

48. Harry Kessler, *Das Tagebuch*, 9 vols (Stuttgart 2004-10), iii.388 (entry of 10 Feb. 1901).

49. NAB (transcript of taped interview between Winifred Wagner and Geoffrey Skelton).

50. See René Martin, *La vie et l'œuvre de Charles Dollfus* (Gap 1934), 175.

51. F. Hoffmann (i.e. Cosima Wagner), 'Courrier politique, littéraire et scientifique', *Revue germanique*, xviii (7 Nov. 1861), 155.

52. F. Hoffmann, 'Courrier politique' (note 51), 150.

53. Hohenlohe, *Erinnerungen* (note 38), 20.

54. Hohenlohe, *Erinnerungen* (note 38), 19.

55. Otto Strobel, *König Ludwig II. und Richard Wagner: Briefwechsel*, 5 vols (Karlsruhe 1936-9), v.115-18 (letter from Cosima von Bülow to Hans von Bülow, 15 June 1869).

56. La Mara, *Franz Liszt's Briefe: Briefe an die Fürstin Carolyne Sayn-Wittgenstein* (note 12), iv. 453 (letter from Franz Liszt to Carolyne von Sayn-Wittgenstein, 2 March 1859).

57. Pretzsch, *Cosima Wagner und Houston Stewart Chamberlain im Briefwechsel* (note 46), 565 (letter from Cosima Wagner to Houston Stewart Chamberlain, 7 May 1899).

58. Bernhard Fürst von Bülow, *Denkwürdigkeiten*, 4 vols (Berlin 1930-1), iv.305.

59. Quoted by John C. G. Röhl, *Die Jugend des Kaisers 1859-1888* (Munich 2001), 265.

60. Kessler, *Das Tagebuch* (note 48), iv.398-9 (entry of 10 March 1911).

61. Bülow, *Denkwürdigkeiten* (note 58), iv.308.

62. Klára Hamburger (ed.), *Franz Liszt: Briefwechsel mit seiner Mutter* (Eisenstadt 2000), 491 (letter from Anna Liszt to Franz Liszt, 11 Sept. 1859).

63. Hamburger, *Franz Liszt: Briefwechsel mit seiner Mutter* (note 62), 492 (letter from Anna Liszt to Franz Liszt, 18 Oct. 1859).

64. Marie von Bülow, *Bülow: Briefe* (note 2), iii.269 (letter from Hans von Bülow to Felix Draeseke, 8 Oct. 1859).

65. La Mara, *Franz Liszt's Briefe: Briefe an die Fürstin Carolyne Sayn-Wittgenstein* (note 12), iv.502 (letter from Franz Liszt to Carolyne von Sayn-Wittgenstein, 15 Dec. 1859).

66. Marie von Bülow, *Bülow: Briefe* (note 2), iii.284 (letter from Hans von Bülow to Joachim Raff, 16 Dec. 1859).

67. NAB (letter from Blandine Liszt to Cosima von Bülow, 19 Dec. 1859).

68. Cosima Wagner, *Die Tagebücher* (note 15), i.288-9; Engl. trans. i.274 (entry of 23 Sept. 1870).

69. Cosima Wagner, *Die Tagebücher* (note 15), ii.679; Engl. trans. ii.611 (entry of 30 Jan. 1881).

70. Cosima Wagner, *Die Tagebücher* (note 15), i.288-9; Engl. trans. i.274 (entry of 23 Sept. 1870).

71. Strobel, *König Ludwig II. und Richard Wagner: Briefwechsel* (note 55), v.117 (letter from Cosima von Bülow to Hans von Bülow, 15 June 1869).

72. Marie von Bülow, *Bülow: Briefe* (note 2), iii.337 (letter from Hans von Bülow to A. Giacomelli, 12 Oct. 1860).

73. SHB (register of births no. 741/1860).

74. Ollivier, *Correspondance de Liszt et de sa fille* (note 48), 271 (letter from Blandine Liszt to Franz Liszt, 30 March 1861).

75. Marie von Bülow, *Bülow: Briefe* (note 2), iii.406–7 (letter from Hans von Bülow to Joachim Raff, 19 July 1861).

76. Richard Wagner, *Mein Leben*, ed. Martin Gregor-Dellin (Munich 1976), 675; trans. by Andrew Gray as *My Life* (Cambridge 1983), 658–9.

77. Marie von Bülow, *Bülow: Briefe* (note 2), iii.418 (letter from Hans von Bülow to Alexander Ritter, 19 Sept. 1861).

78. Marie von Bülow, *Bülow: Briefe* (note 2), iii.432 (letter from Hans von Bülow to Alexander Ritter, 28 Sept. 1861).

79. Marie von Bülow, *Hans von Bülows Leben dargestellt aus seinen Briefen* (Leipzig 1921), 172 (letter from Hans von Bülow to Isidore von Bülow, 24 June 1862).

80. Marie von Bülow, *Bülow: Briefe* (note 2), iii.186–7 (letter from Hans von Bülow to Richard Pohl, 24 July 1858).

81. Marie von Bülow, *Bülow: Briefe* (note 2), iii.481–5 (letter from Hans von Bülow to Richard Pohl, 31 July 1862).

82. Cosima Wagner, *Die Tagebücher* (note 15), i.27; Engl. trans. i.33 (entry of 8 Jan. 1869).

83. Waldberg, *Cosima Wagners Briefe an ihre Tochter* (note 23), 277 (letter from Cosima Wagner to Daniela von Bülow, 7 June 1882).

84. Wagner, *Mein Leben* (note 76), 709; Engl. trans. 692–3 (emended).

85. See Alan Walker, *Franz Liszt*, Vol. 3: *The Final Years 1861–1886* (London 1997), 50.

86. Marie von Bülow, *Bülow: Briefe* (note 2), iii.494 (letter from Hans von Bülow to Joachim Raff, 23 Sept. 1862).

87. Wagner, *Mein Leben* (note 76), 714–15; Engl. trans. 697.

88. Cosima Wagner, *Die Tagebücher* (note 15), i.73–4; Engl. trans. i.75–6 (entry of 19 March 1869).

89. SHB (register of births 270/1863).

90. Wagner, *Sämtliche Briefe* (note 28), xiv.300 (letter from Richard Wagner to Franz Schott, 20 Oct. 1862).

91. Wagner, *Sämtliche Briefe* (note 28), xv.36 (letter from Richard Wagner to Mathilde Maier, 4 Jan. 1863).

92. Wagner, *Sämtliche Briefe* (note 28), xv.190 (letter from Richard Wagner to Mathilde Maier, 16 June 1863).

93. Wagner, *Sämtliche Briefe* (note 28), xv.184 (letter from Richard Wagner to Eliza Wille, 5 June 1863).

94. Wagner, *Mein Leben* (note 76), 745–6; Engl. trans. 729.

95. Cosima Wagner, *Die Tagebücher* (note 15), i.174; Engl. trans. i.168 (entry of 28 Nov. 1869).

96. Cosima Wagner, *Die Tagebücher* (note 15), i.463; Engl. trans. i.435 (entry of 28 Nov. 1871).

97. Cosima Wagner, *Die Tagebücher* (note 15), i.873; Engl. trans. i.807 (entry of 28 Nov. 1874).

98. Wagner, *Sämtliche Briefe* (note 28), xv.325 (letter from Richard Wagner to Mathilde Maier, 3 Dec. 1863).

99. Wagner, *Sämtliche Briefe* (note 28), xv.326–7 (letter from Richard Wagner to Maria Völkl, 6 Dec. 1863).

100. Friedrich von Bernhardi, *Denkwürdigkeiten aus meinem Leben* (Berlin 1927), 166.

101. Eliza Wille, *Erinnerungen an Richard Wagner: Mit 15 Briefen Richard Wagners* (Zurich 1982), 64.

102. Wagner, *Sämtliche Briefe* (note 28), xvi.141 (letter from Richard Wagner to Ludwig II, 3 May 1864).

103. Wagner, *Sämtliche Briefe* (note 28), xvi.144 (letter from Richard Wagner to Eliza Wille, 4 May 1864).

104. Wagner, *Sämtliche Briefe* (note 28), xvi.145 (letter from Richard Wagner to Mathilde Maier, 5 May 1864).

105. Strobel, *König Ludwig II. und Richard Wagner: Briefwechsel* (note 55), i.11 (letter from Ludwig II to Richard Wagner, 5 May 1864).

106. Martin Gregor-Dellin, *Richard Wagner: Sein Leben, sein Werk, sein Jahrhundert* (Munich 1980), 523; trans. J. Maxwell Brownjohn as *Richard Wagner: His Life, His Work, His Century* (London 1983), 335.

107. Quoted in Rupert Hacker, *Ludwig II. von Bayern in Augenzeugenberichten* (Düsseldorf 1966), 212.

108. Martha Schad (ed.), *Cosima Wagner und Ludwig II. von Bayern: Briefe. Eine erstaunliche Korrespondenz* (Bergisch Gladbach 1996), 308 (letter from Ludwig II to Cosima von Bülow, 16 Dec. 1866).

109. Strobel, *König Ludwig II. und Richard Wagner: Briefwechsel* (note 55), i.44 (letter from Ludwig II to Richard Wagner, 31 Dec. 1864). The quotation 'No one went, but someone came' ('Keiner ging – doch Einer kam') comes from the love scene between Siegmund and Sieglinde in Act One of *Die Walküre*.

110. Strobel, *König Ludwig II. und Richard Wagner: Briefwechsel* (note 55), iv.63 (letter from Ludwig von Pfistermeister to Cosima von Bülow, 4 June 1865).

111. Cosima Wagner, *Die Tagebücher* (note 15), ii.135; Engl. trans. ii.110 (entry of 10 July 1878).

112. Strobel, *König Ludwig II. und Richard Wagner: Briefwechsel* (note 55), i.174 (letter from Richard Wagner to Ludwig II, 7 Sept. 1865).

113. Strobel, *König Ludwig II. und Richard Wagner: Briefwechsel* (note 55), iv.134 (letter from Richard Wagner to Constantin Franz, 19 March 1866).

114. Wagner, *Sämtliche Briefe* (note 28), xvi.162 (letter from Richard Wagner to Hans von Bülow, 12 May 1864).

115. BHA (Ludwig von der Pfordten, 'Mein zweites Ministerium: Autobiographische Skizze').

116. NAB (witness deposition from Anna Mrazek, Munich District Court, 20 May 1914).

117. Wagner, *Sämtliche Briefe* (note 28), xvi.215 (letter from Richard Wagner to Hans von Bülow, 1 June 1864).

118. Wagner, *Sämtliche Briefe* (note 28), xvi.227–9 (letter from Richard Wagner to Hans von Bülow, 9 June 1864).

119. Wagner, *Sämtliche Briefe* (note 28), xvi.242–3 (letter from Richard Wagner to Mathilde Maier, 22 June 1864).

120. Wagner, *Sämtliche Briefe* (note 28), xvi.246 (letter from Richard Wagner to Josephine Maier, 25 June 1864).

121. NAB (witness deposition from Anna Mrazek, Munich District Court, 20 May 1914).

122. NAB (witness deposition from Anna Mrazek, Munich District Court, 20 May 1914).

123. Wagner, *Sämtliche Briefe* (note 28), xvi.262 (letter from Richard Wagner to Mathilde Maier, 19 July 1864).

124. Lina Ramann, *Lisztiana: Erinnerungen an Franz Liszt in Tagebuchblättern, Briefen und Dokumenten aus den Jahren 1873–1886/87* (Mainz 1983), 76.

125. Wagner, *Sämtliche Briefe* (note 28), xvi.293 (letter from Richard Wagner to Mathilde Maier, 8 Sept. 1864).

126. Marie von Bülow, *Bülow: Briefe* (note 2), iii.601 (letter from Hans von Bülow to Joachim Raff, 29 Sept. 1864).

3. Wagner (1864–83)

1. Eliza Wille, *Erinnerungen an Richard Wagner: Mit 15 Briefen Richard Wagners* (Zurich 1982), *64*.

2. Marie von Bülow (ed.), *Hans von Bülow: Briefe und Schriften*, 8 vols (Leipzig 1895–1908), iv.6 (letter from Hans von Bülow to Franziska von Bülow, 28 Dec. 1864).

3. Marie von Bülow (ed.), *Bülow: Briefe* (note 2), iv.16–17 (letter from Hans von Bülow to Adolf Jensen, 8 Jan. 1865).

4. Peter Cornelius, *Literarische Werke*, 4 vols (Leipzig 1904–5), i.687 (diary entry of 23 Nov. 1862).

5. Cornelius, *Literarische Werke* (note 4), i.772 (letter from Peter Cornelius to Reinhold Köhler, 24 June 1864).

6. Cornelius, *Literarische Werke* (note 4), i.793 (letter from Peter Cornelius to Carl Cornelius, 26 Nov. 1864).

7. Cornelius, *Literarische Werke* (note 4), i.795 (diary entry of Dec. 1864).

8. Cornelius, *Literarische Werke* (note 4), i.775 (letter from Peter Cornelius to Susanne Cornelius, 24 June 1864).

9. Cornelius, *Literarische Werke* (note 4), ii.6 (diary entry of 1 Jan. 1865).

10. Cornelius, *Literarische Werke* (note 4), ii.20 (letter from Peter Cornelius to Carl Hestermann, 17 Jan. 1865).

11. Cornelius, *Literarische Werke* (note 4), ii.25–6 (letter from Peter Cornelius to Josef Standthartner, 24 Jan. 1865).

12. Otto Strobel (ed.), *König Ludwig II. und Richard Wagner: Briefwechsel*, 5 vols (Karlsruhe 1936–9), i.57 (letter from Ludwig II to Richard Wagner, 14 Feb. 1865).

13. Strobel, *König Ludwig II. und Richard Wagner: Briefwechsel* (note 12), iv.47–51 ('Richard Wagner und die öffentliche Meinung', *Allgemeine Zeitung* [19 Feb. 1865]).

14. Cornelius, *Literarische Werke* (note 4), ii.32 (letter from Peter Cornelius to Carl Hestermann, 27 Feb. 1865).

15. Strobel, *König Ludwig II. und Richard Wagner: Briefwechsel* (note 12), i.72 (letter from Richard Wagner to Ludwig II, 11 March 1865).

16. Strobel, *König Ludwig II. und Richard Wagner: Briefwechsel* (note 12), i.73 (letter from Ludwig II to Richard Wagner, 11 March 1865).

17. AEM (baptismal register of St Boniface's Parish Church, Munich).

18. Marie von Bülow, *Bülow: Briefe* (note 2), iv.24–5 (letter from Hans von Bülow to Carl Gille, 14 April 1865).

19. NAB (minutes of Anna Mrazek's witness statement at the Munich District Court, 20 May 1914).

20. Cornelius, *Literarische Werke* (note 4), ii.253 (letter from Peter Cornelius to Bertha Jung, 6 Sept. 1865).

21. Rosalie Braun-Artaria, *Von berühmten Zeitgenossen: Erinnerungen einer Siebzigerin* (Munich 1918), 97–8.

22. Josefa Dürck-Kaulbach, *Erinnerungen an Wilhelm von Kaulbach und sein Haus* (Munich 1918), 343–4.

23. Dürck-Kaulbach, *Erinnerungen an Wilhelm von Kaulbach* (note 22), 342.

24. BSB, Fasc. germ. 159/5 (undated letter from Cosima Wagner to Malvina Schnorr von Carolsfeld).

25. Braun-Artaria, *Von berühmten Zeitgenossen* (note 21), 99.

26. Braun-Artaria, *Von berühmten Zeitgenossen* (note 21), 101.

27. Richard Wagner, *Sämtliche Briefe*, ed. Gertrud Strobel, Werner Wolf, Werner Breig, and others (Leipzig 1967–2000 and Wiesbaden 1999–), xvi.203–4 (letter from Richard Wagner to Heinrich Porges, 28 May 1864).

28. Cosima Wagner, *Die Tagebücher*, ed. Martin Gregor-Dellin and Dietrich Mack, 2 vols (Munich and Zurich 1976–7), i.126; trans. by Geoffrey Skelton as *Cosima Wagner's Diaries*, 2 vols (London 1978–80), i.123–4 (entry of 11 July 1869).
29. Cornelius, *Literarische Werke* (note 4), ii.316 (diary entry of 9 Dec. 1865).
30. Strobel, *König Ludwig II. und Richard Wagner: Briefwechsel* (note 12), i.129 (letter from Richard Wagner to Ludwig II, 22 July 1865).
31. Wolfgang Golther (ed.), *Richard Wagner an Mathilde Wesendonk: Tagebuchblätter und Briefe 1853–1871* (Berlin 1908), 360 (letter from Mathilde Wesendonck to Richard Wagner, 13 Jan. 1865).
32. Cornelius, *Literarische Werke* (note 4), ii.251–2 (undated letter from Johannes Brahms to Peter Cornelius).
33. Cornelius, *Literarische Werke* (note 4), ii.224 (letter from Carl Tausig to Peter Cornelius, 13 Aug. 1865).
34. Braun-Artaria, *Von berühmten Zeitgenossen* (note 21), 100.
35. Cornelius, *Literarische Werke* (note 4), ii.286–7 (letter from Peter Cornelius to Bertha Jung, 1 Nov. 1865).
36. Cornelius, *Literarische Werke* (note 4), ii.291 (letter from Peter Cornelius to Bertha Jung, 5 Nov. 1865).
37. Strobel, *König Ludwig II. und Richard Wagner: Briefwechsel* (note 12), iv.60 (letter from Franz Seraph von Pfistermeister to Cosima Wagner, 20 May 1865).
38. Strobel, *König Ludwig II. und Richard Wagner: Briefwechsel* (note 12), i.160 (letter from Richard Wagner to Ludwig II, 20 Aug. 1865).
39. Martha Schad (ed.), *Cosima Wagner und Ludwig II. von Bayern: Briefe. Eine erstaunliche Korrespondenz* (Bergisch Gladbach 1996), 455–6 (letter from Cosima Wagner to Ludwig II, 21 Nov. 1867).
40. Schad, *Cosima Wagner und Ludwig II.* (note 39), 458 (letter from Ludwig II to Cosima Wagner, 30 Nov. 1867).
41. Cornelius, *Literarische Werke* (note 4), ii.295–6 (letter from Peter Cornelius to Bertha Jung, 15 Nov. 1865).
42. Strobel, *König Ludwig II. und Richard Wagner: Briefwechsel* (note 12), i.200 (letter from Richard Wagner to Ludwig II, 16 Oct. 1865).
43. Strobel, *König Ludwig II. und Richard Wagner: Briefwechsel* (note 12), iv.106 (*Der Volksbote für den Bürger und Landmann* [26 Nov. 1865]).
44. Strobel, *König Ludwig II. und Richard Wagner: Briefwechsel* (note 12), i.231–3 (letter from Richard Wagner to Ludwig II, 27 Nov. 1865).
45. Strobel, *König Ludwig II. und Richard Wagner: Briefwechsel* (note 12), iv.108–9 (*Neueste Nachrichten* [29 Nov. 1865]).
46. Strobel, *König Ludwig II. und Richard Wagner: Briefwechsel* (note 12), i.84 (letter from Ludwig von der Pfordten to Ludwig II, 1 Dec. 1865).
47. Cornelius, *Literarische Werke* (note 4), ii.318 (diary entry of 11 Dec. 1865).
48. BSB, Fasc. germ. 159/11 (undated letter from Cosima Wagner to Malvina Schnorr von Carolsfeld [Dec. 1865]).
49. Cornelius, *Literarische Werke* (note 4), ii.311–12 (letter from Peter Cornelius to Bertha Jung, 10 Dec. 1865).
50. BSB, Fasc. germ. 159/13 (letter from Cosima Wagner to Malvina Schnorr von Carolsfeld, 6 Jan. 1866).
51. BHA (Ludwig von der Pfordten, 'Mein zweites Ministerium: Autobiographische Skizze').
52. Marie von Bülow, *Bülow: Briefe* (note 2), iv.100 (letter from Hans von Bülow to Felix Draeseke, 4 March 1866).
53. Cornelius, *Literarische Werke* (note 4), ii.368 (letter from Peter Cornelius to Bertha Jung, 22 April 1866).
54. Cornelius, *Literarische Werke* (note 4), ii.370–1 (letter from Peter Cornelius to Bertha Jung, 12 May 1866).

55. Strobel, *König Ludwig II. und Richard Wagner: Briefwechsel* (note 12), iv.146 (*Neuer Bayerischer Kurier* [29 May 1866]).

56. Strobel, *König Ludwig II. und Richard Wagner: Briefwechsel* (note 12), iv.147 (*Der Volksbote für den Bürger und Landmann* [31 May 1866]).

57. BSB, Fasc. germ. 159/18 (letter from Cosima Wagner to Malvina Schnorr von Carolsfeld, 3 June 1866).

58. Schad, *Cosima Wagner und Ludwig II.* (note 39), 233 (letter from Cosima Wagner to Ludwig II, 7 June 1866).

59. BSB, Fasc. germ. 159/19 (letter from Cosima Wagner to Malvina Schnorr von Carolsfeld, 9 June 1866).

60. Cornelius, *Literarische Werke* (note 4), ii.382 (undated letter from Peter Cornelius to Bertha Jung, [June 1866]).

61. Marie von Bülow, *Bülow: Briefe* (note 2), iv.145 (letter from Hans von Bülow to Joachim Raff, 26 Aug. 1866).

62. Strobel, *König Ludwig II. und Richard Wagner: Briefwechsel* (note 12), ii.54 (letter from Ludwig II to Hans von Bülow, 11 June 1866).

63. Pauline Pocknell, 'Princess Carolyne von Sayn-Wittgenstein: Correspondence with Franz Liszt's Family and Friends', *Liszt Saeculum*, il (1992), 59 (undated letter from Carolyne von Sayn-Wittgenstein to Eduard Liszt, [late July 1866]).

64. Schad, *Cosima Wagner und Ludwig II.* (note 39), 239 (letter from Ludwig II to Cosima Wagner, 21 July 1866).

65. Marie von Bülow, *Bülow: Briefe* (note 2), iv.164 (letter from Hans von Bülow to Alexander Ritter, 22 Dec. 1866).

66. Strobel, *König Ludwig II. und Richard Wagner: Briefwechsel* (note 12), v.49 (letter from Ludwig II to Lorenz von Düfflipp, 9 Dec. 1867).

67. Strobel, *König Ludwig II. und Richard Wagner: Briefwechsel* (note 12), v.49 (letter from Ludwig II to Lorenz von Düfflipp, 13 Dec. 1867).

68. Marie von Bülow, *Bülow: Briefe* (note 2), iv.182 (letter from Hans von Bülow to Joachim Raff, 1 May 1867).

69. NAB (letter from Cosima Wagner to Lorenz von Düfflipp, 20 Sept. 1867).

70. Strobel, *König Ludwig II. und Richard Wagner: Briefwechsel* (note 12), ii.11 ('Annals').

71. Strobel, *König Ludwig II. und Richard Wagner: Briefwechsel* (note 12), ii.11–12 ('Annals').

72. Strobel, *König Ludwig II. und Richard Wagner: Briefwechsel* (note 12), ii.12 ('Annals').

73. Strobel, *König Ludwig II. und Richard Wagner: Briefwechsel* (note 12), v.80 (telegram from Cosima Wagner to Richard Wagner, 27 Oct. 1868).

74. Strobel, *König Ludwig II. und Richard Wagner: Briefwechsel* (note 12), v.80 (telegram from Cosima Wagner to Richard Wagner, 27 Oct. 1868).

75. Strobel, *König Ludwig II. und Richard Wagner: Briefwechsel* (note 12), v.83 (telegram from Cosima Wagner to Richard Wagner, 15 Nov. 1868).

76. Cosima Wagner, *Die Tagebücher*, ed. Martin Gregor-Dellin and Dietrich Mack, 2 vols (Munich and Zurich 1976–7), i.313; trans. by Geoffrey Skelton as *Cosima Wagner's Diaries*, 2 vols (London 1978–80), i.296 (entry of 15 Nov. 1870).

77. Cosima Wagner, *Die Tagebücher* (note 76), i.72; Engl. trans. i.76 (entry of 15 March 1869).

78. Cosima Wagner, *Die Tagebücher* (note 76), i.97; Engl. trans. i.97 (entry of 21 May 1869).

79. Marie von Bülow, *Bülow: Briefe* (note 2), iv. 261 (letter from Hans von Bülow to Richard Pohl, 21 Dec. 1868).

80. Cosima Wagner, *Die Tagebücher* (note 76), i.21; Engl. trans. i.27 (entry of 1 Jan. 1869).

81. Cosima Wagner, *Die Tagebücher* (note 76), i.177; Engl. trans. i.171–2 (entry of 11 Dec. 1869).

82. Cosima Wagner, *Die Tagebücher* (note 76), i.160; Engl. trans. i.156 (entry of 16 Oct. 1869).

83. Cosima Wagner, *Die Tagebücher* (note 76), i.342; Engl. trans. i.323 (entry of 16 Dec. 1871).

84. Cosima Wagner, *Die Tagebücher* (note 76), i.1090; Engl. trans. i.999 (entry of 29 Nov. 1877).

85. Cosima Wagner, *Die Tagebücher* (note 76), i.269; Engl. trans. i.256 (entry of 13 Aug. 1870).

86. Cosima Wagner, *Die Tagebücher* (note 76), i.973; Engl. trans. i.895 (entry of 27 Feb. 1876).

87. Cosima Wagner, *Die Tagebücher* (note 76), i.109; Engl. trans. i.108 (entry of 16 June 1869).

88. Cosima Wagner, *Die Tagebücher* (note 76), i.173; Engl. trans. i.167 (entry of 24 Nov. 1869).

89. Cosima Wagner, *Die Tagebücher* (note 76), i.231; Engl. trans. i.219 (entry of 16 May 1870).

90. Cosima Wagner, *Die Tagebücher* (note 76), i.311; Engl. trans. i.295 (entry of 12 Nov. 1870).

91. Cosima Wagner, *Die Tagebücher* (note 76), i.137; Engl. trans. i.134 (entry of 6 Aug. 1869).

92. Cosima Wagner, *Die Tagebücher* (note 76), i.436; Engl. trans. i.410 (entry of 7 Sept. 1871).

93. Cosima Wagner, *Die Tagebücher* (note 76), i.872; Engl. trans. i.806 (entry of 21 Nov. 1874).

94. Cosima Wagner, *Die Tagebücher* (note 76), ii.161; Engl. trans. ii.136 (entry of 16 Aug. 1878).

95. Cosima Wagner, *Die Tagebücher* (note 76), i.465; Engl. trans. i.437 (entry of 3 Dec. 1871).

96. Cosima Wagner, *Die Tagebücher* (note 76), ii.793; Engl. trans. ii.717 (entry of 9 Sept. 1881).

97. Cosima Wagner, *Die Tagebücher* (note 76), i.826; Engl. trans. i.764 (entry of 7 June 1874).

98. Cosima Wagner, *Die Tagebücher* (note 76), i.658; Engl. trans. i.612 (entry of 21 March 1873).

99. Cosima Wagner, *Die Tagebücher* (note 76), i.72; Engl. trans. i.74 (entry of 15 March 1869).

100. Cosima Wagner, *Die Tagebücher* (note 76), i.986; Engl. trans. i.907 (entry of 9 May 1876).

101. Cosima Wagner, *Die Tagebücher* (note 76), i.377–8; Engl. trans. i.355 (entry of 15 April 1871).

102. Dieter David Scholz, *Richard Wagners Antisemitismus: Jahrhundertgenie im Zwielicht. Eine Korrektur* (Berlin 2000), 63.

103. Wilhelm Altmann (ed.), *Richard Wagners Briefwechsel mit B. Schott's Söhne* (Mainz 1911), 121.

104. See Jens Malte Fischer, *Richard Wagners 'Das Judentum in der Musik'* (Frankfurt 2000), 89.

105. Houston Stewart Chamberlain, *Richard Wagner* (Munich 1919), 229.

106. Cosima Wagner, *Die Tagebücher* (note 76), i.29; Engl. trans. i.35 (entry of 11 Jan. 1869).

107. Cosima Wagner, *Die Tagebücher* (note 76), i.129; Engl. trans. i.126 (entry of 17 July 1869).

108. Cosima Wagner, *Die Tagebücher* (note 76), i.151; Engl. trans. i.147 (entry of 15 Sept. 1869).

109. Cosima Wagner, *Die Tagebücher* (note 76), ii.689; Engl. trans. i.620–1 (entry of 11 Feb. 1881).

110. Cosima Wagner, *Die Tagebücher* (note 76), i.104; Engl. trans. i.103 (entry of 6 June 1869).

111. Cosima Wagner, *Die Tagebücher* (note 76), i.106; Engl. trans. i.105 (entry of 8 June 1869).

112. Strobel, *König Ludwig II. und Richard Wagner: Briefwechsel* (note 12), v.116–17 (letter from Cosima Wagner to Hans von Bülow, 15 June 1869).

113. Richard Graf Du Moulin Eckart (ed.), *Hans von Bülow: Neue Briefe* (Munich 1927), 477–84 (letter from Hans von Bülow to Cosima von Bülow, 17 June 1869).
114. NAB (letter from Cosima von Bülow to Claire de Charnacé, 10 Aug 1869).
115. NAB (letter from Cosima von Bülow to Claire de Charnacé, 31 Aug. 1869).
116. Friedrich Nietzsche, *Sämtliche Briefe*, ed. Giorgio Colli and Mazzino Montinari, 8 vols (Munich and Berlin 1986), iv.8–9 (letter from Friedrich Nietzsche to Richard Wagner, 22 May 1869); trans. Christopher Middleton as *Selected Letters of Friedrich Nietzsche* (Indianapolis 1996), 53.
117. Friedrich Nietzsche, *Briefwechsel: Kritische Gesamtausgabe*, ed. Giorgio Colli, Mazzino Montinari and Norbert Miller (Berlin 1974–), ii/2.493–4 (undated letter from Richard Wagner to Friedrich Nietzsche, [early Jan. 1872]).
118. Cosima Wagner, *Die Tagebücher* (note 76), i.405; Engl. trans. i.382 (entry of 25 June 1871).
119. NAB (letter from Cosima von Bülow to Hans Richter, 26 Nov. 1869).
120. NAB (letter from Cosima von Bülow to Hans Richter, 27 Nov. 1869).
121. NAB (letter from Cosima von Bülow to Hans Richter, 26 Nov. 1869).
122. NAB (letter from Cosima von Bülow to Hans Richter, 15 Nov. 1869).
123. NAB (letter from Cosima Wagner to Marie von Schleinitz, 31 May 1871).
124. NAB (letter from Cosima von Bülow to Claire de Charnacé, 26 Nov. 1869).
125. NAB (letter from Cosima von Bülow to Lorenz von Düfflipp, 11 March 1870).
126. Cosima Wagner, *Die Tagebücher* (note 76), i.248; Engl. trans. i.236 (entry of 21 June 1870).
127. Marie von Bülow, *Bülow: Briefe* (note 2), iv.418 (letter from Hans von Bülow to Jessie Laussot, 4 July 1870).
128. Cosima Wagner, *Die Tagebücher* (note 76), i.262; Engl. trans. i.249 (entry of 27 July 1870).
129. Cosima Wagner, *Die Tagebücher* (note 76), i.277; Engl. trans. i.263 (entry of 25 Aug. 1870).
130. NAB (letter from Cosima Wagner to Hans von Bülow, 29 Oct. 1871).
131. Cosima Wagner, *Die Tagebücher* (note 76), i.329; Engl. trans. i.312 (entry of 25 Dec. 1870).
132. Strobel, *König Ludwig II. und Richard Wagner: Briefwechsel* (note 12), ii.319–21 (letter from Richard Wagner to Ludwig II, 1 March 1871).
133. Carl Friedrich Glasenapp, *Richard Wagner: Bayreuther Briefe* (Berlin 1907), 14–15 (letter from Richard Wagner to Friedrich Feustel, 1 Nov. 1871).
134. NAB (undated letter from Cosima Wagner to Hans Richter, [summer 1871]).
135. SBM (letter from Cosima Wagner to Peter Cornelius, 9 June 1871).
136. NAB (letter from Cosima Wagner to Marie von Schleinitz, 28 Dec. 1871).
137. Cosima Wagner, *Die Tagebücher* (note 76), i.523; Engl. trans. i.488 (entry of 22 May 1872).
138. Cosima Wagner, *Die Tagebücher* (note 76), i.571; Engl. trans. i.532 (entry of 3 Sept. 1872).
139. Cosima Wagner, *Die Tagebücher* (note 76), i.572; Engl. trans. i.533 (entry of 6 Sept. 1872).
140. Cosima Wagner, *Die Tagebücher* (note 76), i.581; Engl. trans. i.542 (entry of 17 Oct. 1872).
141. NAB (letter from Cosima Wagner to Hans von Bülow, 29 Oct. 1871).
142. Cosima Wagner, *Die Tagebücher* (note 76), i.587–8; Engl. trans. i.548 (entry of 31 Oct. 1872).
143. Cosima Wagner, *Die Tagebücher* (note 76), i.667; Engl. trans. i.620 (entry of 6 April 1873).
144. NAB (letter from Cosima Wagner to Marie von Wolkenstein, 3 Dec. 1891).
145. Cosima Wagner, *Die Tagebücher* (note 76), ii.200; Engl. trans. ii.172 (entry of 15 Oct. 1878).

146. NAB (letter from Cosima Wagner to Hans Richter, 11 Feb. 1873).

147. Richard Wagner, 'An die Patrone der Bühnenfestspiele in Bayreuth', *Sämtliche Schriften und Dichtungen*, ed. Richard Sternfeld, 16 vols (Leipzig 1911–14), xii.315.

148. Strobel, *König Ludwig II. und Richard Wagner: Briefwechsel* (note 12), iv.211 (letter from Lorenz von Düfflipp to Richard Wagner, 24 Sept. 1873).

149. Cosima Wagner, *Die Tagebücher* (note 76), i.754; Engl. trans. i.700–1 (entry of 22 Nov. 1873).

150. Cosima Wagner, *Die Tagebücher* (note 76), i.786; Engl. trans. i.727 (entry of 27 Jan. 1874).

151. Strobel, *König Ludwig II. und Richard Wagner: Briefwechsel* (note 12), iii.29 (letter from Ludwig II to Richard Wagner, 25 Jan. 1874).

152. Cosima Wagner, *Die Tagebücher* (note 76), i.813; Engl. trans. i.752 (entry of 28 April 1874).

153. Strobel, *König Ludwig II. und Richard Wagner: Briefwechsel* (note 12), iii.14 (letter from Richard Wagner to Ludwig II, 2 June 1873).

154. Cosima Wagner, *Die Tagebücher* (note 76), i.903; Engl. trans. i.833 (entry of 17 March 1875).

155. Cosima Wagner, *Die Tagebücher* (note 76), i.908; Engl. trans. i.837–8 (entry of 7 April 1875).

156. Cosima Wagner, *Die Tagebücher* (note 76), i.1042; Engl. trans. i.956 (entry of 4 April 1877).

157. Strobel, *König Ludwig II. und Richard Wagner: Briefwechsel* (note 12), iii.49 (letter from Richard Wagner to Ludwig II, 1 Oct. 1874).

158. Ludwig Strecker, *Richard Wagner als Verlagsgefährte* (Mainz 1951), 277–81.

159. Cosima Wagner, *Die Tagebücher* (note 76), i.965; Engl. trans. i.888 (entry of 18 Jan. 1876).

160. Lilli Lehmann, *Mein Weg*, 2nd edn (Leipzig 1920), 228; trans. Alice Benedict Seligman as *My Path through Life* (New York and London 1914), 212.

161. NAB (Susanne Weinert, 'Im Hause Richard Wagners: Ein Stück als Beitrag zu dem Familienleben des großen Meisters', typescript, 61).

162. Cosima Wagner, *Die Tagebücher* (note 76), i.269–70; Engl. trans. i.256 (entry of 13 Aug. 1870).

163. Max Freiherr von Waldberg (ed.), *Cosima Wagners Briefe an ihre Tochter Daniela von Bülow 1866–1885* (Stuttgart 1933), 39 (letter from Cosima Wagner to Daniela von Bülow, 11 Sept. 1876).

164. Waldberg, *Cosima Wagners Briefe an ihre Tochter* (note 163), 120 (letter from Cosima Wagner to Daniela von Bülow, 18 Jan. 1881).

165. Waldberg, *Cosima Wagners Briefe an ihre Tochter* (note 163), 44–5 (letter from Cosima Wagner to Daniela von Bülow, 7 Oct. 1876).

166. Waldberg, *Cosima Wagners Briefe an ihre Tochter* (note 163), 91 (letter from Cosima Wagner to Daniela von Bülow, 9 Aug. 1880).

167. Waldberg, *Cosima Wagners Briefe an ihre Tochter* (note 163), 130–1 (letter from Cosima Wagner to Daniela von Bülow, 4 Feb. 1881).

168. Weinert, 'Im Hause Richard Wagners' (note 161), 42.

169. Lehmann, *Mein Weg* (note 160), 228–9; Engl. trans. 212.

170. Cosima Wagner, *Die Tagebücher* (note 76), ii.802; Engl. trans. ii.726 (entry of 2 Oct. 1881).

171. Lehmann, *Mein Weg* (note 160), 230–1; Engl. trans. 213–15.

172. Cosima Wagner, *Die Tagebücher* (note 76), i.964; Engl. trans. i.887 (entry of 12 Jan. 1876).

173. Cosima Wagner, *Die Tagebücher* (note 76), i.970; Engl. trans. i.892 (entry of 14 Feb. 1876).

174. Cosima Wagner, *Die Tagebücher* (note 76), i.975; Engl. trans. i.897 (entry of 7 March 1876).

175. NAB (undated letter from Cosima Wagner to Marie von Schleinitz, [March 1876]).

176. Waldberg, *Cosima Wagners Briefe an ihre Tochter* (note 163), 31 (letter from Cosima Wagner to Daniela von Bülow, 8 March 1876).

177. Richard Fricke, *Bayreuth vor dreissig Jahren: Erinnerungen an Wahnfried und aus dem Festspielhause* (Dresden 1906), 37.

178. Fricke, *Bayreuth vor dreissig Jahren* (note 177), 42.

179. Fricke, *Bayreuth vor dreissig Jahren* (note 177), 55.

180. Fricke, *Bayreuth vor dreissig Jahren* (note 177), 88–9.

181. Lehmann, *Mein Weg* (note 160), 236–7; Engl. trans. 223.

182. Cosima Wagner, *Die Tagebücher* (note 76), i.997; Engl. trans. i.917 (entry of 28 July 1876).

183. Robert Hartford, *Bayreuth: The Early Years* (London 1980), 53. Tchaikovsky's review appeared in *Russky Viedomosti*.

184. Lehmann, *Mein Weg* (note 160), 234–5; Engl. trans. 219–21.

185. Léon Guichard (ed.), *Lettres à Judith Gautier par Richard et Cosima Wagner* (Paris 1964), 57 (undated letter from Richard Wagner to Judith Gautier, [2 Sept. 1876]).

186. Cosima Wagner, *Die Tagebücher* (note 76), ii.45; Engl. trans. ii.27 (entry of 12 Feb. 1878).

187. Cosima Wagner, *Die Tagebücher* (note 76), i.1013; Engl. trans. i.932 (entry of 5 Nov. 1876).

188. Cosima Wagner, *Die Tagebücher* (note 76), i.1003; Engl. trans. i.923 (entry of 23 Sept. 1876).

189. Cosima Wagner, *Die Tagebücher* (note 76), i.1011; Engl. trans. i.930 (entry of 27 Oct. 1876).

190. Cosima Wagner, *Die Tagebücher* (note 76), i.1012; Engl. trans. i.931 (entry of 2 Nov. 1876).

191. Friedrich Nietzsche, 'Ecce homo', *Kritische Gesamtausgabe*, ed. Giorgio Colli and Mazzino Montinari, 15 vols (Munich and Berlin 1988), vi.323–4; trans. R. J. Hollingdale as *Ecce homo* (Harmondsworth 1979), 90–1.

192. Harry Kessler, *Das Tagebuch*, 9 vols (Stuttgart 2004–10) iii.71–2 (entry of 21 July 1897).

193. Nietzsche, *Kritische Gesamtausgabe* (note 191), xiii.16.

194. Nietzsche, *Sämtliche Briefe* (note 116), viii.604 (undated draft of a letter from Friedrich Nietzsche to Cosima Wagner, [early Sept. 1888]).

195. Cosima Wagner, *Die Tagebücher* (note 76), i.1019; Engl. trans. i.937–8 (entry of 21 Dec. 1876).

196. Cosima Wagner, *Die Tagebücher* (note 76), i.1019; Engl. trans. i.938 (entry of 23 Dec. 1876).

197. Cosima Wagner, *Die Tagebücher* (note 76), ii.480; Engl. trans. ii.429 (entry of 18 Jan. 1880).

198. Cosima Wagner, *Die Tagebücher* (note 76), ii.271; Engl. trans. ii.238–9 (entry of 25 Dec. 1878).

199. Cosima Wagner, *Die Tagebücher* (note 76), ii.336; Engl. trans. ii.296 (entry of 25 April 1879).

200. Joachim Thiery and Dietrich Seidel, ' "Ich behage mir nicht": Richard Wagner und seine Ärzte', *Münchener Medizinische Wochenschrift*, cxxxvi (1994), 491–502; trans. Stewart Spencer as ' "I feel only discontent": Wagner and his doctors', *Wagner*, xvi (1995), 3–22.

201. Cosima Wagner, *Die Tagebücher* (note 76), ii.458; Engl. trans. ii.409 (entry of 5 Dec. 1879).

202. NAB (letter from Cosima Wagner to Adolf von Groß, 28 Jan. 1880).

203. Cosima Wagner, *Die Tagebücher* (note 76), ii.580; Engl. trans. ii.520 (entry of 8 Aug. 1880). (Lusch = Daniela; Boni = Blandine; Loldi = Isolde; and Fidi = Siegfried.)

204. NAB (letter from Cosima Wagner to Isolde von Bülow, 19 Aug. 1880).

205. Cosima Wagner, *Die Tagebücher* (note 76), ii.606; Engl. trans. ii.545 (entry of 28 Sept. 1880).

206. Strobel, *König Ludwig II. und Richard Wagner: Briefwechsel* (note 12), iii.226 (letter from Ludwig II to Richard Wagner, 11 Oct. 1881).

207. Cosima Wagner, *Die Tagebücher* (note 76), ii.754; Engl. trans. ii.681 (entry of 29 June 1881).

208. Cosima Wagner, *Die Tagebücher* (note 76), ii.1242; Engl. trans. ii.1116 (note on entry of 1 July 1881, citing Wagner's letter to Levi).

209. Cosima Wagner, *Die Tagebücher* (note 76), ii.755; Engl. trans. ii.682 (entry of 2 July 1881).

210. Cosima Wagner, *Die Tagebücher* (note 76), ii.797–8; Engl. trans. ii.722 (entry of 24 Sept. 1881). (It is unclear which of Liszt's four Mephisto Waltzes Cosima is referring to.)

211. Cosima Wagner, *Die Tagebücher* (note 76), ii.800; Engl. trans. ii.724 (entry of 28 Sept. 1881).

212. Cosima Wagner, *Die Tagebücher* (note 76), ii.804; Engl. trans. ii.728 (entry of 7 Oct. 1881).

213. Cosima Wagner, *Die Tagebücher* (note 76), ii.803; Engl. trans. ii.727 (entry of 5 Oct. 1881).

214. NAB (letter from Cosima Wagner to Hans Richter, 7 Jan. 1882).

215. Cosima Wagner, *Die Tagebücher* (note 76), ii.911; Engl. trans. ii.826 (entry of 15 March 1882).

216. NAB (letter from Daniela von Bülow to Hans von Bülow, 7 July 1882).

217. Cosima Wagner, *Die Tagebücher* (note 76), ii.984; Engl. trans. ii.894 (entry of 26 July 1882).

218. Cosima Wagner, *Die Tagebücher* (note 76), ii.993; Engl. trans. ii.902 (entry of 25 Aug. 1882).

219. Du Moulin Eckart, *Bülow: Neue Briefe* (note 113), 587–8 (letter from Hans von Bülow to Daniela von Bülow, 12 May 1882).

220. Du Moulin Eckart, *Bülow: Neue Briefe* (note 113), 595 (letter from Hans von Bülow to Daniela von Bülow, 21 Aug. 1882).

221. Cosima Wagner, *Die Tagebücher* (note 76), ii.1059; Engl. trans. ii.962 (entry of 28 Nov. 1882).

222. Cosima Wagner, *Die Tagebücher* (note 76), ii.1079; Engl. trans. ii.981 (entry of 24 Dec. 1882).

223. NAB (letter from Daniela von Bülow to Adolf von Groß, 26 Jan. 1883).

224. See Manfred Eger, 'Warum wurde Carries Brief vernichtet?', *Festspielnachrichten 1992: Heft V 'Parsifal'*, 8–10.

225. Henry Perl, *Richard Wagner in Venedig: Mosaikbilder aus seinen letzten Lebenstagen* (Augsburg 1883), VII.

226. See Stewart Spencer, ' "Er starb, – ein Mensch wie alle": Wagner und Carrie Pringle,' *Festspielbuch 2004* (Bayreuth 2004), 72–85; German trans. 86–101; French trans. 102–17.

227. Anon., 'Hermann Levi an seinen Vater: Unveröffentlichte Briefe aus Bayreuth 1875–1889', *Die Programmhefte der Bayreuther Festspiele 1959*, iii: 'Parsifal' (Bayreuth 1959), 6–23, esp. 13.

228. Cosima Wagner, *Die Tagebücher* (note 76), ii.1111; Engl. trans. ii.1008 (entry of 11 Feb. 1883).

229. Cosima Wagner, *Die Tagebücher* (note 76), ii.1114; Engl. trans. 1010–11 (postscript by Daniela von Bülow).

230. NAB (Cosima Wagner to Heinrich von Stein, letter of 12 Feb. 1883).

231. This and the previous quotations are taken from NAB (Daniela von Bülow, 'Tagebuch' [Feb. 1883]).

232. BSB, Nachl. Mottl (Felix Mottl, 'Erinnerungen').
233. Daniela von Bülow, 'Tagebuch' (note 231).

4. The First Lady of Bayreuth (1883–1900)

1. Martha Schad (ed.), *Cosima Wagner und Ludwig II. von Bayern: Briefe. Eine erstaunliche Korrespondenz* (Bergisch Gladbach 1996), 539 (letter from Ludwig II to Ludwig von Bürkel, 19/20 Feb. 1883).
2. Berta Schleicher (ed.), *Briefe von und an Malwida von Meysenbug* (Berlin 1920), 196–7 (letter from Paul von Joukowsky to Malwida von Meysenbug, 22 Feb. 1883).
3. SBB, Nachl. Lilli Lehmann (letter from Daniela von Bülow to Lilli Lehmann, 5 March 1883).
4. NAB (letter from Malwida von Meysenbug to Daniela von Bülow, 12 March 1883).
5. Quoted in Stewart Spencer, ' "Er starb, – ein Mensch wie alle": Wagner and Carrie Pringle,' *Festspielbuch 2004* (Bayreuth 2004), 76; German trans. 91; French trans. 107–8 (letter from Adolf von Groß to Friedrich Keppler).
6. Julius Kniese, *Der Kampf zweier Welten um das Bayreuther Erbe: Julius Knieses Tagebuchblätter aus dem Jahre 1883* (Leipzig 1931), 59.
7. BSB, Nachl. Dispeker (letter from Marie von Bülow to Isolde Beidler, 4 March 1914).
8. NAB (excerpt from the documents relating to Wagner's estate).
9. Cosima Wagner, *Cosima Wagner: Das zweite Leben. Briefe und Aufzeichnungen 1883–1930*, ed. Dietrich Mack (Munich 1980), 33 (letter from Cosima Wagner to Daniela von Bülow, 10/11 April 1883).
10. NAB (letter from Malwida von Meysenbug to Daniela von Bülow, 12 March 1883).
11. NAB (letter from Daniela von Bülow to Malwida von Meysenbug, 23 June 1883).
12. Quoted in Michael Karbaum, *Studien zur Geschichte der Bayreuther Festspiele* (Regensburg 1976), ii.32 (letter from Adolf von Groß to Ludwig von Bürkel, 23 Feb. 1883).
13. Cosima Wagner, *Die Tagebücher*, ed. Martin Gregor-Dellin and Dietrich Mack, 2 vols (Munich and Zurich 1976–7), ii.1110; trans. by Geoffrey Skelton as *Cosima Wagner's Diaries*, 2 vols (London 1978–80), ii.1007 (entry of 9 Feb. 1883). In the original, 'his supporters' has been altered by another hand to 'some of his supporters', and the words '& W[olzogen]' have been added after 'Stein'.
14. Kniese, *Der Kampf zweier Welten* (note 6), 118 (letter from Julius Kniese to Olga Kniese, 26 July 1883).
15. Kniese, *Der Kampf zweier Welten* (note 6), 71 (letter from Julius Kniese to Olga Kniese, 7 July 1883).
16. Kniese, *Der Kampf zweier Welten* (note 6), 116 (letter from Julius Kniese to Olga Kniese, 25 July 1883).
17. NAB (Festspielplan von Mama für 1884–1889). Luise Reuß-Belce (1862–1945) sang a Flowermaiden at every Bayreuth Festival from 1882 to 1886, later adding Eva (1889), Fricka (1899–1912), Siegrune (1896), Gutrune (1896–7 and 1901–2), the Third Norn (1896, 1897) and the Second Norn (1901, 1904) to her repertory. She retired from the stage in 1912 but continued to work as a production assistant at every Bayreuth Festival until 1933.
18. Erich Kloss (ed.), *Richard Wagner an seine Künstler* (Berlin 1908), 405 (letter from Richard Wagner to Hans von Wolzogen, 28 Sept. 1882).
19. Cosima Wagner, *Das zweite Leben* (note 9), 37–8 ('Bemerkungen zu den "Parsifal"-Proben 1884').
20. Anon., 'Hermann Levi an seinen Vater: Unveröffentlichte Briefe aus Bayreuth 1875–1889', *Die Programmheft der Bayreuther Festspiele* 1959, iii: *'Parsifal'* (Bayreuth 1959)', 6–23, esp. 16 (letter from Hermann Levi to Benedikt Levi, 7 Aug. 1884).

21. Karbaum, *Studien zur Geschichte der Bayreuther Festspiele* (note 12), ii.47 ('Statuten-Entwurf für eine Internationale Richard-Wagner-Stiftung').
22. Karbaum, *Studien zur Geschichte der Bayreuther Festspiele* (note 12), ii.47 (letter from Adolf von Groß to Carl Friedrich Glasenapp, 19 Jan. 1885).
23. 'Hermann Levi an seinen Vater' (note 20), 16 (letter from Hermann Levi to Benedikt Levi, 8 Aug. 1885).
24. NAB (letter from Cosima Wagner to Hans Richter, 28 Aug. 1889).
25. Cosima Wagner, *Das zweite Leben* (note 9), 69 (letter from Cosima Wagner to Hermann Levi, 8 Sept. 1886).
26. Frithjof Haas, *Zwischen Brahms und Wagner: Der Dirigent Hermann Levi* (Zurich 1995), 330 (letter from Cosima Wagner to Hermann Levi, 15 Jan. 1887).
27. Cosima Wagner, *Das zweite Leben* (note 9), 250 (letter from Cosima Wagner to Hermann Levi, 3 Sept. 1891).
28. NAB (letter from Cosima Wagner to Marie von Wolkenstein, 27 Feb. 1898).
29. NAB (letter from Cosima Wagner to Marie von Wolkenstein, 12 Dec. 1889).
30. Paul Pretzsch (ed.), *Cosima Wagner und Houston Stewart Chamberlain im Briefwechsel 1888–1908* (Leipzig 1934), 599 (letter from Cosima Wagner to Houston Stewart Chamberlain, 28 June 1900).
31. NAB (letter from Felix Mottl to Cosima Wagner, 9 July 1887).
32. Felix Weingartner, *Lebenserinnerungen*, 2nd edn, 2 vols (Zurich 1928–9), i.266. (The Engl. trans. that appeared in 1937 under the title *Buffets and Rewards* is incomplete and has therefore been ignored by the present translator.)
33. NAB (letter from Felix Mottl to Cosima Wagner, 15 April 1889).
34. BSB, Nachl. Mottl (Felix Mottl, diary entry, 28 July 1892).
35. NAB (letter from Adolf von Groß to Cosima Wagner, 6 Sept. 1893).
36. NAB (undated letter from Adolf von Groß to Cosima Wagner).
37. Schad, *Cosima Wagner und Ludwig II.* (note 1), 541 (letter from Cosima Wagner to Ludwig II, 27 Sept. 1885).
38. Richard Wagner, *Entwürfe, Gedanken, Fragmente: Aus nachgelassenen Papieren zusammengestellt* (Leipzig 1885).
39. NAB (letter from Malwida von Meysenbug to Daniela von Bülow, 18 June 1886).
40. NAB (letter from Eva Wagner to Blandine Gravina, 22 June 1886).
41. NAB (letter from Eva Wagner to Blandine Gravina, 22 June 1886).
42. Weingartner, *Lebenserinnerungen* (note 32), i.260.
43. Weingartner, *Lebenserinnerungen* (note 32), i.249.
44. Weingartner, *Lebenserinnerungen* (note 32), i.260–1.
45. BSB, Fasc. germ. 158 (letter from Hans von Bülow to Fritz Brandt, 3 Aug. 1884).
46. BSB, Fasc. germ. 158 (letter from Hans von Bülow to Fritz Brandt, 11 Aug. 1884).
47. See Anna Maria Szylin, *Henry Thode (1857–1920): Leben und Werk* (Frankfurt 1993).
48. Max Freiherr von Waldberg (ed.), *Cosima Wagners Briefe an ihre Tochter Daniela von Bülow 1866–1885* (Stuttgart 1933), 332 (letter from Cosima Wagner to Daniela von Bülow, 3 June 1885).
49. Weingartner, *Lebenserinnerungen* (note 32), i.264.
50. Marie von Bülow (ed.), *Hans von Bülow: Briefe und Schriften*, 8 vols (Leipzig 1895–1908), viii.42 (letter from Hans von Bülow to Eugen Spitzweg, 25 June 1886).
51. BSB, Nachl. Mottl (Felix Mottl, diary entry, 4 July 1886).
52. NAB (letter from Henry Thode to Daniela Thode, 31 July 1894).
53. Adolf Grabowsky, *Der Kampf um Böcklin* (Berlin 1906), 13.
54. NAB (letter from Cosima Wagner to Henry Thode, 4 Jan. 1894).
55. Harry Kessler, *Das Tagebuch*, 9 vols (Stuttgart 2004–10), iv.398–9 (entry of 6 Jan. 1908).
56. Waldberg, *Cosima Wagners Briefe an ihre Tochter* (note 48), 171 (letter from Cosima Wagner to Daniela von Bülow, 16 March 1881).

57. Waldberg, *Cosima Wagners Briefe an ihre Tochter* (note 48), 218 (letter from Cosima Wagner to Daniela von Bülow, 2 July 1881).

58. BSB, Nachl. Dispeker (letter from Daniela Thode to Isolde von Bülow, 10 Jan. 1894).

59. BAB, Nachl. Schweninger (letter from Blandine Gravina to Ernst Schweninger, 19 Oct. 1912).

60. NAB (Henry Thode, 'Nur für mich geschrieben!', 27 Jan. 1913).

61. NAB (letter from Henry Thode to Daniela Thode, 22 Feb. 1913).

62. 'Hermann Levi an seinen Vater' (note 20), 17–18 (letter from Hermann Levi to Benedikt Levi, 14 July 1886).

63. Weingartner, *Lebenserinnerungen* (note 32), i.264–5.

64. Weingartner, *Lebenserinnerungen* (note 32), i.266.

65. NAB (letter from Eva Wagner to Blandine Gravina, 28 July 1886).

66. Weingartner, *Lebenserinnerungen* (note 32), i.273.

67. See Alan Walker, *The Death of Franz Liszt: Based on the unpublished diary of his pupil Lina Schmalhausen* (Ithaca 2002).

68. Walker, *The Death of Franz Liszt* (note 67), 98.

69. BAB, Nachl. Mottl (Felix Mottl, diary entry, 31 July 1886).

70. See Walker, *The Death of Franz Liszt* (note 67), 133–4.

71. NAB (letter from Eva Wagner to Blandine Gravina, 24 Aug. 1886).

72. Klára Hamburger, 'Ein unbekanntes Dokument über Franz Liszts Tod', *Studia musicologica*, lxvi (2005), 403–12, esp. 410.

73. Hamburger, 'Ein unbekanntes Dokument' (note 72), 410–11.

74. Weingartner, *Lebenserinnerungen* (note 32), i.275.

75. Lina Ramann, *Lisztiana: Erinnerungen an Franz Liszt in Tagebuchblättern, Briefen und Dokumenten aus den Jahren 1873–1886/87* (Mainz 1983), 364.

76. Weingartner, *Lebenserinnerungen* (note 32), i.275.

77. BSB, Nachl. Mottl (Felix Mottl, diary entry, 4 Aug. 1886).

78. Weingartner, *Lebenserinnerungen* (note 32), i.276.

79. BSB, Nachl. Mottl (Felix Mottl, diary entry, 14 Aug. 1886).

80. Weingartner, *Lebenserinnerungen* (note 32), i.278.

81. NAB (letter from Cosima Wagner to Adolf von Groß, 11 March 1887).

82. NAB (letter from Cosima Wagner to Daniela Thode, 21 March 1887).

83. NAB (letter from Cosima Wagner to Adolf von Groß, 27 Aug. 1886).

84. NAB (letter from Cosima Wagner to Daniela Thode, 18 Jan. 1887).

85. NAB (letter from Cosima Wagner to Daniela Thode, 11 Feb. 1887).

86. NAB (letter from Cosima Wagner to Heinrich von Stein, 21 March 1887).

87. NAB (letter from Cosima Wagner to Daniela Thode, 26 Jan. 1887).

88. NAB (letter from Cosima Wagner to Daniela Thode, 3 March 1887).

89. Marie von Bülow, *Bülow: Briefe* (note 50), viii.113–14 (letter from Hans von Bülow to Marie von Bülow, 28 June 1887).

90. Marie von Bülow, *Bülow: Briefe* (note 50), viii.115–16 (letter from Hans von Bülow to Marie von Bülow, 1 July 1887).

91. John C. G. Röhl (ed.), *Philipp Eulenburgs politische Korrespondenz*, 3 vols (Boppard 1976–83), i.231 (letter from Philipp zu Eulenburg to his mother, 4 Aug. 1887).

92. Richard Linsert, *Kabale und Liebe: Über Politik und Geschlechtsleben* (Berlin 1931), 492.

93. See Peter Jungblut, *Famose Kerle: Eulenburg – eine wilhelminische Affäre* (Hamburg 2003).

94. 'Hermann Levi an seinen Vater' (note 20), 21 (letter from Hermann Levi to Benedikt Levi, 3 Feb. 1887).

95. Cosima Wagner, *Das zweite Leben* (note 9), 375 (letter from Cosima Wagner to Ernst zu Hohenlohe-Langenburg, 9 April 1894).

96. Reinhold Conrad Muschler, *Philipp zu Eulenburg: Sein Leben und seine Zeit* (Leipzig 1930), 171–2.

97. Röhl, *Eulenburgs politische Korrespondenz* (note 91), i.265 (Eulenburg's diary entry of 18 Sept. 1887).

98. Röhl, *Eulenburgs politische Korrespondenz* (note 91), i.265 (letter from Philipp zu Eulenburg to Prince Wilhelm, 6 Feb. 1888).

99. NAB (letter from Philipp zu Eulenburg to Cosima Wagner, 24 June 1888).

100. NAB (letter from Kaiser Wilhelm II to Cosima Wagner, 29 July 1888).

101. NAB (letter from Malwida von Meysenbug to Daniela Thode, 4 Aug. 1888).

102. Weingartner, *Lebenserinnerungen* (note 32), i.321.

103. Cosima Wagner, *Das zweite Leben* (note 9), 796 (letter from Felix Weingartner to Hermann Levi, 6 Aug. 1892).

104. Röhl, *Eulenburgs politische Korrespondenz* (note 91), i.308–9 (letter from Count Bolko von Hochberg to Philipp zu Eulenburg, 16 Aug. 1888).

105. Röhl, *Eulenburgs politische Korrespondenz* (note 91), i.305 (Eulenburg's diary).

106. Cosima Wagner, *Das zweite Leben* (note 9), 155–7 (letter from Cosima Wagner to Kaiser Wilhelm II, 23 Aug. 1888).

107. Bernhard Fürst von Bülow, *Denkwürdigkeiten*, 4 vols (Berlin 1931), iv.585.

108. Johannes Haller (ed.), *Aus 50 Jahren: Erinnerungen, Tagebücher und Briefe aus dem Nachlaß des Fürsten Philipp zu Eulenburg-Hertefeld* (Berlin 1923), 58.

109. NAB (letter from Philipp zu Eulenburg to Cosima Wagner, 22 Oct. 1888).

110. NAB (letter from Philipp zu Eulenburg to Cosima Wagner, 10 Nov. 1888).

111. NAB (undated letter from Adolf von Groß to Cosima Wagner, [Nov. 1888]).

112. NAB (letter from Philipp zu Eulenburg to Cosima Wagner, 27 Nov. 1888).

113. NAB (letter from Philipp zu Eulenburg to Cosima Wagner, 4 Jan. 1889).

114. NAB (letter from Philipp zu Eulenburg to Cosima Wagner, 17 Jan. 1889).

115. Quoted in Jungblut, *Famose Kerle* (note 93), 30.

116. Röhl, *Eulenburgs politische Korrespondenz* (note 91), i.265 (diary entry, 18 Sept. 1887).

117. NAB (letter from Daniela Thode to Adolf von Groß, 29 Aug. 1888).

118. 'Hermann Levi an seinen Vater' (note 20), 22 (letter from Hermann Levi to Benedikt Levi, 4 July 1889).

119. 'Hermann Levi an seinen Vater' (note 20), 22 (letter from Hermann Levi to Benedikt Levi, 23 July 1889).

120. Bernhard Sattler (ed.), *Adolf von Hildebrand und seine Welt: Briefe und Erinnerungen* (Munich 1962), 327–8 (letter from Elisabeth von Herzogenberg to Adolf and Irene von Hildebrand, 7 Aug. 1889).

121. BSB, Nachl. Mottl (Felix Mottl, diary entry, 16 Aug. 1889).

122. BSB, Nachl. Mottl (Felix Mottl, diary entry, 17 Aug. 1889).

123. *Bayreuther Taschenbuch mit Kalendarium für das Jahr 1889* (Berlin [1888]), Preface.

124. Waldberg, *Cosima Wagners Briefe an ihre Tochter* (note 48), 185 (letter from Cosima Wagner to Daniela von Bülow, 3 April 1881).

125. Waldberg, *Cosima Wagners Briefe an ihre Tochter* (note 48), 187 (letter from Cosima Wagner to Daniela von Bülow, 4 April 1881).

126. Cosima Wagner, *Die Tagebücher* (note 13), ii.1110; Engl. trans. ii.1007 (entry of 9 Feb. 1883). See also note 13 above.

127. Max Weber, *Wirtschaft und Gesellschaft: Grundriss der verstehenden Soziologie* (Tübingen 1972), 140; trans. and ed. Guenther Roth and Claus Wittich as *Economy and Society: An Outline of Interpretive Sociology* (Berkeley 1978), 241.

128. Weber, *Wirtschaft und Gesellschaft* (note 127), 141; Engl. trans. 243.

129. Quoted in Winfried Schüler, *Der Bayreuther Kreis: Von seiner Entstehung bis zum Ausgang der wilhelminischen Ära. Wagnerkult und Kulturreform im Geiste völkischer Weltanschauung* (Münster 1971), 53 (letter from Carl Friedrich Glasenapp to Ludwig Schemann, 29 April 1883).

130. Schüler, *Der Bayreuther Kreis* (note 129), 71 (letter from Carl Friedrich Glasenapp to Ludwig Schemann, 17 July 1884).

131. 'Hermann Levi an seinen Vater' (note 20), 14 (letter from Hermann Levi to Benedikt Levi, 27 June 1883).
132. Karbaum, *Studien zur Geschichte der Bayreuther Festspiele* (note 12), i.32.
133. Max Millenkovich-Morold, *Cosima Wagner: Ein Lebensbild* (Leipzig 1937), 354.
134. Millenkovich-Morold, *Cosima Wagner* (note 133), 331.
135. Hans von Wolzogen, *Lebensbilder* (Regensburg 1923), 51–2.
136. Wolzogen, *Lebensbilder* (note 135), 60.
137. Kessler, *Das Tagebuch* (note 55), iii.70 (entry of 19 July 1897).
138. NAB (letter from Cosima Wagner to Anna Kekulé, 5 Jan. 1891).
139. NAB (letter from Cosima von Wagner to Adolf von Groß, 21 Feb. 1891).
140. NAB (letter from Adolf von Groß to Cosima Wagner, 22 Feb. 1891).
141. Pretzsch, *Cosima Wagner und Houston Stewart Chamberlain im Briefwechsel* (note 30), 169 (letter from Cosima Wagner to Houston Stewart Chamberlain, 28 June 1890).
142. Pretzsch, *Cosima Wagner und Houston Stewart Chamberlain im Briefwechsel* (note 30), 213 (letter from Cosima Wagner to Houston Stewart Chamberlain, 22 March 1891).
143. Quoted in Max Steinitzer, *Richard Strauss* (Berlin 1911), 72.
144. Cosima Wagner, *Das zweite Leben* (note 9), 807 (letter from Hermann Levi to Cosima Wagner, 30 Aug. 1891).
145. Cosima Wagner, *Das zweite Leben* (note 9), 250–1 (letter from Cosima Wagner to Hermann Levi, 3 Sept. 1891).
146. Cosima Wagner, *Das zweite Leben* (note 9), 808 (letter from Hermann Levi to Cosima Wagner, 21 Sept. 1891).
147. Cosima Wagner, *Das zweite Leben* (note 9), 261 (letter from Cosima Wagner to Hermann Levi, 21 Sept. 1891).
148. Siegfried Wagner, *Erinnerungen* (Frankfurt 2005), 28.
149. NAB (letter from Cosima Wagner to Reinhard Kekulé, 29 Dec. 1891).
150. Quoted in Peter P. Pachl, *Siegfried Wagner: Genie im Schatten* (Munich 1988), 98–9 (letter from Siegfried Wagner to Daniela Thode).
151. NAB (letter from Cosima Wagner to Anna Kekulé, 13 Jan. 1892).
152. NAB (undated letter from Cosima Wagner to Adolf von Groß, [Easter Sunday 1892]). Bahry remains unidentified.
153. NAB (letter from Adolf von Groß to Cosima Wagner, 14 April 1892).
154. Richard Graf Du Moulin Eckart, *Cosima Wagner: Ein Lebens- und Charakterbild*, 2 vols (Berlin 1929–31), ii.413.
155. NAB (Sven Friedrich, 'Siegfried Wagner zum 75. Todestag').
156. BSB, Nachl. Mottl (Felix Mottl, diary entry, 1 July 1896).
157. BSB, Nachl. Mottl (Felix Mottl, diary entry, 3 July 1896).
158. Felix Weingartner, *Bayreuth 1876–1896* (Berlin 1904), 40–1.
159. Claude Debussy, *Debussy on Music*, ed. François Lesure and trans. Richard Langham Smith (Ithaca 1988), 133.
160. Debussy, *Debussy on Music* (note 159), 189.
161. William A. Wellner, 'Wagneriana', *Lustige Blätter*, xix (1904).
162. Karl Kraus, 'Momentaufnahmen', *Die Fackel* (5 Oct. 1912), 33.
163. Weingartner, *Lebenserinnerungen* (note 32), ii.56.
164. NAB (letter from Reinhard Kekulé to Cosima Wagner, 23 Dec. 1893).
165. NAB (letter from Reinhard Kekulé to Cosima Wagner, 26 Dec. 1898).
166. BSB, Nachl. Mottl (Felix Mottl, diary entry, 4 April 1904).
167. BSB, Nachl. Mottl (Felix Mottl, diary entry, 6 Dec. 1904).
168. Kessler, *Das Tagebuch* (note 55), iv.619 (entry of 15 Feb. 1911).
169. SBB, Sammlung Holzblock (undated letter from Siegfried Wagner to Alfred Holzblock).
170. Kessler, *Das Tagebuch* (note 55), iv.612 (entry of 7 Feb. 1911).
171. Alexander Moszkowski, 'Siegfried Wagner gegen Strauss', *Neue Musik-Zeitung*, xxxiii (1912), 107.

172. NAB (letter from Cosima Wagner to Marie von Wolkenstein, 14 June 1906).
173. NAB (letter from Adolf von Groß to Cosima Wagner, 12 Sept. 1901).
174. NAB (undated letter from Cosima Wagner to Marie von Wolkenstein, [early 1905]).
175. Houston Stewart Chamberlain, '1876–1896: Die ersten zwanzig Jahre der Bayreuther Bühnenfestspiele', *Bayreuther Blätter*, xix (1896), 1–67, esp. 42.
176. Du Moulin Eckart, *Cosima Wagner* (note 154), ii.387.
177. Kessler, *Das Tagebuch* (note 55), iii.71 (entry of 20 July 1897).
178. Röhl, *Eulenburgs politische Korrespondenz* (note 91), ii.816–18 (letter from Philipp zu Eulenburg to Kaiser Wilhelm II, 21 March 1892).
179. Maximilian Harden, *Köpfe*, 4 vols (Berlin 1923–4), iv.303 and 305.
180. Kessler, *Das Tagebuch* (note 55), iii.71 (entry of 20 July 1897).
181. Anna Bahr-Mildenburg and Hermann Bahr, *Bayreuth* (Leipzig 1912), 17.
182. Kessler, *Das Tagebuch* (note 55), iii.291 (entry of 15 March 1900).
183. Kessler, *Das Tagebuch* (note 55), iii.291 (entry of 21 March 1900).
184. NAB (letter from Cosima Wagner to Felix Weingartner, 31 March 1893).
185. Leo Slezak, *Song of Motley: Being the Reminiscences of a Hungry Tenor* (London 1938), 95–6.
186. NAB (undated letter from Cosima Wagner to Anna Kekulé, [June 1893]).
187. NAB (letter from Cosima Wagner to Anna Kekulé, 29 June 1893).
188. NAB (letter from Cosima Wagner to Dora Glaser, 1 June 1900).
189. Marie von Bülow, *Bülow: Briefe* (note 50), viii.459.
190. NAB (letter from Cosima Wagner to Anna Kekulé, 14 Feb. 1894).
191. Cosima Wagner, *Das zweite Leben* (note 9), 369 (Cosima Wagner's poem on the death of Hans von Bülow).
192. NAB (undated letter from Cosima Wagner to Adolf von Groß, [Feb. 1894]).
193. Haas, *Zwischen Brahms und Wagner* (note 26), 348 (letter from Hermann Levi to Cosima Wagner, 22 May 1894).
194. NAB (letter from Adolf von Groß to Eva Wagner, 18 Aug. 1893).
195. Weingartner, *Bayreuth* (note 158), 41.
196. Weingartner, *Bayreuth* (note 158), 44.
197. Weingartner, *Bayreuth* (note 158), 39.
198. Anon., 'Die Erbin eines unermeßlichen Vermögens' *Coburger Zeitung* (19 Aug. 1894), 2–3.
199. Weingartner, *Bayreuth* (note 158), 40.
200. Cosima Wagner, *Die Tagebücher* (note 13), ii.795; Engl. trans. ii.719 (entry of 14 Sept. 1881).
201. Cosima Wagner, *Die Tagebücher* (note 13), ii.1000; Engl. trans. ii.908 (entry of 8 Sept. 1882).
202. *Bayreuther Abendzeitung* (9 Aug. 1894).
203. STB (letter from Heinrich Landgraf to the Bayreuth Municipal Authorities, 12 Aug. 1894).
204. SBB, Nachl. Lilli Lehmann (letter from Cosima Wagner to Lilli Lehmann, 17 Dec. 1894).
205. Quoted in Du Moulin Eckart, *Cosima Wagner* (note 154), ii.481 (letter from Cosima Wagner to Theodor Muncker).
206. Pretzsch, *Cosima Wagner und Houston Stewart Chamberlain im Briefwechsel* (note 30), 361 (letter from Houston Stewart Chamberlain to Cosima Wagner, 15 Nov. 1893).
207. Pretzsch, *Cosima Wagner und Houston Stewart Chamberlain im Briefwechsel* (note 30), 363 (letter from Cosima Wagner to Houston Stewart Chamberlain, 18 Nov. 1893).
208. Cosima Wagner, *Das zweite Leben* (note 9), 418 (letter from Cosima Wagner to Ernst zu Hohenlohe-Langenburg, 10 June 1896).
209. BSB, Nachl. Mottl (Felix Mottl, diary entry, 18 June 1896).
210. BSB, Nachl. Mottl (Felix Mottl, diary entry, 1 July 1896).

211. Cosima Wagner, *Das zweite Leben* (note 9), 418 (letter from Cosima Wagner to Ernst zu Hohenlohe-Langenburg, 10 June 1896).
212. NAB (letter from Cosima Wagner to Anna Kekulé, 28 Jan. 1896).
213. NAB (letter from Cosima Wagner to Anna Kekulé, 23 May 1896).
214. NAB (letter from Isolde von Bülow to Malwida von Meysenbug, 14 March 1887).
215. NAB (letter from Cosima Wagner to Adolf von Groß, 3 Oct. 1896).
216. NAB (undated letter from Adolf von Groß to Cosima Wagner, [Sept. 1897]).
217. Ernst zu Hohenlohe (ed.), *Briefwechsel zwischen Cosima Wagner und Fürst Ernst zu Hohenlohe-Langenburg* (Stuttgart 1937), 155 (letter from Cosima Wagner to Ernst zu Hohenlohe-Langenburg, 17 Oct. 1897).
218. NAB (letter from Cosima Wagner to Anna Kekulé, 24 March 1898).
219. SBB, Nachl. Hans von Bülow (letter from Cosima Wagner to Marie von Bülow, 20 Dec. 1897).
220. NAB (letter from Cosima Wagner to Anna Kekulé, 4 Dec. 1899).

5. A New Era (1900–14)

1. *Vossische Zeitung* (2 Feb. 1900), 1.
2. Cosima Wagner, *Das zweite Leben: Briefe und Aufzeichnungen 1883–1930*, ed. Dietrich Mack (Munich 1980), 496 (letter from Cosima Wagner to Bodo von dem Knesebeck, 31 Dec. 1899).
3. Cosima Wagner, *Das zweite Leben* (note 2), 497 (letter from Cosima Wagner to Carl Friedrich Glasenapp, 3 Jan. 1900).
4. Cosima Wagner, *Das zweite Leben* (note 2), 498 (letter from Cosima Wagner to Carl Friedrich Glasenapp, 3 Jan. 1900).
5. Otto Strobel (ed.), *König Ludwig II. und Richard Wagner: Briefwechsel*, 5 vols (Karlsruhe 1936–9) iii.182–3 (letter from Richard Wagner to Ludwig II, 28 Sept. 1880).
6. Cosima Wagner, *Das zweite Leben* (note 2), 524 (letter from Cosima Wagner to Richard von Chelius, 18 June 1900).
7. Cosima Wagner, *Das zweite Leben* (note 2), 570–1 (letter from Cosima Wagner to Bodo von dem Knesebeck, 10 Jan. 1901).
8. Anon., *Stenographische Berichte über die Verhandlungen des Reichstags: x. Legislaturperiode* (Berlin 1901), 2217.
9. *Stenographische Berichte* (note 8), 2222.
10. *Stenographische Berichte* (note 8), 2227.
11. See Eugen Richter, *Politisches ABC-Buch: Ein Lexikon parlamentarischer Zeit- und Streitfragen* (Berlin 1903), 182–3.
12. Willi Schuh (ed.), *Richard Strauss: Briefe an die Eltern 1882–1906* (Zurich 1954), 245.
13. Cosima Wagner, *Das zweite Leben* (note 2), 576–82 (letter from Cosima Wagner to members of the German Reichstag, 9 May 1901).
14. NAB (letter from Cosima Wagner to Pastor Schittler, 14 May 1901).
15. Paul Zschorlich, 'Parsifalomanie', *Die Zeit*, il (Sept. 1902), 728–9.
16. NAB (letter from Cosima Wagner to Feodora von Schleswig-Holstein, 13 May 1901).
17. NAB (letter from Cosima Wagner to Philipp zu Eulenburg, 13 May 1901).
18. Paul Pretzsch (ed.), *Cosima Wagner und Houston Stewart Chamberlain im Briefwechsel 1888–1908* (Leipzig 1934), 620 (letter from Houston Stewart Chamberlain to Cosima Wagner, 31 Oct. 1901).
19. NAB (letter from Cosima Wagner to Marie von Wolkenstein, 19 Feb. 1902).
20. Bernhard Fürst von Bülow, *Denkwürdigkeiten*, 4 vols (Berlin 1931), i.550.
21. Pretzsch, *Cosima Wagner und Houston Stewart Chamberlain im Briefwechsel* (note 18), 628 (letter from Houston Stewart Chamberlain to Cosima Wagner, 17 Feb. 1902).
22. Richard Graf Du Moulin Eckart (ed.), *Cosima Wagner: Ein Lebens- und Charakterbild*, 2 vols (Berlin 1929–31) ii.712.

23. Cosima Wagner, *Das zweite Leben* (note 2), 642–3 (letter from Cosima Wagner to Felix Mottl, 28 Sept. 1903).
24. NAB (letter from Cosima Wagner to Hans Richter, June 1903).
25. NAB (letter from Cosima Wagner to Marie von Wolkenstein, 27 March 1903).
26. BSB, Nachl. Mottl (Felix Mottl, diary entry, 14 April 1905).
27. BSB, Nachl. Mottl (Felix Mottl, diary entry, 14 Oct. 1903).
28. NAB (letter from Cosima Wagner to Felix Mottl, 15 Dec. 1903).
29. ÖNB (letter from Felix Mottl to Countess Christiane Thun-Salm, 24 Jan. 1904).
30. BSB, Nachl. Gravina (letter from Felix Mottl to Blandine Gravina, 25 March 1904).
31. Cosima Wagner, *Das zweite Leben* (note 2), 724 (letter from Cosima Wagner to Hugo von Tschudi, 6 Aug. 1911).
32. Ludwig Strecker, *Richard Wagner als Verlagsgefährte* (Mainz 1951), 328.
33. NAB ('Das Parsifal-Intermezzo', *Morgen-Journal*).
34. NAB (*Morgen-Journal* [18 Sept. 1903]).
35. NAB (*Morgen-Journal* [31 Aug. 1903]).
36. Cosima Wagner, *Das zweite Leben* (note 2), 636 (letter from Cosima Wagner to Adolf von Groß, 12/13 Sept. 1903).
37. BSB, Nachl. Mottl (Felix Mottl, diary entry, 5 Dec. 1903).
38. BSB, Nachl. Mottl (Felix Mottl, diary entry, 24 Dec. 1903).
39. Anon., 'Tageschronik', *Die Musik*, iv (1904/5), 276–7.
40. Hermann Bahr, *Parsifalschutz ohne Ausnahmegesetz* (Berlin 1912), 15. No translator can do justice to Bahr's style. For example, he refers to Michael Georg Conrad as Michel Georg Conrad in order to evoke associations with the expression 'der deutsche Michel', meaning 'a plain, honest German'.
41. Bahr, *Parsifalschutz* (note 40), 17.
42. Franz W. Beidler, 'Cosima Wagner: Eine kulturhistorische Studie', Dieter Borchmeyer (ed.), *Franz Wilhelm Beidler: Cosima Wagner-Liszt. Der Weg zum Wagner-Mythos* (Bielefeld 1997), 244–56, esp. 255.
43. On Eberlein, see Simone Müller-Trumpf, 'Das Richard-Wagner-Denkmal von Gustav Eberlein in Berlin' (MA dissertation, Ruprecht Karl University, Heidelberg, 2004).
44. Cosima Wagner, *Das zweite Leben* (note 2), 625 (letter from Cosima Wagner to Bodo von dem Knesebeck, 28 Nov. 1902).
45. See Henry Thode, *Wie ist Richard Wagner vom deutschen Volke zu feiern?* (Heidelberg 1903).
46. NAB (letter from Cosima Wagner to Henry Thode, 15 Feb. 1903).
47. Anon., 'Internationale Richard-Wagner-Feier', *Germania* (15 Feb. 1903).
48. Cosima Wagner, *Das zweite Leben* (note 2), 627 (letter from Cosima Wagner to Hans Richter, 16 Jan. 1903).
49. 'Hans Richter gegen das Programm der Richard-Wagner-Feier', *Deutsche Zeitung* (8 May 1903).
50. Anon., 'Aus der Reichshauptstadt', *Deutsche Zeitung* (8 May 1903).
51. *Münchner Neueste Nachrichten* (9 May 1903).
52. BSB, Nachl. Mottl (letter from Felix Mottl to Ludwig Leichner, 8 May 1903).
53. BSB, Nachl. Mottl (letter from Ludwig Leichner to Felix Mottl, 9 May 1903).
54. BSB, Nachl. Mottl (letter from Felix Mottl to Ludwig Leichner, 9 May 1903).
55. NAB (letter from Cosima Wagner to Fritz Volbach, 6 March 1903).
56. *Illustriertes Wiener Extrablatt* (16 May 1903).
57. NAB (*Morgen-Journal* [14 Aug. 1903]).
58. Anon., 'Zum Streit über die Wagner-Feier', *Die Post* (13 May 1903, evening edition).
59. Kurt Mey, 'Das Berliner Richard-Wagner-Denkmal', *Wartburgstimmen*, i (1903).
60. BAB, Nachl. Schweninger (telegram from Eva Wagner to Ernst Schweninger, Genoa, 8 Feb. 1906).

61. On Schweninger, see Albert Espach, *Beiträge zur Biographie Ernst Schweninger*s (Munich 1979).
62. Ernst Schweninger, *Der Arzt* (Frankfurt 1906), 39.
63. Schweninger, *Der Arzt* (note 62), 19.
64. Schweninger, *Der Arzt* (note 62), 93.
65. BAB, Nachl. Schweninger (letter from Cosima Wagner to Ernst Schweninger, 14 May 1894).
66. BAB, Nachl. Schweninger (letter from Cosima Wagner to Ernst Schweninger, 24 Feb. 1902).
67. NAB (letter from Cosima Wagner to Adolf von Groß, 21 Feb. 1906).
68. BSB, Nachl. Mottl (Felix Mottl, diary entry, 1 Jan. 1906).
69. NAB (letter from Wilhelm II to Cosima Wagner, 24 July 1906).
70. Cosima Wagner, *Das zweite Leben* (note 2), 685–6 (letter from Cosima Wagner to Franz Beidler, 11 Aug. 1906).
71. Cosima Wagner, *Das zweite Leben* (note 2), 557 (letter from Cosima Wagner to Gustav Mahler, 19 Nov. 1900).
72. NAB (letter from Cosima Wagner to Marie von Wolkenstein, 21 Dec. 1900).
73. BSB, Nachl. Dispeker (letter from Cosima Wagner to Franz Beidler, 17 Dec. 1900).
74. BSB, Nachl. Dispeker (letter from Cosima Wagner to Isolde Beidler, 4 Feb. 1902).
75. BSB, Nachl. Dispeker (letter from Cosima Wagner to Isolde Beidler, 13 Feb. 1902).
76. NAB (letter from Cosima Wagner to Marie von Wolkenstein, 31 Dec. 1900).
77. NAB (letter from Cosima Wagner to Marie von Wolkenstein, 13 Sept. 1901). (The quotation is a paraphrase of Mime's line to Siegfried in Act One of *Siegfried*.)
78. NAB (letter from Cosima Wagner to Marie von Wolkenstein, 18 Oct. 1901).
79. BSB, Nachl. Dispeker (letter from Daniela Thode to Franz Beidler, 18 Oct. 1901).
80. NAB (letter from Cosima Wagner to Frau Beidler, 11 Nov. 1901).
81. NAB (letter from Cosima Wagner to Marie von Wolkenstein, 10 Jan. 1902).
82. NAB (letter from Cosima Wagner to Marie von Wolkenstein, 15 Jan. 1902).
83. BSB, Nachl. Dispeker (letter from Cosima Wagner to Isolde Beidler, 4 March 1902).
84. NAB (letter from Eva Wagner to Adolf von Groß, 4 June 1902).
85. BSB, Nachl. Dispeker (letter from Cosima Wagner to Isolde Beidler, 5 Aug. 1902).
86. NAB (letter from Cosima Wagner to Adolf von Groß, 4 May 1905).
87. NAB (letter from Cosima Wagner to Franz Beidler, 30 April 1905).
88. NAB (letter from Cosima Wagner to Franz and Isolde Beidler, 9 June 1905).
89. NAB (letter from Cosima Wagner to Adolf von Groß, 12 Sept. 1905).
90. NAB (letter from Cosima Wagner to Isolde Beidler, 28 Nov. 1905).
91. Cosima Wagner, *Das zweite Leben* (note 2), 685–6 (letter from Cosima Wagner to Franz Beidler, 11 Aug. 1906).
92. NAB (letter from Daniela Thode to Adolf von Groß, 30 Oct. 1906).
93. NAB (letter from Cosima Wagner to Adolf von Groß, 17 Nov. 1906).
94. HZA (Ernst zu Hohenlohe-Langenburg, diary entry, 6 Dec. 1906).
95. NAB (letter from Daniela Thode to Adolf von Groß, 9 Dec. 1906).
96. BAB, Nachl. Schweninger (letter from Kuno Moltke to Ernst Schweninger, 10 Dec. 1906).
97. BSB, Nachl. Gravina (newspaper article of indeterminate origin).
98. Cosima Wagner, *Das zweite Leben* (note 2), 690 (letter from Cosima Wagner to Hugo von Tschudi, 19 June 1907).
99. NAB (letter from Adolf von Groß to Eva Wagner, 29 April 1907).
100. NAB (undated letter from Adolf von Groß to Eva Wagner, [early May 1907]).
101. NAB (letter from Cosima Wagner to Marie von Wolkenstein, 16 July 1907).
102. NAB (letter from Cosima Wagner to Isolde Beidler, 26 July 1907).
103. SBB, Nachl. Lilli Lehmann (letter from Siegfried Wagner to Lilli Lehmann, 26 Oct. 1908).
104. NAB (letter from Eva Wagner to Anna Kekulé, 15 Oct. 1908).

105. Pretzsch, *Cosima Wagner und Houston Stewart Chamberlain im Briefwechsel* (note 18), 689 (letter from Houston Stewart Chamberlain to Cosima Wagner, 1 Sept. 1908).

106. NTH (letter from Houston Stewart Chamberlain to Blandine Gravina, 13 Dec. 1896).

107. See Brigitte Hamann, *Winifred Wagner oder Hitlers Bayreuth* (Munich 2002), 21. This passage has been omitted from Alan Bance's English translation, *Winifred Wagner: A Life at the Heart of Hitler's Bayreuth* (London 2005). The quotation is taken from Gertrud Strobel's diary entry of 29 June 1946.

108. NAB, Nachl. Chamberlain (Houston Stewart Chamberlain, diary entry, Aug.–Nov. 1908).

109. Pretzsch, *Cosima Wagner und Houston Stewart Chamberlain im Briefwechsel* (note 18), 691 (letter from Houston Stewart Chamberlain to Cosima Wagner, 1 Sept. 1908).

110. BSB, Nachl. Dispeker (Chamberlain's decree of divorce).

111. NAB, Nachl. Chamberlain (Houston Stewart Chamberlain, diary entry, 26 Dec. 1908).

112. Hermann Keyserling, *Reise durch die Zeit: Ursprünge und Entfaltungen* (Vaduz 1948), 126.

113. Keyserling, *Reise durch die Zeit* (note 112), 134.

114. Wolfram Kinzig (ed.), *Harnack, Marcion und das Judentum: Nebst einer kommentierten Edition des Briefwechsels Adolf von Harnacks mit Houston Stewart Chamberlain* (Leipzig 2004), 263 (letter from Adolf von Harnack to Houston Stewart Chamberlain, 24 Nov. 1912).

115. Kinzig, *Harnack, Marcion und das Judentum* (note 114), 267–8 (letter from Houston Stewart Chamberlain to Adolf von Harnack, 9 Dec. 1912).

116. Houston Stewart Chamberlain, *Briefe 1882–1924 und Briefwechsel mit Kaiser Wilhelm II.*, 2 vols (Munich 1928), i.307–8 (letter from Houston Stewart Chamberlain to Major Kotze, 3 April 1915).

117. NAB (letter from Empress Hermine to Daniela Thode, 2 July 1926).

118. Keyserling, *Reise durch die Zeit* (note 112), 135.

119. NAB, Nachl. Chamberlain (letter from Houston Stewart Chamberlain to Hermann Keyserling, 28 March 1908).

120. Cosima Wagner, *Das zweite Leben* (note 2), 761 ('Mama's words, 1929 and 1930, written down by Eva').

121. Houston Stewart Chamberlain, *Die Grundlagen des neunzehnten Jahrhunderts*, 2 vols (Munich 1912), i.278; trans. John Lees as *Foundations of the Nineteenth Century*, 2 vols (Munich 1911), i.277.

122. Pretzsch, *Cosima Wagner und Houston Stewart Chamberlain im Briefwechsel* (note 18), 562 (letter from Cosima Wagner to Houston Stewart Chamberlain, 7 May 1899).

123. Pretzsch, *Cosima Wagner und Houston Stewart Chamberlain im Briefwechsel* (note 18), 569 (letter from Cosima Wagner to Houston Stewart Chamberlain, 25 May 1899).

124. Keyserling, *Reise durch die Zeit* (note 112), 129.

125. Keyserling, *Reise durch die Zeit* (note 112), 130.

126. Chamberlain, *Briefe* (note 116), ii.231 (letter from Houston Stewart Chamberlain to Wilhelm II, 11 Dec. 1908).

127. NAB (letter from Houston Stewart Chamberlain to Adolf von Groß, 26 Oct. 1908).

128. NAB (letter from Houston Stewart Chamberlain to Adolf von Groß, 26 Oct. 1908).

129. NAB, Nachl. Chamberlain (letter from Adolf von Groß to Houston Stewart Chamberlain, 30 Sept. 1911).

130. Keyserling, *Reise durch die Zeit* (note 112), 124.

131. NAB (letter from Daniela Thode to Adolf von Groß, 28 Oct. 1908).

132. *Berliner Börsen Courier* (19 March 1909).

133. NAB, Nachl. Chamberlain (letter from Ernst Schweninger to Eva and Houston Stewart Chamberlain, 26 March 1909).

134. BSB, Nachl. Dispeker (letter from Cosima Wagner to Isolde Beidler, 15 Aug. 1909).

135. BSB, Nachl. Dispeker (letter from Siegfried Wagner to Isolde Beidler, 21 Aug. 1909).
136. NAB (copy of letter from Houston Stewart Chamberlain to Adolf von Groß, 14 Sept. 1909).
137. NAB (declaration of Houston Stewart Chamberlain, 25 Sept. 1909).
138. BAB, Nachl. Schweninger (letter from Henry Thode to Ernst Schweninger, 19 Oct. 1909).
139. NAB, Nachl. Chamberlain (Houston Stewart Chamberlain, diary entry, 16 Sept. 1909).
140. BAB, Nachl. Schweninger (letter from Houston Stewart Chamberlain to Ernst Schweninger, 16 Sept. 1909).
141. BAB, Nachl. Schweninger (letter from Houston Stewart Chamberlain to Ernst Schweninger, 15 Nov. 1909).
142. NAB (undated letter from Daniela Thode to Adolf von Groß).
143. BSB, Nachl. Dispeker (letter from Isolde Beidler to Cosima Wagner, 5 Nov. 1909).
144. BSB, Nachl. Dispeker (letter from Franz Beidler to Cosima Wagner, 5 Nov. 1909).
145. BAB, Nachl. Schweninger (letter from Houston Stewart Chamberlain to Ernst Schweninger, 15 Nov. 1909).
146. BSB, Nachl. Dispeker (letter from Siegfried Wagner to Franz Beidler, 7 Nov. 1909).
147. BSB, Nachl. Dispeker (letter from Isolde Beidler to Siegfried Wagner, 14 Nov. 1909).
148. BSB, Nachl. Dispeker (letter from Siegfried Wagner to Isolde Beidler, 14 Nov. 1909).
149. BSB, Nachl. Dispeker (letter from Siegfried Wagner to Isolde Beidler, 14 Nov. 1909).
150. BSB, Nachl. Dispeker (letter from Siegfried Wagner to Isolde Beidler, 18 Nov. 1909).
151. BSB, Nachl. Dispeker (letter from Isolde Beidler to Siegfried Wagner, 23 Nov. 1909).
152. ÖNB (letter from Felix Mottl to Christiane Thun-Salm, 13 Feb. 1911).
153. NAB (letter from Daniela Thode to Eva Chamberlain, 1 Nov. 1910).
154. Michael Karbaum, *Studien zur Geschichte der Bayreuther Festspiele* (Regensburg 1976), i.58.
155. NAB (letter from Cosima Wagner to Adolf von Groß, 20–2 March 1910).
156. BAB, Nachl. Schweninger (letter from Houston Stewart Chamberlain to Ernst Schweninger, 11 Aug. 1910).
157. HUB, Phil. Fak. 1384 (application from Cosima Wagner).
158. HUB, Phil. Fak. 1384 (letter from Cosima Wagner to the staff of the Faculty of Philosophy).
159. NAB, Nachl. Chamberlain (letter from Adolf von Groß to Houston Stewart Chamberlain, 29 Sept. 1910).
160. NAB (letter from Daniela Thode to Eva Chamberlain, 1 Nov. 1910).
161. BSB, Nachl. Dispeker (letter from Isolde Beidler to Hans von Wolzogen, 6 Oct. 1910).
162. BSB, Nachl. Dispeker (letter from Hans von Wolzogen to Isolde Beidler, 6 Oct. 1910).
163. BAB, Nachl. Schweninger (letter from Houston Stewart Chamberlain to Ernst Schweninger, 8 Sept. 1911).
164. BAB, Nachl. Schweninger (letter from Houston Stewart Chamberlain to Ernst Schweninger, 6 Nov. 1911).
165. NAB ('Cosima's conversations about Isolde, noted down by Eva Chamberlain, Feb. 1911').
166. ÖNB (letter from Felix Mottl to Christiane Thun-Salm, 13 Feb. 1911).
167. See NAB (letter from August Püringer to Hans von Wolzogen, 3 July 1912).
168. NAB (letter from Gerhart Freiesleben to Hans von Wolzogen, 8 Oct. 1912).
169. Michael Georg Conrad, *Wagners Geist und Kunst in Bayreuth* (Munich 1906), 99.
170. See Friedrich Jaskowski, *Volksbildung durch Wagnersche Kunst: Praktische Vorschläge, theoretische Begründungen* (Bühl 1909).
171. Hans von Wolzogen, *Germanisierung der Religion* (Berlin 1911).
172. Hans von Wolzogen, 'Nach 1913', *Bayreuther Blätter*, xxxvii (1914), 3–4.
173. Leopold von Schroeder, *Die Vollendung des arischen Mysteriums in Bayreuth* (Munich 1911), 211–12.
174. See Leopold von Schroeder, *Lebenserinnerungen* (Leipzig 1921), 227.

175. Arnold Schoenberg, 'Parsifal und Urheberrecht', *Neue Musik-Zeitung*, xxxiii (1912), 315–17, esp. 316; trans. Leo Black as '*Parsifal* and Copyright', *Style and Idea*, ed. Leonard Stein (London 1975), 491–6, esp. 493.

176. Paul Bekker, 'Bayreuth und seine Leute', *Frankfurter Zeitung* (11 Aug. 1912, early morning edition).

177. Walther Rathenau, *Schriften aus Kriegs- und Nachkriegszeit* (Berlin 1929), 171.

178. John Maynard Keynes, 'Essays in Biography', *The Collected Writings of John Maynard Keynes*, 28 vols (London 1971–82), x.411.

179. NAB (letter from Cosima Wagner to Isolde Beidler, 23 May 1913).

180. NAB (undated medical report on Isolde Beidler [Oct. 1912]).

181. BSB, Nachl. Dispeker (letter from Isolde Beidler to Eva Chamberlain, 22 June 1913).

182. See Anon., *Adreßbuch deutscher Millionäre* (Leipzig 1909), 268.

183. NAB, Nachl. Chamberlain (letter from Adolf von Groß to Houston Stewart Chamberlain, 25 Jan. 1913).

184. Information kindly supplied by the Deutsche Bundesbank, 18 Nov. 2005.

185. BSB, Nachl. Dispeker (letter from Eva Chamberlain to Isolde Beidler, 29 June 1913).

186. MSB, Nachl. Weil (Siegfried Dispeker, 'Erinnerungen eines Münchner Rechtsanwalts', 87).

187. SAB, Prozessunterlagen Isolde Beidler (letter from Isolde Beidler to Cosima Wagner, 2 Sept. 1913).

188. NAB (letter from Cosima Wagner to Isolde Beidler, 13 Sept. 1913).

189. NAB, Nachl. Chamberlain (letter from Adolf von Groß to Houston Stewart Chamberlain, 4 Feb. 1914).

190. NAB, Nachl. Chamberlain (letter from Adolf von Groß to Eva Chamberlain, 20 Feb. 1914).

191. NAB (letter from Houston Stewart Chamberlain to Josef Stolzing-Cerny, 15 May 1914).

192. NAB, Nachl. Chamberlain (letter from Josef Stolzing-Cerny to Houston Stewart Chamberlain, 18 May 1914).

193. Anon., 'Der Streit im Hause Wagner', *Münchner Neueste Nachrichten* (28 June 1914).

194. BSB, Nachl. Dispeker (letter from Heinrich Wadere to Siegfried Dispeker, 6 June 1914).

195. MSB, Nachl. Weil (Siegfried Dispeker, 'Erinnerungen eines Münchner Rechtsanwalts', 100).

196. Richard Wagner, *Sämtliche Schriften und Dichtungen*, 16 vols (Leipzig 1911–14), v.211.

197. BAB, Nachl. Schweninger (letter from Blandine Gravina to Ernst Schweninger, 19 Oct. 1912).

198. BSB, Nachl. Dispeker (letter from Isolde Beidler to Siegfried Dispeker, 26 March 1915).

199. NAB (medical certificate from the Schweizerhof Sanatorium at Davos, 22 Jan. 1915).

200. NAB (letter from Isolde Beidler to Daniela Thode, 6 July 1918).

201. BAB, Nachl. Schweninger (letter from Eva Chamberlain to Ernst Schweninger, 8 July 1918).

202. NAB (letter from Daniela Thode to Eva Chamberlain, 8 Feb. 1919).

203. SAM (announcement of Isolde Beidler's death).

204. NAB (letter from Daniela Thode to Eva Chamberlain, 11 Feb. 1919).

205. Cosima Wagner, *Das zweite Leben* (note 2), 761 ('Mama's words, 1929 and 1930, written down by Eva', 21 May 1929).

206. Maximilian Harden, 'Tutte le corde: Siegfried und Isolde', *Die Zukunft* (27 June 1914), 406.

207. Harden, 'Tutte le corde' (note 206), 409.

208. Harden, 'Tutte le corde' (note 206), 424.

209. Harden, 'Tutte le corde' (note 206), 426–7.

210. BAB, Nachl. Harden (letter from Franz Beidler to Maximilian Harden, 1 July 1914).

6. The Long End (1914–30)

1. Letter from Siegfried Wagner to Ludwig Karpath, quoted by Zdenko von Kraft, *Der Sohn: Siegfried Wagners Leben und Umwelt* (Graz 1969), 190.

2. Cosima Wagner, *Das zweite Leben: Briefe und Aufzeichnungen 1883–1930*, ed. Dietrich Mack (Munich 1980), 730 (letter from Cosima Wagner to Ernst zu Hohenlohe-Langenburg, New Year 1915).

3. Houston Stewart Chamberlain, *Briefe 1882–1924 und Briefwechsel mit Kaiser Wilhelm II.*, 2 vols (Munich 1928), i.236–40 (letter from Houston Stewart Chamberlain to Leopold Casselmann, 29 Aug. 1914).

4. Houston Stewart Chamberlain, *Kriegsaufsätze* (Munich 1914), 67.

5. NAB, Nachl. Chamberlain (letter from Basil Hall Chamberlain to Houston Stewart Chamberlain, 21 Oct. 1914).

6. NAB (letter from Eva Chamberlain to Anna Kekulé, 8 Jan. 1910).

7. Winifred Wagner quoted by Brigitte Hamann, *Winifred Wagner oder Hitlers Bayreuth* (Munich 2002), 25; trans. Alan Bance as *Winifred Wagner: A Life at the Heart of Hitler's Bayreuth* (London 2005), 11–12.

8. Hamann, *Winifred Wagner* (note 7), 29; Engl. trans. 14.

9. Kraft, *Der Sohn* (note 1), 192–3 (letter from Eva Chamberlain to Siegfried Wagner). Katherlieschen is an intellectually challenged farmer's daughter in the Grimm Brothers' fairytale 'Der Frieder und das Katherlieschen'.

10. Kraft, *Der Sohn* (note 1), 201 (letter from Winifred Williams to Siegfried Wagner, 7 July 1915).

11. NAB (letter from Eva Chamberlain to Anna Kekulé, 28 July 1915).

12. Hamann, *Winifred Wagner* (note 7), 33; Engl. trans. 18 (letter from Winifred Williams to Helena Boy, 6 July 1915).

13. Hamann, *Winifred Wagner* (note 7), 36; Engl. trans. 19 (Franz Stassen's reminiscences).

14. NAB (letter from Eva Chamberlain to Anna Kekulé, 13 Oct. 1915).

15. NAB (letter from Eva Chamberlain to Blandine Gravina, 12 Oct. 1915).

16. Eva Humperdinck (ed.), *Engelbert Humperdinck in seinen persönlichen Beziehungen zu Richard Wagner, Cosima Wagner, Siegfried Wagner*, 3 vols (Koblenz 1996–9), iii.299 (letter from Cosima Wagner to Engelbert Humperdinck, 29 Dec. 1915).

17. NAB (letter from Winifred Wagner to Blandine Gravina, 2 Jan. 1916).

18. Hamann, *Winifred Wagner* (note 7), 40; Engl. trans. 23–4 (letter from Winifred Wagner to Helena Boy, 18 Oct. 1915).

19. Hamann, *Winifred Wagner* (note 7), 39; Engl. trans. 23 (Winifred Wagner's interview with Geoffrey Skelton).

20. Hans Jürgen Syberberg, *Winifred Wagner und die Geschichte des Hauses Wahnfried 1914–1975* (video interview with Winifred Wagner released by Alexander Verlag of Berlin in 1975 and again in 1993 with ISBN 3-923854-85-4).

21. NAB (letter from Eva Chamberlain to Blandine Gravina, 14 June 1916).

22. HZA (letter from Marie Wenden to Alexandra zu Hohenlohe-Langenburg, 28 Sept. 1925).

23. NAB (letter from Eva Chamberlain to Blandine Gravina, 3 Feb. 1916).

24. NAB (letter from Winifred Wagner to Blandine Gravina, 3 Feb. 1916).

25. HZA (letter from Marie Wenden to Alexandra zu Hohenlohe-Langenburg, 6 Aug. 1925).

26. Syberberg, *Winifred Wagner* (note 20).

27. NAB (letter from Eva Chamberlain to Blandine Gravina, 3 Feb. 1916).

28. Syberberg, *Winifred Wagner* (note 20).

29. Syberberg, *Winifred Wagner* (note 20).

30. BAB, Nachl. Schweninger (letter from Winifred Wagner to Ernst Schweninger, 31 Aug. 1916).

31. BAB, Nachl. Schweninger (letter from Winifred Wagner to Ernst Schweninger, 9 Oct. 1916).

32. Friedelind Wagner and Page Cooper, *Heritage of Fire: The Story of Richard Wagner's Granddaughter* (New York and London 1945), 3.

33. Kraft, *Der Sohn* (note 1), 212–13 (letter from Siegfried Wagner to Franz Stassen, 11 Jan. 1917). The meaning of the word 'Goldschniggelchen' is obscure, although it may be related to the noun 'Schniegel', meaning a 'fop' or 'dandy'. For a note on 'Katherlieschen' as a term of dubious endearment, see note 9 above.

34. Kraft, *Der Sohn* (note 1), 214 (Winifred Wagner's reminiscences).

35. Hamann, *Winifred Wagner* (note 7), 50; Engl. trans. 32.

36. Cosima Wagner, *Das zweite Leben* (note 2), 735 (letter from Cosima Wagner to Ernst zu Hohenlohe-Langenburg, 22 Dec. 1916).

37. See Dirk Stegmann, *Die Erben Bismarcks: Parteien und Verbände in der Spätphase des Wilhelminischen Deutschlands* (Cologne 1970), 501.

38. Cosima Wagner, *Das zweite Leben* (note 2), 738 (letter from Cosima Wagner to Ernst zu Hohenlohe-Langenburg, 21 Oct. 1917).

39. Houston Stewart Chamberlain, 'Die Deutsche Vaterlands-Partei', *Der Wille zum Sieg und andere Aufsätze* (Munich 1918), 45.

40. Friedrich Meinecke, *Autobiographische Schriften* (Stuttgart 1969), 354.

41. Ernst zu Hohenlohe (ed.), *Briefwechsel zwischen Cosima Wagner und Fürst Ernst zu Hohenlohe-Langenburg* (Stuttgart 1937), 366 (letter from Cosima Wagner to Ernst zu Hohenlohe-Langenburg, early Jan. 1918).

42. Chamberlain, *Briefe* (note 3), ii.50 (letter from Houston Stewart Chamberlain to Gerhart Hauptmann, 16 March 1918).

43. Hohenlohe, *Briefwechsel zwischen Cosima Wagner und Fürst Ernst zu Hohenlohe-Langenburg* (note 41), 369 (letter from Cosima Wagner to Ernst zu Hohenlohe-Langenburg, 14 Feb. 1918).

44. Cosima Wagner, *Das zweite Leben* (note 2), 740 (letter from Cosima Wagner to Ernst zu Hohenlohe-Langenburg, Maundy Thursday 1918).

45. Cosima Wagner, *Das zweite Leben* (note 2), 742 (letter from Cosima Wagner to Ernst zu Hohenlohe-Langenburg, 28 Nov. 1918).

46. SBB, Sammlung Sternfeld (letter from Siegfried Wagner to Richard Sternfeld, 25 April 1918). (The king of Elis was Augeas, not Euryatheus.)

47. NAB (letter from Siegfried Wagner to Gustav Manz, 15 March 1929).

48. Franz Wilhelm Beidler, quoted by Hans Curjel, *Experiment Krolloper 1927–1931* (Munich 1975), 59.

49. Josephine Baker and Jo Bouillon, *Josephine* (New York 1977), 58.

50. HZA (letter from Daniela Thode to Ernst zu Hohenlohe-Langenburg, 2 Feb. 1930).

51. NAB (Siegfried Wagner, 'Zweierlei Rosa! Ein zeitgenössisches Gedicht', Christmas 1918).

52. Cosima Wagner, *Das zweite Leben* (note 2), 744 (letter from Cosima Wagner to Ernst zu Hohenlohe-Langenburg, 27 Feb. 1919).

53. Cosima Wagner, *Das zweite Leben* (note 2), 746 (letter from Cosima Wagner to Ernst zu Hohenlohe-Langenburg, 11 Sept. 1919).

54. Syberberg, *Winifred Wagner* (note 20).

55. Friedelind Wagner, *Heritage of Fire* (note 32), 3.

56. Syberberg, *Winifred Wagner* (note 20).

57. BAB, Nachl. Schweninger (letter from Winifred Wagner to Ernst Schweninger, 8 Jan. 1919).

58. BAB, Nachl. Schweninger (letter from Cosima Wagner to Ernst Schweninger, 27 Sept. 1919).

59. BAB, Nachl. Schweninger (letter from Winifred Wagner to Ernst Schweninger, 28 Sept. 1919).

60. HZA (letter from Blandine Gravina to Ernst zu Hohenlohe-Langenburg, 20 Jan. 1920).
61. HZA (letter from Blandine Gravina to Ernst zu Hohenlohe-Langenburg, 11 Sept. 1919).
62. HZA (letter from Daniela Thode to Ernst zu Hohenlohe-Langenburg, 16 May 1925). (In her final phrase, Daniela quotes King Wilhelm I's telegram to his wife, reporting the German victory at Sedan in 1870 that spelt the end of the Second Empire in France.)
63. NAB (letter from Eva Chamberlain to Anna Kekulé, 22 March 1919).
64. Cosima Wagner, *Das zweite Leben* (note 2), 750–1 (letter from Cosima Wagner to Ernst zu Hohenlohe-Langenburg, 4 July 1923).
65. NAB, Nachl. Chamberlain (Houston Stewart Chamberlain, diary entry, 29 Sept. 1923).
66. NAB, Nachl. Chamberlain (Houston Stewart Chamberlain, diary entry, 30 Sept. 1923).
67. NAB, Nachl. Chamberlain (Houston Stewart Chamberlain, diary entry, 30 Sept. 1923).
68. NAB, Nachl. Chamberlain (Houston Stewart Chamberlain, diary entry, 1 Oct. 1923).
69. Chamberlain, *Briefe* (note 3), ii.124–5 (letter from Houston Stewart Chamberlain to Adolf Hitler, 7 Oct. 1923).
70. Hamann, *Winifred Wagner* (note 7), 85; Engl. trans. 61.
71. Syberberg, *Winifred Wagner* (note 20).
72. NAB, Nachl. Chamberlain (Houston Stewart Chamberlain, diary entry, 9 Nov. 1923).
73. Hamann, *Winifred Wagner* (note 7), 94; Engl. trans. 68 (letter from Siegfried Wagner to Rosa Eidam, Christmas 1923).
74. Goebbels's diary entry of 8 May 1926 quoted in Hamann, *Winifred Wagner* (note 7), 149; Engl. trans. 115.
75. Syberberg, *Winifred Wagner* (note 20).
76. See Fritz Blaich, *Der schwarze Freitag: Inflation und Wirtschaftskrise* (Munich 1990), 29–31.
77. SBB, Sammlung Holzblock (letter from Siegfried Wagner to Alfred Holzblock, 19 May 1920).
78. NAB (Appeal to Sign Patrons' Certificates for the German Festival Foundation, Bayreuth 1921).
79. See Michael Karbaum, *Studien zur Geschichte der Bayreuther Festspiele (1876–1976)* (Regensburg 1976), i.66.
80. HZA (letter from Daniela Thode to Ernst zu Hohenlohe-Langenburg, 7 Jan. 1924).
81. Lauritz Melchior, 'Die drei Vaterländer', *Das musikalische Selbstporträt von Komponisten, Dirigenten, Instrumentalisten, Sängerinnen und Sängern unserer Zeit*, ed. Josef Müller-Marein and Hannes Reinhardt (Hamburg 1963), 150–1.
82. Kurt Singer, 'Bayreuth: Zur Eröffnung der Festspiele', *Vorwärts*, ccclxxxvi (17 Aug. 1924), quoted by Susanna Großmann-Vendrey, *Bayreuth in der deutschen Presse: Beiträge zur Rezeptionsgeschichte Richard Wagners und seiner Festspiele*, 3 vols (Regensburg 1977–83), iii/2.180.
83. Karl Holl, 'Bayreuth 1924', *Frankfurter Zeitung*, dlxxiv (3 Aug. 1924), quoted by Großmann-Vendrey, *Bayreuth in der deutschen Presse* (note 82), iii/2.183.
84. Syberberg, *Winifred Wagner* (note 20).
85. Friedelind Wagner, *Heritage of Fire* (note 32), 31.
86. NAB, Nachl. Chamberlain (Houston Stewart Chamberlain, diary entry, 12 Nov. 1925).
87. Quoted by Geoffrey G. Field, *Evangelist of Race: The Germanic Vision of Houston Stewart Chamberlain* (New York 1981), 445.
88. NAB, Nachl. Chamberlain (Houston Stewart Chamberlain, diary entry, 6 May 1926).
89. Obituary published in the *Oberfränkische Zeitung und Bayreuther Anzeiger* (21 Jan. 1927).
90. Anon., 'Chamberlains letzte Fahrt mit Hakenkreuzlerbegleitung', *Fränkische Volkstribüne* (12 Jan. 1927).

91. Anon., 'Die Einäscherung Chamberlains', *Coburger Volksblatt* (13 Jan. 1927).

92. HZA (letter from Daniela Thode to Ernst zu Hohenlohe-Langenburg, 20 Jan. 1927).

93. Friedelind Wagner, *Heritage of Fire* (note 32), 32.

94. Hermann Wilhelm Draber, *Der Weg einer deutschen Künstlerin: Erinnerungen an Emmy Krüger* (Munich 1940), 84.

95. NAB (letter from Eva Chamberlain to Anna Kekulé, 12 Sept. 1927).

96. NAB (letter from Siegmund von Hausegger to Cosima Wagner, 25 Dec. 1927).

97. NAB (letter from Gustav Böß to Cosima Wagner, 25 Dec. 1927).

98. NAB (letter from Hans Schemm to Cosima Wagner, 24 Dec. 1927).

99. NAB (letter from Wolfgang Golther to Cosima Wagner, 21 Dec. 1927).

100. NAB (letter from Hugo Patermann to Cosima Wagner, 22 Dec. 1927).

101. HZA (letter from Daniela Thode to Ernst zu Hohenlohe-Langenburg, 7 Jan. 1928).

102. NAB (letter from Eva Chamberlain to Anna Kekulé, 13 Dec. 1928).

103. Cosima Wagner, *Das zweite Leben* (note 2), 752–60 ('Mama's Words, 1925–30').

104. NAB (letter from Blandine Gravina to Dora Glaser, 23 March 1930).

105. Cosima Wagner, *Das zweite Leben* (note 2), 760 ('Mama's Words, 1925–30').

106. Friedelind Wagner, *Heritage of Fire* (note 32), 34.

Epilogue

1. Author's interview with Verena Lafferentz.

2. SAB ('Funeral Service for Dr Cosima Wagner').

3. Hans Jürgen Syberberg, *Winifred Wagner und die Geschichte des Hauses Wahnfried 1914–1975* (video interview with Winifred Wagner released by Alexander Verlag of Berlin in 1975 and again in 1993 with ISBN 3-923854-85-4).

4. SBB, Nachl. Paul Pretzsch (letter from Eva Chamberlain to Paul and Toni Pretzsch, 30 Jan. 1933).

Bibliography

Unpublished Sources

Archiv des Erzbistums München und Freising (AEM)
Baptism register of the Parish of Saint Boniface, Munich, MM 227
Bayerisches Hauptstaatsarchiv (BHA)
    Unpublished papers of Ludwig von der Pfordten ('My Second Ministry: Autobiographical Sketch')
Bayerische Staatsbibliothek München (BSB)
    Ana 452: Unpublished papers of Felix Mottl
    Ana 471: Unpublished papers of Blandine Gravina
    Cgm 8405: Unpublished papers of Siegfried Dispeker
    Fasc. germ. 109: Cosima Wagner to Claire de Charnacé
    Fasc. germ. 158: Hans von Bülow to Fritz Brandt
    Fasc. germ. 159: Cosima Wagner to Malvina Schnorr von Carolsfeld
Bibliothèque nationale de France (BNF)
    NAF 25191: Archives Daniel Ollivier
Bundesarchiv Berlin/Koblenz (BAB)
    Unpublished papers of Maximilian Harden
    Unpublished papers of Ernst Schweninger
Hohenlohe-Zentralarchiv (HZA)
    Unpublished papers of Prince Ernst and Princess Alexandra zu Hohenlohe-Langenburg
Humboldt Universität Berlin (HUB), University Archives
    Phil. Fak. 1384: Appointment to honorary doctorate
Katholisches Dompfarramt St. Hedwig Berlin (SHB)
    Marriage registers
    Birth registers
Münchner Stadtbibliothek (MSB)
    Unpublished papers of Grete Weil
Nationalarchiv der Richard-Wagner-Stiftung, Bayreuth (NAB)
Neill Thornborrow Private Archives (NTH)
    Houston Stewart Chamberlain to Blandine Gravina
Österreichische Nationalbibliothek Wien, Department of Manuscripts (ÖNB)
    Felix Mottl to Countess Christiane Thun-Salm
Staatsarchiv Bamburg (SAB)
    K3 Präs. Reg. Nr. 2160: Funeral service for Cosima Wagner
    K106/VII Nr. 55a: Court records relating to Isolde Beidler
Staatsbibliothek zu Berlin, Preußischer Kulturbesitz, Department of Music (SBB)
    Unpublished papers of Hans von Bülow
    Unpublished papers of Lilli Lehmann

Unpublished papers of Paul Pretzsch
Collection Alfred Holzblock
Collection Richard Sternfeld
Stadtarchiv Bayreuth (STB)
B 2007: Minutes of the Bayreuth Town Council meeting in August 1894
Stadtarchiv München (SAM)
AG München NR 1919/292: Announcement of death of Isolde Beidler
Wissenschaftliche Stadtbibliothek Mainz (SBM)
Unpublished papers of Peter Cornelius

Interview

Author's interview with Verena Lafferentz

Video

Syberberg, Hans Jürgen. *Winifred Wagner und die Geschichte des Hauses Wahnfried 1914–1975* (video interview with Winifred Wagner released by Alexander Verlag of Berlin in 1975 and again in 1993 with ISBN 3-923854-85-4)

Published Sources

Agoult, Marie d'. *Mémoires, souvenirs et journaux*, ed. Charles F. Dupêchez, 2 vols (Paris 1990)
Altmann, Wilhelm (ed.). *Richard Wagners Briefwechsel mit B. Schott's Söhne* (Mainz 1911)
Anon. 'Die Erbin eines unermeßlichen Vermögens', *Coburger Zeitung* (19 Aug. 1894), 2–3
——. *Stenographische Berichte über die Verhandlungen des Reichstags: X. Legislaturperiode*, vol. iii (Berlin 1901)
——. *Adreßbuch deutscher Millionäre* (Leipzig 1909)
——. 'Der Streit im Hause Wagner', *Münchner Neueste Nachrichten* (28 June 1914)
——. 'Chamberlains letzte Fahrt mit Hakenkreuzlerbegleitung', *Fränkische Volkstribüne* (12 Jan. 1927)
——. 'Die Einäscherung Chamberlains', *Coburger Volksblatt* (13 Jan. 1927)
——. 'Hermann Levi an seinen Vater: Unveröffentlichte Briefe aus Bayreuth von 1875–1889', *Die Programmhefte der Bayreuther Festspiele 1959*, iii: *Parsifal* (Bayreuth 1959), 6–23
Bahr, Hermann. *Parsifalschutz ohne Ausnahmegesetz* (Berlin 1912)
Bahr-Mildenburg, Anna and Hermann Bahr. *Bayreuth* (Leipzig 1912)
Baker, Josephine and Jo Bouillon. *Josephine* (New York 1977)
Bandilla, Kai. *Urheberrecht im Kaiserreich: Der Weg zum Gesetz betreffend das Urheberrecht an Werken der Literatur und Tonkunst vom 19. Juni 1901* (Frankfurt 2005)
Bayreuther Taschenbuch mit Kalendarium für das Jahr 1889 (Berlin n.d.)
Beidler, Franz Wilhelm. *Cosima Wagner-Liszt: Der Weg zum Wagner-Mythos*, ed. Dieter Borchmeyer (Bielefeld 1997)
Bekker, Paul. 'Bayreuth und seine Leute', *Frankfurter Zeitung Erstes Morgenblatt* (11 Aug. 1912)
Bernhardi, Friedrich von. *Denkwürdigkeiten aus meinem Leben* (Berlin 1927)
Blaich, Fritz. *Der schwarze Freitag: Inflation und Wirtschaftskrise* (Munich 1990)
Bock, Claus Victor. *Pente Pigadia und die Tagebücher des Clement Harris* (Amsterdam 1962)
Borchmeyer, Dieter and Jörg Salaquarda (eds). *Nietzsche und Wagner: Stationen einer epochalen Begegnung*, 2 vols (Frankfurt 1994)
Bory, Robert (ed.). *Liszt et ses enfants Blandine, Cosima & Daniel* (Paris 1936)
Braun-Artaria, Rosalie. *Von berühmten Zeitgenossen: Erinnerungen einer Siebzigerin* (Munich 1918)
Bülow, Bernhard Fürst von. *Denkwürdigkeiten*, 4 vols (Berlin 1930–1)
Bülow, Marie von (ed.). *Hans von Bülow: Briefe und Schriften*, 8 vols (Leipzig 1895–1908)
——. *Hans von Bülows Leben dargestellt aus seinen Briefen* (Leipzig 1921)

——. *Hans von Bülow in Leben und Wort* (Stuttgart 1925)

Busch, Fritz. *Aus dem Leben eines Musikers* (Zurich 1949); trans. Marjorie Strachey as *Pages from a Musician's Life* (London 1953)

Chamberlain, Houston Stewart. '1876–1896: Die ersten zwanzig Jahre der Bayreuther Bühnen-festspiele', *Bayreuther Blätter*, xix (1896), 1–67

——. *Die Grundlagen des neunzehnten Jahrhunderts*, 2 vols (Munich 1912); trans. John Lees as *Foundations of the Nineteenth Century*, 2 vols (London 1911)

——. *Kriegsaufsätze* (Munich 1914)

——. *Der Wille zum Sieg und andere Aufsätze* (Munich 1918)

——. *Richard Wagner* (Munich 1919)

——. *Briefe 1882–1924 und Briefwechsel mit Kaiser Wilhelm II.*, 2 vols (Munich 1928)

Conrad, Michael Georg. *Wagners Geist und Kunst in Bayreuth* (Munich 1906)

Cornelius, Peter. *Literarische Werke*, 4 vols (Leipzig 1904–5)

Curjel, Hans. *Experiment Krolloper 1927–1931* (Munich 1975)

Debussy, Claude. *Monsieur Croche et autres écrits*, ed. François Lesure (Paris 1987); trans. Richard Langham Smith as *Debussy on Music: The Critical Writings of the Great French Composer* (Ithaca, NY 1977)

Draber, Hermann Wilhelm. *Der Weg einer deutschen Künstlerin: Erinnerungen an Emmy Krüger* (Munich 1940)

Du Moulin Eckart, Richard Graf (ed.). *Hans von Bülow: Neue Briefe* (Munich 1927)

——. *Cosima Wagner: Ein Lebens- und Charakterbild*, 2 vols (Berlin 1929–31)

Dürck-Kaulbach, Josefa. *Erinnerungen an Wilhelm von Kaulbach und sein Haus* (Munich 1918)

Eger, Manfred. 'Warum wurde Carries Brief vernichtet?', *Nordbayerischer Kurier Festspielnachrichten: Parsifal* (1992), 8–10

Espach, Albert. *Beiträge zur Biographie Ernst Schweningers* (Munich 1979)

Eulenburg-Hertefeld, Philipp Fürst zu. *Eine Erinnerung an Graf Arthur Gobineau* (Stuttgart 1906)

Fifield, Christopher. *True Artist and True Friend: A Biography of Hans Richter* (Oxford 1993)

Fischer, Jens Malte. *Richard Wagners 'Das Judentum in der Musik'* (Frankfurt 2000)

Fricke, Richard. *Bayreuth vor dreissig Jahren: Erinnerungen an Wahnfried und aus dem Festspielhause* (Dresden 1906)

Friedländer, Hugo. *Interessante Kriminal-Prozesse von kulturhistorischer Bedeutung: Band XI* (Berlin 1920)

Fröhlich, Elke (ed.). *Die Tagebücher von Joseph Goebbels*, 2nd edn, 3 vols (Munich 1998–2008)

Gewande, Wolf-Dieter. *Hans von Bülow: Eine biographisch-dokumentarische Würdigung aus Anlass seines 175. Geburtstages* (Lilienthal 2004)

Girard, Franz. *Como und der Comersee mit Umgebung* (Munich 1910)

Giroud, Françoise. *Cosima la sublime* (Paris 1996)

Glasenapp, Carl Friedrich (ed.). *Bayreuther Briefe von Richard Wagner (1871–1883)* (Berlin 1907)

Golther, Wolfgang (ed.). *Richard Wagner an Mathilde Wesendonk: Tagebuchblätter und Briefe 1853–1871* (Berlin 1908)

Grabowsky, Adolf. *Der Kampf um Böcklin* (Berlin 1906)

Gregor-Dellin, Martin. *Richard Wagner: Sein Leben, sein Werk, sein Jahrhundert* (Munich 1980); trans. J. Maxwell Brownjohn as *Richard Wagner: His Life, His Work, His Century* (London 1983)

Großmann-Vendrey, Susanna. *Bayreuth in der deutschen Presse: Beiträge zur Rezeptionsgeschichte Richard Wagners und seiner Festspiele*, 3 vols (Regensburg 1977–83)

Guichard, Léon (ed.). *Lettres à Judith Gautier par Richard et Cosima Wagner* (Paris 1964)

Gut, Serge and Jacqueline Bellas (eds). *Franz Liszt – Marie d'Agoult: Correspondance* (Paris 2001)

Haas, Frithjof. *Zwischen Brahms und Wagner: Der Dirigent Hermann Levi* (Zurich 1995)

——. *Hans von Bülow: Leben und Wirken. Wegbereiter für Wagner, Liszt und Brahms* (Wilhelmshaven 2002)

Hacker, Rupert. *Ludwig II. von Bayern in Augenzeugenberichten* (Düsseldorf 1969)

Hagenlücke, Heinz. *Deutsche Vaterlandspartei: Die nationale Rechte am Ende des Kaiserreiches* (Düsseldorf 1997)

Haller, Johannes (ed.). *Aus 50 Jahren: Erinnerungen, Tagebücher und Briefe aus dem Nachlaß des Fürsten Philipp zu Eulenburg-Hertefeld* (Berlin 1923)

Hamann, Brigitte. *Winifred Wagner oder Hitlers Bayreuth* (Munich 2002); trans. Alan Bance as *Winifred Wagner: A Life at the Heart of Hitler's Bayreuth* (London 2005)

Hamburger, Klára (ed.). *Franz Liszt: Briefwechsel mit seiner Mutter* (Eisenstadt 2000)

——. 'Ein unbekanntes Dokument über Franz Liszts Tod', *Studia musicologica*, lxvi (2005), 403–12

Harden, Maximilian. 'Tutte le corde: Siegfried und Isolde', *Die Zukunft* (27 June 1914), 405–31

——. *Köpfe*, 4 vols (Berlin 1923–4)

Herwegh, Marcel (ed.). *Au printemps des dieux: Correspondance inédite de la Comtesse Marie d'Agoult et du poète Georges Herwegh* (Paris 1929)

Herzfeld, Friedrich. *Königsfreundschaft: Ludwig II. und Richard Wagner* (Leipzig 1939)

Hoffmann, F. (i.e. Cosima Wagner), 'Courrier politique, littéraire et scientifique', *Revue germanique* (7 Nov. 1861), 150–7

Hohenlohe, Ernst zu (ed.). *Briefwechsel zwischen Cosima Wagner und Fürst Ernst zu Hohenlohe-Langenburg* (Stuttgart 1937)

Hohenlohe, Marie Fürstin zu. *Erinnerungen an Richard Wagner* (Weimar 1938)

Humperdinck, Eva (ed.). *Engelbert Humperdinck in seinen persönlichen Beziehungen zu Richard Wagner, Cosima Wagner, Siegfried Wagner*, 3 vols (Koblenz 1996–9)

Jaskowski, Friedrich. *Volksbildung durch Wagnersche Kunst: Praktische Vorschläge, theoretische Begründungen* (Bühl 1909)

Jungblut, Peter. *Famose Kerle: Eulenburg – eine wilhelminische Affäre* (Hamburg 2003)

Kapp, Julius. *Richard Wagner und die Frauen* (Berlin 1951); trans. Hannah Waller as *The Women in Wagner's Life* (London 1932) (the incomplete translation is based on the third German edition of 1929)

Kessler, Harry Graf. *Das Tagebuch*, 9 vols (Stuttgart 2004–10)

Keynes, John Maynard. 'Essays in Biography', *The Collected Writings of John Maynard Keynes*, 28 vols (London 1971–82)

Keyserling, Hermann Graf. *Reise durch die Zeit: Ursprünge und Entfaltungen* (Vaduz 1948)

Kinzig, Wolfram (ed.). *Harnack, Marcion und das Judentum: Nebst einer kommentierten Edition des Briefwechsels Adolf von Harnacks mit Houston Stewart Chamberlain* (Leipzig 2004)

Kloss, Erich (ed.). *Richard Wagner an seine Künstler* (Berlin 1908)

Kniese, Julius. *Der Kampf zweier Welten um das Bayreuther Erbe: Julius Knieses Tagebuchblätter aus dem Jahre 1883* (Leipzig 1931)

Kraft, Zdenko von. *Der Sohn: Siegfried Wagners Leben und Umwelt* (Graz 1969)

Kraus, Karl. 'Momentaufnahmen', *Die Fackel* (5 Oct. 1912)

Laforgue, Jules. *Berlin: Der Hof und die Stadt 1887* (Frankfurt am Main 1970)

La Mara (ed.). *Briefwechsel zwischen Franz Liszt und Hans von Bülow* (Leipzig 1898)

——. *Franz Liszt's Briefe: Briefe an die Fürstin Carolyne Sayn-Wittgenstein*, 4 vols (iv–vii) (Leipzig 1899–1902)

Lehmann, Lilli. *Mein Weg*, 2nd edn (Leipzig 1920); trans. Alice Benedict Seligman as *My Path through Life* (New York and London 1914)

Linsert, Richard. *Kabale und Liebe: Über Politik und Geschlechtsleben* (Berlin 1931)

Martin, René. 'Une femme de lettres française à Berlin (1857–1865): Mme Cosima de Bulow', *Revue de littérature comparée*, xi (1931), 687–710

——. *La vie et l'œuvre de Charles Dollfus* (Gap 1934)

Meinecke, Friedrich. *Autobiographische Schriften* (Stuttgart 1969)

Mey, Kurt. 'Das Berliner Richard-Wagner-Denkmal', *Wartburgstimmen*, i (1903)

Millenkovich-Morold, Max. *Cosima Wagner: Ein Lebensbild* (Leipzig 1937)

Müller-Marein, Josef and Hannes Reinhardt. *Das musikalische Selbstportrait von Komponisten, Dirigenten, Instrumentalisten, Sängerinnen und Sängern unserer Zeit* (Hamburg 1963)

Müller-Trumpf, Simone. 'Das Richard-Wagner-Denkmal von Gustav Eberlein in Berlin' (MA dissertation, Ruprecht Karl University, Heidelberg, 2004)

Muschler, Reinhold Conrad. *Philipp zu Eulenburg: Sein Leben und seine Zeit* (Leipzig 1930)

Nietzsche, Friedrich. 'Ecco homo', *Kritische Gesamtausgabe*, ed. Giorgio Colli and Mazzino Montinari, 15 vols (Munich and Berlin 1988); trans. R.J. Hollingdale as *Ecco homo* (Harmondsworth 1979)

Ollivier, Daniel (ed.). *Correspondance de Liszt et de sa fille Madame Émile Ollivier 1842–1862* (Paris 1936)

Pachl, Peter P. *Siegfried Wagner: Genie im Schatten* (Munich 1988)

Perl, Henry. *Richard Wagner in Venedig: Mosaikbilder aus seinen letzten Lebenstagen* (Augsburg 1883)

Pocknell, Pauline. 'Princess Carolyne von Sayn-Wittgenstein: Correspondence with Franz Liszt's Family and Friends', *Liszt Saeculum*, ii (1992), 3–67 and l (1993), 3–35

Pretzsche, Paul (ed.). *Cosima Wagner und Houston Stewart Chamberlain im Briefwechsel 1888–1908* (Leipzig 1934)

Ramann, Lina. *Lisztiana: Erinnerungen an Franz Liszt in Tagebuchblättern, Briefen und Dokumenten aus den Jahren 1873–1886/87* (Mainz 1983)

Rathenau, Walter. *Schriften aus Kriegs- und Nachkriegszeit* (Berlin 1929)

Richardson, Joanna. *Judith Gautier: A Biography* (London 1986)

Richter, Eugen. *Politisches ABC-Buch: Ein Lexikon parlamentarischer Zeit- und Streitfragen* (Berlin 1903)

Röhl, John C. G. (ed.). *Philipp Eulenburgs politische Korrespondenz*, 3 vols (Boppard 1976–83)

——. *Die Jugend des Kaisers 1859–1888* (Munich 2001)

Sattler, Bernhard (ed.). *Adolf von Hildebrand und seine Welt: Briefe und Erinnerungen* (Munich 1962)

Schad, Martha (ed.). *Cosima Wagner und Ludwig II. von Bayern: Briefe. Eine erstaunliche Korrespondenz* (Bergisch Gladbach 1996)

Schleicher, Berta (ed.). *Briefe von und an Malwida von Meysenbug* (Berlin 1920)

Schoenberg, Arnold. 'Parsifal und Urheberrecht', *Neue Musik-Zeitung*, xxxiii (1912), 315–17; trans. Leo Black as '*Parsifal* and Copyright', *Style and Idea*, ed. Leonard Stein (London 1975), 491–6

Scholz, Dieter David. *Richard Wagners Antisemitismus: Jahrhundertgenie im Zwielicht. Eine Korrektur* (Berlin 2000)

Scholz, Hans (ed.). *Richard Wagner an Mathilde Maier* (Leipzig 1930)

Schroeder, Leopold von. *Die Vollendung des arischen Mysteriums in Bayreuth* (Munich 1911)

——. *Lebenserinnerungen* (Leipzig 1921)

Schüler, Winfried. *Der Bayreuther Kreis: Von seiner Entstehung bis zum Ausgang der wilhelminischen Ära. Wagnerkult und Kulturreform im Geiste völkischer Weltanschauung* (Münster 1971)

Schuh, Willi (ed.). *Richard Strauss: Briefe an die Eltern 1882–1906* (Zurich 1954)

Schweninger, Ernst. *Der Arzt* (Frankfurt 1906)

Skelton, Geoffrey. *Richard and Cosima Wagner: Biography of a Marriage* (London 1982)

Slezak, Leo. *Song of Motley: Being the Reminiscences of a Hungry Tenor* (London 1938)

Spencer, Stewart. ' "Er starb, – ein Mensch wie alle": Wagner and Carrie Pringle', *Festspielbuch 2004* (Bayreuth 2004), 72–85

Stargardt-Wolff, Edith. *Wegbereiter großer Musiker* (Berlin 1954)

Stegmann, Dirk. *Die Erben Bismarcks: Parteien und Verbände in der Spätphase des Wilhelminischen Deutschlands* (Cologne 1970)

Steinitzer, Max. *Richard Strauss* (Berlin 1911)

Stempel, Ilse. 'Deutschland in der "Revue Germanique" von Dollfus und Nefftzer 1858–1865' (dissertation, University of Bonn, 1967)

Strecker, Ludwig. *Richard Wagner als Verlagsgefährte* (Mainz 1951)

Strobel, Otto (ed.). *König Ludwig II. und Richard Wagner: Briefwechsel*, 5 vols (Karlsruhe 1936–9)

Stumpf, Gerhard. *Michael Georg Conrad: Ideenwelt, Kunstprogrammatik, Literarisches Werk* (Frankfurt 1986)

Szylin, Anna Maria. *Henry Thode (1857–1920): Leben und Werk* (Frankfurt 1993)

Tchaikovsky, Peter Ilyich. [Review of 1876 *Ring* in the *Russky Viedomosty*], *Bayreuth: The Early Years*, ed. Robert Hartford (London 1980), 53–6

Thiery, Joachim and Dietrich Seidel, ' "Ich behage mir nicht": Richard Wagner und seine Ärzte', *Münchener Medizinische Wochenschrift*, cxxxvi (1994), 491–504; trans. Stewart Spencer as ' "I feel only discontent": Wagner and his doctors', *Wagner*, xvi (1995), 3–22

Thode, Daniela (ed.). *Richard Wagners Briefe an Hans von Bülow* (Jena 1916)

Thode, Henry. *Wie ist Richard Wagner vom deutschen Volke zu feiern? Vortrag, gehalten am 13. Februar 1903 in der Philharmonie zu Berlin* (Heidelberg 1903)

Vetter, Isolde. 'Hans von Bülows Irrfahrt durch die Medizin: Mit Briefen und anderen unveröffentlichten Zeugnissen aus seinem letzten Lebensjahr', *Südthüringer Forschungen 28: Beiträge zum Kolloquium Hans von Bülow, Leben, Wirken und Vermächtnis* (Meiningen 1994)

Wagner, Cosima. *Die Tagebücher*, ed. Martin Gregor-Dellin and Dietrich Mack, 2 vols (Munich and Zurich 1976–7); trans. by Geoffrey Skelton as *Cosima Wagner's Diaries*, 2 vols (London 1978–80)

——. *Cosima Wagner. Das zweite Leben: Briefe und Aufzeichnungen 1883–1930*, ed. Dietrich Mack (Munich 1980)

Wagner, Friedelind and Page Cooper. *Heritage of Fire: The Story of Richard Wagner's Granddaughter* (New York and London 1945)

Wagner, Richard. *Entwürfe, Gedanken, Fragmente: Aus nachgelassenen Papieren zusammengestellt* (Leipzig 1885)

——. *Sämtliche Schriften und Dichtungen*, ed. Richard Sternfeld, 16 vols (Leipzig 1911–14)

——. *Das Braune Buch: Tagebuchaufzeichnungen 1865 bis 1882*, ed. Joachim Bergfeld (Zurich 1975); trans. by George Bird as *The Diary of Richard Wagner: The Brown Book* (London 1980)

——. *Mein Leben*, ed. Martin Gregor-Dellin (Munich 1976); trans. by Andrew Gray as *My Life* (Cambridge 1983)

——. *Sämtliche Briefe*, ed. Gertrud Strobel, Werner Wolf, Werner Breig, and others (Leipzig 1967–2000 and Wiesbaden 1999–)

Wagner, Siegfried. *Erinnerungen* (Stuttgart 1923; new edition by Bernd Zegowitz, Frankfurt 2005)

Waldberg, Max Freiherr von (ed.). *Cosima Wagners Briefe an ihre Tochter Daniela von Bülow 1866–1885* (Stuttgart 1933)

Walker, Alan. *Franz Liszt*, 3 vols (London 1983–97)

——. *The Death of Franz Liszt: Based on the unpublished diary of his pupil Lina Schmalhausen* (Ithaca 2002)

Weber, Max. *Wirtschaft und Gesellschaft: Grundriss der verstehenden Soziologie* (Tübingen 1972); trans. and ed. Guenther Roth and Claus Wittich as *Economy and Society: An Outline of Interpretive Sociology* (Berkeley 1978)

Weingartner, Felix. *Bayreuth 1876–1896* (Berlin 1904)

——. *Lebenserinnerungen*, 2nd edn, 2 vols (Zurich 1928–9)

Wille, Eliza. *Erinnerungen an Richard Wagner: Mit 15 Briefen Richard Wagners* (Zurich 1982)

Wolzogen, Hans von. *Germanisierung der Religion* (Berlin 1911)

——. 'Nach 1913', *Bayreuther Blätter*, xxxvii (1914), 3–4

——. *Lebensbilder* (Regensburg 1923)

Zschorlich, Paul. 'Parsifalomanie', *Die Zeit* (Sept. 1902)

Index